Electronic Visualisation in Arts and Culture

Springer Series on Cultural Computing

For further volumes:
http://www.springer.com/series/10481

Jonathan P. Bowen • Suzanne Keene • Kia Ng
Editors

Electronic Visualisation in Arts and Culture

Springer

Editors
Jonathan P. Bowen
Department of Informatics
London South Bank University
London, UK

Suzanne Keene
Department of Archaeology
University College London
London, UK

Kia Ng
Interdisciplinary Centre for Scientific
Research in Music (ICSRiM)
School of Computing & School of Music
University of Leeds
Leeds, UK

Corresponding e-mail for all editors: evabook2013@eva-london.org

ISSN 2195-9056
ISSN 2195-9064 (electronic)
ISBN 978-1-4471-7235-2
ISBN 978-1-4471-5406-8 (eBook)
DOI 10.1007/978-1-4471-5406-8
Springer London Heidelberg New York Dordrecht

Printed on acid-free paper

Springer is part of Springer Science+Business Media (www.springer.com)

Foreword

The EVA conferences span the 20 years from the early 1990s until now. They began as part of the EU-funded VASARI collaborative research project, which included the National Gallery, London, and its peers in Munich and Paris as well as universities and industrial companies across Europe. EVA stands for *Electronic Visualisation and the Arts*: 'Electronic Visualisation' because the aim of the VASARI project was to develop a digital camera with sufficient resolution to do justice to the two thousand or so paintings in the National Gallery's collection, as the leader of the VASARI project.

James Hemsley led the project's Dissemination Work Package and the progress and results were disseminated by organising the first EVA conference to 'exchange experiences, plans and dreams' with participants in VASARI and other projects. For the first few years, the conferences were held in London but subsequently in many other cities around the world (see Chap. 1). Initially funded by the EU, the meetings proved so popular that they continued afterwards on a self-supporting basis. Since 2008, the Computer Arts Society, a Specialist Group of the British Computer Society (BCS – the Chartered Institute for IT), has been hosting the EVA London conferences at the BCS London headquarters in Covent Garden.

Historically, EVA spans momentous developments in technology and culture. The World Wide Web has revolutionised computing and information technology, the digital camera has revolutionised the way we image ourselves and the world around us, social networks have revolutionised how we relate to each other, the mobile phone has revolutionised how we talk to each other and search technologies are revolutionising our relationship to knowledge and its creation and preservation. Even those of us who lived through and took part in some of these developments wonder how on earth we managed in the bygone days without these tools. But the next generation of professionals and leaders will have grown up with them since early childhood. Generation Xbox, Facebook and Kinect will be completely adapted to these environments as fish are to water. However, these developments have not escaped criticism; while these technologies have matured, the economies that spawned them have sunk into recession or at best undergone slow growth. Cause and effect – very doubtful! While the nineteenth-century technologies – railways, engines, sewers, telegraphy, aircraft, etc. – had truly major economic and life-changing effects, there is an argument that these late twentieth-century developments have had marginal, incremental effects on the economy rather than being fundamental game changers. But if the quantifiable economic benefits are rather less than the fanfares suggest, it may be that more people are doing more things which are not economically measurable or 'productive', for example talking to each other, helping each other and having fun, enjoying immersion in the new open culture which these new technologies have seeded and exploring qualitative, human possibilities. And, being of its time, eclectic in its coverage, this is precisely what the EVA conferences have tried to achieve, with major success, as you will discover from the following chapters.

Although EVA is of modern times, we now know that concerns with images, movement and interactions, in the sense of performances, were present from the very beginnings of *Homo sapiens*. That combination of language, tool making, empathy, socialisation, playfulness and inventiveness which distinguishes our species made its mark early. Recent analyses of cave paintings have suggested that the makers of these were using animation techniques at least 30,000 years ago. Flickering light and subtle use of line and 3D features of the cave wall could give a sense of movement. It is tempting to speculate that these early efforts at animations, if such they are, are a manifestation of the brain's capability for prediction – to consider what might happen next and to act accordingly – so vital to our evolution and survival (so far).

But as we edge nervously into the twenty-first century, our scientific understanding of the problems of climate, water, food and disease does raise the spectre that our governance systems are not up to acting on the sombre predictions from the knowledge base. What then of the playful inventiveness from the interdisciplinary arts and technologies described by EVA contributors? The message that I take from these chapters is one of hope; although the outputs from these are not yet quantifiable in economic metrics, they are hugely important in helping create new modes of social interaction that will encourage people in joint efforts to overcome the poverty of the dispiriting hierarchies of power which do seem to be failing us in the face of gloomy predictions. My optimism is that the kinds of innovations and developments described in the EVA conferences are steps towards new ways of articulating and sharing knowledge, which in turn will feed into more open and responsive forms of governance.

The EVA London conferences from 2009 to 2012 have produced around 400–500 contributions, papers, demonstrations and workshops. To distil from this an essence which also projects a sense of what the overall programme has been about and might do has been a challenge to which, as you will see, the editors have risen with great insight and skill.

For me, these EVA chapters are a real contribution to twenty-first-century arts and culture, and Springer is to be congratulated for publishing them.

London, 2013 George Mallen

Preface

To accomplish great things we must first dream, then visualize, then plan... believe... act!

– Alfred A. Montapert

In this book, we present selected revised and extended papers from the EVA London Conference on Electronic Visualisation and the Arts held between 2009 and 2012. These conferences provide an interdisciplinary forum for people with a wide range of backgrounds, ranging from visual artists to computer scientists. The initial selection of chapters was largely by the audience during 'best presentation' competitions at these conferences, with some additions by the editors for a more rounded overall selection. Each chapter was then peer-reviewed by experts.

George Mallen has provided a summing up at recent EVA London conferences and provides a thoughtful foreword for this book. James Hemsley is the progenitor of the EVA conferences, which began in London, but are now held annually in a number of other venues around the world, including Berlin, Florence and Moscow. In Chap. 1, he provides a history of EVA by way of background to this book.

The rest of the book is divided into themed parts. Each has been shepherded by an editor during the reviewing and revision process and includes a short introduction summarising the theme and the rest of the chapters in that part, together with some suggested reading where appropriate.

The annual EVA London conferences are held on behalf of the Computer Arts Society, a British Computer Society (BCS) Specialist Group of the Chartered Institute for IT. We gratefully acknowledge the assistance and support of both organisations. The editors thank the EVA London organising and programme committees for the years 2009–2012, especially the organising chairs and proceedings editors (for the proceedings for these conferences, see http://www.eva-london.org).

James Hemsley and George Mallen have been stalwarts of the EVA London Conference series for many years. Finally, thank you to all the participants at EVA London conferences for making them such exciting and successful events.

London, 2013

Jonathan P. Bowen
Suzanne Keene
Kia Ng

Contents

Contributors

Joanne Armitage ICSRiM – University of Leeds, School of Electronic and Electrical Engineering & School of Music, Leeds, UK

Matt Benatan ICSRiM – University of Leeds, School of Computing & School of Music, Leeds, UK

Emma Bevan Nonsense Ltd., London, UK

Dominique Boutet UMR 7023 SFL, CNRS, Université Paris 8, France

Andy Clarke Lincoln School of Media, University of Lincoln, Lincoln, UK

Fernanda D'Agostino Fernanda D'Agostino Studio, Portland, OR, USA

Claire Danet GestuelScript, ESAD Amiens, Amiens, France

Stephen Boyd Davis Royal College of Art, London, UK

Harry Dawson Dawson Media Group, USA

Raphël de Courville GestuelScript, ESAD Amiens, Amiens, France

Steve DiPaola Simon Fraser University, Surrey, BC, Canada

Graham Diprose London's Found Riverscape Partnership, Redhill, Surrey, UK

Patrick Doan GestuelScript, ESAD Amiens, Amiens, France

Stuart Dunn Department of Digital Humanities, King's College London, London, UK

Jeremy Gardiner Ravensbourne, London, UK

Murat Germen Sabanci University/Visual Arts and Communication Design Program, Sabanci University, FASS, Orhanli, Tuzla, Istanbul, Turkey

Marion Harney Centre for Advanced Studies in Architecture, Department of Architecture and Civil Engineering, University of Bath, Bath, UK

Anthony Head Bath Spa University, Bath, UK

James Hemsley EVA Conferences International, London, UK

Aleksei Kudikov SRL Global, London, UK

Michael Lesk Rutgers University, New Brunswick, NJ, USA

Roman Miletitch GestuelScript, ESAD Amiens, Amiens, France

Grethe Mitchell Lincoln School of Media, University of Lincoln, Lincoln, UK

Kia Ng ICSRiM – University of Leeds, School of Computing & School of Music, Leeds, UK

Gordana Novakovic Computer Science Department, University College London, London, UK

Jeremy Pilcher Independent scholar, London, UK

Morgane Rébulard GestuelScript, ESAD Amiens, Amiens, France

Paul Richens Centre for Advanced Studies in Architecture, Department of Architecture and Civil Engineering, University of Bath, Bath, UK

Mike Seaborne London's Found Riverscape Partnership, Redhill, Surrey, UK

Sophy Smith Institute of Creative Technologies, De Montfort University, Leicester, UK

Amir Soltani Department of Architecture, DIGIS – Cambridge University, Cambridge, UK

Chris Alen Sula Pratt Institute, School of Information & Library Science, New York, NY, USA

Bret W. Tobalske Division of Biological Sciences, University of Montana, Missoula, MT, USA

Kirk Woolford School of Media, Film and Music, University of Sussex, Falmer, UK

Chapter 1
The EVA London Conference 1990–2012: Personal Reflections

James Hemsley

Abstract This chapter focuses on the origins and early history of the EVA London Conference, as well as embracing its numerous EVA siblings across Europe and internationally. The EVA London Conference was born in the pre-web age. Its precursors lay in early work in architecture and engineering and work on colour change analysis in major museums. The EVA conferences were initiated from the European Commission funded research project, VASARI. For many years EU research funding supported EVA conferences to support innovation through networking between key people and organisations. EVA conferences have been held worldwide, and there are currently annual conferences in EVA London, Berlin, Jerusalem, Florence and Moscow.

Introduction

Born in the pre-web era, the EVA London Conference has, perhaps surprisingly, continued to survive and creatively evolve. In 2013, there is just over one year to its 25th annual event in July 2014. Its beginnings in 1990 at Imperial College of Science & Technology, London were quite modest with fewer than 50 art historians, conservation scientists, engineers, computer scientists and mathematicians gathered together, mainly from the UK but with a sprinkling from across Europe. This gathering was testimony to EVA's roots in the European-supported VASARI research project, as George Mallen describes in the Foreword. It is tempting to look both forward as well as backward on the context and history of EVA London. This chapter presents the beginnings and history of the EVA London Conference as well as its related EVA events in Europe and around the world.

J. Hemsley (✉)
EVA Conferences International, Tavistock Court,
Tavistock Square 32, London WC1H 9HE, UK
e-mail: jrhemsley@hotmail.com

J.P. Bowen et al. (eds.), *Electronic Visualisation in Arts and Culture*,
Springer Series on Cultural Computing, DOI 10.1007/978-1-4471-5406-8_1,

Before EVA

The precursors of EVA London may be characterised as largely separate streams of scientific engagement with the cultural sector, to try to apply the promising capabilities of the rapidly developing Information and Communication Technologies (ICT) to bridge the great divide. These efforts notably included those of the Museum Documentation Association (MDA) in Cambridge. For a number of years the MDA had played a key role in the application of computers for the operational improvement of museum information systems, including establishing standards of vital importance. At that time these were limited mainly to alphanumeric systems.

From architecture (and engineering), serious work was already underway, with Computer-Aided Design (CAD) and Computer-Aided Engineering (CAE) entering the 3D world, and such approaches began to be applied early to archaeology as well. Notably, most early work was conducted in black and white and this, for the purists, was also the case for serious art history, but colour digital images were arriving and increasingly became dominant. Computer research for art history itself was driven by real problems such as computer aided recognition of an artist's works. In particular, Professor Will Vaughan's pioneering MORELLI system at Birkbeck College in the 1980s was arguably in advance of the competing IBM research of the period. However, the longest-standing relationship between art and computers had been initiated early on by computer artists and merits careful historical attention, for instance the study of pioneering British computer artists in the CACHE Project [1]. For the EVA Conferences, however, the research stream which primarily led to their creation was the new digital signal processing technologies, including those used for colour change analysis and its display, being carried out by conservation scientists in the laboratories of major museums.

The VASARI Project

Motivated by the complementary aims of Europe, and, even more strongly, to contribute to closer union between arts and sciences, planning was initiated for a "Beyond the State of the Art" research project to be supported by the European Commission. Preparatory work continued for nearly two years before a proposal was submitted to the ESPRIT Programme (the computing forerunner to the later European Commission ICT Framework programmes). This initiative became the VASARI research project on ultra-high quality imaging of paintings for conservation purposes and also for computer support of art history education. Partners were an industry museum/university partnership from France, Germany, Italy and UK including scientists from the Doerner Institute, Munich (Andreas Burmester), the Louvre, Paris (Christian Lahanier), and the National Gallery, London (David Saunders), led by a small UK company. The project was skilfully baptised by

David Saunders as Visual Arts System for Archiving & Retrieval of Images in homage to the great Giorgio Vasari, the father of art history. A specific aim of the project was to help open the way for subsequent ICT research projects, to be driven by stimulating requirements from the heritage world. Key to achieving this goal was not just to disseminate the project's results but to facilitate networking between key people and organisations enabling them to share experiences, plans and dreams: a *leitmotiv* of EVA London.

The EVA Conferences

The context of the 1990 EVA London Conference (Electronic Imaging & The Visual Arts, subsequently evolving to its current title) included dramatic technology advances resulting from increasing efforts to build the European Union towards the Single Market of 1992, pushed by the Cold War and the fall of the Berlin Wall. In pursuit of international openness, the first EVA London Conferences were scheduled in late July to increase participation by North American and Japanese researchers visiting Europe in the summer; this worked well, especially at the second EVA London in 1991 at University College London, UCL, which included an impressive exhibition of new advances organised by the Co-chair, Anthony Hamber of Birkbeck College. A further step proved decisive for EVA London's success from 1992 to 1997: the move to holding these annual EVAs in the beautiful surroundings of the National Gallery, London, which was also launching its acclaimed Micro-Gallery Electronic Visitor Information System, sponsored by American Express.

International Diffusion

During the mid to late 1990s the EVA Conferences spread across the EU – Berlin, Brussels, Florence, Madrid and Paris. Many of the enthusiastic local organising committees and supporter groups had participated in one of the early EVA London events. The events were supported by apparently never-ending waves of new computer and telecommunications technologies as well as continuing support from the European Commission. In 1998, the EC requested a regional approach regarding Europe, and EVA Florence (1998) and EVA Berlin (1999) were selected in turn to be the main EVA Conference site. This provided, inter alia, a solid foundation for their continuation as annual EVAs up to the present, led by the University of Florence (Professor Vito Cappellini) and GfAI (Professor Gerd Stanke). Simultaneously the EC also decided to support the expansion of the EVA Conferences outside the EU and in dizzying succession, EVA Conferences were held in Japan (Gifu Prefecture), Austin, Texas and Moscow. The latter (led by Nadia Brakker and Leonid Kubyshev) continues to retain its place as the largest single EVA with some 600–700 participants, an astonishingly wide range of cultural areas covered, and a major focus on students. However, the record-holder is still the first EVA Japan with some 1,000 participants due to massive local and national support.

This significant international diffusion, with networking facilitation, exchange of experiences, plans and dreams and face-to-face communication continued until 2002, with EVA Conferences in Beijing, Mumbai (New Delhi) as well as Los Angeles and New York and a think-tank symposium at Harvard. However, the times for such generous EC support then ended, and similar events were springing up across the world. Now, the principal EVA conferences in Berlin, Florence, London, and Moscow, continue annually on their own initiative, together with EVA MINERVA, Jerusalem (Israel Museum, Susan Hazan and Dov Wiener), which has resulted from the EVA Harvard Symposium and the EC MINERVA project. Each reflects particular priorities and individualities such as 3D, as well as general international trends in innovation in the field [2].

EVA Conferences in the UK and London

During the late 1990s, UK EVA conferences were held in Cambridge (1998) and then Edinburgh (1999 and 2000, hosted by the National Museums of Scotland), and Glasgow (2001, Hunterian Museum, University of Glasgow) and then returned to London for the 50th EVA held again at Imperial College with training and workshop sessions at the Victoria & Albert Museum. The subsequent history of EVA London was one of undiminished brilliance of innovative papers, as shown by a first print publication of EVA papers [3] covering the period 2000–2003. Of particular note at EVA London from modest beginnings in 2000, inspired by the Edinburgh Festival, has been the increasing role of the performing arts, especially music, with the University of Leeds (led by Kia Ng) an enthusiastic supporter and more recently computer art, thus bringing together in an increasingly eclectic creative mix the various streams discernible in the 1980s.

Most importantly, leadership of EVA London passed into the fresh hands, from co-chairs Suzanne Keene, Jonathan Bowen and Lindsay MacDonald to George Mallen, Suzanne Keene and presently Stuart Dunn, ably supported by active organising and programme committees. The future of the conference is now assured by the support of the British Computer Society and its specialist group the Computer Arts Society (CAS). They are to be thanked and congratulated for maintaining EVA London at the forefront of the technology wave in the arts, and for maintaining the series of published proceedings for each year of the conference [4–7]. Last but not least, thanks to all over the years that have played a role in EVA London from Val Duncan and Monica Kaayk in the early days to Stuart Dunn, current Chair of EVA London. Good luck to future EVAs and similar events internationally as well as, most of all, to the readers of these chapters who will pursue their own dreams building on, extending, and breaking away from the initial efforts in this exciting and worthwhile field of international cooperation in culture and computers.

References

1. CACHE Project. http://www.e-x-p.org/cache/. Accessed 24 Apr 2013.
2. EVA Conferences International. http://www.eva-conferences.com. Accessed 24 Apr 2013.
3. Hemsley, J., Cappellini, V., & Stanke, G. (Eds.). (2005). *Digital applications for cultural and heritage institutions*. Farnham: Ashgate. ISBN 978–0754633594.
4. Seal, A., Keene, S., & Bowen, J. P. (Eds.) (2009). *EVA London 2009 conference proceedings*. Electronic workshops in computing (eWiC). London: British Computer Society. ISBN 978-1-906124-17-5. http://www.bcs.org/ewic/eva2009. Accessed 26 May 2013.
5. Seal, A., Bowen, J. P., & Ng, K. (Eds.) (2010). *EVA London 2010 conference proceedings*. Electronic workshops in computing (eWiC). London: British Computer Society. ISBN 978-1-906124-65-6. http://www.bcs.org/ewic/eva2010. Accessed 26 May 2013.
6. Dunn, S., Bowen, J. P., & Ng, K. (Eds.) (2011). *EVA London 2011 conference proceedings*. Electronic workshops in computing (eWiC). London: British Computer Society. ISBN 978-1-906124-88-5. 12http://www.bcs.org/ewic/eva2011. Accessed 26 May 2013.
7. Dunn, S., Bowen, J. P., & Ng, K. (Eds.) (2012). *EVA London 2012 conference proceedings*. Electronic workshops in computing (eWiC). London: British Computer Society. ISBN 978-1-78017-159-3. http://www.bcs.org/ewic/eva2012. Accessed 26 May 2013.

Part I
Imaging and Culture

Suzanne Keene

Visualisation might be taken to imply a focus on the pictorial, but to the contrary: it can be and is used for an almost infinite variety of cultural expressions and activities [1]. The chapters in this Part offer varied perspectives on some of the less obvious applications. As early as 1949, academic researchers have found computer analysis and visualisation invaluable for text-based studies [2]. Visualising cultural data can help in extracting information and building understanding, as Tufte and Candless have eloquently demonstrated [3, 4]. Early map makers used graphics and illustrations so that their maps were not just sterile diagrams of roads but offered a flavour of the experience of the places depicted [5] – now, visualisation techniques can recreate that presentation, whether via Google Streetview or through enhanced aerial imagery. But will this newly created wealth of digital culture last for centuries and millennia, as have conventional graphic media? As electronic visualisations become universally prevalent and fundamental to culture, this issue becomes ever more compelling [6].

Michael Lesk argues that it is the quantity and availability of cultural materials in digital form that influences use and research (Chap. 2). In the early days individual scholars keyed in and studied text. Now, digitised texts and images of documents and books, artworks and, increasingly, 3D works, music and performance are ubiquitous. As more and different digital materials become available scholars use and analyse them in ever more sophisticated ways. From finding aids (catalogues), which were the initial focus, now enormous amounts of the data that comprises digitised cultural objects can be analysed using computers, offering new avenues of research. The use of visualisation for studying and learning music, dance and performance (see Part III) is growing, but still in the early stages.

Data visualisation, the graphic representation of data, relates to cognitive science, computer visualisation and data analysis (Chris Alen Sula, Chap. 3). It is designed to assist human perception in comprehending large-scale information. The benefits of visualising data include the cognitive – improved memory, easier search, enhanced pattern recognition and perceptual inference. Visualised data can also engage the emotions, through the use of colour – this can be beneficial, but it may be manipulative. Visualisations can be social objects – an example is also described by Pilcher in Chap. 14, *Legal Networks*, below. The power of visualisation should be taken seriously by cultural institutions – for instance, it can confer a false impression of objectivity. However, these visual techniques greatly facilitate the presentation of data and datasets.

Referring to early maps such as those by John Speed, which are illustrated with figures, aerial perspectives and other images that enhance the perception and understanding of their mapped content, Soltani describes the benefits of adding 'embodiment' to otherwise sterile aerial imagery of cities and places (Chap. 4). Google maps, for example, sterile and detached as normally accessed, can be enhanced by using cinematographic techniques such as low altitude oblique images. It has been shown that we perceive different spaces (the geometry of a room, city streets) in relation to our bodies. The introduction of pictorial cues such as depth can help us to understand the places depicted: mechanically made aerial maps are not the true representation of physical reality.

Vast amounts of digital images and text documents now exist. It is improbable that the majority will exist for more than a matter of years, yet it is the responsibility of museum curators and those in other memory institutions such as archives and libraries to think in terms of centuries when selecting for the future. We are in danger of losing creative cultural materials including artworks such as those described elsewhere in this volume (Part II), as the processes and costs of copying, reformatting and managing the enormous and growing quantities of data that constitute these materials escalate. While acknowledging that this is not the only viable approach, Diprose and Seaborne in Chap. 5 report their development of the use of printing using durable inks and paper, materials that we know to survive for millennia, to preserve the data that comprises these cultural (and other) objects.

References

1. The EVA conferences have, during their 24 years, presented what we might claim to be the entire spectrum of the cultural (and even scientific) uses of electronic visualisation. The EVA archive is housed in Birkbeck College, University of London, and recent publications can be found via: http://www.eva-conferences.com. Accessed 29 May 2013.
2. Hockey, S. (2004). The history of humanities computing. In S. Schreibman, R. Siemens, & J. Unsworth (Eds.), *Companion to digital humanities. Blackwell companions to literature and culture*. Oxford: Blackwell Publishing Professional.
3. Tufte, E. R. (1986). *The visual display of quantitative information*. Cheshire: Graphic Press.
4. McCandless, D. (Ed.). (2009). *Information is beautiful*. London: Collins.
5. There are many examples of illustrated early maps online, for instance http://www.maphistory.info. Accessed 29 May 2013.
6. For example by the Alliance for Digital Preservation, http://www.alliancepermanentaccess.org, and in the Handbook, *Preservation management of digital materials*, Digital Preservation Coalition, 2008. http://www.dpconline.org/advice/preservationhandbook/. Accessed 29 May 2013.

Chapter 2
From Descriptions to Duplicates to Data

Michael Lesk

Abstract Scholarly use of digital material moves from catalogues (locator services) to digital duplicates intended for human study to digital versions intended for computer analysis. We have been through this entire path for text, the easiest material to digitise, and we are now fairly far along with artistic imagery. More difficult content, such as costume and dance, will move through the same stages in the future. Perhaps the most important question is whether the nature of critical research changes as the tools change. Many early applications of computers were authorship studies, for example. More generally, does research based on computer analysis ask the same kind of questions as other research? Is it done on the same materials? So far, it would appear that the same materials are considered, and the same questions asked, but there are newer tools to apply. Algorithmic research can also study larger quantities of material, perhaps reducing the single-work focus of much cultural study.

Introduction

Two different forms of progress take place in digital cultural studies. First, we move from simpler to more complex media; text is easiest and is done first, followed by images and then video, sculpture, and specialised materials such as costumes. Second, we move from just listing the items available in catalogues, to providing substitute digital forms that may be suitable for human study, to doing the research automatically. This chapter compares the progress in both media and in study methods, dealing with previously existing objects, not "born-digital" items.

M. Lesk (✉)
Rutgers University, New Brunswick, NJ, USA
e-mail: lesk@rci.rutgers.edu

J.P. Bowen et al. (eds.), *Electronic Visualisation in Arts and Culture*,
Springer Series on Cultural Computing, DOI 10.1007/978-1-4471-5406-8_2,

Digital collections may be larger than any traditional museum or library, and thus permit very wide-ranging comparisons and complete surveys. It is perhaps easier in the digital world to look at details rather than conceptual properties of works. It is easier to measure the size of a work than to say what it is about and still harder to say what emotions it will evoke in a person. Surprisingly, perhaps, it has been possible in textual studies to infer a surprising number of advanced properties, such as authorship or sentiment, from the statistical analysis of simple words. Such techniques are now appearing in research on images or sculptures as well as with text.

This chapter first looks at the problems of creating digital materials from historic objects, and then at their use. In each area, we tend to begin with very small amounts of material; in the 1960s, individuals would start by keying and studying one text, and by 1990 researchers would have large text libraries but only one video. As the amount of material increases, so does what we can learn.

Creating Digital Materials

The technology to digitise and analyze materials is easiest for text and cultural studies began there, but it has moved from text to images and then to video and sculpture, as displayed in this abbreviated chart (Fig. 2.1).

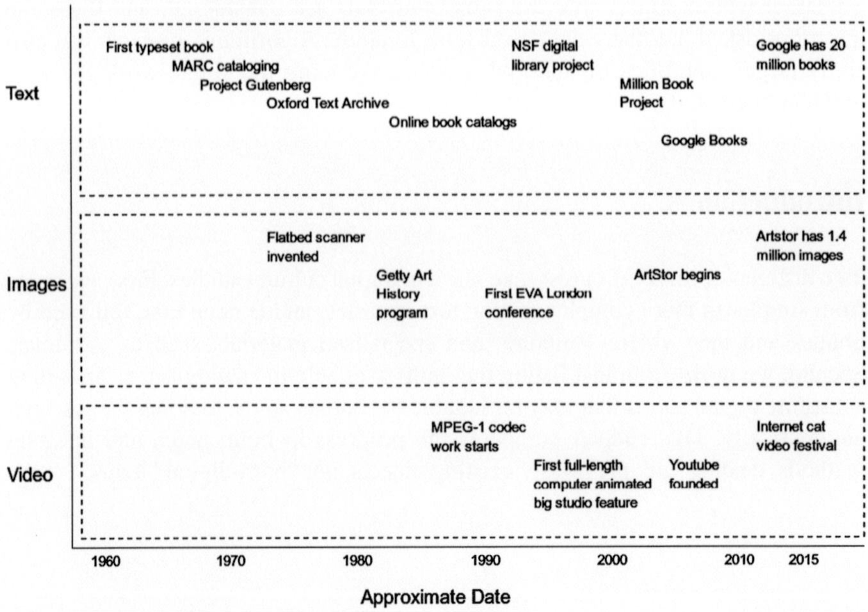

Fig. 2.1 Some milestones in computers and scholarship

In each area, we find that initially people have one item on which they work, and scholars deplore the inability to have full context. Efforts are made to have full descriptions and provide finding aids to let people know what is available where. Then, we start to have large enough collections with good enough reproductions that people start to do their actual work online. Finally, people start writing code to do studies of one or another level.

Books. The techniques to create digital materials have changed over the decades. In the 1950s and 1960s we converted text to machine-readable form by keystroking. Although a number of important works were completely converted, in the earliest days only some aspects of the text were done, for example the metrical patterns of poetry. Often a researcher would work on a single author or one book; I can recall from the 1960s conversions of Roman authors and of Icelandic sagas.

Libraries did the earliest broad conversion projects as they worked on catalogues. There was a long history of libraries maintaining locator services that reported which books were held in which libraries. For example, even 80 years ago Pollard and Redgrave [1] published their Short Title Catalog to locate pre-1640 books, and supplemented by Wing with the next 60 years [2]. Larger catalogues followed, including the *National Union Catalog*, whose hundreds of volumes were available in research libraries around the world.

Thanks to workers such as Henrietta Avram at the Library of Congress and Fred Kilgour at OCLC, in the 1960s we began to acquire machine-readable shared cataloguing [3]. Today OCLC WorldCat. a successor to both the original OCLC and the analogous Research Libraries Group's RLIN system, provides access to the largest catalogue of books that has ever existed.

As time went on, it became feasible to convert the actual books. At first conversion meant keystroking, whether on to punch cards or paper tape. The first effort completed was the Thesaurus Linguae Graecae, which did all the important works of classical literature, employing staff in Korea, China and the Philippines [4]. Project Gutenberg began in the mid 1970s, with a goal of 10,000 books.

Today books are often born-digital, but earlier works still needed to be converted. Several large conversion projects such as the Million Book Project, the Open Content Alliance, and Google Books, the largest of all, soon reached the point where the main barrier was copyright law. The average nineteenth century printed book has now been scanned multiple times. Although most of these projects have used manual page turning to present new pages to the cameras, Google has recently announced that they have been using a mechanical page turner. An explanation of how you could do this yourself using a vacuum cleaner even made it on to the web [5].

For some particularly valuable or difficult works to scan, unusual technologies can be used; these include IR and UV scanning, low-incidence light, and transmitted light illumination. For example, the British Library's manuscript of Beowulf, which was damaged in a fire in 1731, has been scanned so carefully [6] that the images are easier to read than the original. Cuneiform writing may now be scanned in 3-D to help see what has been worn down over time; this is the modern equivalent of rubbing or tracing over the letters.

Flat artistic works. Once we had scanners, it became possible to scan some kinds of artwork such as prints, and digital cameras made it possible to scan paintings as well. Again, scholars had traditionally prepared directories to keep track of which works existed and where they were, such as Hind's 1912 [7] list of locations for all of Rembrandt's etchings.

The creation of online indexes to artistic works followed, of course. Howard Besser describes the Berkeley "imagequery" system planned in 1986–1990, to combine metadata access with images of artistic works [8]. As he writes, art materials are more difficult to catalogue than books; they do not come with a title page identifying the work and its creators, and may not even be signed. So art library catalogues have been a challenge to put online.

Obviously, once we had graphic display terminals, it became attractive to show the works themselves, rather than just their titles. The Andrew W. Mellon Foundation supported the ARTSTOR project which provided access to reproductions of art works. As of early 2013 it contains 1.4 million images [9]. In the United Kingdom the Public Catalogue Foundation has listed 145,000 of the estimated 200,000 oil paintings in the country, with images and locations for each artwork.

Digitising 3-D. There is also a history of cataloguing sculptures, but they are even less well organised than image cataloguing. Typically these are combined, since often the sculptural catalogue is illustrated with flat images, and many sculptors also did drawings or other flat works. The Public Catalogue Foundation, mentioned above, will add some 60,000 indoor sculptures to its files, while the National Recording Project of the Public Monuments and Sculpture Association will index outdoor objects.

The technology to scan 3-D objects is complex but includes "feeler" devices, photogrammetry from multiple cameras, structured light, and laser scanning. An early important project is the Digital Michelangelo work of Marc Levoy [10]. Using laser scanners, his team prepared 3-D images of many of Michelangelo's carvings. The "David" in Florence was scanned to an accuracy of 0.25 mm, letting scholars see individual chisel marks. Figure 2.2 shows a detail of a scan.

Still more difficult tasks. Many objects pose additional problems in digitisation. Costumes, for example, are not just 3-D objects, but they have insides and outsides. Some viewers wish to look at the whole garment, and some wish to examine details of fabric, stitching and decoration. For some scholars, it may be important to view the garment by transmitted light rather than direct light.

Similarly, recording 3-D motion for the study of choreography is still ambitious and difficult. Takeo Kanade [11] and others have shown how to capture multiple people in motion with multiple cameras, but it is far from a routine procedure. The movie industry is now using motion capture, as in the film *Happy Feet* where Savion Glover's dancing was captured and transferred to an animated penguin. In time, this technology should become affordable for dance groups.

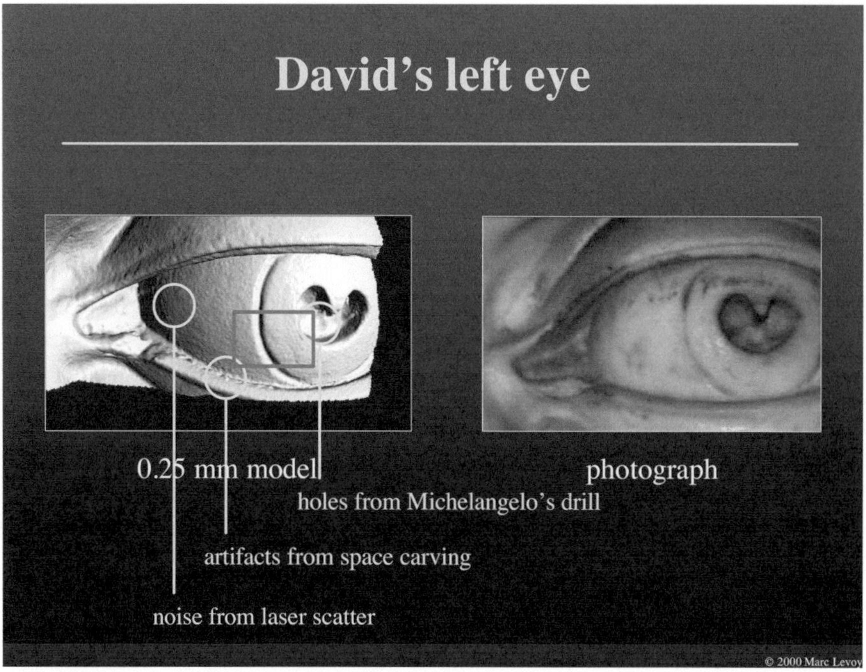

Fig. 2.2 Left eye of Michelangelo's *David*, Florence (Image by Marc Levoy, Stanford; used with permission)

Substitutes

Once digital material is available, the question is whether this substitute or "surrogate" is suitable for study. In the past, scholars demanded to see the original of anything being discussed. Microfilm, for example, was unpopular with generations of historians who much preferred to see the actual documents. Art historians have been even more insistent that they must do their work with originals.

Books. For books, we are well past the time when people insisted on paper copies. Robert Hayes reported in 1987 (quoted by Baker [12]) that half the readers he surveyed insisted on paper books, while today Amazon sells more e-books than paper books, and most scientists, certainly, do almost all their reading of research papers online. In 1990 chemists who were part of an early experiment on the use of digital journals [13] told us that they not only liked the arrangement of the articles in the journals they read but also liked the feel of the paper and even the smell of the brand-new issue (I offered to pour a bottle of PVA glue over the computer to provide the same experience). By 2009, the American Chemical Society had decided to publish only online in the future. Electronic texts are searchable, enlargeable, and more flexible. Most of the physical properties of the paper book are not the work of the author, anyway; many more scholars study literature than study the way publishing houses used to design and compose books. Any instructor knows that students today resist all attempts to make them read paper.

Although the success of the Kindle seems sufficient to prove that people are happy reading on line, there are evaluations of both reading speed and comprehension [14–16]. Both speed and comprehension are so similar across devices that differences are within the standard error. Although the Harris paper noted that the Kindle might offer a slight increase in comprehension at the cost of a slight decrease in reading speed, the authors noted that the differences were not significant.

Other studies have shown differences in the way people read even if they take the same time and have the same performance. Wacholder [17] asked students to judge the utility of books for writing undergraduate papers, with some students skimming the books on paper and others on screens. They were both given the same time limit for the task. Although both groups of students performed comparably well at choosing the best books for a paper topic, the pages read as they examined the books were quite different. Readers who had the books on paper relied heavily on the table of contents and the index, and read only a small number of pages within the book. Those who had a PDF file, which they could search, looked at a larger number of pages in the book.

Do computer systems encourage the reading of "snippets?" Modern students are commonly criticised for superficiality, reading widely rather than deeply. Jidong Wang [18] noted that until about 100 years ago scholars of traditional Chinese literature were expected to memorise the books they were studying, and that the use of digital search systems had encouraged misunderstandings when people read without reading in context.

This complaint is not new. Plato in the *Phaedrus* had complained that writing was being used as an inadequate substitute for memory. Nor is griping about attention span limited to writing. As part of the 2012 election campaign there was an early debate in which each speech was limited to 30 s. The Lincoln-Douglas debate schedule was an opening speech of an hour, an opponent's speech of 90 min, and a final 30 min reply by the first speaker. The use of photography instead of sketching also reduces the amount of time spent on each individual object, and presumably therefore the appreciation of its detail. However, the modern technologies permit the consideration of far more material, particularly when searching is available, and presumably if scholars did not like this, they would not use it.

Text processing has had the advantage of very generally applicable technology. We use the same formatting and searching algorithms on virtually all documents, whether they are letters, journal articles, or monographs. We can even share methods across multiple languages. By contrast, image processing methods are often quite specialised: we have software and even whole companies dealing with maps, CAD drawings, handwriting, and artworks [19]. The cataloging methods of libraries, museums and archives are converging, and as these groups continue to use digital methods and accumulate data, we may see more widely applicable algorithms.

Flat artistic works. Art historians have been more attached to the original image. Aby Warburg, immortalised by his library (now in London) seems to have pioneered the idea of using surrogate images for study [20]. He would lay out, in a large space, reproductions of works that he wished to compare or look at side-by-side. Even photographic reproductions were slow to be accepted in scholarship.

Quality is obviously a key consideration for images to be studied. Michael Ester [21] evaluated different image qualities and concluded that a 1 megapixel image (i.e. a 1,000 × 1,000 image) was an appropriate size. Now that cellphone cameras deliver 5 megapixel imagery, that seems pitiful, although megapixels are far from everything. Many visitors in front of Van Gogh's "Starry Night" today hold up a phone and take a picture of it, but no matter how many pixels in their cellphone, the low quality lenses, camera shake, viewing angle, and illumination result in an image inferior to what they could buy on a postcard in the MOMA store.

Lindsay MacDonald [22] asked about the ultimate resolution required for art study. His measurements found that a brush with a single sable or mouse hair might be 20 μm across, and that the smallest artifacts in paintings appeared to be in the neighborhood of 50 μm. Similarly, a person with good vision might be able to see features of about that size (but not smaller). He suggested that 1,200 dpi would be adequate to resolve features that are 40 μm wide and thus be "enough" for any practical problem. For a 20 × 30 in. object, that is almost a gigabyte of image, but today that's easily handled. Gigapixel images are routinely used now in panoramas.

Michael Ester [23] discusses a number of reasons why surrogates are deprecated. They do not give a sense of scale, for example; if everything is the size of your computer screen, you do not know what was originally large and what was originally a miniature. Another problem is context. Seeing Michelangelo's "David" in a museum in Florence, surrounded by other sculptures and by paintings, is different from a screen view or holding a small-size copy, although our context is not the context Michelangelo had. He thought originally that it was going to be on the cathedral roof and would have seen it placed in a public square; it was not moved to the museum until more than 200 years after his death.

Perhaps the most ambitious recent scanning project is the Google Art project, which now includes more than 30,000 images from more than 150 collections. The project also includes views of the galleries in which the artworks are presented, so that one can see the works in their actual context, and "walk through" the museum. Although not a 3-D model of the museum, it gives a similar feeling.

3-D. Perhaps the quickest adoption of 3-D digitising was in architecture. Architects use CAD models of buildings to generate the construction blueprints and help with structural engineering [24]. Often architects create a physical 3-D scale model of the building to show the clients, just as they once built models of cardboard or wood; the CAD drawings and 3-D printers build these more easily.

Models of historic buildings are also useful for studying structural as well as artistic issues. Beauvais, for example, has a cathedral that is in danger of collapse. It has been scanned in detail with the aim of doing careful modeling of the structure [25], remembering that many times in the past engineers who thought they were helping to stabilise a building actually made things worse. Cathedral structures are very complex and computer modeling is helping in the structural analysis.

The virtual reconstruction of destroyed buildings is now an active area of research. For example, a number of historic synagogues destroyed in Germany have been modeled and it has become possible to "view" them in full 3-D, rather than just look at photographs [26, 27]. An excellent example of remote access is the International Dunhuang Project [28] using virtual reality to both (a) let people look at wall paintings in caves in the Chinese desert, and (b) to let people look at objects which are now scattered around the world.

Research

The step after relying on digital copies rather than originals is to have the research done by computer algorithms. At first this "research" concentrated on mechanical tasks, such as the preparation of concordances [29]. Now we see relatively sophisticated studies being done by algorithms, involving syntactic and semantic analysis. Technology to help scholars comes from natural language applications such as sentiment analysis or machine translation. Although we are not yet in a comparable state those areas of scientific research where data processing is essential, increasingly computation appears in cultural and artistic research.

Books. Early high-profile research done with digitised texts included authorship studies. The first work in this area was done by hand; it is the famous study by Mosteller [30] on authorship of the *Federalist* papers. Morton [31] and Wake [32] were other early authorship studies. Other early work was on poetry, such as Milic [33] and Sowa [34]. Some of these projects were done without full text; the metrical patterns alone sufficed.

Robert Harris [35] described simple ways of doing literary analysis with computers. For example, Mark Twain made fun of James Fenimore Cooper for his repeated use of a character stepping on a dry twig and thus disclosing his presence. Harris suggests that one can easily count the instances of *twig, stick,* or *branch* and check whether Twain's ridicule was justified.

More advanced work has followed, especially now that large collections of texts are available. Even the *New York Times* [36] has recently published an article about "big data" in literary research, showing that Jane Austen and Sir Walter Scott were the most influential nineteenth century writers, comparing the number of times that other works shared words and themes with them. To do this, more than 3,500 novels in machine-readable form were analyzed.

Michel [37] introduced the term "culturomics" and reviewed many cultural changes in terms of searches over the Google Books corpus. He demonstrates one instance of censorship in Nazi Germany by noticing that references to Marc Chagall disappear from German literature between 1936 and 1944, and also covers topics ranging across medicine, science, religion and cooking using the book data.

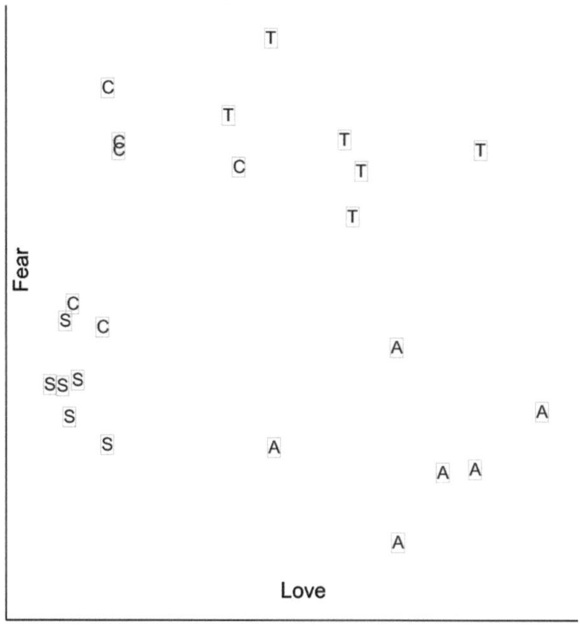

Fig. 2.3 Plot of thesaurus category occurrences. Books are as follows. (*A*) Jane Austen: Emma, Mansfield Park, Northanger Abbey, Persuasion, Pride and Prejudice, Sense and Sensibility. (*C*) Willkie Collins: After Dark, Armadale, The Evil Genius, The Moonstone, No Name, The Woman in White. (*S*) Sir Walter Scott: Guy Mannering, The Heart Of Mid-Lothian, Ivanhoe, Quentin Durward, Rob Roy, Waverley. (*T*) Anthony Trollope: Can You Forgive Her, The Duke's Children, The Eustace Diamonds, Phineas Finn, Phineas Redux, The Prime Minister

As a very simple example of grouping literary works by genre, Fig. 2.3 is a plot of the relative occurrences of words in the Roget categories "Fear" and "Love" in six works by each of four authors: Jane Austen, Willkie Collins, Sir Walter Scott and Anthony Trollope. This is actually a visualisation and extension of an exercise in a first programming course. For both categories, the words listed in the category in a 1911 Roget's Thesaurus were counted in each novel. The results are plotted; to nobody's surprise, Jane Austen scores high on "love" and low on "fear" while Willkie Collins is high on "fear" and low on "love". The Jane Austen novel that scores highest on "fear" is of course *Northanger Abbey.*

Flat artistic works. Research into paintings has been slower to develop, but James Z. Wang has done several provocative studies. One of these [38] looked at the ability of algorithms to recognise esthetically pleasing images. Features extracted from the images which had been rated for aesthetic appeal were used to fit the ratings; important features for this purpose included color saturation, round shapes, and image similarity (whether the image had components similar to components of other images in the data set).

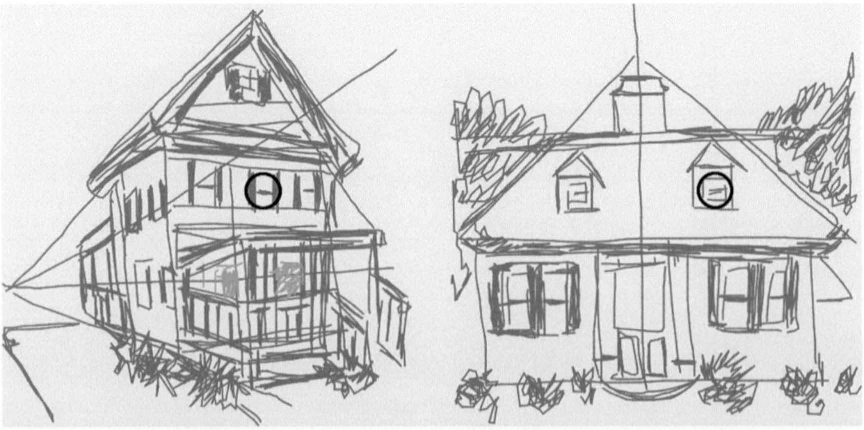

Fig. 2.4 Image matches across sketches (Drawings by Annamarie Klose, used with permission)

In another study [39] the brushstrokes in Van Gogh paintings were extracted automatically and his paintings were found to have longer and more regular brushstrokes than those of his contemporaries. This confirmed earlier art historical opinion but provided numerical measurements for the features. The work was not successful, however, at detecting a known forgery. Just as authorship studies have been of great significance in literary research, forgery detection matters in art history. Polatkan [40] describes promising work on forgery detection using wavelets.

Similarly Li [41] was able to extract brushstrokes from traditional Chinese painting. Graham [42] tried to extract stylistic features by spatial frequency analysis and analogised the problem to both the study of human perception and to the kinds of literary analysis described in the previous section. The paper attempted to distinguish naturalistic representations from more diagrammatic imagery, and talked about the new field of "visual stylometry."

Figure 2.4 shows some very preliminary work on finding common elements in sketches. Drawings for which we know the stroke sequence were segmented by both time and space and then visually similar portions were found automatically.

Just as genres of novels can be distinguished by elements, Shamir [43] has been able to plot relations between artistic works. In his tree of painters, Rembrandt and Rubens are close as are Renoir and Monet, but those two pairings are far apart.

Other uses of image technology include Crandall [44], who has an ambitious discussion of tracking human motion and finding landmarks in general imagery. Manovich [45] also writes about applications of "big data" in cultural contexts. He discusses the role of computation for exploring massive data, to be followed by human analysis, and reviews the wide variety of data now available, ranging over social media, photographic sites, and commercially produced materials.

3-D Sculptures. Less has been done on sculptures, of course. As one example, Rodriguez-Echevarria [46] is building a 3-D inventory of sculpture with detailed tags on the elements of the sculpture, but the tags are assigned manually. Flaherty [47] explains how 3-D printing techniques are being used to repair sculptures; but in this work, the decisions are made by scholars.

Today we can create 3-D maps of cities based on aerial photography, and 3-D databases of buildings. A remarkable recent study is Agrawal's "Building Rome in a Day" [48], which used vast numbers of amateur photographs for photogrammetric modeling. Once data is available, we can expect algorithms that identify features characteristic of different sculptors and different sculptural subjects.

Has Research Changed?

Inclusion. A colleague of mine, Marc Donner, suggested that the most important aspect of digitisation would be the large number of items rescued from obscurity. Tens of thousands of nineteenth century books have heretofore been available only in the largest libraries, and the typical art museum can only display a small fraction of its paintings. Wider availability of little-known material might redirect research.

I skimmed the titles of articles in *English Literary History* for the years 1936, 1961, and 2010–2011. The subjects of study remain the traditional corpus: Spenser, Shakespeare, Chaucer and Milton continue to dominate. I saw only one author who had been obscure and but had been the subject of a recent article (James Hogg). I then checked the most recent issues of the journal *Literary and Linguistic Computing*, which of course contains a great many articles about tools rather than about authors. Its list of authors studied is more inclusive, since it includes non-English writers and more modern authors (including Agatha Christie and P. D. James) but it still contains Bacon, Bentham, Darwin, and Shakespeare. There are of course, some authors whose popularity rises and falls; see Fig. 2.5.

It may be too soon to make conclusions here. It has only been a few years since we have had millions of books online, and the barriers to commercial content still make it difficult for many scholars to do very wide-ranging studies, so that, for example,

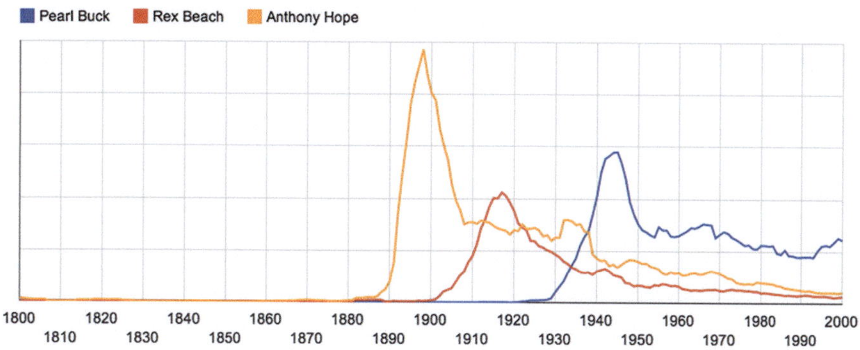

Fig. 2.5 Google "ngram" showing references to Anthony Hope, Rex Beach and Pearl Buck

the work on literary influence described by Lohr [36] was done on nineteenth century books that are out of copyright.

A subject that is particularly popular in computer literary studies is still authorship, even beyond text. Dobrzynski [49] discusses attribution of Native American artworks, often collected a century ago with no attempt to record the name of the carver or other creator. For example, the Denver Art Museum identified someone known previously as the Master of the Chicago Settee (a wooden object in the Field Museum). Widespread access to multiple images, just as with multiple texts, is critical to such studies.

Questioning. Sometimes authors using computers address new styles of research problems. Consider three kinds of questions:

1. Those only suitable for computers (e.g., counting the number of superlatives in Dickens and Smollett).
2. Those that could be done either with traditional or with algorithmic methods, such as tracing influences by Jane Austen in the work of other writers.
3. Those that it is still hard to address algorithmically, such as discussing the role of religion in Keats' poetry or the importance of gold in the research of Michael Faraday.

The perceived danger is that research which is easy to do will supplant work that is more important. Looking at literary research, where the most progress has been made, we see traditional questions such as authorship, influence, and literary style still dominating. In artistic research, we see work on brushstrokes and composition. The academic community seems to maintain its focus, perhaps following Lord Balfour's aphorism "History does not repeat itself. Historians repeat each other." In science, "big data" is changing the way we study protein chemistry or flu epidemics.

The humanities are also benefitting from data analysis, including techniques such as quantitative historical methods, or Schilit's paper [50] on quotations from one book to another in a million book collection. Perhaps the most remarkable success has been statistical machine translation. If Google Translate can succeed based on statistical methods, so can stylistic or thematic analysis.

Conclusions

What sequence of research projects should we expect? There are techniques in commercial and government applications, such as sentiment analysis and social network analysis, now being introduced to cultural studies. The wide scope of cultural materials available cannot yet be easily exploited for practical reasons: Google may have scanned 20 million books, more than all but a few libraries, but copyright bottlenecks prevent access for researchers. Academic inertia also impedes new studies, including a perception that there are greater rewards for inventing a new theory than for accumulating or analyzing data, a problem that also exists in the sciences.

Image and sculpture study will follow behind literary studies, and will in turn be followed by film and dance. We can anticipate authorship studies based on comparisons of details, and similar stylometric analysis. We can expect emotional analysis to follow, just as sentiment analysis is now widespread with text. The kinds of image analysis done for searching and scanning – face recognition, feature extraction, analysis of differences – will be applied in cultural studies, just as statistical methods moved into historical research. This is the model of the intelligence agencies, which try to integrate information over millions and billions of messages and images.

The most relevant aphorism may be "more data beats better algorithms" [51]. The style of textual research that relies on huge collections and answers questions by statistical methods rather than individual item analysis can be applied to other media as well. Once we can recognise the features of cultural objects, and collect these features over millions of items, we can hope to reach some level of conceptual and intellectual understanding.

References

1. Pollard, A. W., & Redgrave, G. R. (1926). *A short-title catalog of books printed in England, Scotland, and Ireland, and of English books printed abroad, 1475–1640*. London: The Bibliographical Society.
2. Wing, D. *Short-title catalogue of books printed in England, Scotland, Ireland, Wales and British America and of English books printed in other countries, 1641–1700*, 3 vols. New York: The Index Society, 1945–51.
3. Borgman, C. L. (1997). From acting locally to thinking globally: A brief history of library automation. *The Library Quarterly, 67*(3), 215–249.
4. Brunner, T. F. (1991). The thesaurus Linguae Graecae: Classics and the computer. *Library Hi Tech, 9*(1), 61–67.
5. Quay, A. (2012). Google engineer builds automatic 'page-turning scanner', uses vacuum cleaner. Taxi, 13. http://designtaxi.com/news/354337/Google-Engineer-Builds-Automatic-Page-Turning-Scanner-Uses-Vacuum-Cleaner/. Accessed 28 Jan 2013.
6. Kiernan, K. S. (1991). Digital image processing and the Beowulf manuscript. *Literary and Linguist Computing, 6*(1), 20–27.
7. Hind, A. M. (1912). *A catalogue of Rembrandt's etchings*. New York: Fred Stokes.
8. Besser, H. (1990). Visual access to visual images: The UC Berkeley image database project. *Library Trends, 38*(4), 787–798.
9. ARTstor Blog. *About ARTstor*. http://artstor.wordpress.com/about-2/. Accessed 28 Jan 2013.
10. Levoy, M., Pulli, K., Curless, B., Rusinkiewicz, S., Koller, D., Pereira, L., Ginzton, M., Anderson, S., Davis, J., Ginsberg, J., Shade, J., & Fulk, D. (2000). The digital Michelangelo project: 3D scanning of large statues." In *Proceedings of the 27th annual conference on computer graphics and interactive techniques (SIGGRAPH'00)*, (pp. 131–144). New York: ACM Press/Addison-Wesley.
11. Kanade, T., Rander, P., Vedula, S., & Saito, H. (1999). Virtualised reality: Digitizing a 3D time-varying event as is and in real time. In Y. Ohta & H. Tamura (Eds.), *Mixed reality, merging real and virtual worlds* (pp. 41–57). Heidelberg, Germany: Springer.
12. Baker, N. (2001). *Double fold: Libraries and the assault on paper*. New York: Random House.
13. Egan, D. E., Lesk, M. E., Ketchum, R. D., Lochbaum, C. C., Remde, J. R., Littman, M., & Landauer.T. K. Hypertext for the electronic library? CORE sample results. In *Proceedings Hypertext '91* (pp. 299–312). San Antonio, 15–18 December 1991.

14. Nielsen, J. iPad and Kindle reading speed. Jakob Nielsen's Alertbox, 2 July 2010. http://www.nngroup.com/articles/ipad-and-kindle-reading-speeds/. Accessed 29 Jan 2013.
15. Siegenthaler, E., Wurtz, P., Bergamin, P., & Groner, R. (2011). Comparing reading processes on e-ink displays and print. *Displays, 32*(5), 268–273.
16. Harris, P. (2012). Reading speed variations on paper vs. computer vs. Kindle. In *6th annual conference, vision performance institute*. Pacific University College of Optometry, OR. http://commons.pacificu.edu/cgi/viewcontent.cgi?article=1006&context=vpir6. Accessed 29 Jan 2013.
17. Wacholder, N., Liu, L., & Liu, Y-H. (2006). User behavior during the book selection process. *Proceedings American Society for Information Science and Technology*, *43*:1–16.
18. Wang, J. (2006). Approaching pre-modern China through the computer: The impact of full-text databases on Sinological research. Private communication.
19. Lesk, M. (1985). Graphical information resources: Maps and beyond. In *Proceedings of 8th annual ACM SIGIR conference on Research and Development in Information Retrieval (SIGIR'85)*, (pp. 2–8). New York: ACM.
20. Humphries, T., & Thompson, S. (2012). *A Hippocratic Intuition for Balance in Warburg's Mnemosyne Atlas*. Transtechnology Research Reader, Plymouth University. http://trans-techresearch.net/wp-content/uploads/2010/11/Humphries-and-Thompson.pdf. Accessed 23 May 2013.
21. Ester, M. (1990). Image quality and viewer perception. Digital Image Digital Cinema. Supplemental Issue. *Leonardo*, *1*(23), 51–63.
22. Macdonald, L. The limits of resolution. In A. Seal, J. P. Bowen, & K. Ng (Eds.), *EVA London 2010 conference proceedings*. Electronic Workshops in Computing (eWiC), British Computer Society, 2010. http://ewic.bcs.org/content/ConWebDoc/36085. Accessed 23 May 2013.
23. Ester, M. (1993). Image use in art: Historical practice. Gateways, gatekeepers and roles in the information omniverse, Association of Research Libraries, Washington DC. http://web.archive.org/web/20110602124423/www.arl.org/resources/pubs/symp3/ester.shtml. Accessed 23 May 2013.
24. Boland, R. J., Lyytinen, K., & Yoo, Y. (2007). Wakes of innovation in project networks: The case of digital 3-D representations in architecture, engineering, and construction. *Organization Science, 18*(4), 631–647.
25. Allen, P. K., Troccoli, A., Smith, B., Stamos, I., & Murray, S. (2003). The Beauvais Cathedral Project. In *Computer Vision and Pattern Recognition Workshop* (p. 10), Madison. Los Alamitos: IEEE Computer Society.
26. Krebs, F., & Brück, E. (2002). Historical buildings in 3D. In *EVA London 2002*. Electronic Visualisation and the Arts, London. http://www.memo38.de/root_IE/main/d/d_01/3d-visualisation_of_lost_jewish_heritage.pdf. Accessed 23 May 2013.
27. McNamara, M. Destroyed German synagogues reconstructed on web page. *The New York Times*, 24 September 1998.
28. Lutz, B., & Weintke, M. (1999). Virtual Dunhuang art cave: A cave within a CAVE. *Computer Graphics Forum*, *18*(3):257–264. See also the International Dunhuang Project, idp.bl.uk.
29. Packard, D. W. (1968). *A concordance to Livy* (Vol. 4). Cambridge, MA: Harvard University Press.
30. Mosteller, F., & Wallace, D. (1963). Inference in an authorship problem. *Journal of the American Statistical Association, 58*(302), 275–309.
31. Morton, A. Q. (1965). The authorship of Greek prose. *Journal of the Royal Statistical Society, Series A, 128*(2), 169–233.
32. Wake, W. C. (1957). Sentence length distributions of Greek authors. *Journal of the Royal Statistical Society, 120*, 331–346.
33. Milic, L. T. Winged words: Carieties of computer applications to literature. In *Proceedings Fall Joint Computer conference* (pp. 321–326). New York: ACM, 14–16 November 1967.
34. Sowa, C. A., & Sowa, J. F. (1974). Thought clusters in early Greek oral poetry. *Computers and the Humanities, 8*, 131–146.

35. Harris, R. The personal computer as a tool for student literary analysis. VirtualSalt, 30 December 1994. http://www.virtualsalt.com/comptool.htm. Accessed 29 Jan 2013.
36. Lohr, S. Dickens, Austen and Twain, through a digital lens. *The New York Times*, p. BU3, 27 January 2013.
37. Michel, J., Shen, Y., Aiden, A., Veres, A., Gray, M., Pickett, J., Hoiberg, D., Clancy, D., Norvig, P., Orwant, J., Pinker, S., Nowak, M., & Aiden, E. (2011). Quantitative analysis of culture using millions of digitised books. *Science, 331*(6014), 176–182.
38. Datta, R., Joshi, D., Li, J., & Wang, J. Z. (2006). Studying aesthetics in photographic images using a computational approach. In *Proceedings of European conference on computer vision*, Part III (pp. 288–301), Graz, Austria, May 2006. Springer, Lecture Notes in Computer Science, Vol. 3953. Heidelberg, Germany: Springer.
39. Li, J., Yao, L., Hendriks, E., & Wang, J. Z. (2012). Rhythmic brushstrokes distinguish van Gogh from his contemporaries: Findings via automated brushstroke extraction. *IEEE Transactions on Pattern Analysis and Machine Intelligence, 34*(6), 1159–1176.
40. Polatkan, G., Jafarpour, S., Brasoveanu, A., Hughes, S., & Daubechies, I. Detection of forgery in paintings using supervised learning. In 16th *IEEE international conference on image processing (ICIP)* (pp. 2921–2914), Cairo, 7–10 November 2009. Piscataway: IEEE.
41. Li, J., & Wang, J. Z. (2003). Studying digital imagery of ancient paintings by mixtures of stochastic models. *IEEE Transactions on Image Processing, 13*(3), 340–353.
42. Graham, D. J., Hughes, J. M., Leder, H., & Rockmore, D. N. (2012). Statistics, vision and the analysis of artistic style. *WIREs Computational Statistics, 4*, 115–123.
43. Shamir, L., & Tarakhovsky, J. (2012). Computer analysis of art. *Journal on Computing and Cultural Heritage*, *5*(2), 1–11, article 7.
44. Crandall, D., & Snavely, N. (2012). Modeling people and places with internet photo collections. *ACM Queue*, *10*(5), 30–44.
45. Manovich, L. Trending: The promises and the challenges of big social data. 28 April 2011. http://www.manovich.net/DOCS/Manovich_trending_paper.pdf. Accessed 5 Apr 2013.
46. Rodriguez-Echavarria, K., Morris, D., & Arnold, D. (2009). Web based presentation of semantically tagged 3D content for public sculptures and monuments in the UK. In S. N. Spencer (Ed.), *Proceedings of 14th international conference on 3D Web technology (Web3D'09)* (pp. 119–126). New York: ACM.
47. Flaherty, J. Harvard's 3D-printing archaeologists fix ancient artifacts. *Wired*, 10 December 2012. http://www.wired.com/design/2012/12/harvard-3d-printing-archaelogy/. Accessed 29 Jan 2013.
48. Agarwal, S., Yurukawa, Y., Snavely, N., Simon, I., Curless, B., Seitz, S. M., & Szeliski, R. (2011). Building Rome in a day. *Communications of the ACM, 54*(10), 105–112.
49. Dobrzynksi, J. Honoring art, honoring artists. *The New York Times,* p. AR1, 6 February 2011.
50. Schilit, B. N., & Kolak, O. (2008). Exploring a digital library through key ideas. In *Proceedings of 8th ACM/IEEE-CS Joint Conference on Digital Libraries (JCDL'08)* (pp. 177–186), Pittsburgh. New York: ACM.
51. Rajaraman, A. More data usually beats better algorithms. *Datawocky*, 24 March 2008. http://anand.typepad.com/datawocky/2008/03/more-data-usual.html. Accessed 4 Apr 2013.

Chapter 3
Quantifying Culture: Four Types of Value in Visualisation

Chris Alen Sula

Abstract As cultural heritage work increasingly involves quantitative data, the need for sophisticated tools, methods and representations becomes ever more pressing. The field of information visualisation can make a helpful intervention here. This chapter explores four types of value associated with visualisation (cognitive, emotional, social and ethical/political) and discusses their prospects and limitations, including examples. The chapter concludes with a case study illustrating the value of visualisation.

Cultural Heritage Institutions and Quantitative Data

Cultural heritage institutions have undergone major changes in the past few decades, marked by a noticeable shift toward the digital. Items once preserved carefully in archives – largely sealed from the general public – have now been given new life in digital collections; access, use and sharing have become central values at the most progressive institutions. Within this digital turn, there are two moments of significance. The first is the creation of digital objects (or the capture of "born-digital" ones), which opens up new possibilities for accessing, sharing and using content.

This chapter is an updated and extended version of the following paper, published here with kind permission of the Chartered Institute for IT (BCS) and of EVA London Conferences: C.A. Sula, "Quantifying Culture: The value of visualization inside (and outside) libraries, museums, and the academy." In S. Dunn, J. P. Bowen, and K. Ng (eds.). *EVA London 2012 Conference Proceedings*. Electronic Workshops in Computing (eWiC), British Computer Society, 2012. http://www.bcs.org/ewic/eva2012 (accessed 26 May 2013).

C.A. Sula (✉)
Pratt Institute, School of Information & Library Science,
144 West 14th Street, Sixth Floor, New York, NY 10011, USA
e-mail: csula@pratt.edu

J.P. Bowen et al. (eds.), *Electronic Visualisation in Arts and Culture*,
Springer Series on Cultural Computing, DOI 10.1007/978-1-4471-5406-8_3,

The second moment, which is the occasion of this chapter, is the point at which these scans, digital images, digital recordings, etc. become *data*.

Two types of data may be involved with cultural heritage work. One is metadata, which describes these digital objects in a structured format and facilitates information retrieval, organisation and architecture. The second type is the data present in the *content* of items themselves, especially in the case of digitised records. Birth certificates, census counts and other ambient records are physical instruments for collecting and storing information. They have fields for "given name" or "race" or for more administrative metadata, such as record number or preparer. This information may be transformed into digital data by employing character recognition and also by exploiting the fact that these records are *visual* materials, whose layouts provide important clues about the types of information being recorded. Names are tagged as "Name," letters and numbers become "Date of birth," and so on. These values may even enter into databases where they can be aggregated, compared, merged and reconciled with other datasets.

Born-digital artifacts are even richer in quantitative information. Many photos, tweets and posts now carry embedded geospatial data, and the platforms that host them capture relationships between people and groups, forming large-scale social networks, the scope and documentation of which is unprecedented in human history.

Though data comes in various types (e.g., numerical, geospatial, relational), it may all be discussed under the rubric of "quantitative" information. The defining characteristic of quantitative data is regularisation through fields, value formats and validation. Qualitative data, or "document-centric" information [1], lacks these structures and is open in length and format, often preventing validation. Part of the reason why it is worth considering both types of information as "data" is that both are susceptible to analysis through computational means: statistical processing in the former case and natural language, image, or audio processing in the latter. These analytical methods also bring with them the need for more advanced representations of results. In the case of large collections, one simply *cannot* process such high-volume longitudinal data in a textual form. Attempting to do so would exhaust limits of human memory and attention long before trends could be noticed.

The field of information visualisation can make a helpful intervention here. Visualisation, broadly defined, sits at the centre of cognitive science, computer visualisation and data analysis. Colin Ware defines the term 'visualisation' as "a graphical representation of data or concepts," specifically designed to harness and augment basic powers of human perception for the task of comprehending large-scale information [2]. Current information visualisations allow viewers to browse through complex datasets, noting top-level patterns and trends and often drilling down into more detailed information. Lin [3] reviews several early studies that identify contexts in which information visualisation is particularly useful: where there is an organisational structure that brings related items together [4], when users are unfamiliar with a collection [5] or its organisation [6], when users have trouble describing their information needs [7], or when information is easier to recognise than describe [8]. All of these instances have wide application to the materials found in cultural heritage institutions and many are especially relevant to the case of structured, quantitative data.

Though cognitive enhancements are the most frequently discussed benefits of visualisation, they do not exhaust a theoretical account of the value of visualisation. After all, many trends, groupings and hypotheses generated through visualisations require independent, statistical confirmation. Though visualisation may help show the way, or, "answer questions you didn't know you had" [9], it is not the final or only approach to large data and its value is not limited strictly to its interaction with human cognitive systems. A more complete account would recognise other types of value added by visualisation, including emotional and social value, as well as ethical and political value. The following four sections each develop one type of value associated with visualisation. Each section also highlights examples of visualisation related to cultural information and suggests future areas of research to enhance our understanding of the development, use and evaluation of visualisation.

The Cognitive Benefits of Visualisation

Information visualisation attempts to harness quick perceptual systems for the purpose of processing information. Card, Mackinlay and Shneiderman even *define* 'visualisation' as "the use of computer-supported, interactive visual representations of data to amplify cognition" [10]. In discussing this definition, they list a number of cognitive benefits associated with visualisation:

- Increasing memory and processing resources available,
- Reducing search for information,
- Enhancing the recognition of patterns,
- Enabling perceptual inference operations (which are much faster than logical ones),
- Using perceptual attention mechanisms for monitoring and
- Encoding info in a manipulable medium.

According to Larkin and Simon, many of these benefits are achieved by substituting rapid perceptual inferences for more difficult logical ones [11]. This switch is made possible by preventive processing: low-level tasks in the human visual system that occur less than 200–250 milliseconds from the time an observer sees a visual stimulus. Healey and Enns summarise the range of these tasks as:

- *Target detection:* users rapidly and accurately detect the presence or absence of a "target" element with a unique visual feature within a field of distractor elements,
- *Boundary detection:* users rapidly and accurately detect a texture boundary between two groups of elements, where all of the elements in each group have a common visual property,
- *Region tracking:* users track one or more elements with a unique visual feature as they move in time and space, and
- *Counting and estimation:* users count or estimate the number of elements with a unique visual feature [12].

Visualisations that make good use of pre-attentive processing often help viewers to grasp large, complex datasets for the first time. This characterisation is reflected in Franco Moretti's *Graphs, Maps, Trees: Abstract Models for a Literary History* [13]. As opposed to the close readings of a single text that typify literary scholarship, Moretti employs a "distance reading" method: "instead of concrete, individual works, a trio of artificial constructs – graphs, maps, trees – [is used] in which the reality of the text undergoes a process of deliberate reduction and abstraction…. fewer elements, hence a sharper sense of overall interconnection. Shapes, relations, structures. Forms. Models" (p. 1). In particular, Moretti's graph of the rise of the novel in Britain and Japan (1700s), Italy and Spain (1800s) and Nigeria (1900s) provokes new questions about the development of the genre and the underlying forces of industrialisation that account for these trends. "[M]ost radically," he says of quantitative visualisations, "we see them *falsifying* existing theoretical explanations, and ask for a theory" (p. 30).

In addition to amplifying cognition, visualisation has also been discussed in the context of aiding decision-making [2], as well as facilitating collaboration, engaging new audiences and fostering higher levels of understanding [14]. Additional social uses of visualisation are discussed in section "Visualisations as Social Objects" of this chapter.

A helpful example of cognitive enhancement applied to cultural materials is "Mapping the Republic of Letters: Exploring Correspondence and Intellectual Community in the Early Modern Period (1500–1800)," based at Stanford University (http://republicofletters.stanford.edu). The primary source material for the project includes over 2,000 correspondents who formed a communication network across Europe, Asia, Africa and the Americas and different project interfaces leverage mapping and network analysis techniques to trace interactions across space and time (Fig. 3.1). A key macroscopic component of this effort is its focus on high-level trends, structures and patterns, rather than the individuals that compose and exist within those larger elements. Such visualisations are no substitute for detailed analysis of primary source documents but rather an alternative method for understanding a set of material. The hundreds of individuals and thousands of connections between them could not be apprehended in textual form, yet visualisation renders these documents quite saliently at a glance.

Visualisation and the Emotions

Cognitive benefits are the most commonly discussed advantage of visualisation, receiving two to three times more attention than emotional and social advantages [15]. Bresciani and Eppler do discuss emotional *dis*advantages through studies of disturbing content [16, 17], boringness and ugliness [17], personal preferences [18], prior experiences [19] and wrong use of colour [2, 20, 21]. A closer examination of these sources, however, shows only casual reference to the role of emotions; none of the studies are specifically about the role of emotion in visualisation.

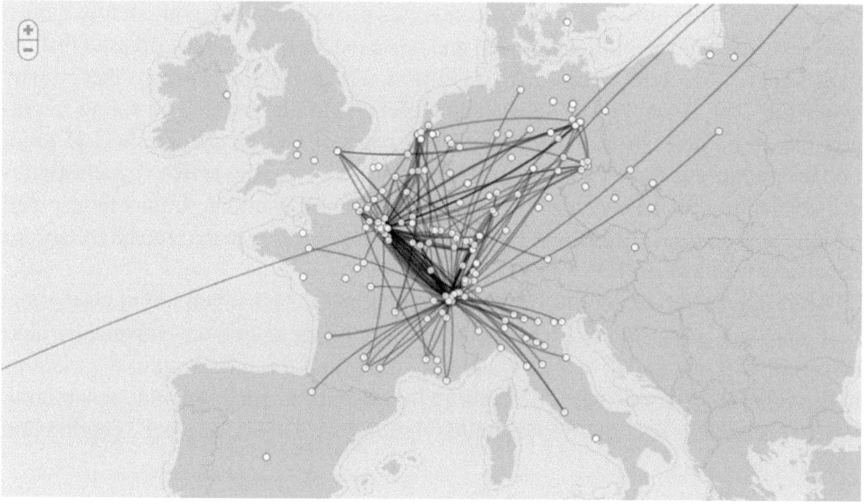

Fig. 3.1 Ink interface for the Republic of Letters showing all the letters sent and received by Voltaire (Image courtesy of Mapping the Republic of Letters, Stanford University and DensityDesign Research Lab, Milan)

Even in-depth studies of visualisation aesthetics examine general features such as "beauty" and "ugliness" [22, 23].

Though research into visualisation and the emotions is sorely lacking, emotions have been found to play an important (although infrequently discussed) role in information processing generally [24] and it is reasonable to suspect that emotions enter into perceptions of visualisations, either alone or (more likely) in tandem with cognitive and other factors. Visual elements such as shape, flow, texture, position and colour are likely to elicit emotional responses from viewers, much in the same way that those elements engage preattentive processing to amplify cognition. More extensive studies of emotion and visualisation might explore the ways in which emotions bind to particular visual elements (perhaps differentially); interact with preattentive processing and Gestalt effects; facilitate cognition, meaning and understanding; and influence decision-making and action with respect to visualisation.

Chief among considerations of visualisation and emotions would be inquiries into the special role of colour, widely regarded as having emotional connotations – and one of the most problematic elements of visualisation. MacDonald [25] discusses the three ways that colour perception may vary across instances of observation, all of which involve cultural factors: individual differences, both genetic and developmental; group-level effects, such as gender and expert training; and the context of presentation itself, such as the display medium and colour calibration. Though earlier research attempted to discover universal colour names and associated emotional reactions, the most successful studies found only six to seven cross-cultural colour names [26] and very general emotional valences, such as positive/negative and active/passive [27]. In a controlled experiment, Post and

Greene found that only eight colour categories plus white were consistently named with better than 75 % probability [28] and more recent studies have stressed that the meaning of colour terms varies across cultures, along with the emotions that colours evoke [29, 30]. An ambitious (if questionable) attempt to understand colour in culture has come through David McCandless's chart of 13 colours and their 85 emotional associations across 10 cultural groupings [31]. (An interactive visualisation is also available [32].) This chart is based on data from "Pantone, ColorMatters, and various web sources," making it hard to fully evaluate its research methodology for consistency and reliability.

More rigorous research into colour, emotion and visualisation might also reveal best practices for using colour to convey certain messages or, conversely, alert researchers to manipulative uses of colour – all with reference to cultural variations in the emotional significance of colour. In the absence of such research, it is premature to speculate about more systematic relationships between colour, emotion and visualisation.

Visualisations as Social Objects

IBM researcher Martin Wattenberg was among the first to discuss the "social life of visualizations," [33] in which audience members participate in social data analysis through shared discussions, hypotheses testing and even gameplaying. These and other social uses of visualisation draw attention to the sense in which visualisations, once created, are social objects – artifacts, documents, *things* – that can be held up, examined, critiqued and shared. Heer similarly notes that such objects can establish shared interpretations (e.g., "do you see what I see?"), create spaces for conversation and break conventional boundaries through expected uses and reinventions of technology [34]. Both researchers point to NameVoyager, an interactive visualisation of baby name data from the 1880s to the present [35], which sparked widespread discussion well beyond the intended user community of prospective parents.

More recent research has explored visualisation-based collaboration, both synchronous and asynchronous. This literature generally recognises the complex and specialised nature of information processing in the present day, hoping to meet this task with the joint forces of visualisation, collaboration and social intelligence. Collaborative contexts for visualisation may range from viewing visualisations in group environments (e.g., lectures, presentations), to collaborative interaction/exploration and sharing/creating of visualisations [14]. Specific tasks accomplished by visualisation include dividing and allocating work; establishing common ground and awareness; providing reference and deixis (context); offering incentives for engagement; promoting identity, trust and reputation; mediating group dynamics; and facilitating consensus and decision making [36]. Specific attention has also been paid to design elements and affordances that facilitate usability and group interaction, including segmented discussion spaces, pointing and annotation mechanisms, collection creation and linked views [37]; the wide range of skill level different viewers may bring with them to the same visualisation [38]; and "casual" visualisation, including ambient visualisation, artistic visualisation and other examples [39].

In some cases, visualisation also facilitates data *collection*. A common example is rating and commenting interfaces that also display aggregated feedback through visualisations. Another example is the Transborder Immigrant Tool, a digital art project by Micha Cardenas and Jason Najarro at the University of California San Diego, which uses hacked Nextel cell phones to track immigrant geolocations across the Mexico/U.S. Border. As well as providing undocumented immigrants with access to map information, the application's creators hope it will "add an intelligent agent algorithm that would parse out the best routes and trails on that day and hour for immigrants to cross this vertiginous landscape as safely as possible" [40].

The Ethics and Power of Visualisation

The problem of bias has long been discussed with reference to acts of collection and curating, especially where cultural materials are concerned. Decisions over which items to collect, preserve and digitise, as well as how to categorise and disseminate them, all position cultural heritage institutions as contested sites of power. How visualisation might change, mediate, or interact with such power is a pressing ethical question.

The data foundation of visualisations often bestows a false air of objectivity and neutrality upon them. As Huff pointed out long ago, it is always possible to lie with statistics [41] and so too is it possible to lie with the datasets that form the basis of visualisations, if not the visual representations themselves. No matter how neutral or objective a dataset or collection purports to be, there may be residual biases in measurement design, modelling techniques or background assumptions. Cathy Davidson puts the point nicely: "Data transform theory; theory, stated or assumed, transforms data into interpretation. As any student of Foucault would insist, data collection is really data selection. Which archives should we preserve? Choices based on a complex ideational architecture of canonical, institutional, and personal preferences are constantly being made" [42]. In this respect, a more robust "ethics of visualisation" is needed to guide practitioners toward transparent and critical approaches to their data.

On occasion, visualisation can be of help in bringing questionable data to the fore of discussion. If large portions of continuous trend data are missing or a significant number of outliers present, such omissions or deviations will be plainly visible in faithful representations. These visual cues invite questions about whether trends are indeed as they appear, whether outliers are genuine outliers or something else (e.g., perhaps nothing more than an innocent keystroke error during data entry). Visualisations can even be used to represent imperfect data, as shown in a recent study that examined uncertainty across 18 different subject domains [43]. Though the arts and humanities were largely absent from this study, the five cross-domain categories for understanding uncertainty (measurement, completeness, inference, credibility and disagreement) are easily transferable to many disciplines. Visual techniques may not be able to address all types or degrees of uncertainty, but they can represent many of them more fully than statistical measures – especially measures of central tendency – and help to reduce the impression that findings are determinate or at least more certain than they are. Such techniques must be incorporated in the design process more frequently to be successful and Boyd Davis et. al. (Chap. 17) note how unusual it is for historical visualisations to bother representing imprecision or uncertainty.

Still, we must be on guard about the power of visualisations to misrepresent and mislead – as all representations can. Though some resources exist for visualisers, especially journalists [44–46], their guidance is mainly confined to case-based design studies and question of accuracy. Similar examples are found outside the world of journalism [47, 48], but they go little beyond questions of accuracy and design. Subtler effects of omission, framing, emotional manipulation and other ticks are rarely discussed – nor anything about the way in which visualisation might be used to good purpose by raising awareness, providing insight, or correcting false beliefs.

At present, it is worth noting that the shift toward quantitative data provides a level of empirical verifiability that is not found in many non-quantitative forms of visualisation. This shift provides wronged parties with a framework within which to question claims, seek redress and present counter-narratives, in much the same way that human rights advocates have historically advanced empirical realities in the service of greater equality. This process is far from perfect; evidence can be ignored and powerful bodies often have more resources to produce data than those with less privilege. Nevertheless, an empirical framework is, in principle, more disinterested on the whole. The victors can still write history, but only insofar as they can measure it – and cannot avoid *all* measurements of it, even those that challenge established narratives.

Visualisation, however, can do more than just reduce harm through minimising bias, error and false completeness; it can also *help* individuals and groups, especially those that are unrepresented or underrepresented in the past or present. A prominent example here is Invisible Australians (http://invisibleaustralians.org), which documents Indigenous Australians and thousands of non-Europeans – including Chinese, Japanese, Indians, Afghans, Syrians and Malays – who faced discriminatory laws and policies. The site draws together government records of these individuals, including archival photos (Fig. 3.2) and attempts to "link together their lives." While the site currently focuses on more qualitative aspects of their lives, the quantitative possibilities abound, from frequency charts and line graphs of their history to geospatial mapping and network graphs of their activities and connections.

These and other such uses of visualisation belong to a broader study of "liberation technology" [49–51]. As Diamond [52] points out, though internet and communications technology can be used for censorship, it can also allow individuals to "report news, expose wrongdoing, express opinions, mobilise protest, monitor elections, scrutinise government, deepen participation, and expand the horizons of

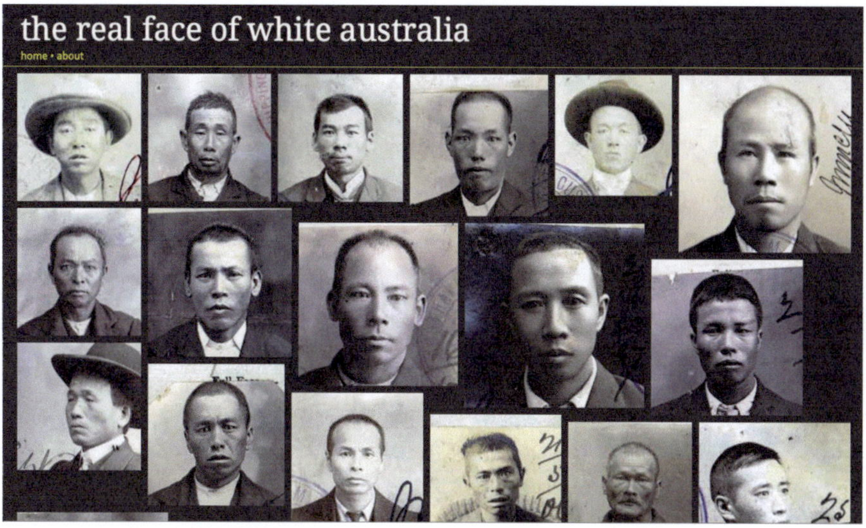

Fig. 3.2 Randomly ordered portraits from the National Archives of Australia extracted using a face detection script. Clicking on a portrait reveals the document it came from, as well as a link to explore the context of the document in the National Archives's RecordSearch database (Image courtesy of http://invisibleaustralians.org/faces/; used under Creative Commons license (CC BY 3.0))

freedom" (p. 70). More generally, it can help create a pluralistic sphere of public discussion before democratic rights are even present. Though much of this literature is centred around contemporary notions of democracy, it should also be noted that the vast amount of cultural heritage materials available for visualisation speak to a range of political, economic and social arrangements of power.

A Case Study of the *Occupy Wall Street Project List*

On September 17, 2011, an encampment protest began in New York City's Zuccotti Park, blocks away from Wall Street and the New York Stock Exchange. Occupy Wall Street, as it came to be known, drew in thousands of residents and tourists for conversations, criticism and direct actions, and generated solidarity groups in all 50 states before its forcible eviction two months later. Reflecting on this movement in December 2012, *Time* magazine noted a shift toward what it dubbed "Occupy 2.0," a transition from physical occupation to partnerships with local communities and community organisations: "less than a year after the last protester was removed from New York City's Zuccotti Park, the movement has re-emerged as a series of laser-focused advocacy groups that, loosely organised under the Occupy umbrella, are trying to effect change in a variety of sectors, financial and otherwise" [53].

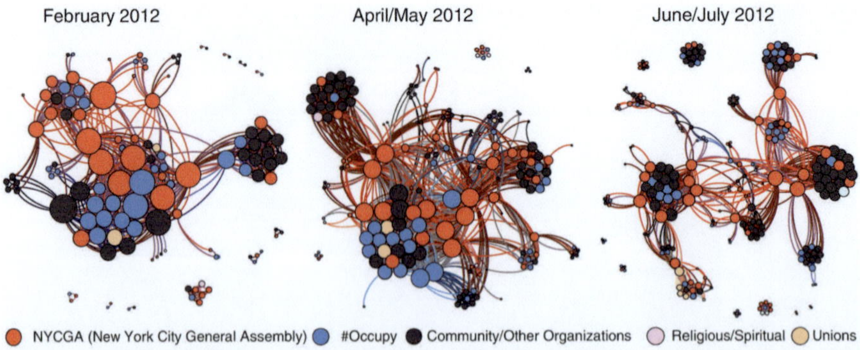

Fig. 3.3 Network diagrams of partner organisations from the Occupy Wall Street Project List, Issues #1 (February 2012), #2 (April/May 2012) and #3 (June/July 2012). An interactive colour version is available at http://occupydatanyc.org/2013/02/27/occupy-1-5

Such a claim has obvious importance, both for those interested on the legacy of the Occupy movement and for the American political landscape in general. Though many have offered speculations about the ultimate impact of Occupy, compelling empirical data has yet to fully emerge. Part of this effort has been taken up by branches of the Occupy movement, including OccupyData NYC, which hosts regular hackathons to analyze and visualise data produced by and about the Occupy movement and related issues.

This case study, led by the author over several hackathons, investigates three moments in the Occupy movement drawn from three issues of the *Occupy Wall Street Project List* published between February and July 2012. Each issue lists several dozen projects and participating organisations, including Occupy-related groups, community organisations, political organisations, religious/spiritual organisations and unions. From these lists, relational data was extracted about partner organisations, providing a window into the shifting structure of the Occupy movement within the larger American landscape. Organisations listed in the directory of the New York City General Assembly (oriented around the physical occupation of Zuccotti Park) were categorised separately from larger Occupy-related groups to study the special role of space in the movement. Notably, the data was all generated by the Occupy community itself, which provides a degree of ethological validity lacking in external interpretations of the movement. Non-Occupy organisations were classified through web research.

In a series of network visualisation (Fig. 3.3), each project is represented as set of lines between partner organisations. The resulting force-directed network graphs provide powerful, macroscopic views of (sub)cultures arising from these projects and hint at larger patterns of growth, development, division and perhaps even replication within the movement.

Two trends are particularly noticeable across these visualisations. The first is a shift in structural relationship between NYCGA and Occupy-related groups and community organisations (shown in black). In February 2012, NYCGA and Occupy-related groups are found in dense clusters, often separated from community organisations on the fringe of the movement. By the end of the period, these organisations are more fully integrated into topical clusters around financial, political, educational, health care, labour, arts and culture and other areas of advocacy (all viewable in the detailed online version). The second trend is a shift in the overall structure of partnership from a highly centralised network to a looser, chain-and-link model, with major NYCGA and Occupy-related groups connecting the various issue-based clusters. Such observations seem to support the description of Occupy 2.0 presented in *Time* and raise further questions about the causes and significance of these shifts.

These images again underscore the social nature of visualisations: the sense in which they and their contents may be discussed and disseminated among broader audiences. Colour versions of these images were exhibited at the James Gallery at the Graduate Center of the City University of New York in March 2013 along with other materials produced by OccupyData NYC. Each image was printed and placed in a small petri dish, evoking themes of surveillance, monitoring and control as well as the use of visualisation for self-reflection, understanding and intentional practice. Informal observations of visitors noted a range of reactions to these images, with some seeing fragmentation and discord and others noting a broader base of support and work with community organisations.

Conclusion

Though cultural heritage institutions are faced with a deluge of digital information, the process of presenting such materials is greatly facilitated by visualisation, which holds vast potential for providing context, insight and perspective with large-scale datasets. The empirical foundations of such datasets also support visualisations that reduce bias and represent individuals, groups and events more fully. While significant work remains in developing and preserving visualisations, the field provides exciting ground for the task of quantifying – and visualising – culture.

References

1. Pitti, D. (2004). Designing sustainable projects and publications. In S. Schreibman, R. Siemens, & J. Unsworth (Eds.), *Companion to digital humanities* (Blackwell companions to literature and culture). Oxford: Blackwell Publishing Professional.
2. Ware, C. (2004). *Information visualization: Perception for design* (1st ed.). San Francisco: Morgan Kaufmann.
3. Lin, X. (1997). Map displays for information retrieval. *Journal of the American Society for Information Science, 48*(1), 40–54.
4. Thompson, R. H., & Croft, W. B. (1989). Support for browsing in an intelligent text retrieval system. *International Journal of Man–Machine Studies, 30*(6), 639–668.

5. Motro, A. (1986). BAROQUE: A browser for relational databases. *ACM Transacions on Information Systems, 4*(2), 164–181.
6. Marchionini, G. (1997). *Information seeking in electronic environments*. Cambridge: Cambridge University Press.
7. Belkin, N. J., Oddy, R. N., & Brooks, H. M. (1982). ASK for information retrieval: Part I. Background and theory. *Journal of Documentation, 38*(2), 61–71.
8. Bates, M. J. (1986). An exploratory paradigm for online information retrieval. In B. C. Brooks (Ed.), *Intelligent information systems for the information society: Proceedings of 6th IRFIS conference* (91–99). New York: North-Holland.
9. Plaisant, C. (2004). The challenge of information visualization evaluation. In *Proceedings of working conference on advanced visual interfaces* (109–116), New York.
10. Card, S. K., Mackinlay, J. D., & Shneiderman, B. (1999). *Readings in information visualization: Using vision to think*. New York: Morgan Kaufmann.
11. Larkin, J. H., & Simon, H. A. (1987). Why a diagram is (sometimes) worth 10,000 words. *Cognitive Science, 11*, 65–99.
12. Healey, C. G., & Enns, J. T. (2012). Attention and visual memory in visualization and computer graphics. *IEEE Transactions on Visualization and Computer Graphics, 18*(7), 1170–1188.
13. Moretti, F. (2005). *Graphs, maps, trees: Abstract models for a literary history*. Brooklyn/New York: Verso.
14. Isenberg, P., Elmqvist, N., Scholtz, J., Cernea, D., Ma, K.-L., & Hagen, H. (2011). Collaborative visualization: Definition, challenges and research agenda. *Information Visualization, 10*(4), 310–326.
15. Bresciani, S., & Eppler, M. J. (2009). The risks of visualization. In P. J. Schulz, U. Hartung, & S. Keller (Eds.), *Identität und Vielfalt der Kommunikations-wissenschaft* (pp. 165–178). Konstanz: UVK Verlagsgesellschaft.
16. Tufte, E. R. (1990). *Envisioning information*. Cheshire: Graphic Press.
17. Cawthon, N. (2007). Qualities of perceived aesthetic in data visualization. In *Proceedings of 2007 conference on designing for user experiences* (p. 9:1), New York.
18. Tversky, B. (2005). Visuospatial reasoning. In K. J. Holyoak (Ed.), *The Cambridge handbook of thinking and reasoning* (pp. 209–240). New York: Cambridge University Press.
19. Chen, C. (2005). Top 10 unsolved information visualization problems. *IEEE Computer Graphics and Applications, 25*(4), 12–16.
20. Wainer, H. (1984). How to display data badly. *The American Statistician, 38*(2), 137–147.
21. Tufte, E. R. (1986). *The visual display of quantitative information*. Cheshire: Graphic Press.
22. Cawthon, N., & Moere, A. V. (2007). The effect of aesthetic on the usability of data visualization. In *Information visualization, 2007. IV'07. 11th international conference* (pp. 637–648).
23. Cawthon, N. (2009). *Aesthetic effect: Investigating the user experience of data visualization*. Australia: University of Sydney.
24. Lopatovska, I., & Arapakis, I. (2011). Theories, methods and current research on emotions in library and information science, information retrieval and human–computer interaction. *Information Processing and Management, 47*(4), 575–592.
25. MacDonald, L. W. (1999). Using color effectively in computer graphics. *IEEE Computer Graphics and Applications, 19*(4), 20–35.
26. Berlin, B., & Kay, P. (1969). *Basic color terms: Their universality and evolution*. Berkeley: University of California Press.
27. Adams, F. M., & Osgood, C. E. (1973). A cross-cultural study of the affective meanings of color. *Journal of Cross-Cultural Psychology, 4*(2), 135–156.
28. Post, D. L., & Greene, F. A. (1986). Color name boundaries for equally bright stimuli on a CRT: Phase I. *Society for Information Display, Digest of Technical Papers, 86*, 70–73.
29. Gao, X.-P., Xin, J. H., Sato, T., Hansuebsai, A., Scalzo, M., Kajiwara, K., Guan, S.-S., Valldeperas, J., Lis, M. J., & Billger, M. (2007). Analysis of cross-cultural color emotion. *Color Research and Application, 32*(3), 223–229.
30. Hupka, R. B., Zaleski, Z., Otto, J., Reidl, L., & Tarabrina, N. V. (1997). The colors of anger, envy, fear and jealousy: A cross-cultural study. *Journal of Cross-Cultural Psychology, 28*(2), 156–171.

31. McCandless, D. (2009). Colours & cultures [infographic]. In D. McCandless (Ed.), *Information is beautiful* (p. 0076). London: Collins. See also "Colours in culture." http://www.informationisbeautiful.net/visualizations/colours-in-cultures/. Accessed 2 May 2012.
32. Hodges, P. (2011). Interactive colours in culture. *Zoho: Lab*, UK, 23 March. http://lab.zoho.co.uk/lab/interactive-colours-in-culture. Accessed 11 Dec 2012.
33. Wattenberg, M. (2005). *The social life of visualizations*. Berkeley: University of California.
34. Heer, J. (2006). Socializing visualization. In *CHI 2006 workshop on social visualization*, Montréal.
35. Generation Grownup, LLC. (2010). NameVoyager. *The Baby Name Wizard*, 10 October. http://www.babynamewizard.com/voyager#. Accessed 31 Jan 2013.
36. Heer, J., & Agrawala, M. (2008). Design considerations for collaborative visual analytics. *Information Visualization, 7*(1), 49–62.
37. Heer, J., Viégas, F. B., & Wattenberg, M. (2009). Voyagers and voyeurs: Supporting asynchronous collaborative visualization. *Communications of the ACM, 52*(1), 87–97.
38. Heer, J., van Ham, F., Carpendale, S., Weaver, C., & Isenberg, P. (2008). Creation and collaboration: Engaging new audiences for information visualization. In A. Kerren, J. T. Stasko, J.-D. Fekete, & C. North (Eds.), *Information visualization*. Berlin: Springer.
39. Pousman, Z., Stasko, J., & Mateas, M. (2007). Casual information visualization: Depictions of data in everyday life. *IEEE Transactions on Visualization and Computer Graphics, 13*(6), 1145–1152.
40. Electronic Disturbance Theater. (2012). About this project. *Transborder Immigrant Tool*. Internet Archive, 2 May. http://web.archive.org/web/20120502200742/bang.calit2.net/xborderblog/?page_id=2. Accessed 14 May 2013.
41. Huff, D. (1954). *How to lie with statistics*. New York: Norton.
42. Davidson, C. N. (2008). Humanities 2.0: Promise, perils, predictions. *PMLA, 123*(3), 707–717.
43. Skeels, M., Lee, B., Smith, G., & Robertson, G. G. (2010). Revealing uncertainty for information visualization. *Information Visualization, 9*(1), 70–81.
44. Gray, J., Bounegru, L., & Chambers, L. (Eds.). (2012). *The data journalism handbook: How journalists can use data to improve the news*. Sebastopol: O'Reilly Media.
45. The New York Times Company. (2013). The New York Times Company policy on ethics in journalism. http://www.nytco.com/press/ethics.html. Accessed 30 Jan 2013.
46. Society of Professional Journalists. (2013). Society of Professional Journalists: SPJ code of ethics. http://spj.org/ethicscode.asp. Accessed 30 Jan 2013.
47. Kosara, R. (2011). Visualization is growing up. *eagereyes*, 6 November. http://eagereyes.org/blog/2011/visualization-is-growing-up. Accessed 31 Jan 2013.
48. Lima, M. (2009). Information visualization manifesto. *VC blog*, 30 August. http://www.visualcomplexity.com/vc/blog/?p=644. Accessed 7 Jan 2013.
49. Diamond, L., & Plattner, M. F. (Eds.). (2012). *Liberation technology: Social media and the struggle for democracy*. Baltimore: The Johns Hopkins University Press.
50. Chopra, S., & Dexter, S. D. (2007). *Decoding liberation: The promise of free and open source software* (1st ed.). London: Routledge.
51. Deibert, R., & Rohozinski, R. (2010). Liberation vs. control: The future of cyberspace. *Journal of Democracy, 21*(4), 43–57.
52. Diamond, L. (2010). Liberation technology. *Journal of Democracy, 21*(3), 69–83.
53. Matthews, C. (2012). Occupy 2.0. *Time*, 3 December 2012.

Chapter 4
Embodied Airborne Imagery: Low-Altitude Cinematic Urban Topography

Amir Soltani

Abstract Aerial photography has been the leading method for collecting and mapping topographic information from environments such as cities via remote sensing. Usually the qualitative analysis of aerial images is performed through descriptive pattern recognition and manual spatial associations, using human observations. Other techniques for remote sensing have been through software analysis of photographic or satellite data. The subsequent graphical products, such as Google maps, are disembodied and detached from the visual reality that is evident at human scale. The purpose of this study is to examine low-altitude topographical techniques and to utilise new visualisation methods that can benefit urban and architectural appreciation. The outcomes show that low-altitude oblique images via cinematic modes of representation can particularly exhibit urban aesthetics, vitality and other qualitative data, revealing sensory information such as spatial perception and expressive modes that can be easier for people to appreciate.

Introduction

For centuries aerial imagery and mapping have been utilised in drawings, paintings and photography. We have seen maps decorated with expressive human body features, describing places and activities; these early maps were embodied versions of what today's maps are similarly portraying to us. Today Google maps are among

---

This chapter is an updated and extended version of the following paper, published here with kind permission of the Chartered Institute for IT (BCS) and of EVA London Conferences: A. Soltani. "Embodied airborne imagery". In S. Dunn, J. P. Bowen, and K. Ng (eds.). *EVA London 2011 Conference Proceedings*. Electronic Workshops in Computing (eWiC), British Computer Society, 2011. http://www.bcs.org/ewic/eva2011 (accessed 26 May 2013).

A. Soltani (✉)
Department of Architecture, DIGIS – Cambridge University, Cambridge CB2 1PX, UK
e-mail: amir@metrowave.co.uk; www.expressivespace.org

J.P. Bowen et al. (eds.), *Electronic Visualisation in Arts and Culture*,
Springer Series on Cultural Computing, DOI 10.1007/978-1-4471-5406-8_4,

the most commonly used aerial map systems, competing with Microsoft Bing aerial imagery and OpenStreetMap. Google Maps, alongside its many useful features, lacks the presence of human activities: it would be difficult to qualitatively identify lived spaces just by looking at the aerial maps. This is somewhat addressed by using Google's Street View. With regard to aerial topography the purpose of using low-altitude filmic imagery is to create a method which considers typically unreachable views of the city from new dynamic vantage points, using a variety of angles in aerial perspective that can be assembled simultaneously and synchronised inside a virtual 3D space. This creates an informative way of dealing with a city's topography at a human scale in relation to a ground level view, similar to the way movies use aerial shots.

In filmmaking the perceptions of cinematic aerial experience are created using spatial narrative methods of *creative geography* and *topographical coherency* [1], which give symbolic and embodied meaning to places in the form of *cinematic mapping* and storytelling. The bird's-eye view in a film reveals to the spectator new imaginative aspects of urban spaces. This project's hypothesis argues that in cinema we have been able to negotiate an embodied aerial mapping method for urban topography, creating graphic bird's-eye views at a human scale, that expose the narratives of lived-experiences along with the characteristics of places.

Historical and Theoretical Contexts

In the seventeenth century Queen Elizabeth granted John Speed permission to use a room in the Custom House where he was encouraged by William Camden to begin his *Historie of Great Britain* [2]; it was published in 1611. Speed, besides working on historical accounts, did some important map-making; his town plans represented a significant contribution to historic records, as he provided many of the first visual records of the British towns. They are a combination of aerial perspectives and maps with descriptive drawings, notes, and symbols (Fig. 4.1).

Since the invention of photography, aerial images have had a significant fascination for urban planners, as they envision a projected Utopian image of the earth for city planning [3]. Anthony Vidler describes the aerial images of the earth and the city as a cross between surreal and real pictures via privileged instruments of vision [3]. French literary theorist and semiotician Roland Barthes stated that panoramic aerial vision recognises nothing other than a nicely connected space [4]. In contrast, Giuliana Bruno considers an aerial view as an encounter between map and landscape, thus rejecting the 'totalising perspective' that is often associated with the bird's-eye view as 'superior eye'; rather, considering aerial views as from the imagined 'nowhere and now here.' She describes the creative elements of early artist-cartographers, such as Leonardo da Vinci's bird's-eye view, as 'an imaginary perspective taken from an impossible viewpoint' [5]. Da Vinci's early attempts were 'to turn earthbound observation into aerial vision in his oblique map of Milan' [5]. Bruno quotes Louis Martin who suggested that the artist-cartographer is

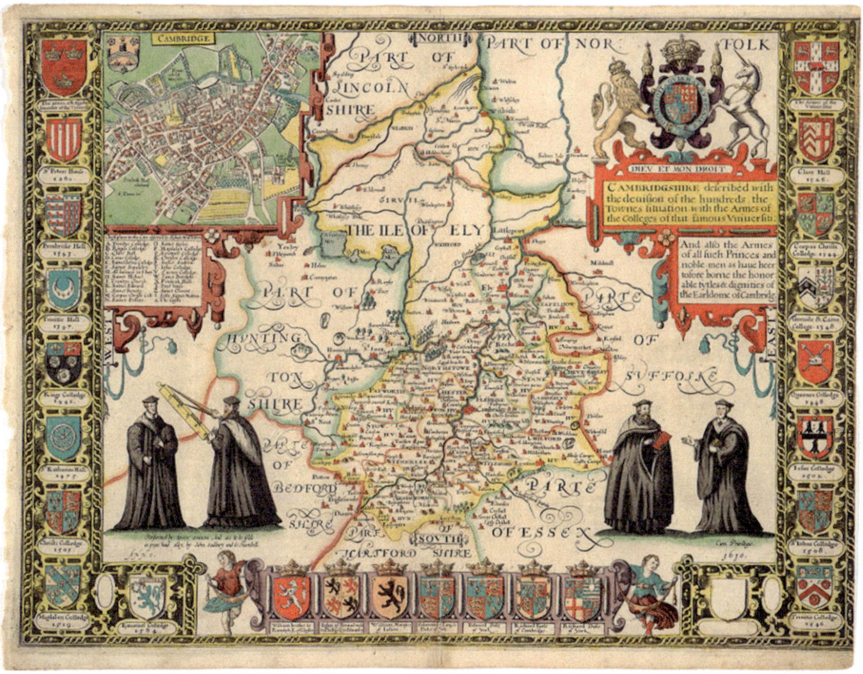

Fig. 4.1 An early map of Cambridge by John Speed c.1610, decorated with expressive human features and shields defining the place through its scholarly activities (© 2013 Reproduced by kind permission of the Syndics of Cambridge University Library, Atlas.2.61.1)

depicting places travelled in bird's-eye view which 'gives us a snapshot of the city.' She continues that this is an imaginative 'dislocated view, made possible much later by the *spatiovisual* techniques of cinema, which attempted to free vision from a singular, fixed viewpoint and imaginatively mobilising the visual space' [5].

Aerostat (Balloon) and Kite Platforms

Low-altitude filming and photography have become more popular since digital cameras become widely accessible to the public: they are no longer a specialised tool. Environmental and scientific research using aerial imaging have not been prominent until recent decades. Historically, the first known attempt to take aerial photographs was by Colonel Aimé Laussedat of the French Army Corps of Engineers [6]. He tried both balloon and kite methods but neither was successful, until in 1858 Nadar, using a balloon, managed to photograph the village of Petit Bicetre in Clamart near Paris (Fig. 4.2).

In the early twentieth century the kite was the most widely used platform for lifting cameras into the sky. It replaced the balloon, which had been the main instrument

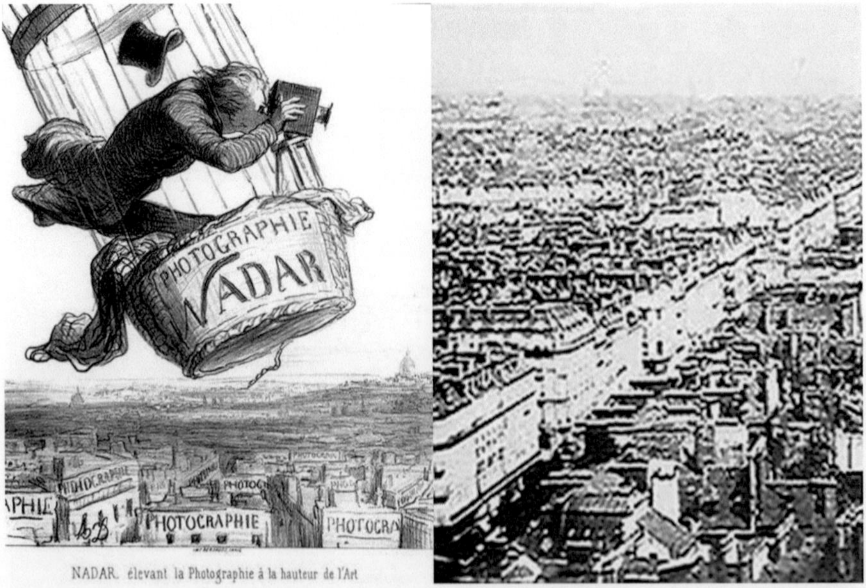

Fig. 4.2 Early aerial photography by Nadar c.1856, and a self-portrait caricature titled: *Nadar Élevant la Photographie à la Hauteur de l'Art* or 'Nadar Raising Photography to the Height of Art' published in *Le Boulevard*, May 25, 1862, France (Copyright free, images in the public domain)

for aerial photography since the mid-nineteenth century. This was due to the balloon (aerostat) method being too costly and dangerous; airplanes had also been tried but were also risky. Hence, kite aerial photography (KAP) become the favored platform and was used as a 'utilitarian method for scientific surveys, military applications, and general viewing of the Earth's surface.' [7]. After WWII in the United States there was a renewed interest in kite photography, and eventually in 1985 the Kite Aerial Photography Worldwide Association (KAPWA) was founded. As interest in kite photography increased a quarterly journal, *Aerial Eye* [8], was published, from 1994–1999. Currently, interest in aerial imagery is popular due to the advance of technologies in flying kites, the availability of personal aerostats, multi-motor aerial model planes and multicopters (small aircraft with multiple rotors).

The Sense of Embodied Perception

The embodied perception of space has been described in detail by Merleau-Ponty. He states that we embody the space and objects which exist according to our personified subjects, and experience our bodies in relation to space. He cites as an example the moon appearing in different sizes: when it is seen at the horizon it appears larger than when it is seen in the sky directly above us [9]. This is because when we look at the moon on the horizon we may compare it to many other objects in the foreground, such as trees, houses, hills, mountains. Therefore we judge its size when perceived at the level of the horizon to be larger than when it is seen in a vast empty sky overhead, when it appears smaller, creating a psychological illusion [9]. Thus, this example of how we embody the different experiential properties of space while seeing the moon depends on our perceptual fields of view. Likewise, the geometry of a room changes its shape psychologically, when we privilege certain gestures or actions in different situations and as a result we mentally alter its spatial regions. Therefore, mind 'and' body, in the phrase, are not separate. Rather, mind is 'with' body, gaining access to thought, body, and objects through the qualities our different senses perceive.

Pictorial Cues: Depth in Aerial Perspective

Various parameters related to aerial perspective views are affected by the visual experience; for instance, the light, the contrast and the vividness of the colors in an image are changed according to the distance. When traditional aerial maps and photography were enhanced they lost some of the visual nuances that are actually representations of distance. We know that when objects are far away, there is a perception of spatial distance between the eyes and the object, the light is more scattered, contrast and vividness of colour are reduced and objects may appear blurred. This information indicates to us the relevant distance and proximity of the objects in a scene; therefore, "contrast is a function of the distance from the object to the viewer and of the degree of clarity of the atmosphere" [10].

O'Shea et al. (1994) have written that it is not only objects such as dust and particles that affect a viewpoint; even in a perfectly clear day distance creates phenomena such as lower contrast. Hence, aerial perspective gives us many *pictorial cues* for the perception of depth in a scene. In experiments that O'Shea et al. conducted, samples of scenes were captured with different contrasts to see whether changing contrast or altering tonal variation resulted in a simulation of distance. They concluded that "contrast is a pictorial cue to depth that acts by simulating aerial perspective" [10]; in those scenes with higher contrast objects were perceived as closer than in those with lower contrast. By considering pictorial cues we can examine in aerial imagery some of the perceptual phenomena such as parallax vision, proximity, and depth of view.

Cinematic Aerial Mapping

In today's typical satellite aerial maps the idea of aerial perspective has been almost completely erased, because clarity of the map is considered the most important factor. We see pictorial cues replaced with technological cues, because the aerial maps are meant to be used as analytical tools in the spatial understanding of maps. We can conclude that these mechanically made aerial maps, and in many ways what we see in them, are not in fact the true representation of the physical reality.

Olivo Barbieri is a contemporary artist exploring the aerial filmic mapping, who uses a tilt-shift lens in his filmic and photographic works, purposely altering our perception of landscapes, cityscapes and crowds; they appear as dramatic graphic toy models (http://www.olivobarbieri.it). Giuliana Bruno points out that staged bird's-eye scenes depicted by the hands of early artists created "spatial observation that opened the door to narrative space," and made the city become "part of the sequence of imaginative survey." Later, aerial views of the city in cinema became reconstructed mobile maps of the city [5] and at the same time a symbolic aid in illuminating its design. Like those early maps where peoples' narratives and actions were an integral part of the topography, *cinematic mapping* uses various ways of negotiating mobile views by combining overlapping camera movements, zooming, panning, tracking and traversing shots with other montage methods to give the perception of an embodied map of a city.

Project Specifications

This project started in the Digital Studios for Research in Design, Visualisation and Communication (DIGIS) at the Department of Architecture, University of Cambridge, as part of an exploration of images of the city from different points of view. The concept is to combine aerial perspectives with the human ground level viewpoint and to recognise the potential of associative parameters between viewpoints and the activities of people. The American city planner Kevin Lynch suggested that one of the most interesting parts of a map is what is not there, the people. By using filmic topography we put people back in the maps. Through combining low-altitude aerial imagery, particularly oblique and vertical shots, we can simultaneously correlate the spatial qualities of the city with its corporeal representations. This project is also an experimental attempt to examine the possibilities of incorporating alternative methods of visualisation by revealing urban topographies that can include features like sensory and gestural analysis amongst others.

For the purpose of this project, which demanded a steady, slow survey of architectural features and the capture of city street events, a kite was not the best choice. Rather, a balloon aerostat served as a better platform for low-altitude aerial filming. This was because, unlike a kite that needs wind to navigate, a balloon hand controlled through one or two tethered lines worked well enough on a calm day (Fig. 4.3), allowing the attached camera cradle to get close to buildings without much risk. In addition, the balloon camera-rig utilised a suspension dampening system, *Picavet,* first designed by Pierre Picavet in France (1912). This enabled it to stay level to the plane of the ground at all times despite any movement caused by wind. Helium gas was used to lift the 5–7 ft diameter meteorological latex balloon, a camera, a GPS tracker and the Picavet rig (Fig. 4.4).

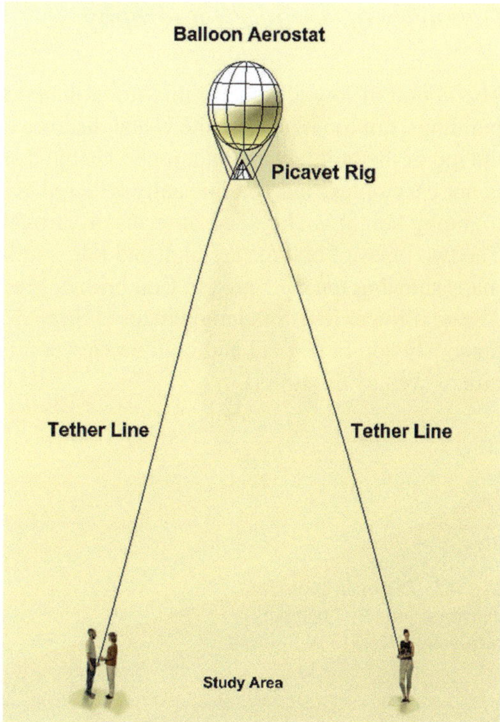

Fig. 4.3 Two tethered lines for controlling the height as well as traversal path of the aerostat (© 2011 A. Soltani)

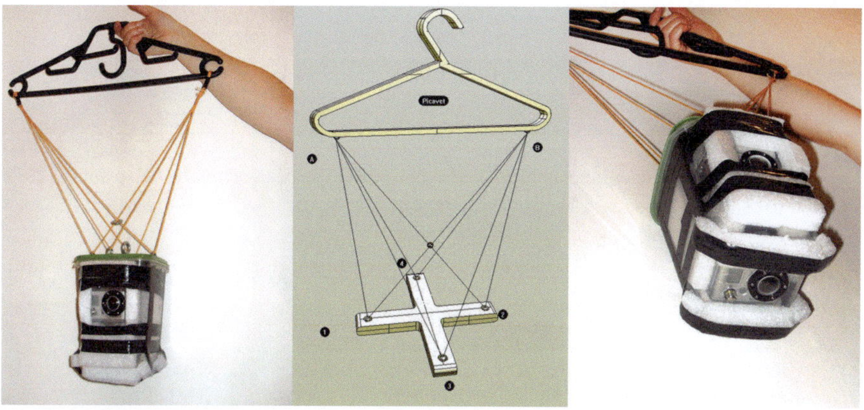

Fig. 4.4 Picavet suspension dampened system keeps camera level to the ground plane (© 2011 A. Soltani)

Geometry of Aerial Photography

The notion of low-altitude in this study meant specific heights from the top of the buildings, not too high as in the visual distance of a hot air balloon or too low where the top of the buildings would not be visible. Lower altitude photographic mapping is not easy unless using a manually tethered balloon or kite. In general aerial photography height is classified in terms of vertical and oblique geometries (Fig. 4.5). The two types of oblique are high and low, similarly in Google's multi-level satellite maps showing the MIT area in Cambridge, Massachusetts (Figs. 4.6, 4.7, and 4.8). The next lower level in Google maps is Street View. Our experiment tries to simultaneously depict vertical and oblique viewpoints, as tangible views of the architecture as well as the streets.

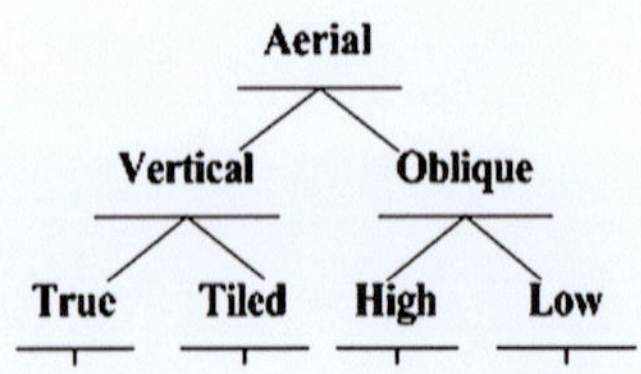

Fig. 4.5 The main geometric categories of aerial mapping viewpoints (© 2013 A. Soltani)

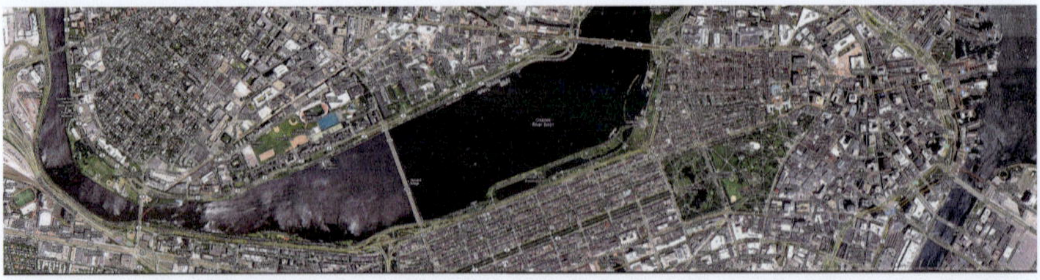

Fig. 4.6 Google aerial satellite map of MIT area in Cambridge, Massachusetts (Map data © 2012 Google, INEGI)

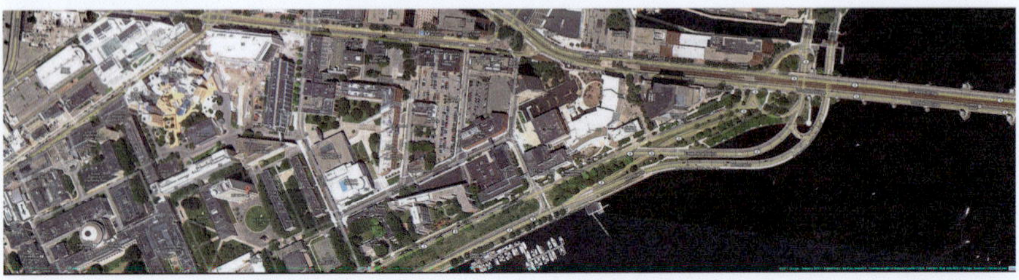

Fig. 4.7 Google aerial map of the same area but zoomed to the next semi-oblique level (Map data © 2012 Google, INEGI)

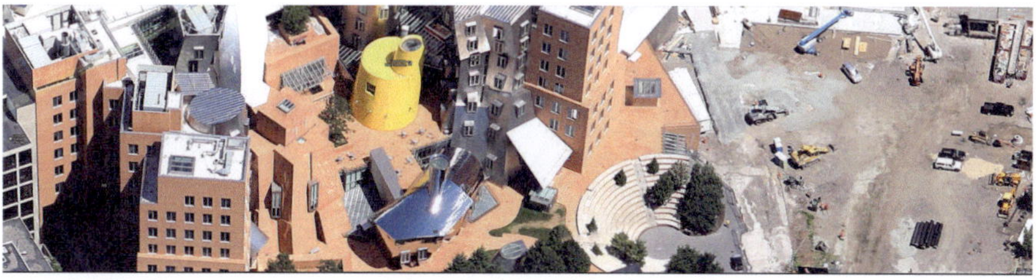

Fig. 4.8 Maximum zooming-in of Google aerial map before street view, a low-oblique level (Map data © 2012 Google, INEGI)

Vertical Versus Oblique: Flat Versus Perspectival

Traditional aerial photography is either vertical or oblique, and usually the photographs are slightly overlapped or tiled to create coverage of the whole area. The majority are vertical views with less than three degrees from the tilt angle to the ground (Fig. 4.9). In the oblique view we have angles of 3–90° from the *Nadir* direction which creates a perspectival aerial photograph of the area [11]. Another method is stereoscopic: two photographs taken simultaneously to create 3D depth imagery. This is viewed using a stereo image viewer similar to a stereogram.

We are interested not only in the urban surfaces, but also in spatial and sensory qualities achieved from real-time combinations of aerial and ground data. We combine the traditional analysis of vertical and oblique aerial photography with a low-altitude airborne system where we can get close to features of the built environment. The three different viewpoints are a flat filmic mapping based on the vertical view, an oblique perspective view of the city which can also be achieved through stereo imagery, and finally, adding the ground level images that are taken concurrently. These combined views are synchronised to create one-to-one correlations, giving a range of dynamic information rather than just statistics or density. Synchronised spatial, temporal and sensual information are possible, using split-screen cinematic methods of mapping spatiotemporal information.

Spatial Strategies: Flight Lines and Altitudes

Aerial photography has used various types of platforms such as helicopter, balloon, kites, and even tall buildings – "the advent of powered flight disclosed a boundless field of vision centered on a ubiquitous and omnivoyant aerial gaze. The primary bearer of this gaze, the airplane, soon became an unrivalled viewing platform" [12]. An early historic example of high resolution aerial views is a series "of 164 large format, sharp, black and white vertical aerial photographs of San Francisco taken in 1938 from an airplane by Harrison Ryker, a pioneer in aerial photography;" in this

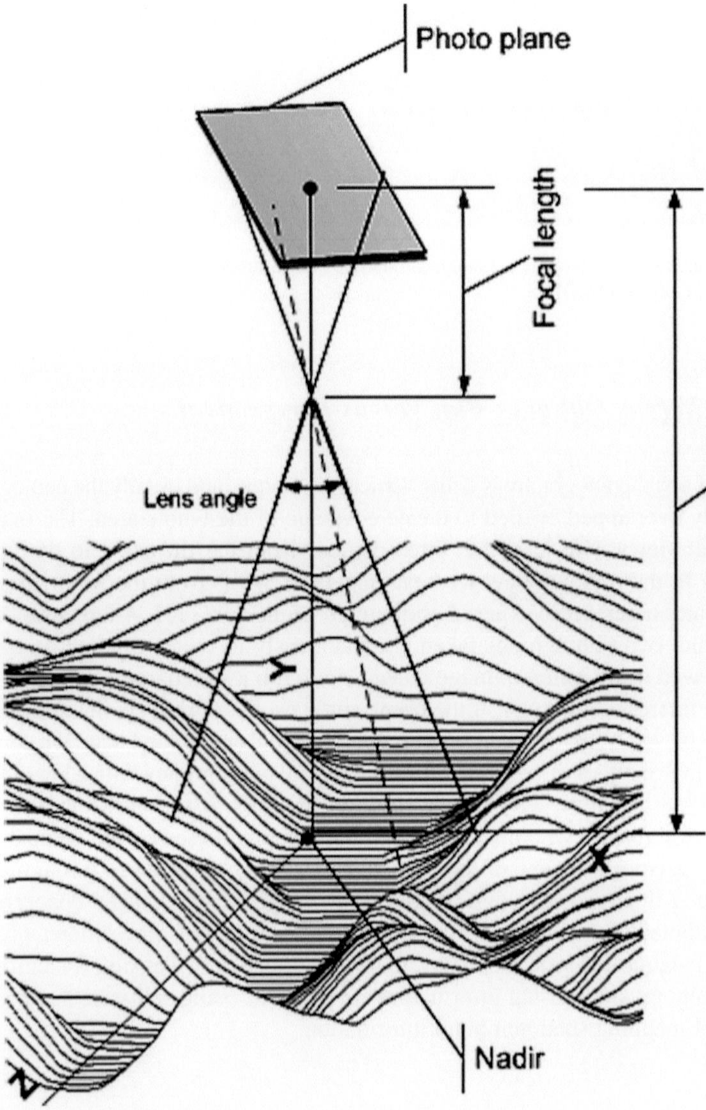

Fig. 4.9 Geometry of a vertical aerial photography (© 2011 A. Soltani)

series we can see how he overlapped the images to cover the complete city [13]. By using small weather balloons instead we can create ideal conditions such as a slow moving camera, close proximity to tall places, high resolution low-altitude bird's-eye imagery and controlled navigation through specific city streets, including areas where it is impossible to use an airplane or helicopter.

The project's end results uses multi-viewpoint projection mapping, and two different views are compared simultaneously with the ground footage, creating a new spatial representation of the map using *oblique, vertical*, and *ground* points-of-views. Furthermore, the 3D stereoscopic oblique shots can be utilised to explore the 3D texture-space of the buildings from close-up, similar to the way in which we perceive 3D depth through binocular vision. In an ideal setting it is possible to derive a variety of useful qualitative and quantitative information regarding the behavior of the built environment, including the size, shape, texture, patterns and *gesture* among others. People will associate the data with a narrative as an embodied spatial technique for urban mapping analysis. The camera becomes a sensor that through detail observation and *cinematic-aided design* narrative techniques, can decipher a range of meanings from manually combining and digitally visualising the images in a whole map.

Visualisation Interfaces

One of the project's aims is to juxtapose different types of information in a single viewpoint visualisation, comparable to a computer generated 3D architectural model, from an architect's viewpoint. Computer modeling and ultimately digital projection mapping of aerial views generate different kinds of representational information regarding a city and its architecture. The resulting footages are shared between four different methods for interfacing with the visualisation phase:

1. Split-screen montage of viewpoints
2. Multi-viewpoint projection mapping
3. Sequential framing matrix
4. Layered spatiotemporal zones

Case Study

This initial study of low-altitude aerial mapping started in mid-2011. Streets in Cambridge, UK, were chosen as the subject. The diverse styles of architecture and picturesque historical viewpoints in Cambridge become part of the test area (Fig. 4.10). How will the filmic mapping of the city from above contribute new knowledge and understanding of its spatial and formal structure? Furthermore, low-altitude aerial imagery was tested in comparison with existing maps for the level of errors in automated versus manual mapping.

Visualisation Layouts

In order to compare different types of viewpoints simultaneously, a few different methods were selected, offering alternative visual results. The three main viewpoints were the *oblique* which was recorded at 30–60 frames per second, the *vertical* view

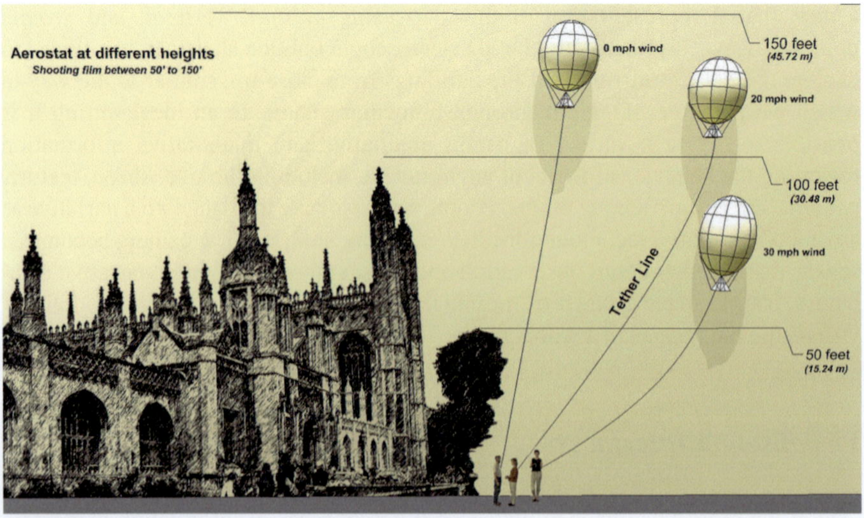

Fig. 4.10 King's College, Cambridge was one of the targets areas for the low-altitude mapping (© 2011 A. Soltani)

which was time-lapse sequential photography every 3–5 s, and the *ground* view which was filmed by a separate observer. In the next stage the footages were analyzed and categorised into multiple methods of visualisation, revealing various temporal impressions of the city. The following section explains three of the methods – split-screening, multi-viewpoint projection mapping in 3D and sequential juxtaposition of the images as a matrix arrangements.

Split-Screen Montage of Viewpoints

In an attempt to concurrently incorporate data from qualitative and quantitative information, the *split-screen* method is utilised, commonly used in the cinema. Data is assembled side-by-side within a single frame creating the impression of simultaneous action. In the 1950s and 1960s, cinematic split-screen was often used, for instance, to depict both sides of telephone conversations as well as in classic horror films. Today in Hollywood cinema split-screen is not limited to genre and in many ways it has been revived. Jennifer Van Sijll describes split-screen as a way to exploit "the elasticity of time and place […] to heighten the suspense of the scene" [14]. Therefore, using split-screen with the aerial shots created a sense of narrative that revealed both the temporal and the spatial nuances of the events; its aim is to highlight the qualities of the environment and the levels of temporal elasticity between the objects and characters.

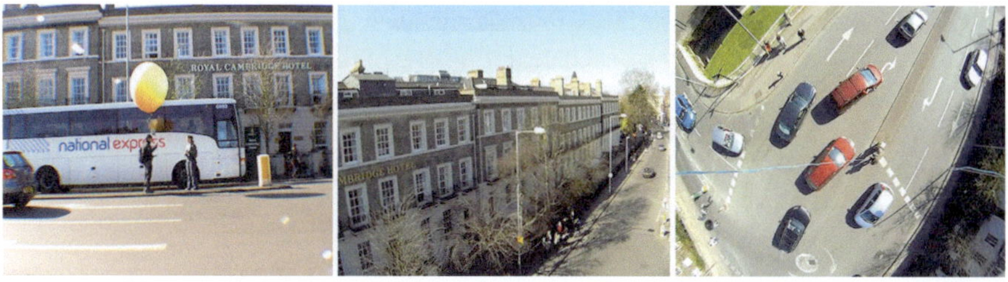

Fig. 4.11 *Ground, Oblique,* and *Vertical* shots depicting the terrain, collage layered masses of buildings, the patterns of street objects, and the effects of time and change (© 2011 A. Soltani)

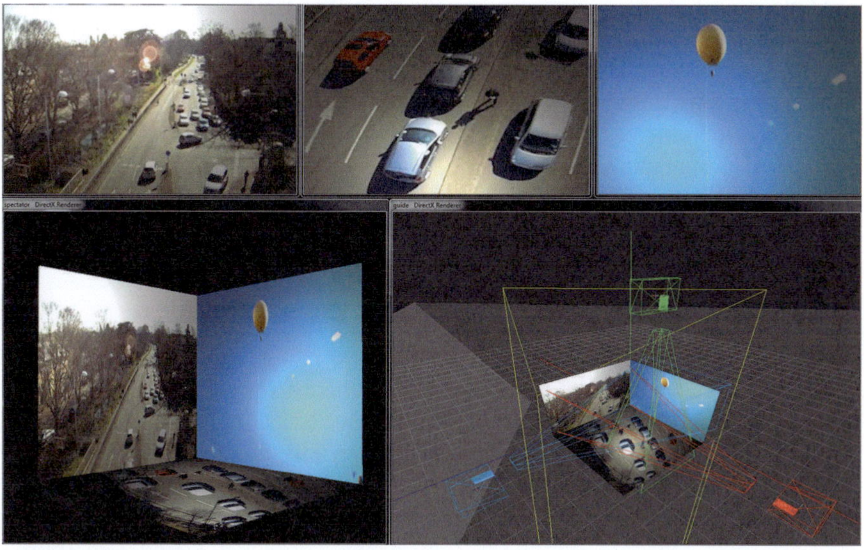

Fig. 4.12 Projection mapping interface of three simultaneous views using vvvv programming tool (© 2011 A. Soltani)

Multi-viewpoint Projection Mapping

Similar to split-screen, *projection mapping* explores the idea of presenting simultaneous events using multiple views (Figs. 4.11 and 4.12). The visual results can be used in an installation for physical space where audiences' bodies can interact with the results. In the last few years projection mapping on architectural façades has become popular. Computational innovations in graphical programming and the accessibility of the projectors enable visual artists to explore the spatial domains of projecting onto architectural surfaces, thus altering their appearances in non-permanent ways. By using three projectors, each depicting one of the views, virtually positioned along XYZ axis, the projected imagery is spatially translated and mapped onto the planar space or a façade, using vvvv (a graphical programming environment, http://www.vvvv.org), which then can be interactively embodied by the audience.

Sequential Framing Matrix

The third method is mainly employed to examine the temporal framing of aerial footage using selected individual frames. Landscape and architectural forms similar to people have *gestures* suggesting the trajectory of meaning through analyzing motion and form. The sequential framing of a landscape exposes various patterns and topographic changes in the city streets, as well as the behavior of people, with a gestural quality. The results create a framing of gestural motion as visual structures from the city's dynamic textures and forms, especially in vertical viewpoints.

There are other multidimensional cinematic-aided methods which can reveal yet more new opportunities for visualising topographic information; what these methods share is the embodied *cinematic-aided design* strategy for mobilising, synchronising, and simulating time space of urban lived-experiences.

Alternative Platforms, Problems and Future Prospects

In the last decade technology has shifted its interest towards the Natural User Interface (NUI) and mobile computing, which have influenced the next generation of aerial imaging techniques as well as the platforms for taking the camera into the sky. There are many new websites that organise, describe and promote aerial mapping methods. Two sites that are active since 2011 in the field of DIY aerial imaging are Grassroots Mapping (http://grassrootsmapping.org) and Public Lab (http://www.publiclaboratory.org). They are activists, educators, technologists, and community organisers working on issues like the Gulf Oil (spill) Mapping project (http://publiclaboratory.org/place/gulf-coast) and open-source tools for environmental exploration through accessible do-it-yourself techniques. Companies such as DroneMapper (http://dronemapper.com) deal with geo-referencing and 3D modeling directly from digital image products acquired from the drones. The future of aerial topography using photograph and film has never been brighter (or, some would say, more sinister, as there are serious implications for the surveillance of peoples' activity, as the UK police already do) [15].

In the last few years robotic drone quadcopters with four or more propellers have flourished, such as DJI Phantom [16], operated via GPS and gyroscope. There has been a surge in the number of aerial photography enthusiasts due to quadcopters' ability to combine low-altitude flying with telemetry. This is a new platform for aerial photography and filming that adds remarkable new possibilities, including surveying difficult to reach areas with precision.

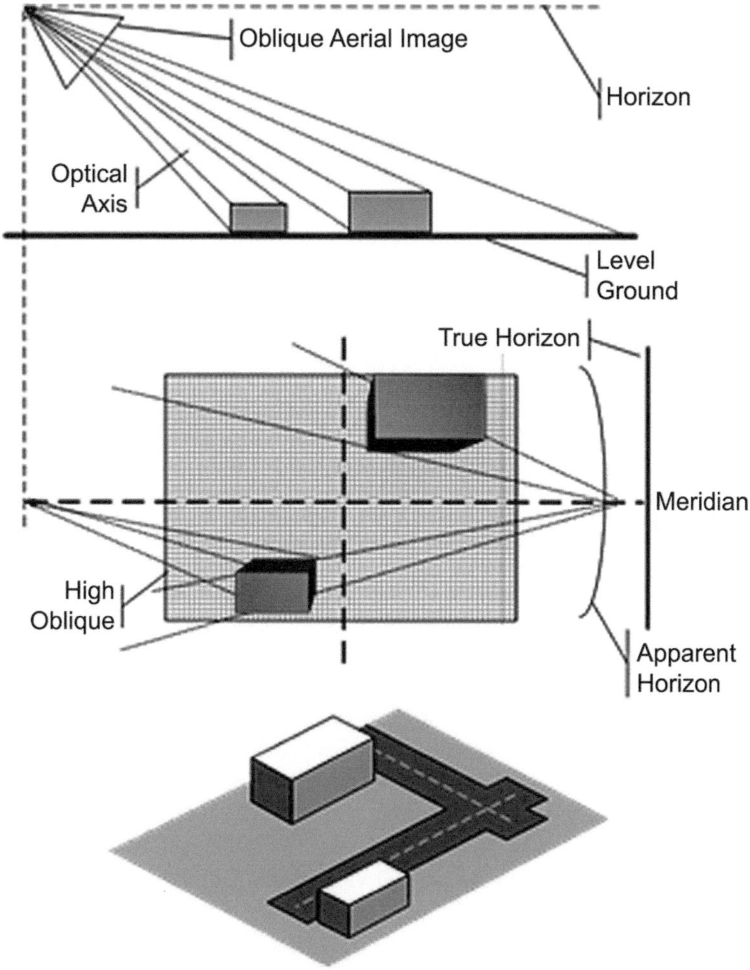

Fig. 4.13 Accuracy of the oblique aerial shots depends on the height and angle of the optical axis (© 2011 A. Soltani)

Low-Altitude Visual Accuracy Versus Parallax Error and Google Maps Anomalies

When high-altitude aerial images are not taken from the same pivotal point of the camera lens it can lead to parallax errors in the final tiled assembly of images (Fig. 4.13). This combined with fast motion dynamics while capturing could result in temporal and spatial artifacts due to time differences in the image sequences. *Blind stitching* using automated methods instead of manual stitching can also cause faultiness in the final representation.

Google map's imperfections have already caused some political complications. In 2010 Nicaraguan troops crossed the San Juan River that divides Costa Rica from Nicaragua and planted a flag on Costa Rica's Calero Island, which has been recognised as part of Costa Rica since 1897. In error Google Maps placed the border in Nicaragua instead of Costa Rica. Eden Pastora, a former Sandinista guerrilla commander who led the troops told a Costa Rican newspaper, "see the satellite photo on Google and there you see the border." [17]. Laura Chinchilla, Costa Rica's president, said the presence of Nicaraguan troops on Calero Island was "the invasion of one nation to another," mainly fueled by the error in Google maps [18].

The high number of visual errors as well as Google mapping faults in directions and boundaries prompted Google to ask users to report problems via a dedicated webpage that mainly applies to business listings on the maps [19]. Automated mapping can indeed cause flaws; however, a low-altitude approach is slower and more precisely captures the representation of the landscape and the built environment. Both vertical and oblique aerial imagery at low altitude produce more accurate geometries which depend on the manual handling of the camera's height and the angles of optical axis.

Conclusion

In Hollywood movies aerial shots have been used to portray bird's-eye views, creating graphic renditions of various scenes "which easily lend themselves to symbolic use" [14]. These types of shots graphically depict the narrative at a particular moment by showing eye catching, riveting aerial images [14]. Cinema has managed to capture our emotions through different senses to produce unique meanings of our environment, through creating perceptual viewpoints. Different layers and changes in space and objects are defined through these sensory perceptions according to our individual lived experiences.

The goal of this project is to achieve close-up observation of these aerial views through embodied cinematic-aided methods, triggering new creative models for reconsidering our bodies' sensory perceptions. Utilising the properties of cinema, the low-altitude aerial mapping experiment and its post-visualisation techniques of simultaneous viewpoints parallel the ways we perceive the space in films, with our bodies and our senses. We collect different views and information from the environment through spatial and sensory perceptions, combining perspective information such as scale, direction, proximity and trajectory to create an integral understanding of our world. Production of aerial imagery has come a long way and it's no longer an uncommon practice; now it's available to general public, yet with it brings new challenges and obstacles that we must transcend in order to ethically benefit from its possibilities.

Alternative visualisation processes are popularised by today's scientist-visual-artists. Aerial mapping, using new improved methods and platforms, enables sophisticated results through multi-viewpoint projection mapping methods; we can capture the multiplicity of concurrent spatial characteristics of urban spaces. Unlike automated vision satellite mapping, low-altitude oblique aerial imagery materialises the geometries of space more truthfully through a combination of cinematic experience and spatial visuality.

References

1. Penz, F. (2010). The real city in the reel city: Towards a methodology through the case of Amélie. In R. Koeck & L. Roberts (Eds.), *The city and the moving image urban projections*. London: Palgrave Macmillan.
2. Heninger, J. S. (2005). John Speed 1551/2–1629. Rocky Mountain Map Society, Denver, CO, USA, Spring. http://jhensinger.home.comcast.net~jhensinger/John_Speed/Speed_Biography.html. Accessed 23 May 2013.
3. Vidler, A. (2000). Photourbanism: Planning the city from above and from below. In G. Bridge & S. Watson (Eds.), *A companion to the city* (Blackwell companions to geography, pp. 35–45). Oxford: Blackwell.
4. Leach, N. (Ed.). (1997). *Rethinking architecture: A reader in cultural theory*. London: Routledge.
5. Bruno, G. (2002). *Atlas of emotion: Journeys in art architecture and film*. London/New York: Verso.
6. Wolf, P. R., & Dewitt, B. A. (2000). *Elements of photogrammetry with applications in GIS*. Boston: McGraw Hill.
7. Aber, J. S. (2008). History of kite aerial photography. Great plains kite aerial photography, USA, January. http://www.geospectra.net/kite/history/history.htm. Accessed 23 May 2013.
8. Benton, C. C. (2010). The aerial eye: Background and information on CD-ROM. Kite aerial photography, USA. http://www.arch.ced.berkeley.edu/kap/background/kapae.html. Accessed 23 May 2013.
9. Merleau-Ponty, M. (2004). *The world of perception*. New York: Routledge.
10. Hershenson, M. (1999). *Visual space perception: A primer*. Cambridge, MA: MIT Press.
11. Grass GIS. Photo.init. http://grass.osgeo.org/grass62/manuals/photo.init.html. Accessed 23 May 2013.
12. Deriu, D. (2006). The ascent of the modern planeur: Aerial images and urban imaginary in the 1920s. In C. Emden et al. (Eds.), *Imagining the city, vol. 1: The art of urban living* (pp. 189–212). Oxford: Peter Lang.
13. Rumsey, D. San Francisco aerial photographs 1938. David Rumsey Map Collection. http://www.davidrumsey.com/blog. Accessed 23 May 2013.
14. Van Sijll, J. (2005). *Cinematic storytelling: The 100 most powerful film conventions every filmmaker must know*. Studio City, CA: Michael Wiese Productions.
15. Doward, J. (2012). Rise of drones in UK airspace prompts civil liberties warning. *The Guardian*, 7 October. http://www.guardian.co.uk/world/2012/oct/07/drones-uk-civil-liberty-fears. Accessed 26 Apr 2013.
16. DJI. Phantom tutorials. DJI Innovation. Ghttp://www.dji-innovations.com/tutorial/phantom-tutorial/. Accessed 23 May 2013.
17. Swain, J. (2010). Google maps error sparks invasion of Costa Rica by Nicaragua. *The Telegraph*, 8 November. http://www.telegraph.co.uk/news/worldnews/centralamerica andthecaribbean/nicaragua/8117902/Google-maps-error-sparks-invasion-of-Costa-Rica-by-Nicaragua.html . Accessed 26 Apr 2013.
18. Walker, P. (2010). Nicaragua to deep troops in disputed territory after Google Maps error. *The Guardian*, 11 January. http://www.guardian.co.uk/world/2010/nov/11/nicaragua-troops-calero-island-google-maps. Accessed 26 Apr 2013.
19. Google Inc. Google maps. Google support, USA. http://support.google.com/maps/. Accessed 23 May 2013.

Chapter 5
Back to Paper? An Alternative Approach to Conserving Digital Images into the Twenty-Third Century

Graham Diprose and Mike Seaborne

Abstract Many museums and other archives worldwide are digitising their collections. However, it does not follow that the digitised data files are likely to survive any longer than the artefact that has been copied. Curators have centuries of experience in the conservation of paper and pigments, but there are many unpredictable factors in the preservation of digital archives, which implies digital storage and data migration hundreds of years into the future. This chapter explores an alternative proposal to archive vital images and documents as hard copy inkjet prints. We suggest that this will increase their chances of survival into the twenty-third century. We are not advocating this method in place of digital materials, but rather as a sound form of insurance, based on existing well-known methods of the conservation of acid free paper and pigments.

Introduction

The best archiving and curatorial practices for traditional silver halide photographs are very well established worldwide. Even before the introduction of silver gelatine prints in the 1880s, Victorian photographers were concerned to take steps to avoid their photographs fading, and one of the most successful processes developed in this

---

This chapter is an updated and extended version of the following paper, published here with kind permission of the Chartered Institute for IT (BCS) and of EVA London Conferences: G. Diprose and M. Seaborne, "An Alternative Approach to Conserving Digital Images into the 23rd Century." In S. Dunn, J. P. Bowen, and K. Ng (eds.). *EVA London 2011 Conference Proceedings*. Electronic Workshops in Computing (eWiC), British Computer Society, 2011. http://www.bcs.org/ewic/eva2011 (accessed 26 May 2013).

G. Diprose (✉) • M. Seaborne
London's Found Riverscape Partnership, Heathfield Drive 13, Redhill, Surrey RH1 5HL, UK
e-mail: grahamdiprose@gmail.com; mickey_vista@yahoo.co.uk

J.P. Bowen et al. (eds.), *Electronic Visualisation in Arts and Culture*, Springer Series on Cultural Computing, DOI 10.1007/978-1-4471-5406-8_5,

regard was the carbon pigment print. That the dyes used in post-world war II colour negatives and transparency films would begin to fade in as little as 30 years was probably less anticipated by photographers of their particular era [1].

The vast majority of the world's digital image files are presently stored outside professional archives, and their makers will be very lucky indeed if they can still be accessed and viewed in a mere five or ten years' time. Since the technology continues to evolve rapidly, there is no certainty that the image creation, storage and retrieval devices of the future will continue to be based on today's popular digital platforms [2]. We may therefore conclude that Victorian black and white photographs could outlive the majority of those colour dye images shot by our parents, which may themselves last longer than most of the digital images that we shoot today. From an archiving point of view, we seem perhaps to be going backwards.

The authors are researching the idea of selecting and then sending our most significant artworks, digital photographs and documents forward into the twenty-third century as smaller, high-resolution inkjet prints as an alternative to digital data. The image can be recovered from the print-out with minimal loss, using whatever capture or scanning technology may be available in the future.

We are not arguing that this method should replace archiving images as digital data, rather we propose that it could be an additional technology-proof form of insurance. While not everything can or should be archived in this way, at least with this method today's curators can select what they wish to send forward into the future and use technology most likely to ensure its survival. The alternative is to hope that our grandchildren's sons or daughters will be discerning when it comes to wiping data to free up space on whatever storage devices are used in 2099 or 2199. There is a serious risk in relying on them to decide what digital records and images from today's culture get migrated or deleted.

The Digital Print Debate

We are all indebted to the work of Wilhelm Imaging Research, Inc. for its pioneering investigations into the causes of fading of different kinds of photographic and digital prints [3]. Over the past 25 years, using simulated aging tests, it has meticulously mapped the expected fade resistance of both silver and dye-based colour photographic prints and the more recent dye and pigment-based inkjet digital prints. A simplistic summary would be that ten years ago the life of a dye-based inkjet print was around a third of that of a photographic colour coupler print. Then, about five years ago, both technologies could claim a life expectancy of around 60–90 years, given careful storage. Now certain combinations of acid free papers and pigment-based inks can lay claim to a possible fade-free life of over 250 years. This may be longer still for a monochrome image printed exclusively with carbon-based black pigments onto acid free cotton rag paper. A process not so very different from the highly fade-resistant carbon printing method developed in the 1850s!

To this day, some participants in the fine art market for photographic prints, particularly in the US, appear to remain sceptical that inkjet prints can be longer-lasting than traditional C-type prints (where less fade resistant dyes are chemically synthesised when making the colour print). However, this argument is no longer tenable, as pigments will always be more lightfast than dyes due to their inherent chemistry and only the ‘hand made’ nature of these C-type prints remains as a reason for the value that they attract. The debate about fine art media has led a number of technologists to suggest that prints may be an alternative way to archive digital images into the distant future [4].

Unfortunately, up until now this has looked like a massive and prohibitively expensive task and has thus received limited support. The dilemma is that digital preservation, requiring the need for long term secure data storage and regular migration as technology changes, looks equally risky and possibly even more expensive in the longer term. Andrew Green, former CEO of the National Library of Wales explained the problem:

> Will it be possible to use emulation software to mimic the software available to us now, but obsolete within ten years, let alone thirty? Or will we have to migrate our collections from one format to another over and over again, in order to keep them alive for each succeeding generation? What is certain is that national libraries will need to invest far more than they have till now, especially in staff and expertise, to even start to get to grips with the challenge of digital preservation. [5]

Digitising Images to ‘Save’ Them

Many of us are aware of, and have bid for, funding to ‘digitise’ existing photographs and artworks to ‘save’ them for posterity. While this usually achieves the goal of wider public access for visitors or online, it actually does nothing for the long-term survival of the original images. The National Lottery funding of English Heritage’s *‘Viewfinder’* project and website is one example from many thousands world-wide, that enables massive collections to be explored using our PCs tablets and smart phones [6].

So What Can Possibly Go Wrong?

The issues of digital preservation are the subject of well established debate, and there are now accepted ways to solve the main issues [7]. However, in our experience the approved processes are still likely to be too resource and process intensive for many smaller archives to afford. It would be wrong to say that best efforts are not being made to preserve these virtual, digital data files. Yet however advanced our technology, our world is subject to uncontrollable natural events such as extreme weather, earthquake, floods and solar flares. Political cyber attacks are serious threat.

Those of us who have suffered from a hard drive failure will already be well aware of the ultimate fragility of digital data. The natural degradation of data (sometimes referred to as bit rot) [8] and data corruption during migration are less familiar issues. Even if we store our valuable files across many RAID disks and servers in different corners of this planet, there is no guarantee that evolving technology, such as the storage of bits on strings of DNA [9], for example, will not be so radical that today's files are totally unreadable by the computers in use in 50 or even 25 years' time.

The challenges are huge, from simultaneously migrating and translating digital data on numerous websites worldwide, to writing data to archival gold DVD-R optical discs (with no guarantee there will be any devices able read them in 50 years time). Tape drives provide long-term storage of massive amounts of data, but require regular re-winding to maintain their readability. Once the durability of the tapes has surpassed the support life-time for the tape readers, the tapes are rendered unreadable unless migrated to new types of tapes or other media.

Any lack of standardisation from one present or future digital format to another will lead to considerable difficulties in consolidating or migrating collections. Thus, rather like the game of 'Chinese Whispers', during the course of repeated migrations necessitated by updates in software or hardware changes to the image data may well occur. Many smaller image archives are already finding that they are storing a mixture of TIFF, JPEG and RAW files, collected from different sources. How long will these formats survive before, like JPEG2000 before them, they fail due to lack of industry-wide support? Our conclusion is that vast swathes of our contemporary history and culture are at risk either of being randomly consigned to the twenty-first or twenty-second century digital recycle bin or of becoming inaccessible as the last hardware readers of long-outdated formats cease to function.

Other Non Digital Solutions

Many believe that 'The Cloud' is the answer to all digital preservation, but issues have already arisen concerning security and intellectual property rights. These include hacked passwords, data interception and the fact that in the US, any cloud storage company could be served with a subpoena requiring them to open their clients' data for government examination. Apple Inc. co-founder Steve Wozniak recently said "I really worry about everything going to the cloud, I think it's going to be horrendous. I think there are going to be a lot of horrible problems in the next 5 years." [10] In 2012 an accident while backing-up Royal Bank of Scotland software wiped many thousands of clients accounts to zero. It was caused by human error during a 'routine' software upgrade outsourced to India and serves as a warning to any organisation that one day, if it can go wrong, it probably will go wrong [11].

These and similar concerns have led others to research hard copy techniques for the long-term storage of digital data documents. These include the use of microfilm, where binary data is encoded in printable form [12] and the NanoRosetta process, where either analogue or digital information (PDF, TIFF or DDP files) is laser etched onto a glass wafer from which usable derivatives on nickel plates are created [13].

While microfilm offers the advantage of dense data storage, it is at the expense of wholly accurate data recovery due to the small physical size of the microfilm formats employed (typically 16 mm). However, in contrast to other storage media, such as hard discs, flash memory or SSDs, tapes, CDs or DVDs, the technology to read microfilm is simple and generic unlike the sophisticated technologies required to recover data from any of the complex storage systems in use today.

Nevertheless, while microfilm may offer a viable and cost-effective archival method of storing text files, its data recovery limitations pretty much preclude its use for true photographic quality images. On the other hand, our process of printing full tonal range photographic images on 100 % rag paper with pigment inks provides both a high degree of data recovery and the same level of archival permanence for all images, both monochrome and full colour. It may not offer the same high storage density as microfilm but – and this is especially true of photographic images – it does provide a much more acceptable level of image quality. As with microfilm, the actual storage medium is completely de-coupled from the IT systems needed to read it, and so a future-proof archiving system is guaranteed.

Anne Kenney, a digital preservation pioneer from Cornell University Library who has extensively researched microfilm and other alternative hard copy solutions makes the same point "I've always thought that it's not how much you can capture, it's how little you can capture and get away with doing the things that you need to do. It's always been how you make managerial decisions where there are trade-offs." [14]

Archiving Projects as Inkjet Prints Example: "London's Changing Riverscape"

In 1997, London's Found Riverscape Partnership (LFRP) was formed by Mike Seaborne, Charles Craig and Graham Diprose to make a continuous photographic panorama of both banks of the River Thames from London Bridge to Greenwich, 5 miles downstream [15].

This was to be a remake of a panorama first photographed in black and white in 1937 for the Port of London Authority (PLA). In 1997, LFRP shot the new panorama on 6×17 cm Fujichrome colour film, as at the time this was considered to be one of the most archival dye-based films available. In 2008, LFRP was invited by the PLA to make a new digital version of the panorama to celebrate its centenary in March 2009. Shooting digitally, LFRP was faced with the dilemma of how to archive its new digital files alongside the existing silver gelatine prints from 1937 and the colour transparencies from 1997. Despite some slight discolouration

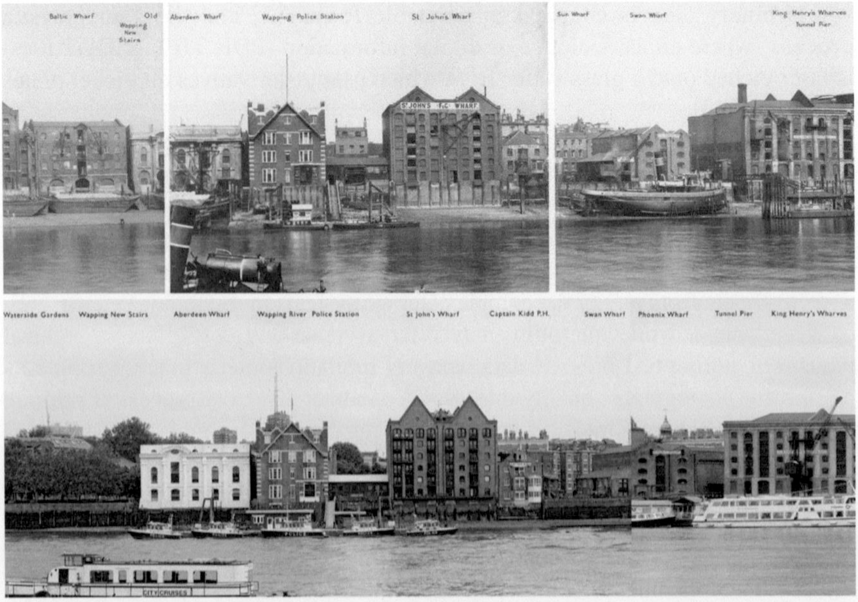

Fig. 5.1 Panoramas of Wapping, London: silver gelatine from 1937 (Courtesy of Port of London Authority) and from digital files, 2008 (Courtesy of London's Found Riverscape Partnership)

in places, the silver gelatine prints still seemed very likely to outlast the newly created TIFF files.

The black and white prints comprising the 1937 panorama (each approximately 12 in. × 10 in.) are mounted on strips of linen made up into fourteen sections for the north riverbank and thirteen for the south side, with each section being about 2.5 m long or 35 m long in total, if laid end to end. LFRP convinced the PLA that the safest way to ensure that that the new digital panorama would survive for their bi-centenary in 2109 was to have a physical version of the new panorama, to match that from 1937, with the same lengths of sections and locations. Prints were made using the Hewlett Packard HP Z3100 printer on Hahnemühle 188gsm Photo Rag paper. The joined 1937 panorama of jointed prints was replicated by cutting and mounting the digital prints using archival dry mounting linen. This allowed any location on the panorama to be viewed simultaneously in both versions placed side-by-side (Fig. 5.1).

Once completed, the new 2008 panorama was placed in blue leather folders similar to those made to house the 1937 panorama. It was then presented as a complete package to the Museum of London in 2009, as one of the PLA's centenary events. LFRP handed over the TIFF files as well, but we are much more confident that the printed version will survive to be part of the PLA's future centenary celebrations.

Project Methodology 1: Archiving Images

No doubt many curators may conclude that, while they can see the advantage of making full-size high quality archival inkjet prints, this is unlikely to be economically viable for their archives, and requires more storage space.

We therefore explored the idea of reducing the size of the printed images to about a half or a quarter of the original, so that several could be fitted onto a single sheet of paper. This would considerably reduce both production costs and storage requirements. The constraint is that the images should be capable of being scanned or photographed using whatever equipment and file format is available in the future without an unacceptable loss of image information. While they will not be 100 % perfect replicas of the original image, if the digital files have been lost or become corrupted then at least the prints will provide useable and reproducible images (Fig. 5.2).

The choice of digital printer for this work was straightforward as the Hewlett Packard Z3100 provides the most fade-resistant prints of any pigment inkjet printer currently available (March 2013). Wilhelm Imaging Research, Inc. still rates this printer and its slightly modified successor the Z3200 as yielding longer-lasting prints on a range of archival papers than any other printer. We used these inks

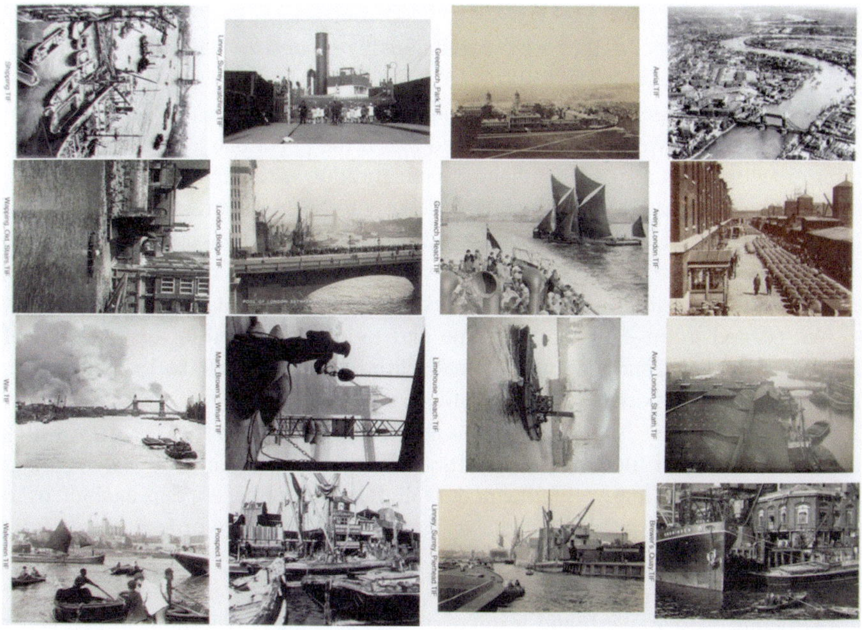

Fig. 5.2 PLA collection images ink-jet printed 16 up on A2 paper

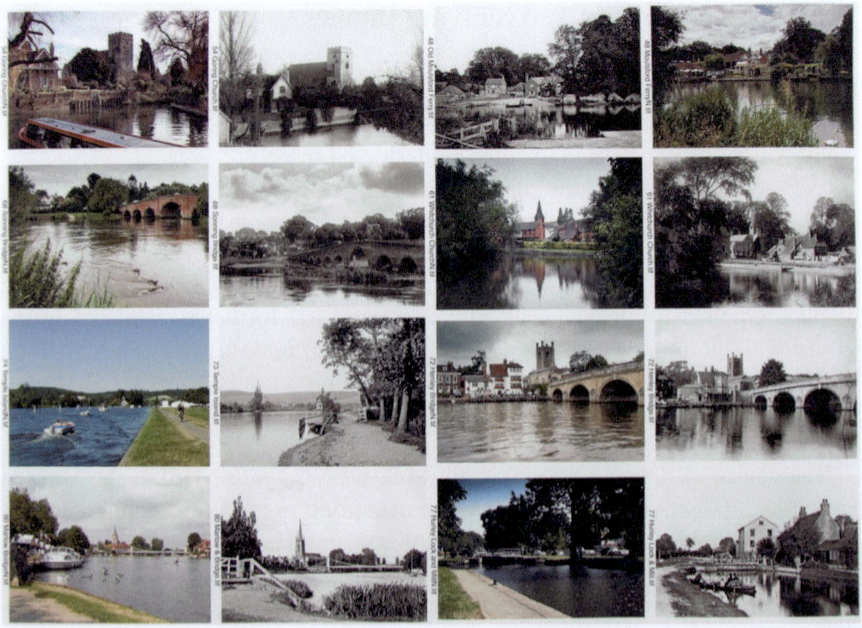

Fig. 5.3 English Heritage Henry Taunt and "...in the footsteps of Henry Taunt" Digitised Silver gelatine and contemporary digital images printed side by side 16-up on A2 paper

throughout the project as they were continuously reported to be the most permanent available from any company [16] (Fig. 5.3).

The choice of paper was much less straightforward and hence a number of different types were tested. We correctly suspected that if the paper had a texture this might interfere with the quality of the image created through scanning or copying. We also thought that the sharpness of the dot was likely to be an important factor, particularly if we intended to print images at a much reduced size. To assess how the nature of the paper surface affected dot sharpness we tested several fibre-based and resin coated papers to determine the differences, if any, in dot bleed.

We printed a range of monochrome and toned images from the Museum of London's Port of London Authority collection onto A2 sheets so that they were reproduced at approximately A4, A5 and A6 (see Technical Details below).

English Heritage's National Monuments Record allowed us to experiment with a collection of digital files made from 1860s silver gelatine prints by Henry Taunt, and we interspersed these with the modern digital colour images. This enabled us to see whether or not a full colour image would reproduce more or less successfully than a toned or pure black and white one.

However, from these tests, using only a high magnification loupe to assess the dot structure by eye, we found it impossible to accurately determine which paper gave the sharpest dot or the best quality image for re-copying and enlargement back to A4 from the reduced A5 and A6 prints. We needed a more accurate, objective and repeatable method of assessment.

Project Methodology 2: Type

We were also interested in exploring this method to archive vital business documents, using inkjet technology as an alternative to microfilm. We made TIFF files of 64, 96 and 128 A4 pages from the Microsoft Word files of a photographic textbook. The files were loaded into Photoshop™, using Contact Sheet II, and printed out. Even at a scale of 128 A4 pages per A2 sheet the text was still readable with a magnifying glass. We then used optical character recognition (OCR) software (see Technical Details below) as an objective assessment of readability. Once a single tiny page was scanned and read into OCR Software, we could count the number of errors as a measure of ink dot sharpness. OCR works by recognising the 'shape' of words that are in its dictionary. All that it can read correctly are printed out as black, editable text. Those it cannot recognise are flagged in green by the software. The sharper the ink jet dot, the fewer green flagged errors occur on the page. We counted errors for different varieties of paper, but generally we could tell at a glance if a paper surface was likely to be suitable for follow-up experiments. (Obviously there would always be some proper nouns or technical words not in the OCR dictionary that we would need to factor out (Fig. 5.4).)

In our own continuing tests on a range of gloss, rag and matt coated papers from manufacturers Harman, Hahnemühle, and Felix Schoeller we concluded that all matt papers tend to cause the dot to bleed into the paper fibres, and on most gloss or lustre papers the ink tends to form tiny bubbles on the paper surface that gave a less accurate, dot shape. Ortiz and Mikkilineni (Purdue University) reported on Inkjet Forensics in 2007, and reached the same conclusion: that smooth Rag papers produced the sharpest dot [17]. We were keen also to avoid choosing papers containing artificial brighteners (baryte) as these have been considered by a number of researchers to risk reducing archival life [18]. If a paper has a very slight warm tone base that does not change over a long period of time, this seems advantageous over a paper where changes in brightness are likely.

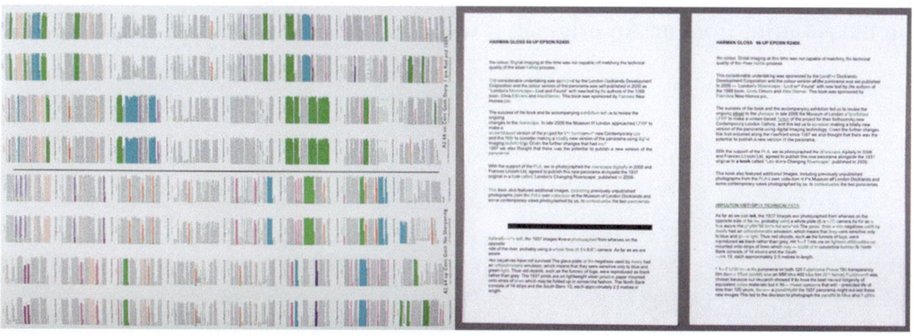

Fig. 5.4 Experiments with type to measure dot accuracy. Harman Baryta gloss fibre-based A2 with pages of type in Arial 64-up and then selecting two single pages to OCR from 64-up and 96-up, showing measurable errors. There are fewer from the 64-up page (*left*) than from the 96-up page (*right*)

The Canson paper company were among the paper suppliers with whom we discussed our research. Their Infinity Rag Photographique paper, while not containing any optical brighteners, did have a special barrier layer that prevented the ink from sinking into the paper base; it fully met the archival standards specified in ISO 9706 [19]. This paper gave us by far the best result of all the papers tested. The 96-up showed about 30 very minor errors as green words in the OCR file, but the 64-up was almost faultless. Additionally, this paper is internally buffered to resist gas fading, and is totally acid free to avoid any long term paper degradation.

Project Methodology 3: Back to Images Again

We next tested the Canson Rag Photographique paper with our photographic images. We printed a set of the PLA's monochrome pictures once again as 8-up and 16-up on A2 size paper (for sizes see Technical Details below), and did the same with a set of digital colour pictures from our project, '…in the footsteps of Henry Taunt'. Once printed, we scanned one A5 and one A6 image from each reduced format set, enlarged the files to A4, and printed them together with the original A4 files for direct visual comparison.

Figure 5.5 shows a ship entering Surrey Docks by crossing Rotherhithe Street, London (1928) by A.G. Linney. The A4 print from the A5 reduced image was excellent and the A4 from the A6 was still usable for most purposes, including small-scale reproduction in books and journals. There are many hundreds of beautiful historical images in the Port of London collection in The Museum of London, and in our opinion it would be much better to have them preserved as slightly lower resolution ink jet prints than to try to send huge digital files forward in time and risk losing many of them. It may also benefit future scholars to be able to view many small images, for context or comparison.

For a colour image, we selected a photograph of Moulsford Ferry (2004), on the River Thames in Oxfordshire (Fig. 5.7). The A4 print from an A5 original was again good enough for many reproduction purposes, and although there was some loss on the A4 print from an A6 original, it was still acceptable and looked similar to a

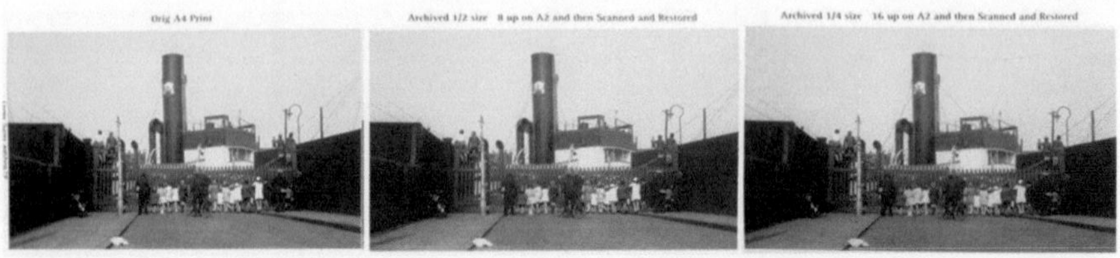

Fig. 5.5 Comparison of original A4 (*left*) and images re-copied and enlarged from A5 (*middle*) and A6 (*right*) in monochrome

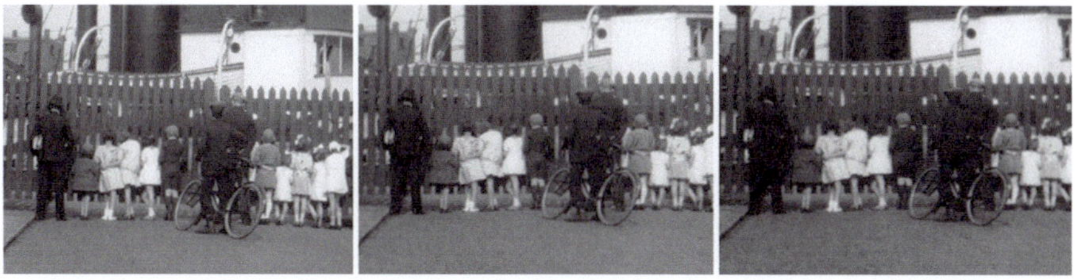

Fig. 5.6 *Left*: a small close-up taken from the original A4 print (*top left*). *Centre*: same section from archived half size at A5 and then copied and enlarged to match the A4 original. *Right*: same section printed at A6 and then copied and enlarged to match the A4 original

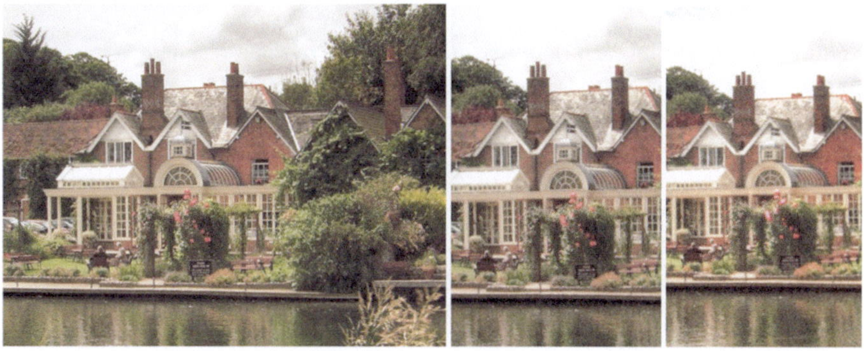

Fig. 5.7 Moulsford Ferry: comparison of original A4 and images re copied and enlarged from A5 and A6 in colour from digital original "...in the footsteps of Henry Taunt"

JPEG that had been re-saved a few too many times. We are continuing to research the use of image enhancement software to improve the quality of the reproduction from images archived as smaller A6 prints (Figs. 5.6 and 5.7).

Project Methodology 4

Our paper at the EVA London Conference 2011 [20] was met with a mixture of polite applause and scepticism, from delegates who relied on the preservation of digital data from their research, and others who had possibly spent a fortune on high-end RAID systems, or were employed to develop data storage. However, after seeing our results first-hand, the audience at least began to appreciate our right to question the data migration approach. This did lead us to seek out other expert opinion, as described below, 'New Developments'.

One of us (Mike Seaborne) had worked on a project at the Museum of London called 'Snapshop London', using digital photography to document the landmarks,

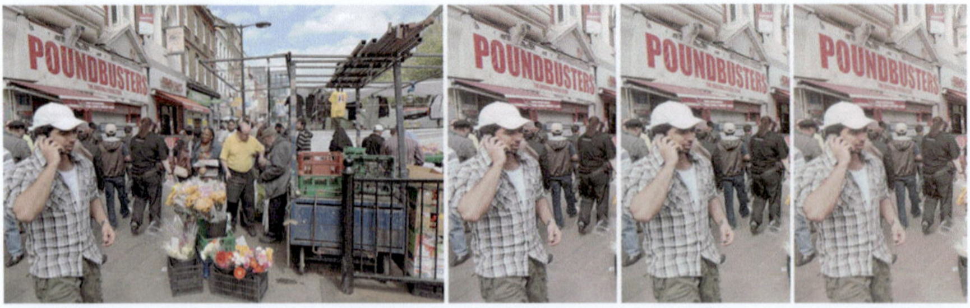

Fig. 5.8 This original image by Mike Seaborne of Whitechapel High Street from 'Snapshot London' is a high quality 73Mb TIFF file and will be archived by the Museum of London as digital data, plus printouts retrieved from 8up, 16up and 32up on A2

culture and people of each borough in London, which had resulted in more than 4,000 digital images. The MoL allowed us access to these files to develop our research and to calculate some costings, important to assessing if our project was financially viable.

This, and the massive number of digital images in other similar projects and archives, led us to question whether all images needed to be archivally printed at the same size. Up until now it had seemed reasonable to follow the path of standardisation in file-size and formats, because altering some data files but not others during any data storage or migration would be time-consuming and expensive. But surely many images now, let alone in the future, will only ever be viewed on tablets, websites or e-books, rather than large high resolution uncompressed TIFF files needed for exhibition prints or high quality book reproductions? If we try to archive all our digital images as high-resolution TIFFs we risk adding to the problems of future generations.

This thought prompted research in two related directions: first, to examine the quality of images printed at a much smaller size, 32-up on A2, and second, how this could reduce the costs of archiving larger numbers of less significant images, but still with enough quality to be a useful reference.

The image above, copied back from an A5 print (8-up on A2 sheet) produces a reasonable quality A3 print and is easily good enough for any normal book or screen output. The same image recovered from an A6 print (16-up on A2) is still good enough for any smaller book or column width reproduction, as well as any screen-based output. The A4 copy of the A7 print (32-up on A2) does however clearly reproduce the pattern of ink dots, particularly in areas of light even tone such as the forearm of the man with the mobile phone (Fig. 5.8). Even that would probably be useable on a web page and it certainly retains enough of its historical context for reference use by future scholars.

The current cost (March 2013) of materials (paper and ink) to print in this way is £1,500 to print out 2,000 images at A7 size (32-up on A2 sheet) or £3,000 to print out the same number of images at A6 size (16-up on A2 sheet).

New Developments

We are presently running a pilot project with The Sir John Cass School of Art, to print images from its East End Archive, which records the area over the past 50 years, with a wide range of file types and sizes. The archive's curators are thinking from the outset about different sizes of print according to what they consider to be the importance of the artists, the aesthetic significance of the images and their value as historical documents and sources of documentary information about East London. Archival printing at a range of sizes will help to keep overall costs down and embody within the archive a hierarchy of importance as determined by its present curators.

There is interest in our proposal from The National Archive (UK) (TNA). Whilst the TNA is confident they have the resources and expertise to manage their own massive digital archive over the long term, it recognises that our proposal has potential value in relation to smaller and less well resourced digital archives. Consequently it has offered to publish on its archive network the results of our pilot project with the East End Archive as a formal case study. Similarly, English Heritage's National Monuments Record has indicated to us that our method could provide a useful insurance for many smaller archives.

In April 2013, a feature on our work was published in the British Journal of Photography (BJP) [21]. The editor felt that many professional photographers, particularly those working in the genres of documentary and reportage, were concerned about the long-term survival of their digital images but do not have the necessary IT skills to achieve this. Making and keeping prints is something much more familiar to photographers.

Conclusion

This project has never been intended to replace attempts at data storage and migration for archiving digital photographs, artwork or documents, but by showing how relatively small prints can capture a great deal of image information in an IT-independent and relatively incorruptible form we believe that it does offer a viable alternative, or back-up, solution for many smaller archives. Developing a policy of keeping humanly-readable analogue prints in addition to attempting to store and migrate digital data, where the potential risks may not be well understood, would significantly reduce the impact of any data losses arising from whatever circumstances.

Aside from the technical and economic aspects of this project, our methodology allows curators and archivists to have a lot more control over what gets archived. They are in a position to decide which works and images from our present culture should be printed larger, and thus be preserved to a higher quality, rather than attempting to keep huge digital files of everything. There is no reason, in fact, why a particularly important digital image could not be printed out much larger if it was felt that even more information should be captured on paper.

With a purely digital data migration strategy we run the risk of saddling future curators with all the debts and dilemmas of selecting what they can afford to continue to preserve from our era, and what they will be forced to delete as migration costs increase from one technological leap to the next. This is why we believe that it is much safer to send digital images into the future as archival inkjet prints rather than solely as easily erasable and corruptible digital data.

Technical Details

"London's Chaging Riverscape" Project

Archival printing paper: Hahnemühle Photo Rag 100 % Cotton

Surface: Fine Smooth Matt Finish, Weight 188 gsm

Printer and details: Hewlett Packard – HP Z3100, 12 Pigment Ink 24" wide

Printing Resolution: 1,200 × 1,200 dpi

Printheads: Two inks in each printhead: gloss enhancer and gray, blue and green, magenta and yellow, light magenta and light cyan, photo black and light gray, and matte black and red

Ink Cartridges: Cartridges containing 130 ml of ink: gloss enhancer, gray, blue, green, magenta, yellow, light magenta, light cyan, photo black, light gray, matte black, and red

Archiving Images

Papers: Various tested, see text Harman, Hahnemühle, and Felix Schoeller

Canson Rag Photographique 100 % Rag

Surface: Extra Smooth Matt Surface

Weights: 310 gsm (for testing) and 210 gsm for pilot project

Printer and Details: As above

Note: While some recently launched Epson printers use a higher resolution than the HP Z3100, this appears, from their own specification sheets, to be to the detriment of archival life, which they predict at below 100 years

Image sizes 4, 8 and 16-up images on A2 paper (42.0 × 59.4 cm, 16.53 × 23.39 in.),

A4: 4up, 21.0cm × 29.7 cm, 8.27 × 11.69 in.

A5: 8up, 14.8cm × 21.0 cm, 5.8 × 8.30 in.

A6: 16 up, 10.5 cm × 14.8 cm, 4.1 × 5.80 in.

Acknowledgements We are grateful to the following for their support or sponsorship: Hewlett Packard for the long term loan of an HP Z3100, 12 Pigment Ink 24" wide printer; Fujifilm UK, Ilford Harman, Felix Schoeller, for supplying test sample and paper for the projects; Canson Paper Company for supplying paper for our pilot project and further research; The National Monuments Record, English Heritage, for allowing us to use the digital image files from Henry Taunt's original prints for our research; The Museum of London, for allowing us to make digital copies and then use these image files from their PLA collection for our research.

References

1. Wilhelm, H. (2002). How long will they last: An overview of the light-fading stability of ink-jet prints and traditional colour paper. In *IS & T 12th international symposium on photofinishing technology*. Wilhelm Imaging Research Inc. Grinnal.
2. Library of Congress. How long will digital storage media last? *Digital preservation*, Personal Digital Archiving Series. http://www.digitalpreservation.gov/personalarchiving/documents/media_durability.pdf. Accessed 22 May 2013.
3. Wilhelm Imaging Research Inc. (2013). *The collected technical papers of Henry Wilhelm and Wilhelm imaging research, 1969–2013,* Vol. 1.
4. Eastman Kodak Company. (2006). *Kodak photographic papers compatible with new wide format printers*. Press release.
5. Green, A. (2008). Series III: ePublications of the Institute ILS of the Jagiellonian University. In M. Kocójowa (Ed.), *No 5. Library: The key to users' success*. National Library of Wales.
6. English Heritage. *Viewfinder: Basic search*. http://viewfinder.english-heritage.org.uk/search/basic.aspx. Accessed 22 May 2013.
7. Digital Preservation Coalition. *Digital preservation handbook*. (2012). http://www.dpconline.org/advice/preservationhandbook Accessed: 2 May 2013.
8. van der Werf, B. Bit rot & long term access. Open Planets Foundation. 28 February 2011. http://preservationmatters.blogspot.co.uk/2012/07/bit-rot-long-term-access.html. Accessed 22 May 2013.
9. Church, G. M., Gao, Y., & Kosuri, S. (2012). Next-generation digital information storage in DNA. *Science, 337*(6102), 1628.
10. Allsopp, A. Apple co-founder Woz thinks cloud will soon have "horrible problems". Macworld, 6 August 2012. http://www.macworld.co.uk/digitallifestyle/news/?newsid=3374153. Accessed 22 May 2013.
11. Scuffham, M. RBS could face 100 million pounds bill or more after IT failure. Reuters, London, 25 June 2012. http://uk.reuters.com/article/2012/06/25/uk-rbs-it-bill-idUKBRE85O0YR20120625. Accessed 22 May 2012.
12. Schilke, S. W., & Rauber, A. (2010). Long-term archiving of digital data on microfilm. *International Journal of Electronic Governance, 3*(3), 237–253. doi:10.1504/IJEG.2010.036900.
13. Stamper Technology Inc., & Norsam Technologies, Inc. Information on NanoRosetta Archival Processing. NanoRosetta. http://www.norsam.com/nanorosettawp.html. Accessed 04 Jan 2013
14. Kenney, A. R., & McGovern, N. (2001). Digital preservation: Short term solutions to long term problems. Cornell University Library.
15. Diprose, G. *London's changing riverscape*. London http://www.londonschangingriverscape.co.uk. Accessed 22 May 2013.
16. Wilhelm Imaging Research Inc. HP designjet Z3100 – print permanence ratings. Grinnal, IA, 28 December 2007. http://wilhelm-research.com/hp/Z3100.html. Accessed 22 May 2013.
17. Ortiz, M. V., & Mikkilineni, A. K. (2007). Inkjet forensics. Purdue Sensor and Printer Forensics (PSAPF), School of Electrical and Computer Engineering, Purdue University, Lafayette. https://engineering.purdue.edu/~prints/outreach/EDEWG06.pdf. Accessed 22 May 2013.
18. Fischer, M. Creating long-lasting inkjet prints. In *Photographs*, 5.4. Northeast Document Conservation Center, Andover. http://www.nedcc.org/free-resources/preservation-leaflets/5.-photographs/5.4-creating-long-lasting-inkjet-prints. Accessed 22 May 2013.
19. ISO International Organization for Standardization. *Information and documentation – paper for documents – requirements for permanence*. ISO 9706, 1994.
20. Diprose, G., & Seaborne, M. (2011). An alternative approach to conserving digital images into the 23rd century. In S. Dunn, J. P. Bowen, & K. Ng (Eds.), *EVA London 2011 conference proceedings*,.Electronic Workshops in Computing (eWiC), British Computer Society. http://ewic.bcs.org/content/ConWebDoc/40582. Accessed 22 May 2013.
21. British Journal of Photography. *Archives of the Future* (pp. 79–80). Incisive Media Investments Limited, April 2013.

Further General Reference Concerning Digital Print Permanence

22. Wilhelm, H. A 15-year history of digital printing technology and print permanence in the evolution of digital fine art photography – from 1991 to 2006. In *Final Program and Proceedings: NIP22, The 22nd international conference on digital printing technologies* (pp. 308–315). Wilhelm Imaging Research, Inc. Grinnell, September 2006. http://www.wilhelm-research.com/ist/WIR_IST_2006_09_HW.pdf. Accessed 22 May 2013.

Part II
New Art Practice

Jonathan P. Bowen

In this part of the book, we consider artistic practice with respect to the use of information technology. Art and science have always been related [1]. As technology has advanced, so artists have been able to capitalise on new possibilities due to changes in available technology. For example, the Impressionists were able to paint outside effectively in the nineteenth century due to improvements in paints that became available in portable tube containers.

In the second half of the twentieth century, computers developed rapidly as the capabilities of the electronic age advanced exponentially. Art using computers as a medium has existed for as long as computers have been able to generate visual output. Early examples of computer art date back to the 1950s, with more significant artistic activity from the 1960s onwards [2]. However, considerable technological expertise was needed initially, thus limiting it to those with access and knowledge of the then expensive computer hardware. This led to the development of digital art as a recognised art form, as availability widened and costs reduced [3, 4].

In the early twenty-first century, the Internet and World Wide Web have developed even more rapidly, opening up yet more possibilities for artistic creativity and interaction [5]. In a more general sense, new media art, including technologies such as video and filmmaking, often making use of Information Technology, has also been an important strand of modern and contemporary art [6, 7].

The EVA conferences have deliberately set out to connect art and electronic media [8] as part of its interdisciplinary remit. A unique feature of EVA is the breadth of participants, from visual artists to computer scientists. As well as conventional presentations of papers, the conferences have also included exhibits of electronic artworks. In this Part, we present some selected topics on the theme of art and electronic media.

The Jurassic Coast immersive landscape project of Jeremy Gardiner and Anthony Head invokes an interpretation of the World Heritage site coastline of great geological interest and beauty in southern England. The artwork was exhibited (and presented) at the EVA London 2009 conference, using a room of its own for its display, which included audiovisual effects. The view presented to the onlooker moves around the virtual coastline on land and at sea with varying weather conditions and associated sound effects in a dreamlike manner. Chapter 6 presents the development of this artwork over a decade. It can be displayed on a variety of platforms with varying degrees of quality.

Aura is an artwork that consists of a set of high-dynamic-range images. This photographic technique captures both the lightest and darkest areas of an image at optimum exposure. The artwork is composed of multiple layers with a highly textured effect, based on these photographic images. The author, Murat Germen, is an experimental artist from Turkey who utilises his expertise in photography as part of the artistic process. Chapter 7 explains Germen's approach to producing the *Aura* artwork, with striking colour illustrations of the work. In the course of the presentation the relationship of painting and photography is explored. The chapter is in the form of a personal artist's statement on Murat's approach to and philosophy of producing art.

Gordana Novakovic has been the artist in residence at the computer science department of University College London, with a background as a professional painter. Chapter 8 describes an audiovisual artwork produced by Novakovic, at the crossover of art and science, inspired by the human immune system. The piece has been developed for a number of years and continues to develop further. It is aimed at both the public and scientists, including interactive and immersive aspects as part of the experience. The piece has been successful in helping to break down the barriers between art and science.

References

1. Smith, C. S. (1980). *From art to science: Seventy-two objects illustrating the nature of discovery*. Cambridge, MA: The MIT Press.
2. Brown, P., Gere, C., Lambert, N., & Mason, C. (Eds.). (2008). *White heat cold logic: British computer art 1960–1980*. Cambridge, MA: The MIT Press.
3. Wands, B. (2007). *Art of the digital age*. London: Thames & Hudson.
4. Paul, C. (2008). *Digital art* (World of art 2nd ed.). London: Thames & Hudson.
5. Greene, R. (2004). *Internet art* (World of art). London: Thames & Hudson.
6. Rush, M. (2005). *New media in art* (World of art 2nd ed.). London: Thames & Hudson.
7. Jana, R., & Tribe, M. (2009). *New media art*. London/Cologne: Taschen.
8. Shanken, E. A. (2009). *Art and electronic media*. London: Phaidon Press.

Chapter 6
Light Years: Jurassic Coast: An Immersive 3D Landscape Project

Jeremy Gardiner and Anthony Head

Abstract *Light Years: Jurassic Coast* is a three-dimensional temporal arena of a UNESCO (United Nations Educational, Scientific and Cultural Organisation) World Heritage Site, a mixture of both old and new, hybrid techniques that combine characteristics of painting, drawing, computer graphics, landscape data and immersive 3D virtual reality. Inside this virtual space is a topographical landscape of the Jurassic Coast in three dimensions. *Light Years: Jurassic Coast* uses technology normally associated with computer games in creative and innovative ways. *Light Years: Jurassic Coast* can be transmitted in scalable formats to allow the work to be viewed on different platforms: a portable device, plasma panel, stadium-sized screen or experienced in remote locations with a portable projector. This chapter explores the evolution of this artwork created through a ten-year collaboration.

Introduction

Jeremy Gardiner is a painter who, for the last three decades, has utilised the convergence and combination of different technologies to produce visually and intellectually challenging artworks. His artistic exploration has taken him from the Jurassic Coast

---

This chapter is an updated and extended version of the following paper, published here with kind permission of the Chartered Institute for IT (BCS) and of EVA London Conferences: J. Gardiner, "Light Years: Jurassic Coast – an immersive 3D landscape project." In A. Seal, S. Keene, and J. P. Bowen (eds.). *EVA London 2009 Conference Proceedings*. Electronic Workshops in Computing (eWiC), British Computer Society, 2009. http://www.bcs.org/ewic/eva2009 (accessed 26 May 2013).

J. Gardiner (✉)
Ravensbourne, 6 Penrose Way, London SE10 OEW, UK
e-mail: j.gardiner@rave.ac.uk

A. Head
Bath Spa University, Sion Hill, Bath BA1 5SF, UK
e-mail: a.head@bathspa.ac.uk

J.P. Bowen et al. (eds.), *Electronic Visualisation in Arts and Culture*,
Springer Series on Cultural Computing, DOI 10.1007/978-1-4471-5406-8_6,

of Dorset to the rugged coast of Cornwall, the rough volcanic islands of Brazil, the arid beauty of the island of Milos in Greece and more recently the Lake District and its numerous waterfalls. His paintings become a symbolic map, simultaneously interpreting and capturing the impact of human and natural events, the activities in time and space that have shaped, textured and coloured the landscape to give it a unique, contemporary depth and beauty.

At the same time he has managed to extend common notions of narrative, place and identity beyond that of his abstract landscape paintings, using cutting edge digital media. In 2001 Jeremy Gardiner and Anthony Head began working in collaboration as 'Light Years Projects', together the painter and software artist have challenged and explored the nature of pictorial space through their work. They collaborated in order to bring an extra dimension beyond their individual experiences. This is the case for the strong partnership that has helped define and refine *Light Years*: *Jurassic Coast*.

Head began working as a software artist due to his longstanding interest in 2D and 3D graphics generated by coding. He had been fascinated by the possibilities of programming, graphics and computers since the 1990s. For him, technology provides an upper limit to what computer systems are capable of creating, beneath which there is a world of possibility. In his Light Years Projects work, his approach is to use code creatively to produce an experience, governed by logic, but representing the unpredictability of life. A measure for success is when the audience feels a sense of touch from the immersive experience, gained from a multi-sensory approach to the artworks without any touch interface. The multi-sensory experiences in question are time-based audio-visual real-time artworks and can be experienced as an interactive participant, or as an observer to interactive events.

The collaboration between Gardiner and Head has continued with several long-term projects created and exhibited nationally and internationally (Fig. 6.1).

The Jurassic Coast

The Jurassic Coast is England's first natural World Heritage Site, a 95 mile long stretch of coastline running from Orcombe Point in East Devon to Old Harry Rocks in East Dorset. Its geology spans the Triassic, Jurassic and Cretaceous periods about 185 million years of the Earth's history.

Along most of the coast, massive bands of rock have been heaved up into a near vertical orientation by unimaginable forces within the earth. In general, the strata of this stretch of coast dip gently to the east. Its classic geomorphological features have an intrinsic beauty which derives directly from erosion which has resulted in a huge variety of different landforms, beaches, landslides, arches, cliffs and caves, which provide an incredibly rich visual and scientific resource [1].

Gardiner's interest in the geology of this unique location inspired him to develop ideas for a collaborative project, using the Dorset coast [2] and Dorset County Museum and Natural History Museum as resources. The research centred on exploring parts of the coast-path on foot, by sea and even by air. Access to the archives of the

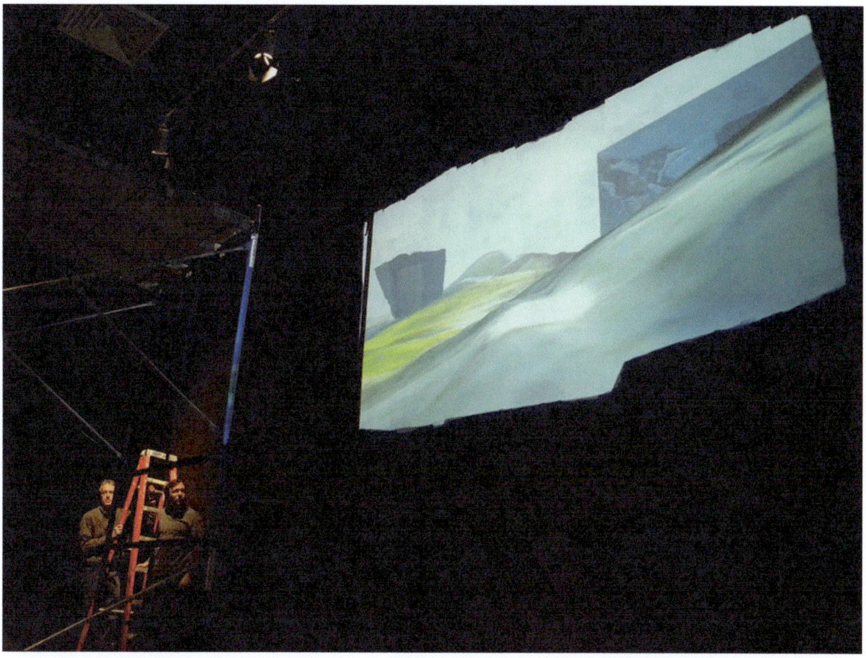

Fig. 6.1 Gardiner and Head (*Light Years*: *Jurassic Coast*, installation, Chelsea Art Museum, New York city 2009)

Dorset County Museum, supplemented by the support of the curators, facilitated his investigations and allowed him to highlight the connections between the physical characteristics of the landscape and related artefacts in the Museum. There were visually significant turning points as the project progressed. The opening of a forgotten cardboard box revealed hand-coloured maps [3] intended to record the geology, but which were beautiful artworks in their own right. A boat trip along the coast provided a vantage point from which to observe the dramatic contrasts of geology and colour. A tangible sense of history was generated by the nineteenth century museum library and by the densely shelved museum stores stacked with neatly labelled boxes of artefacts.

The partnership with the Dorset County Museum has allowed Gardiner to make a careful investigation in order to understand the area with an informed perspective, leading to work that represents another layer in the documentation of the history of the coastline.

A Painterly Approach

What the surface of the world looks like depends on where you are in history; every landscape is merely a phase. Gardiner's paintings of the Jurassic Coast reflect a journey of 185 million years back in time to revisit specific places that he has known

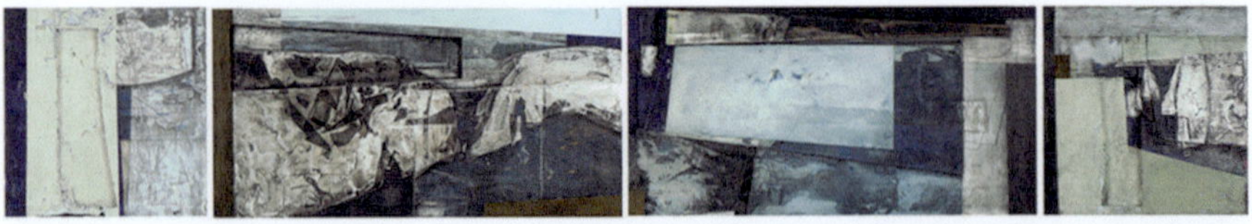

Fig. 6.2 *Morning Tide, Old Harry,* – Acrylic and jesmonite on poplar panel (©Jeremy Gardiner. 2007. 24 cm × 144 cm)

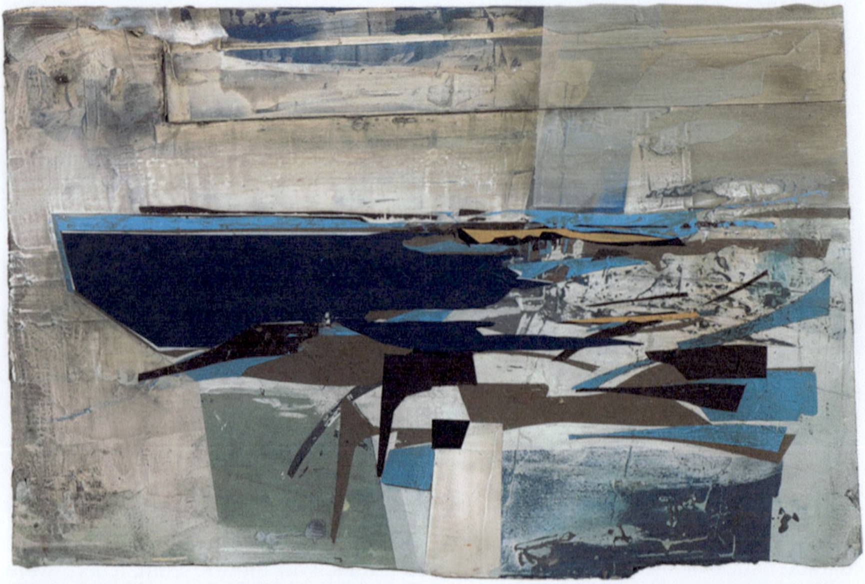

Fig. 6.3 *Clavell Tower.* Acrylic and jesmonite on poplar panel (©Jeremy Gardiner. 2009. 60 cm × 90 cm)

since he was a boy, drawn from a subjective experience of places where land, sea and sky converge (Fig. 6.2). His sense of atmosphere and form has been strongly influenced by this natural environment on the Dorset coast while his colour palette reflects this connection; sometimes the methods used for constructing a painting are forced in new directions by a desire to honour specific features in the landscape [4].

In exploring new visual directions and media, Gardiner has tried to remain responsive to these origins; to an area now re-christened the Jurassic Coast, but celebrated for its fossils [5] and its beauty since the mid-nineteenth century. A careful observer may delight in finding recognisable features incorporated in his paintings and prints, in an attempt to mirror the effects of time on this landscape.

All the images of *Light Years*: *Jurassic Coast* that feature in the digital projection (for example Fig. 6.3) are painted in the studio. Starting with a prepared wooden panel on which the entire development of an image takes place, each one is a subtle

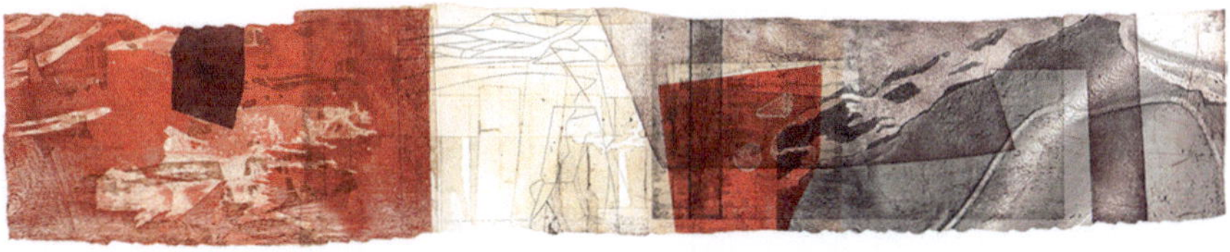

Fig. 6.4 *Swyre Head, March.* Monoprint (©Jeremy Gardiner. 2012. 26 cm × 155 cm)

relief constructed of large flat poplar panels. Many layers of paint are applied which are then scraped down and over-painted so that the intermingled strata echo the multiplicity of memories that inform the work. The complex physical construction of the panels reflects the accretions of memory that have helped Gardiner build a mental image of the place he sets out to portray. The painted surfaces have been inspired by visits to boatyards, where the patina of hulls are examined for their shape, colour and, above all, surface properties.

When transported to the digital project, these painted panels are endowed with transparency in the virtual space; that is, they are able to interpenetrate without optically destroying one another. Transparency however implies more than an optical characteristic; it implies a broader spatial order. Transparency means a simultaneous perception of different spatial locations. Space not only recedes but fluctuates in a continuous activity. The position of the transparent planes has an equivocal meaning as one sees each figure now as the closer, now as the further one.

There are certain parallels with the animated and lenticular landscapes created by Julian Opie, such as *View of Mount Fuji with daises from route 300* (2009).

Painting is a process of finding out, and landscape can be its thesis, the catalyst to map out our universal view of the world. Painting, like science, cannot discover the same things twice. The artist is therefore compelled to take those directions that the still undiscovered and unexplored dictate. It is these directions that Gardiner's artwork is following at the moment.

One of the virtues of the visual arts is their ability to capture and encapsulate feelings, memories and opinions and preserve them beyond their fleeting instant (Fig. 6.7). Interactive installations offer the additional feature of transporting the viewer into the work as it develops. Unlike still paintings or sculptures, interactive installations unfold in real time [6].

Everything a painter does in the studio, from mixing colours, to creating shading and blending elements into formal arrangements involves spending hours working on an image, and the end result is usually a static finished piece (Fig. 6.4). The elements themselves could be used to create their own form of poetry in a virtual temporal space. Kandinsky said 'Artistic composition has two elements. The composition of the whole picture and the creation of the various forms which, by standing in different relationships to each other, decide the composition of the whole' [7].

Unlike painting, digital media can create the illusion of time-travel, in which the viewer has the illusion of entering some other place and period through a virtual

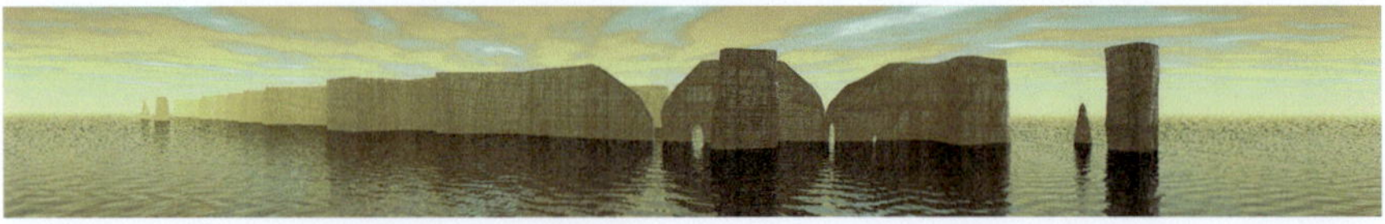

Fig. 6.5 *Isle of Purbeck*. CD ROM Quicktime VR node (©Jeremy Gardiner. 1996)

window. Time and space travel is purely speculative, encouraging daydreams and reverie. Travelling in this manner is an imaginative act, an act of memory and reflection. The new variable is audience choice, which can take users in unexpected directions and combine elements of the artwork in unpredictable ways. This requires a greater commitment to planning or preparation, interface design and finally to making all the elements work together.

Virtual Views

In the last 20 years the full promise of interactivity has started to be realised through digital technology. In 1999 the National Trust launched 'Virtual Views', a project that Gardiner had initially started while developing a CD-Rom of 3D models in 1996 entitled *The Isle of Purbeck – an interactive sketchbook of topographical landscapes* (Fig. 6.5). This concept later grew into *Purbeck Light Years,* and today *Light Years*: *Jurassic Coast* is an example of a contemporary interactive artwork that manages to create a unique aesthetic experience while taking full advantage of the latest computer graphics technologies. *Light Years*: *Jurassic Coast* presents a three-dimensional temporal world that can be dynamically viewed from different angles and at different times of day. This world evokes a contemplative atmosphere based on real and abstract elements, but also offers some playful elements such as the sound of the birds, wind and waves. Created with a mixture of techniques that combine painting, drawing, computer animation and immersive virtual reality, this interactive installation recreates a segment of the Jurassic Coast World Heritage Site that stretches from Dorset to Devon.

Learning from Purbeck Light Years

Purbeck Light Years was the first collaborative interactive project created by the two artists, utilising Gardiner's paintings as source material for Head's programmed environment. It was the precursor to *Light Years*: *Jurassic Coast*, and the first digital work to win the Peterborough Art Prize in 2003 (Fig. 6.6).

The Peterborough Prize is the only major contemporary art award shortlisted by experts and then decided by public vote. It was possible to gather audience responses while the piece was on display both in Peterborough and later at the Lighthouse

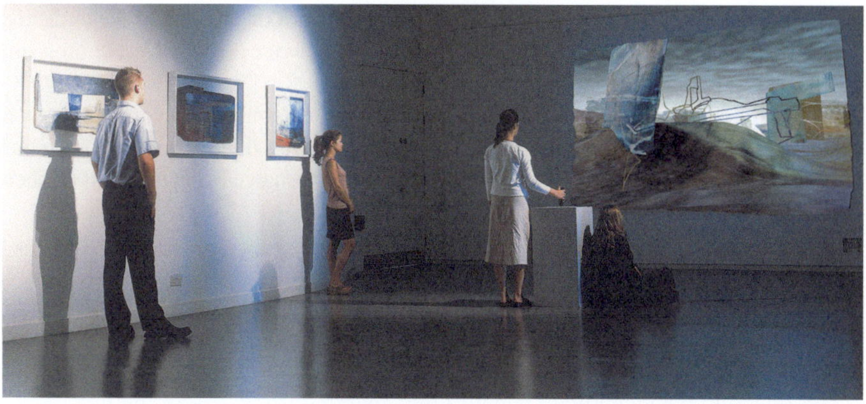

Fig. 6.6 *Purbeck Light Years* installation (The Lighthouse, Poole, Dorset. 2003)

Centre for the Arts in Poole, for 2 months. In Poole it was also possible to display the drawings and paintings that are the content for the piece. Reactions to the exhibit were overwhelmingly positive, many on the theme of "at last a piece of digital art that's beautiful and moving and not just clever".

Purbeck Light Years Sound

Audience feedback showed that sound has had a tremendous influence on users' perception of the content. Sound designers believe that sound accounts for more than half of the experience of using an interactive product. Successfully integrating sound into *Purbeck Light Years* required special attention to mixing and timing. Recorded sounds of nature (birds, bees, crickets) were played at quiet moments; wind was always there, but in different strengths depending on the height of position of the traveller in the space; rain sounds played when it rained; even the sound of a local steam train could be heard when the visitor was positioned in the correct part of the scene. These sounds were all balanced at every moment to produce the correct emphasis and mood. Synchronising sound to changes on screen was technically demanding but added substantial impact to the installation.

Purbeck Light Years Motion

The motion in *Purbeck Light Years* was controlled by different methods: mouse, joystick and camera. It was shown in different locations and formats (different projection sizes) and each gave the audiences a slightly different experience.

For many, controlling the route in the virtual landscape was neither necessary nor desirable. Only those who felt very confident using new technology tended to use the joystick (exhibitions at Peterborough Museum, UK and Poole Arts Centre, UK 2003). The camera-based control method (Bargate Monument Gallery, Southampton

2006), involved a ceiling mounted camera, tracking the floor position of the audience (individual or group). An individual user could soon work out what was going on, but when a group was involved it was less clear.

We had chosen to use this method for aesthetic reasons (to have a clear open space in front of the projection), and also because we felt that by having to use our bodies to walk around the world, a potentially more intensive immersive experience was being created.

Light Years: Jurassic Coast (2009)

When selecting the technology behind *Light Years: Jurassic Coast*, the first objective of both artists was to consider which software methods would allow the flexibility to develop and communicate an idea/experience. Their second objective was to decide whether the specific aesthetic qualities and limitations of the software and hardware technology would enable them to build a work of art to their specifications, and allow a 'painterly' approach to the making. The third was to experiment with the software platform, explore making techniques and aesthetic results. These three objectives were all considered prior to the actual making of the artefact.

All the vistas of the location in *Light Years*: *Jurassic Coast* can be reached easily by 'floating' 'walking' or 'sailing'. Just as you move about within a picture with your eyes, the sensation that you have here is one of being enclosed by order and yet at liberty to navigate within it (Fig. 6.7). The immersive environment represents one

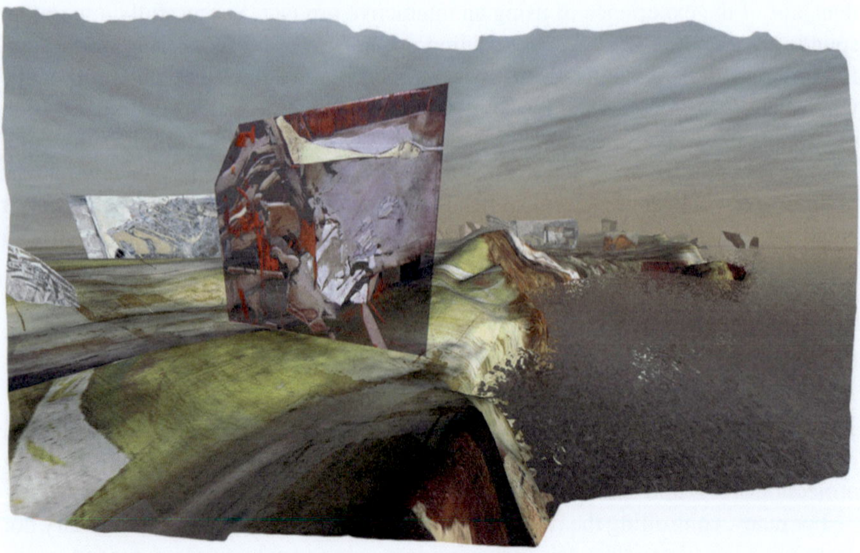

Fig. 6.7 Screen grab (*Light Years: Jurassic Coast*. 2009)

moment, continually. Painting shows a static moment that captures how the artist perceives the world to be. The characteristic of reality is that it is made up of frozen moments or discrete fragments of time perceived one after another, like the continuous movement in this digital artwork [8].

The hardware behind *Light Years*: *Jurassic Coast* consists of a fast personal computer running the Unity 3D game engine with a powerful OpenGL graphics card that is capable of rendering life-like images in real time. This is similar to the games systems used by young audiences at home, but with an artistic rather than ludic intention. The projection of images is done through an HD projector with a brightness of at least 5,000 lm, which is more than enough light for a ten-metre projection in a darkened room. This work has been shown on large LCD screens, which works well for smaller room environments, but this is generally a less immersive experience for the audience, unless they are very close to it.

Motion

The experiences and feedback from audiences viewing the earlier project, *Purbeck Light Years*, where the viewer had access to a joystick that encouraged them to move around through the virtual space, led us to believe that a new, more passive, computer generated approach would establish a richer visual experience for the viewer. Several ideas were possible: a bird's-eye flight, a ground based walk, a sea based boat trip. Head could program movements that would be randomly generated or controlled by events or paths.

The motion that Gardiner and Head decided upon was a smoothed out flight, similar to a seagull flying from one random position and height to another. However, instead of following this realistically, as if a simulation, the flight pattern changed, from being flight, to a land or boat journey. The camera would be allowed to even pass through the land, to reveal the geometry that represented the geology under the terrain.

This decision allowed the artists to deal with the issue of interaction with the audience. In *Purbeck Light Years* only the audience member who pushed the joystick was actively interacting; the rest of the audience was passive, but seemed to gain equal enjoyment and understanding from the experience. Computer control enables the whole audience to have an equal experience. In fact, the piece gains from this kind of unpredictability. *Jurassic Coast* is not, therefore, "interactive" in a direct sense but by using movement through the landscape, it enables a larger group of viewers to experience the immersive nature of the artwork.

Real-Time 3D Computer Rendering

The 3D graphic rendering that drives *Light Years: Jurassic Coast* consists of customised routines developed by Head using Gardiner's paintings and prints as departure points. Through a process of scanning, colour adjustment, cutting out and adding transparency, the paintings, prints and *plein-air* studies are transformed into computer 'textures'. These textures completely fill the scene, covering the land, creating the sky and reflecting off the sea. There are no photographs in the work, interspersed throughout the environment are planes of details from paintings and prints.

The shapes representing the coastline and geology of the coast were built with computing-efficient vertical planes onto which different types of image maps were applied. The juxtaposition of these planes allows the viewer, as they pass through the landscape in real-time, to form two-dimensional compositions. This dichotomy between 3D and 2D provides a visual tension between dimensions, playing with the flatness of the projection screen and the illusion of three dimensions in the virtual world.

The resulting shapes and colours of the textures in the environment are the result of real-time calculations of how sunlight and ambient light reflect, scatter, and refract through the luminous atmosphere, along with artistic interpretation. To add to the mood, simulated weather systems come and go, night follows day and seasons change in real time (Fig. 6.7). The combination of all of these factors creates a work that never repeats, and hence each spectator's journey is unique.

Weather and Geography

The weather system consists of changing waves, wind, rain and atmospheric perspective. The waves, wind and atmosphere are controlled from a live internet feed of meteorological measurements (including wave height, sea temperature, wind speed, air temperature). The use of this data (updated every 10 min) provides another temporal element to the work. Additionally, the rain is an example of a programmed random event. This represents the unpredictable nature of weather in Dorset. The light changes when it rains in *Light Years*: *Jurassic Coast*, the scene becomes darker and the fog increases.

Not only does the virtual landscape represent the countless millennia of the geology that created the actual coastline (Fig. 6.8), the live and randomised weather represents the reminder of the processes that are constantly reshaping it, through erosion [9]. All of the above aspects of *Light Years* represent our painterly approach to 3D computer graphics [10].

The locations along the 90-mile heritage coast are always identifiable, but it is the way colour is used that excites the emotions, making the spectator acutely aware of the changes brought about by season, time and weather, which affect its appearance and the surrounding atmosphere. The visual language of *Light Years: Jurassic Coast* includes richly worked surfaces, and a strong sense of light is suggested not only by contrasts of value and hue, but also by the use of surface effects that emulate stained pigment, chalk and translucent washes in a way that light seems to come both from a source external to the picture space and from within the surface of the picture itself (Fig. 6.9).

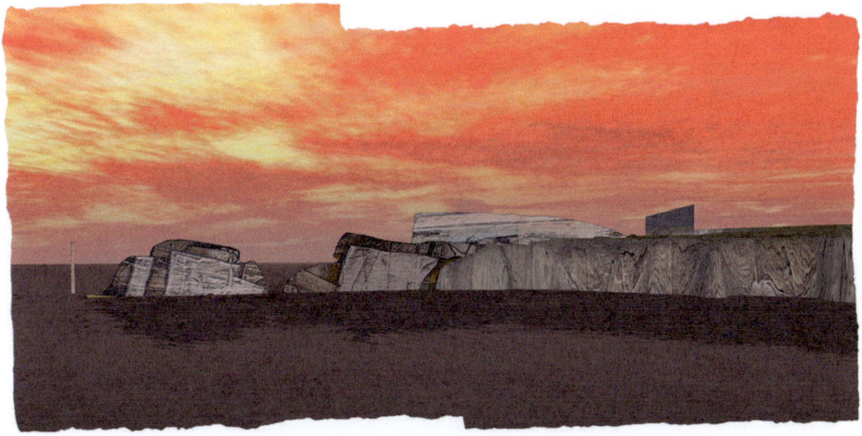

Fig. 6.8 Old Harry Rocks (Screen Grab of Light Years: Coast. 2010)

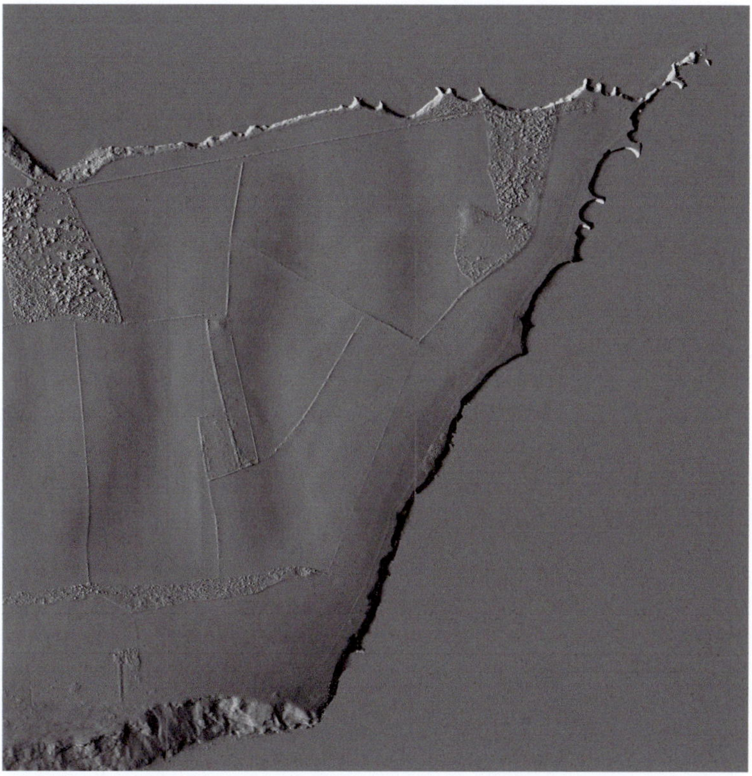

Fig. 6.9 Old Harry Rocks, rendered LIDAR image. The topography of virtual landscape is formed from scientific data. LIDAR (Light Detection And Ranging) scanning, conducted by the Channel Coast Observatory, was used to create the terrain heights, with measurements taken every 2 m. The painting textures were virtually painted onto the undulated surface

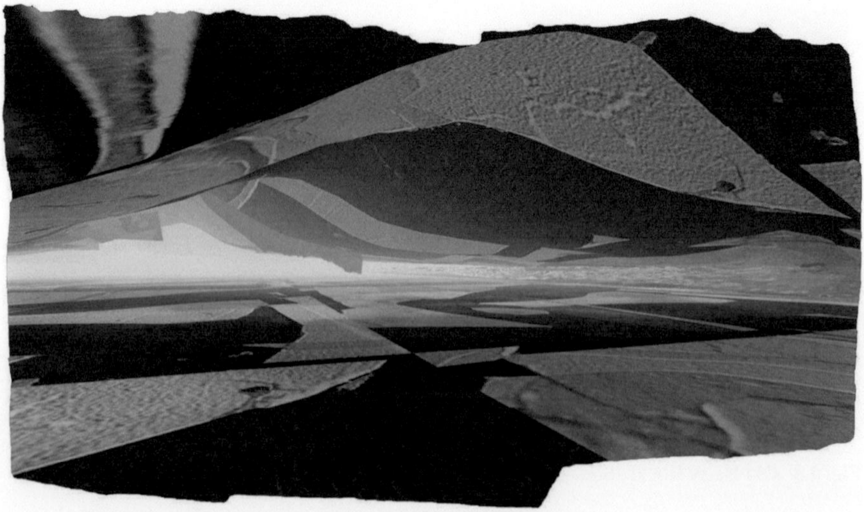

Fig. 6.10 Screen grab (*Light Years: Jurassic Coast*, 2009 (sub surface))

Feelings, memories and impressions change with time because we keep in our memory only certain facets of events and ideas. The best-preserved and clearest memories are usually those based on the most significant aspects of a moment. Much of the emotional crispness and aesthetic steadiness of *Light Years*: *Jurassic Coast* has to do with the elegant simplicity with which the environment and the interactions were conceived and built. The overall scale, height and polygonal density of the mesh was adjusted and optimised for a real-time situation where the impression of movement is paramount.

The location for *Light Years: Jurassic Coast* is Worbarrow Bay, Dorset. The previous *Purbeck Light Years* project had a single focal point (Corfe Castle, Dorset). Hence, in *Light Years: Jurassic Coast* the use of planes to fill the screen area worked differently. Part of the *Purbeck Light Years* experience was the forming and reforming of 2D compositions. *Light Years: Jurassic Coast* was about travelling along the coast, with 2D compositions occurring less frequently.

Challenging Perceptions

Another new aspect was the fact that the viewer (or virtual camera) actually passes through the ground, deliberately shattering the reality of the topographical landscape, and having access to the subterranean world (Fig. 6.10). In computer games, crashing through the landscape would be considered a mistake. However in *Light Years: Jurassic Coast*, this exposing of the underlying geometry is deliberate. It is another way in which we challenge the perceptions of the viewer who might be conditioned to the excessive realism found in many contemporary 3D computer games.

Sound

The sound in *Light Years*: *Jurassic Coast* enhances the atmospheric nature of the environment. Some sounds are activated as the viewer approaches a specific location, using surround sound techniques. The noise that the wind makes, for example, increases in volume as one moves along into to sea. The sound of the sea and additional natural sounds all occur randomly, interspersed with silence. This additional sensory element increases the immersion of the work. Sound is a very evocative medium, triggering memories, and a sense of place. In a similar manner to *Purbeck Light Years*'s recording of a train, *Light Years: Jurassic Coast* has a recording of a tour-guided boat trip along the coast. This can be fleetingly heard as the audience passes through specific locations along the coast.

Representing Time

The splendour and mystery of this 160 million year-old landscape, eroded by weather to create the coastline, permeates the experience. However, this interactive installation does not seek to create an accurate model of the past, or to recreate vanished moments. *Light Years*: *Jurassic Coast* is about the passing of time, time past and time present. It hints towards the issues of Climate Change, not as a new phenomenon, but as a process as old as the Earth itself [11].

Evolution

Since 2009 and the original paper presentation at EVA 2009, *Light Years: Jurassic Coast* has evolved through experimentation and increased ambition. In January 2010 its creators received an Arts Council England grant to develop the work into an even more ambitious piece: *Light Years: Coast.* This featured a ten-mile stretch of the Jurassic Coast from Old Harry Rock to Chapman's Pool, Dorset (Fig. 6.8). Once again it used LIDAR and weather data along with recent paintings and prints. The work focuses on a boat journey that continually travels back and forth along the coast. The recurring themes explored by Gardiner and Head, those of constantly changing light and weather conditions, as well as subtle variations in composition, make this version another unique experience each time it is viewed.

Conclusion

One of the key questions in the continued evolution of *Light Years: Jurassic Coast* is the way that the collaborators' roles interchange, with the visual input of the painting and algorithmic input of the software also revealing the technical aspects of painting and the visual processes at work in the virtual realm. *Light Years* is a long term project, it has been running for over 10 years, and the experiments of both artists will continue into the future, as they explore issues of aesthetics, time, representation, multiple dimensions, technology, experience, audience, art and science. Their experiments will lead them forward to the next *Light Years* project.

Our agenda for ongoing research has led Gardiner to collaborate with Dr Gary Priestnall in the Department of Geography at Nottingham University to develop a geographic visualisation technique where the vertical dimension of landscape is represented literally in the form of a physical relief model, and where the dynamic or interactive element can be provided by projection map-based data vertically down onto the model. This is referred to as the projection augmented relief model (PARM) technique [12].

Head's research has developed some of the digital techniques involved in *Light Years* to create 3D graphics based weather simulation software. In effect he is taking the same kind of data sources that were used before, but is representing the skyscape in a more scientific manner, looking at representing cloud forms and movements, precipitation types and temperature [13].

We believe that immersive 3D landscape environment techniques offer a dynamic and interactive form of engagement for artistic and scientific installations. When displayed in a gallery, this form of immersive environment can communicate diverse themes from pictorial space to the passing of geological time in a dynamic and engaging way that static installations cannot.

Acknowledgements Denys Brunsden, Professor Emeritus of Geology at Kings College for his advice on the geomorphology of the Jurassic Coast.

Nick Lambert for his technological support and suggestions.

Amanda Wallwork for her collaboration on the 'Mapping the Coast' project.

Nina Colosi for curating the exhibition *Imaginalis* at the Chelsea Art Museum, New York City.

Jem Main for curating the exhibition *Light Years: Jurassic Coast* at the Lighthouse, Poole Centre for the Arts.

Paul Thirkell for curating the exhibition *3D2D: Object and Illusion in Print* at the Edinburgh Printmakers Gallery.

Jon Murden and Jenny Cripps for their curatorial advice at the Dorset County Museum.

Arts Council England for their support of *Light Years: Jurassic Coast.*

References

1. Brunsden, D., & Goudie, A. (1999). *Classic landforms of the West Dorset Coast*. Sheffield: The Geographical Association Press.
2. Davies, G. (1935). *The Dorset Coast*. London: A& C Black.
3. Winchester, S. (2001). *The map that changed the world*. New York: Viking.
4. Payne, C. (2013). *The art of Jeremy Gardiner: Unfolding landscape*. Farnham: Lund Humphries.
5. Fortey, R. (2002). *Fossils: The key to the past*. Washington, DC: Natural History Museum Publications.

6. Bimber, O., & Raskar, R. (2005). Spatial augmented reality: A modern approach to augmented reality. In *Proceedings of the annual conference on computer graphics and interactive techniques (SIGGRAPH'05)*. New York.
7. Kandinsky, W. (1980). *Point and line to plane*. New York: Dover Books.
8. Wineman, J. D., & Peponis, J. (2010). Constructing spatial meaning: Spatial affordances in museum design. *Environment and Behaviour, 42*(1), 86–109.
9. Dodge, M., McDerby, M., & Turner, M. (2008). *Geographic visualization: Concepts, tools and applications*. Chichester: Wiley.
10. Head, A. (2011). *A painterly approach to 3D computer graphics*. In *Proceedings of the 17th international symposium on electronic art (ISEA 2011)*, Istanbul, 14–21 Sept 2011.
11. Mitsova, H., Mitas, L., Ratti, C., Ishii, H., Alonso, J., & Harmon, R. S. (July 2006). Real-time landscape model interaction using a tangible geospatial modelling environment. *IEEE Computer Graphics and Applications, 26*(4), 55–63.
12. Priestnall, G., Durrant, J., Goulding, J., & Gardiner, J. Projection Augmented Relief Models (PARM): Tangible displays for geographic information. In S. Dunn, J. P. Bowen, & K. Ng (Eds.), *EVA London 2012 Conference Proceedings*. Electronic Workshops in Computing (eWiC), British Computer Society, 2012. http://ewic.bcs.org/content/ConWebDoc/46124. Accessed 22 May 2013.
13. Head, A. 3D weather – Towards a real-time 3D simulation of localised weather. In S. Dunn, J. P. Bowen, & K. Ng (Eds.), *EVA London 2011 Conference Proceedings*. Electronic Workshops in Computing (eWiC), British Computer Society, 2011. http://ewic.bcs.org/content/ConWebDoc/40563. Accessed 22 May 2013.

Chapter 7
Photography as a Tool of Alienation: *Aura*

Murat Germen

Abstract Regular photographic imaging records volumetric planes with smooth surfaces. The reason is the camera's deficiency in perceiving and documenting the visual richness of "persuasive" details in life. HDR imaging methods used in creating the artwork series titled *Aura* helped invisible textures to emerge through different exposures and layering multiple surfaces in an image. A major objective in this series was to facilitate the experiential visual complexity between the animate and inanimate to emerge that cannot otherwise be recorded. The intention was to achieve a new symbiotic painterly visual relationship between biological (humans) and non-biological (space) through the rich textures achieved after high-dynamic-range-imaging (HDRI) procedures. The chapter will focus on photography as a tool of personal world making, instead of photography as witnessing. In unfolding this practice notions of superimposition, palimpsest, painting vs. photography, truth and photography as an apparatus to provoke de-familiarisation will be covered. The aim is to confirm photography as a visual language that enriches and transforms human perception.

This chapter is an updated and extended version of the following paper, published here with kind permission of the Chartered Institute for IT (BCS) and of EVA London Conferences: M. Germen, "Photography as a tool of alienation: Aura." In A. Seal, J. P. Bowen, and K. Ng (eds.). EVA *London 2010 Conference Proceedings*. Electronic Workshops in Computing (eWiC), British Computer Society, 2010. http://www.bcs.org/ewic/eva2010 (accessed 26 May 2013).

M. Germen (✉)
Sabanci University/Visual Arts and Communication Design Program,
Sabanci University, FASS, Orhanli, Tuzla, Istanbul 34956, Turkey
e-mail: muratgermen@sabanciuniv.edu; www.muratgermen.com

J.P. Bowen et al. (eds.), *Electronic Visualisation in Arts and Culture*,
Springer Series on Cultural Computing, DOI 10.1007/978-1-4471-5406-8_7,

Introduction

Aura series is a digital experiment to study the advantages of using computational imaging tools to create a novel photography aesthetic. This is alien to the classical perception of photography where straight evidential images are assumed.

Photography is a creative field in which technological advances greatly influence artistic expression. The ease of manipulation offered by software and the new functions available in cameras have caused artists who use photography as a tool to reconsider their visions, themes, narration, syntax and ways to share their artwork. Photography sharing sites such as Flickr, which facilitate encounters with individuals from different cultures, help to change the perception of time geographically and enable artists to get faster feedback, revelation, exposure and layering of information to be conveyed.

While some photographers are deeply engaged with analogue processes and deny digital technology many artists, aware of the complexity and particular advantages, do indeed adopt the novel aesthetics of photography. The familiar methods of montage and collage used in the old analogue days are still available but digital imaging techniques additionally enable artists to work with concepts such as augmented perception, chronophotography, subreal encounters, pictorialism, palimpsest-like superimposition, interlacing, simplification or minimisation, the creation of new worlds, delusion, synthetic realism or artificiality and appropriation.

Superimposition: The Notion of Palimpsest

The painterly effect obtained as the result of digital superimposition reminds us of the analogue concept of palimpsest (from the Greek *palin*, again; *psëstos*, scraped) – a re-used papyrus, parchment or other manuscript where the original text has been washed or scraped off and a new one substituted. The modern version of this archaic surface of knowledge, which allows the accumulation of information, is the Photoshop canvas, where details of layers behind the current can still be visible. The ability to layer various data from different sources onto one plane is a more complex form of analogue collage and montage that enables artists to achieve richer expression through superimposed pluralities (Fig. 7.1).

Layering different photographic planes into one is not the only way to create visual superimposition. "Also very common in photographs are disjunctions caused by reflections. While reflections in mirrors create discontinuities, reflections in glass can create an intermingling of spaces. This prevalence of reflections in photographs is matched by prevalence in photo-realist paintings, but in each medium the effects are very different. This is not just because the image of reflection is generally flatter, more broadly defined, and more opaque in paint." [1]. This sort of optical

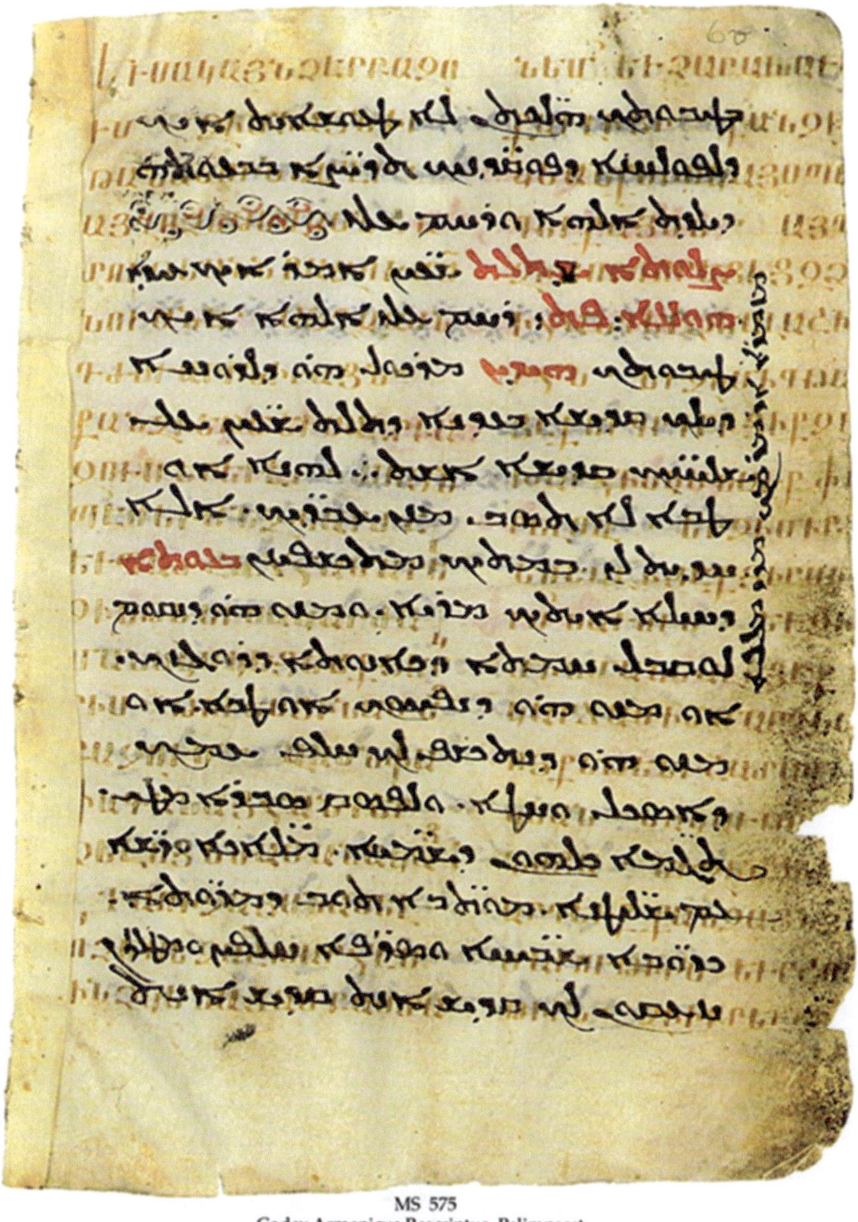

MS 575
Codex Armenicus Rescriptus. Palimpsest,
Monastery of St. Catherine, Mt. Sinai, 6th c. and 1st half of 10th c.

Fig. 7.1 A palimpsest is created when writing on a surface is partially erased and a new text is inscribed on it (Image reprinted from http://analepsis.wordpress.com/2008/04/24/this-is-a-palimpsest/, captured on Dec. 6, 2008)

superimposition is unique and yields a cumulative result different to that from layering multiple images in the digital environment. When analogue and digital visual layerings are combined it is possible to create renderings of the "real" world that are almost impossible to decipher spatially.

The *Aura* series consists of photo-composites created using a combination of Photoshop and Photomatix Pro in order to perform HDR (High Dynamic Range) imaging. Four or more images taken from the same viewpoint are used for each of the plates from the series. As in all multiple image groups, inanimate objects are captured as still while animate subjects are imaged in different positions with movements recorded as blurs, due to slow shutter speeds and the lapse of time between shots. Superimposing four images resulted in particular aesthetics, with immobile objects appearing constant and mobile subjects dynamically intricate, as a consequence of layering. In using multiple photographic renderings of these mobile subjects the aim is to achieve a complex result similar to that described above, arising from merging the reflective analogue visual image with the reflexive digital one.

Superimposition of Contexts: The Concept Text of the *Aura* Series

The *Aura* series does not focus only on the visual complexity of the world surrounding us: there is also a social concern that can be expressed only in words. Therefore, it is essential to take account of the concept text. As Barthes states in his book, *Image-Music-Text*, "the structure of the photograph is not an isolated structure; it is in communication with at least one other structure, namely the text – title, caption or article."[2]. The following paragraphs constitute the departure point of the series and explain why images of different places were superimposed to create the photographs: museums and galleries with market places…

In galleries, museums and art fairs or bazaars and markets alike, items on display are usually preferred if they have a certain "aura." This aura, beyond a pristine "beauty" of the self may depend on current trends that are in vogue, the identity of the particular exhibit venue, the specific person or the brand that exhibits, the arbitrary daily mood of the audience or buyers, the symbiotic relationship between the exhibitor and the positive critique of the promoter, and sometimes the exhibitor's statement and the perception of this statement by the audience or buyers. What renders something beautiful is not always its intrinsic qualities; it can easily be rendered "attractive" externally by cosmetic retouching or remodelling, not integral to the original (Figs. 7.2, 7.3, 7.4, and 7.5).

This series of artworks, focusing on the difference between the intrinsic soul of artworks and their extrinsic perception determined by conditions was created in galleries, museums and market places in Paris, Bologna, Hong Kong, London and Istanbul in the year 2009. The work is conceived as a reminder and critique of the ever-present (but recently peaked) market economy mindset, which is concealed in

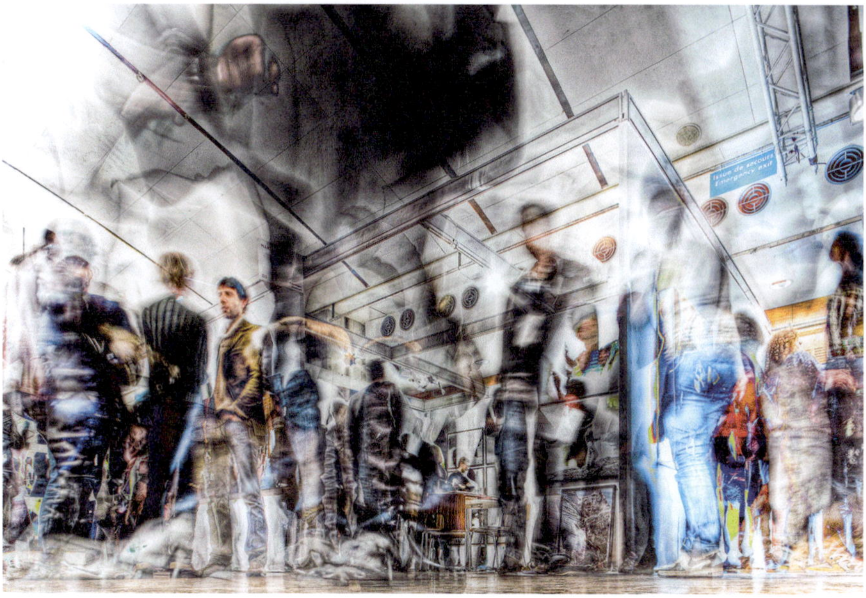

Fig. 7.2 Aura #2, Paris Photo fair, Murat Germen, 2009

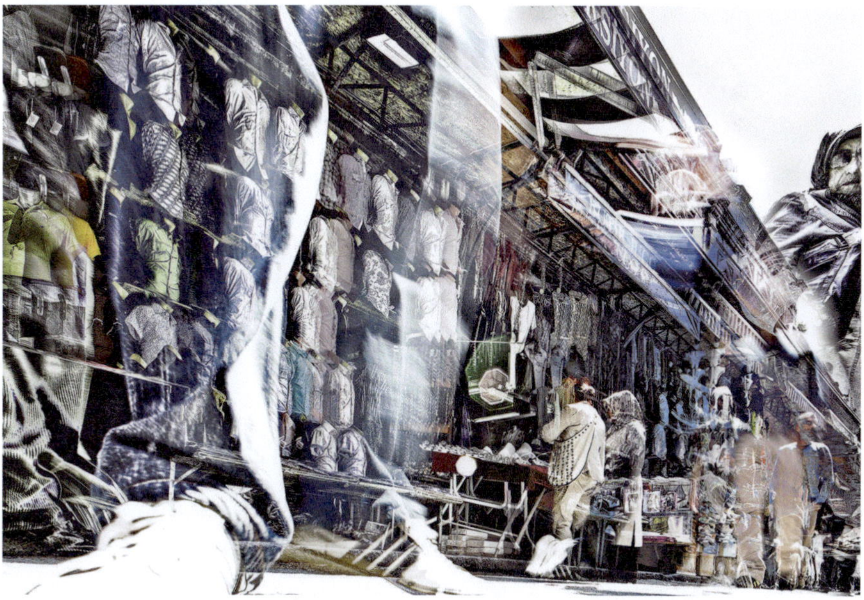

Fig. 7.3 Aura #3, Market place – Istanbul, Murat Germen, 2009

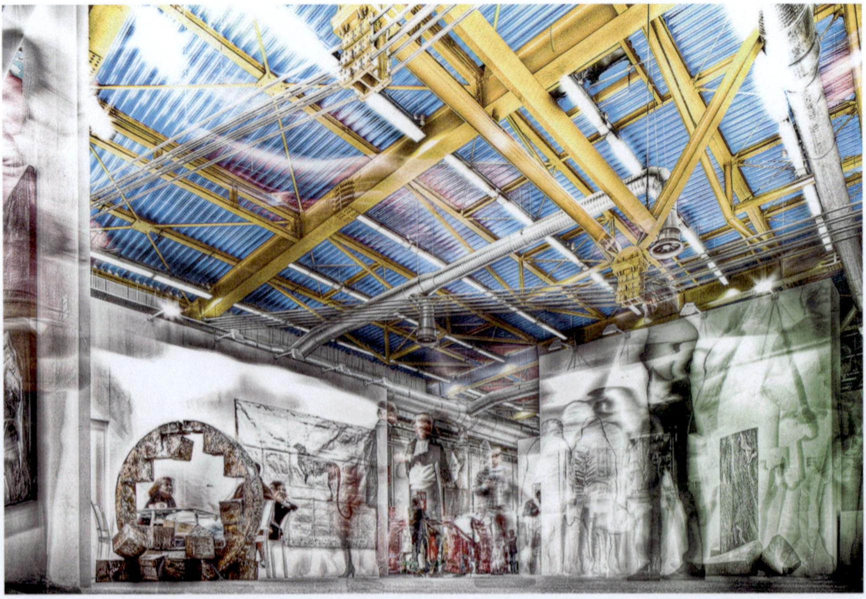

Fig. 7.4 Aura#12, Bologna Art Fair, M. Germen

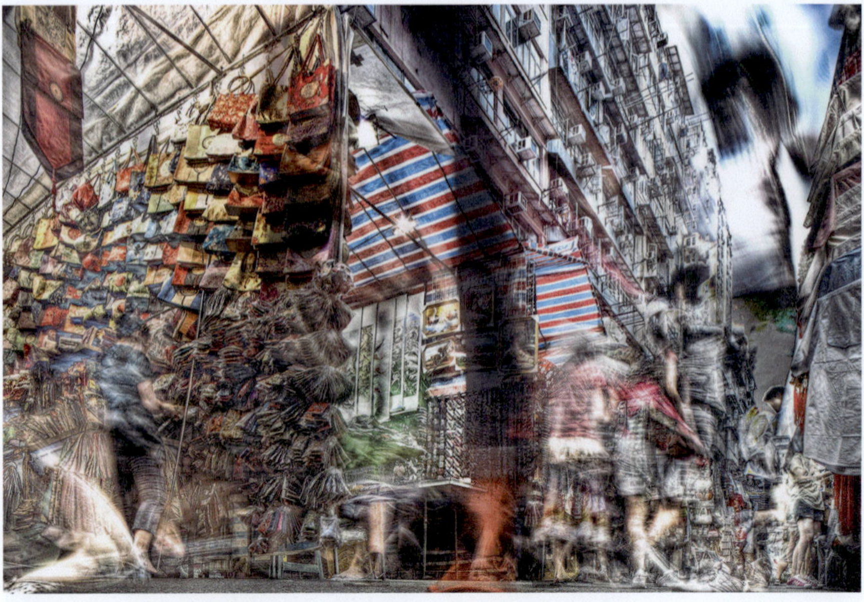

Fig. 7.5 Aura#5, Market place – Hong Kong (*bottom*), M. Germen

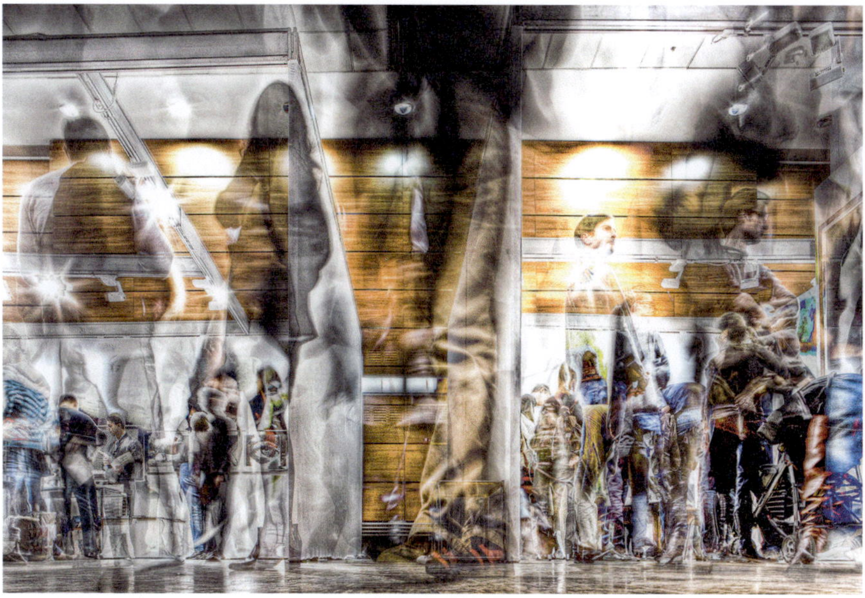

Fig. 7.6 Aura #1, Paris Photo fair, Murat Germen, 2009

artists' statements with a range of arguments and awareness. Important art events draw much attention due to the delusional presence of wild parties, discourses, allegations, lobbying and pathetic self-promotion efforts in exhibition openings, the pursuit for sponsors and influence they exert, artists competing with each other for auction prices, and the focus of attention and press coverage of celebrities at openings as opposed to artworks themselves. These surprising carryings-on perhaps indicate that art has lost its freedom, and is now situated right in the middle of the system it allegedly criticises, but which it finally disingenuously exalts. In the commercial art milieu it seems there is no longer much difference between art venues and shopping malls (Figs. 7.6 and 7.7).

The *Aura* series can be understood as a study created from a desire to make artworks independent of peripheral conditions and to embody their inherent value. Nevertheless, work on this series stopped after its exhibition in 2009, because after a solo exhibition galleries expect a new series.

There are a few reasons why this series is titled *Aura*. First of all, the initially invisible pictorial character of a space can be made visible. HDR technology enables light fields of different intensities to be equally visible on photographic images. Secondly, the ghostly appearances of moving people in the photographs are reminiscent of the so-called aura photographs that claim to document people's otherwise invisible spiritual powers.

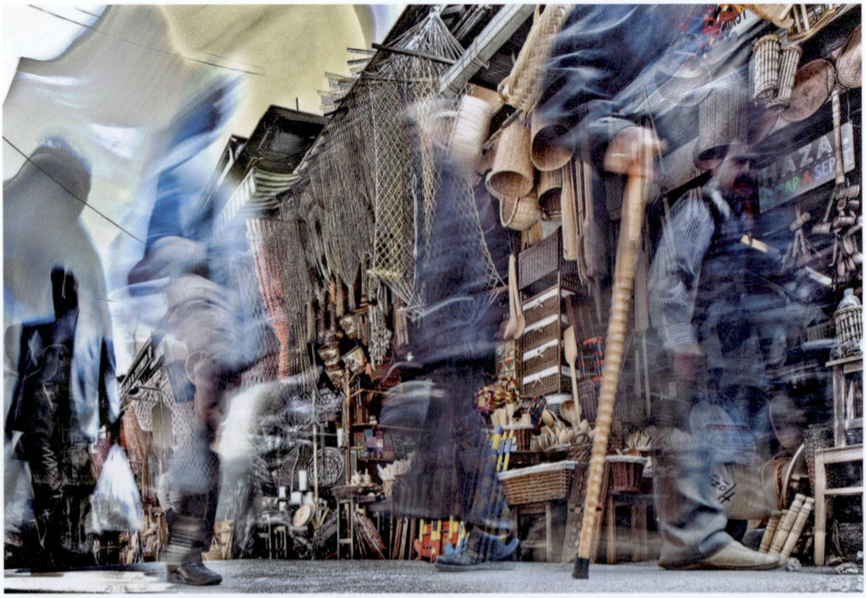

Fig. 7.7 Aura #4, Market place – Istanbul, Murat Germen, 2009

Relationship Between Painting and Photography

There is an ongoing relationship between photography and painting. When photography was invented, it annexed painting's function of recording history and was trusted more as a documentary tool, since it bore witness to experiences more realistically than paintings, which are always constructs. Some time after that, photography proved its independence and stopped being viewed purely as evidence. This is when it found the opportunity to evolve into an apparatus of fiction, like painting. This new relationship gave birth to "pictorial" photos that emulated the optical qualities of paintings, which in turn paved the path for hyper-realistic paintings that are easily mistaken for photographs.

Technological advances in the image processing capabilities of computers and the amazingly rich variety of image editing software allow for the utmost manipulation in photography and seem to weaken its credibility as evidence. Thus, the photograph has been able to lose the heavy weight of the representation of the truth for the public and to begin to represent the photographer, i.e. the self, just like the painter.

Barthes speaks of the painterly potential in photography as a way to consider it as art: "For if one can talk of aestheticism in photography, it is seemingly in an ambiguous fashion: when photography turns into painting, composition or visual substance treated with deliberation in its very material 'texture', it is either so as to signify itself as 'art' (which was the case with the 'pictorialism' of the beginning of

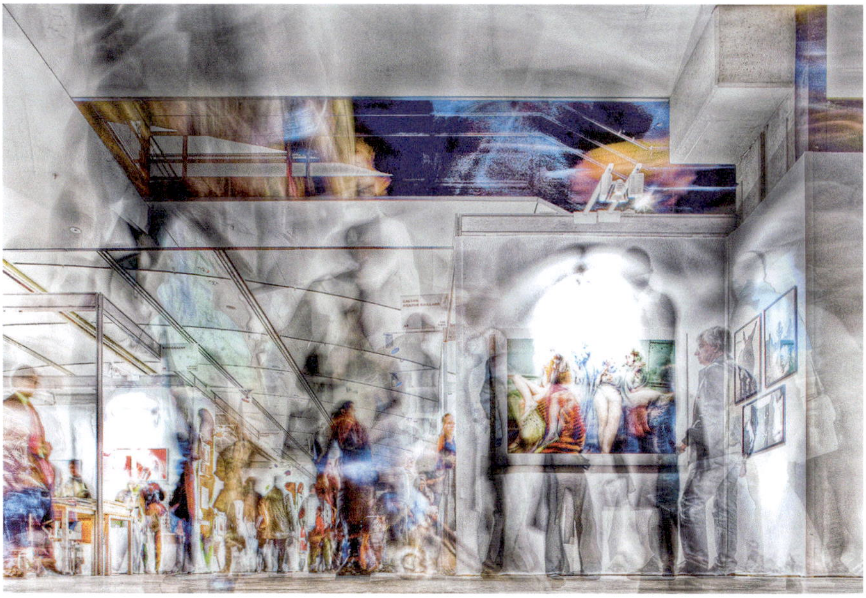

Fig. 7.8 Aura #26, Paris Photo fair, Murat Germen, 2009

the century) or to impose a generally more subtle and complex signified than would be possible with other connotation procedures." [2].

The pictorialism used in the past is nowadays replaced by the digital alchemy of two different forms of images: photography and three-dimensional synthesised images. "Computerised design systems that flawlessly combine real photographed objects and objects synthesised by the computer." [3]. The photographic image obtained from witnessing 'what is there' can easily be turned into an image recreated from scratch and made to express 'what is here', i.e. in the creator's mind. As William Mitchell claims, "a digital image is radically different [from an analogue counterpart] because it is inherently mutable: 'the essential characteristic of digital information is that it can be manipulated easily and very rapidly by computer. Computational tools for transforming, combining, altering, and analysing images are as essential to the digital artist as brushes and pigments to a painter.' Furthermore, in a digital image, the essential relationship between signifier and signified is one of uncertainty." [3]. This uncertainty offers the possibility for multiple readings of artworks and is much appreciated by most of artists (Figs. 7.8 and 7.9).

The association of photography with (so-called) reality seems to constrain its expressive promises but the ambiguity of digital image in the relationship between signifier and signified (discussed above) takes it beyond the boundary: "Unlike paintings, photographs are seen as having a special connection with reality, and this gives the transformations of photography a compelling force and surreal power unavailable to painting. This difference between painting and photography can also

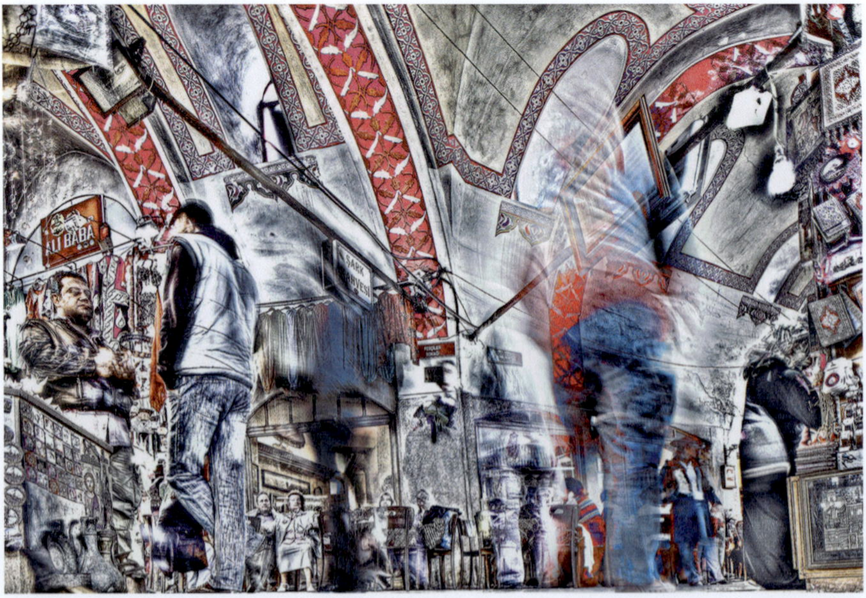

Fig. 7.9 Aura #23, Historical Grand Bazaar – Istanbul, Murat Germen, 2009

he observed in the comparison of animated and live film." [1]. In painting the signifier has to be defined realistically as far possible, since paintings are taken to be constructs resulting from the artist's imagination. But in photography, which is assumed to record the world as seen, the realistic rendering of the signifier/phenomena is not of prime importance: this is how it is possible to focus on the meaning/presence of the signified. As Barbara Savedoff puts it, "the difficulty in painting is to make the image seem alive. Photography, though, has a different starting point. Because it provides a direct record of an animate being, it can be a triumph of photographic art to make us see that person in a new way." [1].

Barthes says "painting can feign reality without having seen it" [4] in his famous 'Camera Lucida'; photography on the contrary, can pretend reality *after* having seen it. This pretended reality is actually the photographer's subjective "framed" reality and is sometimes presented as objective. Despite this subjectivity and false objectivity, photography can keep its documentary connotations, as "digital manipulation might seem particularly conducive to photographic transformation, since very complicated alterations can be achieved without destroying the image's documentary feel [1] (Figs. 7.10 and 7.11).

Paintings describe personal worlds created from imagination and are not expected to be evidence of reality as they are created from personal interpretation and are not instant recordings of objects/subjects. On the other hand photography, in addition to sustaining its duty of pure documentary, has also begun to be used as an apparatus

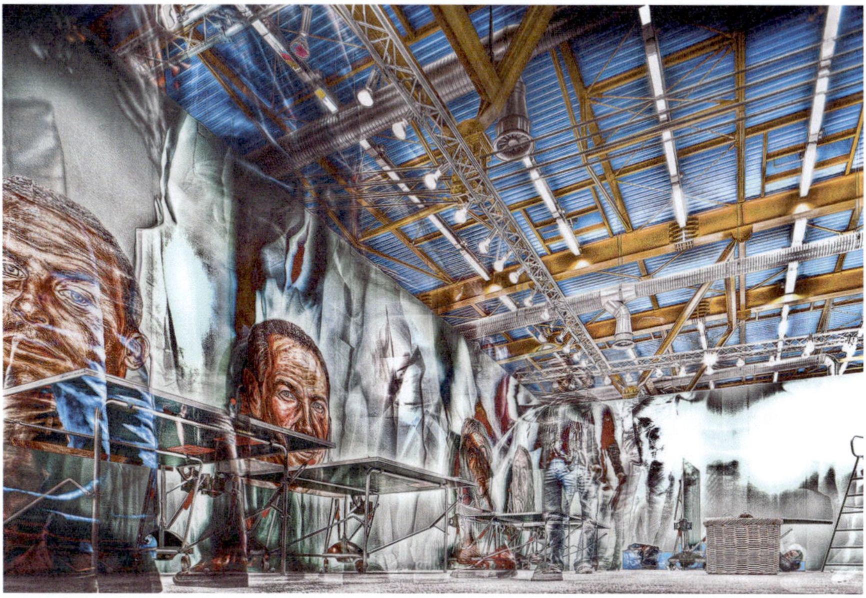

Fig. 7.10 Aura #24, Bologna Art Fair, Murat Germen, 2009

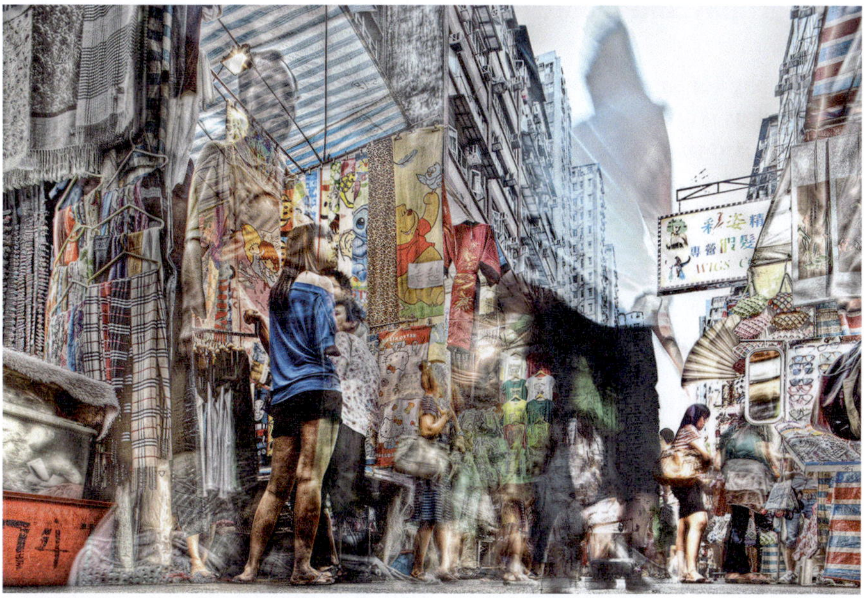

Fig. 7.11 Aura #18, Market place – Hong Kong, Murat Germen, 2009

for portraying constructed personal worlds, reminiscent of paintings. Its potential for augmented perception, chronophotography, subreal encounters, pictorialism, palimpsest-like superimposition, interlacing, simplification or minimisation, creation of new worlds, delusion, synthetic realism or artificiality, or appropriation, discussed at the outset of this article, is used by many artists to create unique aesthetics in photography. Below are some of these artists, using the categories mentioned above (no visuals are provided due to copyright issues):

- Augmented perception: Andreas Gursky (German), Chris Jordan (American), Jean-François Rauzier (French)
- Pictorialism: Jeff Wall (Canadian), Desirée Dolron (Dutch), Yao Lu (Chinese), Alessandro Bavari (Italian), Helena Blomqvist (Swedish)
- Palimpsest-like superimposition: Michael Najjar (German), Jo Teeuwisse (Dutch), Sergey Larenkov (Russian), Kay Kaul (German)
- Chronophotography: Pablo Zuleta Zahr (Chilean), Thomas Weinberger (German), Peter Langenhahn (German)
- Simplification/minimisation: Jesper Rasmussen (Danish), Josef Schulz (German), Pavel Maria Smejkal (Slovakian), Josh Azzarella (American), Matt Siber (American), Liddy Scheffknecht (Austrian)
- Creation of new worlds: Ruud van Empel (Dutch), Anthony Goicolea (American), AES + F Group (Russian), Filip Dujardin (French), David Trautrimas (American)

Photography and the Rendering of Truth

Photography for some is the factual manifestation of reality. Yet, the illusion of a single reality, is criticised by V. Flusser: "The [observer] trusts [technical images] as he trusts his own eyes. If he criticises them at all, he does so not as a critique of image, but as a critique of vision; his critique is not concerned with their production, but with the world 'as seen through' them. Such a lack of critical attitude towards technical images is dangerous in a situation where these images are about to displace texts. [It] is dangerous because the 'objectivity' of the technical image is a delusion. They are, in truth, images, and as such, they are symbolical…" [5]. Some artists take this critical attitude to an extreme to defy 'reality' and create a new synthetic reality.

As William Mitchell states in his 'The Reconfigured Eye: Visual Truth in the Post-Photographic Era'; "because of the difficulty involved in manipulating them, photographs were comfortably regarded as causally generated truthful reports about things in the real world." Yet developments in digital image processing made manipulation ever more easily available to more people, not only to experts. This deconstructionist attitude to defying reality and the ease of manipulating images led to new trends to create personal worlds. Mark Kingwell asserts that "photographs are not multiple depictions of some single reality, waiting out there to be cornered and cropped, and somehow regulating, even in the cornering and cropping, how/what the image means. Rather, photographs offer multiple meanings. The presented image is not a reflection, or even an interpretation, of singular reality. It is, instead, the creation of a world." [6]. This trend should not be seen as a dangerous direction in the present day visual culture, since photographs have in fact never been autonomous entities but have always depended on specific local/contextual historic, social, political and cultural interpretations by the people producing and consuming them.

With this in mind, potential individuals, institutions and nations have started using photography as an illustrative tool to construct reality as opposed to representing reality, since photography can transform the way we see representations. "Media, being in between the segments of the society, have a certain influence in the construction of social reality. Media put issues on the agenda, provide information about facts and events, and offer a cognitive framework for society's interpretation" [7]. "Construct" is a temporary process that exists for a while and finally transforms itself into an end "product": A building, a culture, a society, an idea, a freedom, a dogma, etc. Not only buildings and structures are built; the major components that constitute the spine of the society we live in, such as tradition, culture and identity can also be constructed.

Photography as an Apparatus to Provoke Dis-appearance, Ambiguity and De-familiarisation

Life is so full of idiosyncrasies that the famous saying "truth is stranger than fiction" was coined. Consequently, conveying 'real' appearances through photographs, striving for certainty in image making or communicating familiarities may not always turn as "artful" as expected. Instead, de-familiarisation of the subject to be presented in the eyes the audience offers alternative ways to communicate with them. De-familiarisation is a strategy used especially by radical modernist artists in various fields to challenge our habitual ways of seeing and understanding, allowing or forcing us to see afresh. The key technique for artists attempting to convey strangeness or to create an alienation effect, as de-familiarisation is also called, is to foreground the various devices of artistic language in such a way as to bring attention to the language itself and prevent habitual ways of seeing and reading. Pioneered by the Russian Formalists of the early twentieth century, de-familiarisation was meant to disturb life's habitual ideologies [8]. Viktor Shklovsky introduced the concept of de-familiarisation in his seminal essay, 'Art as Device' (often translated as 'Art as Technique') and claimed that art de-familiarises objects by presenting them as if seen for the first time and thus removes them from the automation of human perception.

When a photograph de-familiarises, it is as though something new to the accustomed perception is being revealed through ambiguity; the resulting observation can turn out to be highly stimulating. This approach makes the familiar disappear and allows us to focus on the notion of *dis-appearance*. This can be described as the depiction of the subject, object or scene as experienced and or felt and not only as seen.

Conclusion

My artist's statement, set out above, will clarify my position. Photography is an opportunity for me to find things people ignore and bring them forward to make people reconsider their ideas. I am not interested in extraordinary things since they are always covered and receive more attention due to mankind's unending interest in celebrities, fame, and sensation… I try to concentrate more on ordinary things and catch possible latent extraordinariness in regularity. It is easy to take ordinary photos of extraordinary things but more challenging to take extraordinary photos of ordinary things. It is possible to say I tend to concentrate on extracting beauty out of ordinary. I attempt to de-familiarise ordinariness, render it ambiguous by alienating it from its familiar context and finally make people see it afresh. Photography records surface information, where one can only depict the exterior features of objects (colour, texture, shape, etc.) and the resulting visual representation cannot incorporate the internal condition, content, even soul. This is why I additionally aim to make photos that carry the many traces of time, multiple dimensions of space and finally create photos usually invisible to the naked eye. The basic idea is to form a personal visual accumulation through time and space that supposedly give us more insight and clues than a single photograph. I see multi-layered photography/chronophotography as gates to augmented perception, surreal encounters, creation of new worlds and self appropriation, since I do not believe in ultimate objectivity in photography and "Truth" with the capital T. Personal delineations of temporary yet experienced smaller realities are truer than imposed institutional "realities." The key is reflecting the inner world with a genuine, idiosyncratic way: "Do not follow the suggested agenda/trend, do your own thing…"

References

1. Savedoff, B. E. (2000). *Transforming images: How photography complicates the picture*. Ithaca: Cornell University Press.
2. Barthes, R. (1978). *Image-music-text*. New York: Hill and Wang.
3. Manovich, L. The paradoxes of digital photography. In *Photography after Photography,* exhibition catalogue, Germany, 1995. http://www.manovich.net/TEXT/digital_photo.html. Accessed 5 Apr 2013.
4. Barthes, R. (1982). *Camera Lucida: Reflections on photography*. New York: Hill and Wang.
5. Flusser, V. (2000). *Towards a philosophy of photography*. London: Reaktion Books.
6. Kingwell, M. (2006). *The truth in photographs: Edward Burtynsky's revelations of excess* (pp. 16–19). Gottingen, Germany: Steidl Publishers.
7. Kempf, W. (2003). Constructive conflict coverage – A social psychological research and development program. *Conflict & Communication Online*, 2(2), 4.
8. Patin, T., & McLerran, J. (1997). *Artwords: A glossary of contemporary art theory*. Westport: Greenwood.

Chapter 8
Fugue and Variations on Some Themes in Art and Science

Gordana Novakovic

Abstract This paper describes the development over several years of *Fugue*, an art|science audio-visual piece inspired by the human immune system. It has been presented in a number of different contexts – as an artwork, as an aid to the public understanding of science, and as a potential tool for scientists – and it is still under development. Stimulated by the response of some participants to the interactive and immersive version of *Fugue*, by recent discoveries in the field of neuroplasticity, and by contemporary analysis and criticism of some adverse effects of the digital revolution, a possible new category of art, neuroplastic art, is identified and briefly discussed.

Prelude

I began my professional life as a painter, but when computers became available from 1984 or so, I began to use them in various ways as tools and media. I made my first computer-controlled interactive piece in 1994 (Fig. 8.1), and was immediately struck by the powerful and unexpected responses shown by some participants.

This stimulated my interest in perception, and in the psychological aspects of the complex experience of interactivity, but also introduced me to the broader

---

This chapter is an updated and extended version of the following paper, published here with kind permission of the Chartered Institute for IT (BCS) and of EVA London Conferences: G. Novakovic, "Fugue and some Variations in Art and Science." In A. Seal, J. P. Bowen, and K. Ng (eds.). EVA *London 2010 Conference Proceedings*. Electronic Workshops in Computing (eWiC), British Computer Society, 2010. http://www.bcs.org/ewic/eva2010 (accessed 26 May 2013).

G. Novakovic (✉)
Computer Science Department, University College London,
Malet Place, London WC1E 6BT, UK
e-mail: gordana.novakovic@cs.ucl.ac.uk; www.gordananovakovic.org

J.P. Bowen et al. (eds.), *Electronic Visualisation in Arts and Culture*,
Springer Series on Cultural Computing, DOI 10.1007/978-1-4471-5406-8_8,

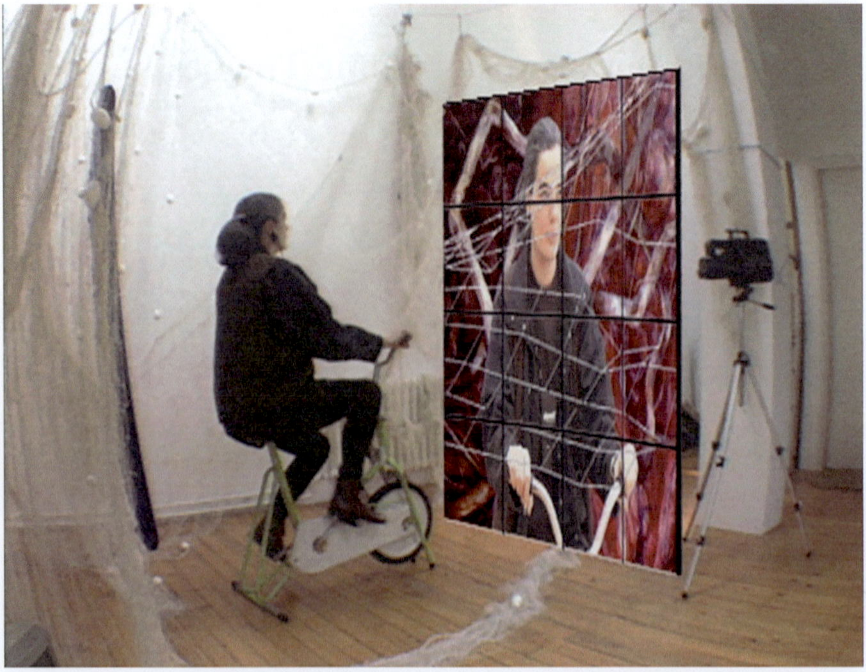

Fig. 8.1 Under the shirt of a happy man (Interactive installation 1994–96)

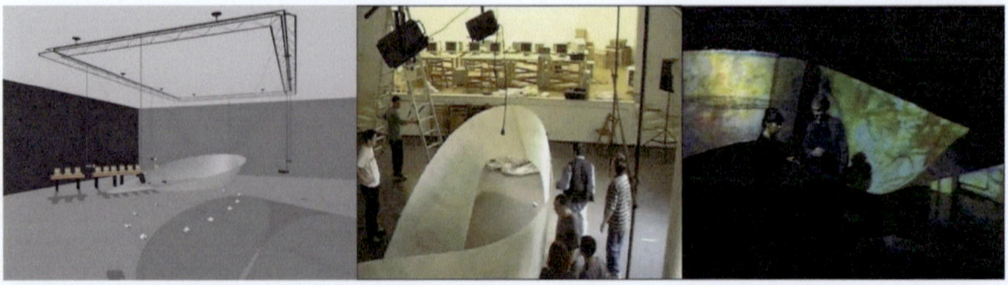

Fig. 8.2 Infonoise (Interactive installation 1998–2001). *Left*: 3D simulation. *Centre*: building the installation. *Right*: inside the installation

framework of the digital revolution, media criticism, sociology, philosophy, and so on. In 2001, several participants in my large-scale interactive installation Infonoise [1] (Fig. 8.2) showed puzzling signs of distorted consciousness, and so I began to explore the transdisciplinary field of consciousness studies [2]. It was against this background that I began work on another large-scale interactive piece, *Fugue*, and once again found myself asking questions about the strange effects of digital interactive technology.

Fugue

An Arts Council England Individual Grant in 2004 brought modest funding for Algorithmica, originally titled City Portrait. Firmly grounded in research, it aimed to critically address the form of the mass-media industry. A spontaneous, non-tactile interaction was to be based on the biological principles of interaction among cells, and a game-based software architecture would operate within the set of a 3D London Tube map. Dr Peter Bentley, a UCL-based expert on computational models of the human immune system, joined the project, along with Anthony Ruto, an expert on 3D modelling also from UCL, and my long-term collaborator Rainer Linz, the Australian new music composer. We agreed to develop the piece in phases, and to present and exhibit each step as a different stand-alone integral work within the overall conceptual framework. Largely because of Peter's influence, the piece soon came to focus on the complex cellular interactions within the immune system, with the core engine being a specially written version of his artificial immune system software.

Algorithmica then evolved into *Fugue* [3], a project with two potentially conflicting goals: creating an artwork, and developing an audiovisualisation of the immune system for scientists. In my view, audiovisualisation offers significant advantages for understanding complex systems, because, as Dombois [4] notes, it offers a much wider bandwidth than vision alone, and engages both serial and parallel modes of perception. I was also keen to explore the potential of interactive technologies for enabling users to engage with the production of phenomena, rather than merely observing them passively.

We decided that our focus in *Fugue* would be on understanding and applying the principles of biological processes rather than creating photo-realistic 'beautiful imagery', or merely re-representing scientific findings as visualisations or sonifications. My friend, the immunologist Dr Nada Pejnovic, a research fellow at St. Mary's Hospital, gave me a detailed introduction to the field, and I was able to discuss with her my artistic interpretations of scientific subjects, my sketches inspired by medical sources, and the concept for the eventual piece. Real-time generated images originating in computational processes would set the framework for the visuals, with a major practical requirement being to reduce the typically heavy computation to a minimum. To meet this condition, and to achieve an abstract, symbolic representation of the actors in the immune system drama, I looked back to the cell-like egg-shaped and spherical structures that had appeared in my paintings from the 1990s (Fig. 8.3) and I suggested making some clay models, as I had done for my early paintings. Anthony scanned the clay models in 3D as the starting point for the final look of the inhabitants of our virtual immune system. To emphasise the focus on processes, and the distinction from the aesthetics of the gaming industry and commercial computer graphics, I suggested a black-and-white approach. Both scientists found this idea problematic, because, in their own words, they 'could think of the immune system only in red'. As a compromise, our first prototype was indeed monochromatic, but in red.

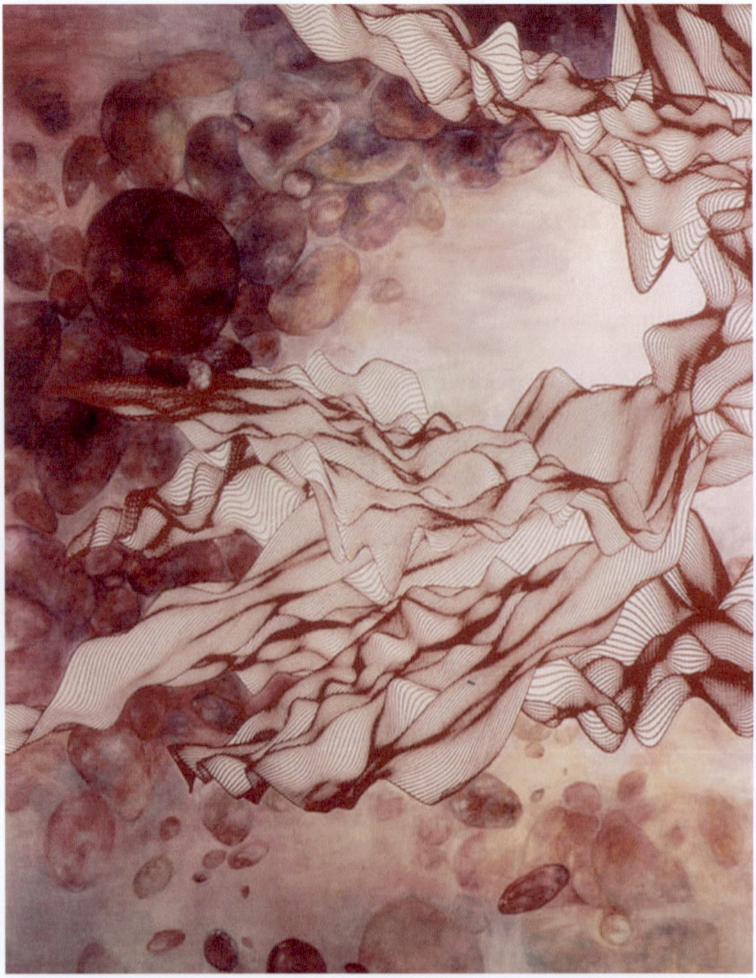

Fig. 8.3 12th view (Oil on canvas, silk screen print computer generated algorithm)

The combination of Anthony's expertise in creating 3D wire-frame models of the human body, his taste for abstract visual art, and my experience as a trained painter of using techniques of perspective, colour and *sfumato* to suggest depth, and to upgrade the crudeness of the computer generated image with the attributes of traditional visual aesthetics, gave rise to an enjoyable creative process. We replaced the red with a greyscale approach, which was now accepted as being congruent with the overall conceptual framework (Fig. 8.4). To complete the basic system, Rainer designed the sound software around a series of customised audio players that he called Fugue Players, which responded in real time to changes within the artificial immune system.

The first outcome of the team's collaboration was a paper [5] presented at a scientific conference. However, our concept received little attention, as most of the scientists categorised it as 'non-scientific', although a small number praised its fresh approach.

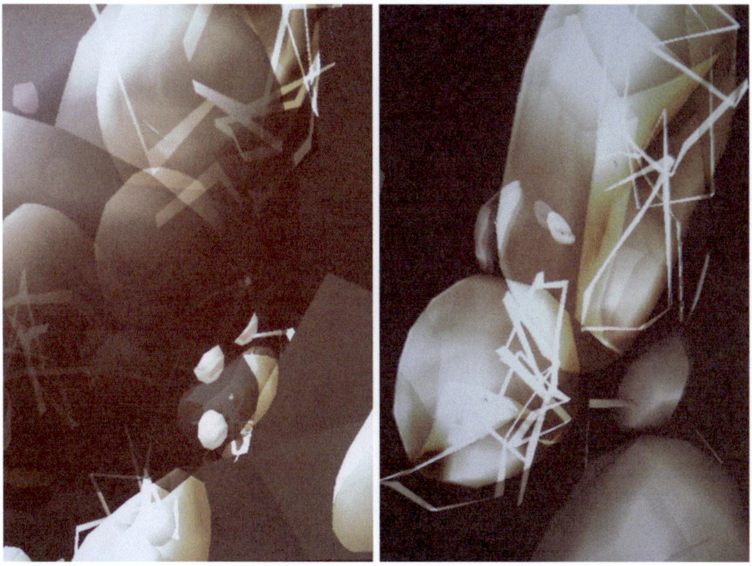

Fig. 8.4 *Fugue* (Images generated in real time by the computational model of the immune system)

Variations on the Theme of Interactivity

After this encounter with scientists, we concentrated on developing the artwork. At the time, I wrote:

> The title '*Fugue*' is a metaphor for the trans-disciplinary nature of the work, and for the method applied: interweaving the different perspectives of artists and scientists. The emergent, evolving nature of the artificial immune system algorithm, the use of repetition in the form of a succession of variations of immune system 'events', and the complex structural and functional interrelationships between the individual elements and processes are strongly related to the musical form of counterpoint, which formed one of the inspirations for the artistic concept for *Fugue*. The Artificial Immune System software creates the dynamics of the virtual immune system drama, and also constructs and implements the architecture of the *Fugue* by providing the functional structure for the communication channels between the visuals and the sound. [5]

We were engaged in intensive online work shaping the architecture and aesthetics of the installation. Online communication imposes numerous limitations, from the inevitable time lag to the lack of direct face-to-face discussion. After a period of excitement and enthusiasm, we entered a phase when tensions ran high. This was caused by conflicts between the demand for scientific accuracy, and the artistic interpretation of scientific data, and it escalated to a level that threatened to end the collaboration, and the project. It took a lot of effort from all of us to reach a consensus, and we decided from then on to limit our comments to our own area of expertise.

Rainer and I had conceptualised the interactive component of *Fugue* as a dialogue between the rhythms of the piece and the biological rhythms of the participants – between the computational model and the living body. The engineer Zoran Milkovic

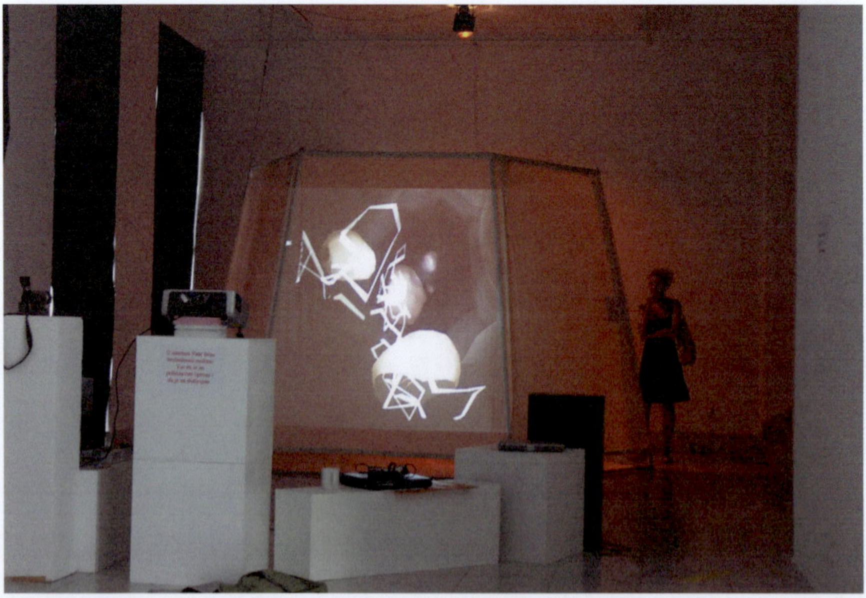

Fig. 8.5 *Fugue*. A participant is about to enter the Belgrade installation

designed the sculptural form for the set – a screen system shaped like a truncated hexagonal pyramid, and large enough to contain several participants, with the visuals being back-projected onto three adjacent walls to achieve an immersive effect. Zoran also produced a 3D computer model that served both as a virtual maquette for designing the interaction software, and as a guide for the final production. This brought a much needed new impetus. Richard Newcombe, a University of Essex computer scientist now at the University of Washington, designed the hardware and software to support the interactive component of *Fugue*. The participants were lit from above by an infrared light source, and the resulting images were streamed from an infrared video camera. Richard then modified his particle filtering and computer vision software, originally designed for scientific research, to track the positions and movements of the participants, and to send the data in real time to the immune system algorithm, which would then respond in a complex time-delayed way through the visuals and the sound. After a few more weeks of intense work on the project, developing a common language with our new collaborating scientist in the process, we had our piece fully developed and tested.

The usual venues for art|science projects are of two kinds: a closed circle of specialised events with well informed audiences, which never engage with the wider art scene; or science education events, which usually target a very young audience and address scientific issues in a predominantly pedagogical manner. The first large-scale interactive *Fugue* installation (Fig. 8.5) in Belgrade in August 2006 was rather different, as it took place in the ULUS fine art gallery. Exhibiting the piece in a fine arts context produced both expected and unexpected results. The expected responses came mainly from artists and scientists, each group initially seeing the piece as the province of the other – a perennial problem with art|science. What was quite unexpected was the degree of suspicion and fear showed by some members of the public, who hesitated at the threshold of the enclosure and refused to enter it, demanding to know what personal data were being collected from them, on whose behalf, and for what purpose. The causes of the intensity of their reaction, and their suspicion of the medical establishment, has become a topic for investigation in future developments of *Fugue*.

Variations on the Theme of Immersion

Fugue was also exhibited in the large-scale group show entitled "Infectious: Stay Away" at Trinity College Dublin's Science Gallery. Oddly enough, it was the first time that *Fugue* had been shown in the context of the public engagement with science. The curatorial concept for this intriguing exhibition was marked by spectacular design and an imaginative theatrical script. An excellent balance of varied and clearly distinct takes on the theme of infection included straight scientific demonstrations along with artworks of a more reflective nature, and provided a perfect framework for both the artistic and scientific aspects of *Fugue* to unfold and communicate.

The Science Gallery exhibitions always attract the general public in large numbers (nearly 9,000 came in the first week or so of Infectious), and the 3 month duration of the show demanded a robust, durable and safe design. We therefore decided to show a new version of *Fugue*, a screen-based presentation of the free-running real-time generated sounds and visuals in a non-interactive and non-immersive environment. For this show, we wanted to guide the audience towards the meditative properties of the piece, and to focus on the complexity of the interplay between the artistic expressions, and the free-running real-time generated dialogue between the artificial immune system components. The intimate set consisted of a large plasma screen in a small cubicle, juxtaposed with the overall spectacular setting of the gallery and the other pieces. We invited visitors to "watch and listen, and become attuned to the processes and rhythms that are mirroring what might be happening right now, inside your own body"; this invitation had a certain immediacy, as the outbreak of the swine flu epidemic coincided with the opening of the exhibition. The response from both the visitors and the curatorial team was very positive, with every indication that we had achieved our aims.

However, what was most remarkable was that the senior scientists curating the exhibition took *Fugue* into the heart of the scientific establishment by interviewing me, and publishing the outcome in the prestigious journal Nature Immunology [6]. I believe this showed that they had accepted that the legitimacy and value of the art|science concept for science goes beyond public engagement with science, and that it is capable of making a distinctive contribution to both of its core disciplines in its own right. A similar softening of disciplinary boundaries can be seen in subsequent invitations to present *Fugue* as an artistic contribution to "Risk inSight", an exhibition dealing with the scientific and social aspects of risk [7], and also at "State of Mind", an exhibition on aspects of consciousness [8] presented by the Sackler Centre for Consciousness Science at the University of Sussex.

Quodlibet

Although the content and form of *Fugue* has attracted most attention, it is perhaps the nature of the technologies employed that carries the deepest message. It is becoming clear that the digital revolution has changed the nature of our perceptual processes, and this in turn has changed our conscious experience of the physical world, inducing changes in cognition on a scale that is still unknown. Some of the most radical insights into the essence of the problems arising from a digital culture come from the media critic Paul Virilio. He identifies the economic and political origins and aspects of the digital revolution, and its socio-political effects, particularly globalisation and global militarisation, mediated perception and new forms of alienation. He paints a dark and accurate picture of the current world, with an even darker vision of the future: "One day the day will come when the day won't come" [9]. His disturbing, dramatic warnings about the potential remodelling of humans by means of technology carry a strong message and call for a revolt against the tyranny of real time interactivity and media, questioning the ethics of both the arts and the sciences.

But of course, issues similar to these have been explored across all art disciplines. An increasing number of artists working with technology are investigating and experimenting with the phenomena arising directly from the interplay between our senses and technology – for example, Stelarc through his concepts of obsolete bodies and exoskeletons [10], Char Davies with her pioneering bio-feedback VR [11], Rainer Linz analysing the physiological aspects of electronic music [12], and Margaret Dolinsky using digital art to study cognitive recognition and perceptual shifts [13].

We might think that science should provide some answers to these questions, but with very few exceptions, mainstream science has ignored the possible cognitive consequences of these dramatic environmental changes. For example, the majority of scientists investigating perception, particularly within the discipline of neuroscience, still refer to the 'real world' as a constant, an axiom, unchanged through time. But there is a further problem within neuroscience itself: the dominant doctrine, recognising slow evolutionary processes as the only way for qualitative changes to happen in a species, has combined with the established view that the brain is a closed and static system with fixed locations for particular functions, leaving no space to consider changes occurring within periods of 10 years – or even less. It is assumed that we come into this world with a genetically predetermined design for the brain, with exact locations for different functions, and that this structure remains constant throughout our lives.

However, over many years, a small number of scientists have been breaking out of this rigid context to show that the brain is not a closed, unchangeable system. We are now seeing growing scientific evidence that the brain is in fact almost nakedly open to external influences, and is capable of rapid and radical change by remodelling itself through learning and interaction with the environment. The field of neuroscience is now yielding evidence that may revolutionise not only the science of cognition, but also the wider view of the relationship between humans and the environment, and even the role and nature of culture. The brain can no longer be regarded as a fixed, closed, passive receiver of information from the senses – a mere processor for the information that controls our body through a kind of one-way communication. Rather, it is intrinsically plastic, in a process of constant change and growth through its interaction with the environment, and through a variety of learning processes.

It is certainly too extensive and complicated a matter to be reviewed adequately in this brief paper, but we can pick out some pioneers. The late Dr. Paul Bach-Y-Rita [14] was one of the first neuroscientists to work on what is now called neuroplasticity. His approach was not just theoretical, but practical: he worked with technical experts to construct electronic devices that would enable the brain of a patient with severe sensory problems to recover the lost functions. His method was to provide the patient's brain with the missing information through a different sensory channel. In 1969 he provided blind people with 'visual' information by transferring a camera image to the patients' skin using an array of vibrating pins, and his success led to the radical concept of 'seeing with the brain'.

We also now have a wealth of scientific evidence that shows that the way in which we use and exercise our brains really does matter. Another neuroplasticity pioneer, the neuroscientist Michael Merzenich [15], argues that learning and practising certain skills can rapidly change hundred of millions of connections in our brain, improving and speeding up a wide variety of cognitive abilities. His experiments over the years have delivered strong arguments against the idea of fixed functions in fixed locations in the brain. He has been particularly active in discovering how new learning can stimulate the brain to counteract age-related deterioration, or the effects of serious brain injury, or language impairment in children. Most importantly, he has found that the most powerful way of delivering the learning tasks is through the use of digital technology: the speed and flexibility of his interactive computer-based training scheme enable the delivery of more effective rewards, in turn speeding up the rate of learning.

In a recent book on neuroplasticity, "The Brain that Changes Itself", Norman Doidge [16] seems to offer a roadmap for future connections between disciplines grounded in neuroplasticity. In the chapter 'The Culturally Modified Brain' he writes:

> As we use an electronic medium, our nervous system extends outwards, and the medium extends inwards. [...] Because our nervous system is plastic, it can take the advantage of this compatibility and merge with the electronic media, making a single, larger system. Indeed, it is the nature of such systems to merge whether they are biological or man-made. [16], p. 311

In the case of an electronic device playing the role of a substitute for a lost capacity, or as an assistant in its regeneration, our body's response can take a dramatic form, because the way in which electronic and digital devices transmit information is in essence quite similar to the basic function of our nervous system – the almost instantaneous transmission of electrical impulses. Due to its capacity for plastic changes, our nervous system easily rewires itself and makes use of this alternative nervous system. In a passage that could have come from the filmmaker and media critic Peter Watkins, Doidge notes that it is actually the form of electronic media, and not so much the content, that affects our cognitive processes:

> It is the form of the television medium—cuts, edits, zooms, pans and sudden noises—that alters the brain, by activating what Pavlov called the 'orienting response', which occurs whenever we sense a sudden change in the world around us, especially a sudden movement. [...] The response is physiological [...]. [16], p. 309

Elsewhere, Merzenich emphasises the unprecedented opportunities that now exist for digital technologies to affect our brains:

> The internet is just one of those things that contemporary humans can spend millions of 'practice' events at, that the average human a thousand years ago had absolutely no exposure to. Our brains are massively remodelled by this exposure—but so, too, by reading, by television, by modern electronics, by contemporary music, by contemporary 'tools', etc. [15]

Merzenich's remarks date from 2005. Since then we have seen the introduction of the iPhone (2007) and other smartphones, and the development of the iPad (2010) and other tablets. In conjunction with developments in social networking, such as the opening of Facebook to anyone over 13 with an email address (2006 – it was previously limited to students), and Twitter (2006), these changes have created an explosion in the use of 'always-on' mobile devices, especially among young people, and so Merzenich's comments are now more relevant than ever.

Because we now have this solid evidence that interaction with electronic media can not only affect our perception and cognition, but can also produce rapid and irreversible changes in our brains, the potentially damaging nature of this aspect of modernity confronts and challenges humanity with a set of serious problems. However, as far as I am aware, the true nature and extent of the influence of the modern urban environment, whether private, public, or workspace, has not yet been the subject of an in-depth scientific analysis. We can, of course, exercise choice even in the face of this onslaught – and neuroplasticity also tells us that the extent to which we can shape our own lives through the ways we choose to use our brains is far larger than we once thought it was.

Coda

It is clear that as artists we must continue to engage with this theme, although we know that this is a difficult task in this age of immaturity, kindergarten states and the hyperreality of the profit-driven post-digital revolution. For artists, however, there may be problems closer to home. This new understanding of cognitive processes is warning us that experiencing art, and especially electronic art, or technology-enabled art, is far from being an innocently entertaining or aesthetically pleasing experience extending for a limited period of time. The disturbing evidence of neuroplasticity raises the possibility that experiencing particular forms of art may itself affect and mark our cognition – perhaps with irreversible and unknown changes. But of course we cannot abandon technology: we must instead seek a deeper understanding of its effects on humanity by looking at all its aspects, positive, negative, and unknown. And here, the dramatic shift in neuroscience brings with it a fascinating opportunity to explore and analyse the effects of electronic media through scientifically informed art, which could give rise to an entirely new art form: neuroplastic art [17].

The concept of neuroplastic art opens a future for scientifically articulate artists and artistically articulate scientists to work closely together, with a full awareness of both the potential and the danger that emerges from the parallels between the nature of our nervous system and the characteristics of digital technology and electronic media. It may be possible to structure artworks according to new scientific evidence, and to fuse scientific knowledge with imagination to exploit the nature of electronic media to create platforms for experiences that have never existed before. Bringing together the scientists' knowledge about the brain, and our knowledge of the properties of electronic media, we can envisage art works that will become in a way tuneable complex instruments, serving both art and science. Only then will imagination and creativity transcend today's mere fascination with state-of-the-art technology, and use both technology and brain science as a means to express ideas. And perhaps this will even uncover new and benign ways of linking our brains with, and through, technology.

However, there is a hidden danger lurking within the concept of neuroplastic art. Does its involvement with neuroscience conceal a tacit acceptance that neuroscience alone can bring the final answers to all perception-related questions, the enigma of digitally enabled artefacts included? This is not necessarily the case, and it is reassuring that a new and strong critique that challenges many current dogmas of neuroscience has now appeared from the field of neurophenomenology, a discipline embracing recent research in neuroscience but also firmly grounded in the philosophy of Maurice Merleau-Ponty. A key figure in neurophenomenology is Alva Noë, who is part philosopher, part cognitive scientist, and part neuroscientist. Together with Evan Thompson and others, he offers a hypothesis about perception in action which builds on Merleau-Ponty's idea of perception as a process of interaction between the embodied and situated human and the world. He also rejects the idea that artists should just be objects of scientific investigation, as they are in neuroaesthetics, and believes that they should actively contribute to the fields of perception and consciousness studies.

Noë's iconoclastic views can be sampled in his recent book 'Out of our Heads' [18]. A key passage reads:

> Our culture is obsessed with the brain—how it perceives; how it remembers; how it determines our intelligence, our morality, our likes and our dislikes. It's widely believed that consciousness itself, that Holy Grail of science and philosophy, will soon be given a neural explanation. And yet, after decades of research, only one proposition about how the brain makes us conscious—how it gives rise to sensation, feeling, and subjectivity—has emerged unchallenged: we don't have a clue.

Among other things, he strongly criticises the limitations of current brain scanning technologies, emphasising the fact that they are incapable of accessing the processes occurring during an individual's freely moving spontaneous interaction with the environment. This is significant, because such a technology is precisely what is needed for enabling a deeper understanding of the nature of interactive environments and artistic installations – especially if they involve neuroplasticity.

In our future development of *Fugue*, we intend to continue our earlier explorations of intuitive interactivity, focusing on the situation of a participant engaged in a spontaneous communication with another entity, in the form of a non-verbal dialogue with the largely virtual body of the digital interactive installation. The technological and scientific aspects of the work will concentrate on turning *Fugue* into a tuneable interactive instrument, like those mentioned above, which will allow the visual and aural elements to be calibrated in terms of the participant's response. If successful, this will give us a way of controlling the audio-visual and kinaesthetic experiences and provide us with a specific tool for analysing the phenomena in question from both the artistic and scientific points of view. Our main problem, identified by Noë, is that the technology that we need for monitoring the relevant brain responses of a freely moving participant is not yet available. (However, wearable technologies for the real-time remote monitoring of major physical and physiological variables have been developed in a number of contexts, including their use in interactive media installations [19].)

But help may be at hand, because we are not the only group with these requirements. The current European project CEEDS 'The Collective Experience of Empathic Data Systems' [20] is committed to developing 'unobtrusive multi-modal wearable technologies to measure people's reactions…including users' heart rate, skin conductance, eye gaze, observable behaviours, speech characteristics, and brain activity.' We have opened a dialogue with one of the project partners (the University of Sussex) and we hope to have access to this equipment within a reasonable time-frame. This will not solve all of our problems – it is unlikely to extend to direct readings of brain activity at the levels sought by Noë, at least initially – but it should be capable of testing and validating our approach, and preparing the way for our ultimate vision.

In summary, what have we learned from *Fugue* so far? Firstly, in relation to the tensions between art and science, many scientists are increasingly ready to accept the validity of artistic contributions, and no longer see them as being limited to a role in the public understanding of science. Such scientists make excellent collaborators for artists, as long as each group respects the discipline-specific expertise of the other. Secondly, we must accept that the way a piece is perceived and experienced will differ for different audiences, and we must actively seek and respond to those perceptions and experiences – for example by accepting invitations to exhibit in unusual contexts – rather than trying to impose our own reading. And thirdly, some scientific ideas, such as neuroplasticity, can have a power and a relevance for technologically-enabled art that goes well beyond serving as the inspiration for individual artworks, and we must engage with this science as well as with the technology.

In conclusion, as a last comment on our responsibility and opportunity as artists to engage with these issues, we should perhaps recall the prophetic words of Heidegger in one of the most frequently analysed philosophical texts on technology [21]:

> …essential reflection upon technology and decisive confrontation with it must happen in a realm that is, on the one hand, akin to the essence of technology and, on the other, fundamentally different from it. Such a realm is art.

Acknowledgments The author gratefully acknowledges the support of the Computer Science Department, University College London; School of Computer Science and Electronic Engineering, University of Essex; Arts Council England; Arts and Humanities Research Council; Leverhulme Trust; Australian Network for Arts and Technology; ULUS (Serbian Association of Fine Arts); and Trinity College Dublin Science Gallery.

References

1. Novakovic, G., Milkovic, Z., & Linz, R. Infonoise: interactive gallery installation and web-connected theatre event. http://www.rainerlinz.net/infonoise/. Accessed 18 Apr 2013.
2. Novakovic, G. (2006). Electronic cruelty. In R. Ascott (Ed.), *Engineering nature*. Bristol: Intellect.
3. Novakovic, G. *Fugue: Art and science collaboration*. http://www.fugueart.com. Accessed 18 Apr 2013.
4. Dombois, F. (2001). Using audification in planetary seismology. In *Proceedings of the 2001 international conference on auditory display* (pp. 227–230). Espoo.
5. Bentley, P. J., Novakovic, G., & Ruto, A. (2005). Fugue: An interactive immersive audiovisualisation and artwork using an artificial immune system. In *Artificial immune systems* (Lecture Notes in Computer Science, Vol. 3627, pp. 1–12). Springer Berlin Heidelberg.
6. O'Neill, L. A. J., & O'Farrelly, C. (2009). The immune system as an invisible, silent Grand Fugue. *Nature Immunology, 10*, 104–1045.
7. November, V. (Ed.). (2012). *Risk inSight*. Lausanne: Presse Polytechnique et Universitaires Romandes.
8. Schwartzman, D. *State of mind: A consciousness expo*, Brighton, UK, 30 June 2012. http://www.consciousnessexpo.co.uk. Accessed 18 Apr 2013.
9. Virilio, P. (1995). *Open sky*. London: Verso.
10. Smith, M. (Ed.). (2007). *Stelarc: The monograph*. Boston: MIT Press.
11. McRobert, L. (2007). *Char Davies' immersive virtual art and the essence of spatiality*. Toronto: University of Toronto Press.
12. Linz, R. Altering consciousness through music: A speculative methodology. http://www.rainerlinz.net/NMA/articles/altering.html. Accessed 18 Apr 2013.
13. Dolinsky, M. *Dolinsky, M. CAVE Research Artist*. http://dolinsky.fa.indiana.edu. Accessed 18 Apr 2013.
14. Bach-Y-Rita, P., Tyler, M., & Kaczmarek, K. (2003). Seeing with the brain. *International Journal of Human-Computer Interaction, 15*(2), 285–295.
15. Olsen, S. Are we getting smarter or dumber? *CNET*, 2005. http://news.cnet.com/Are-we-getting-smarter-or-dumber/2008-1008_3-5875404.html. Accessed 18 Apr 2013.
16. Doidge, N. (2007). *The brain that changes itself*. New York: Viking.
17. Novakovic, G. *Neuroplastic arts*. http://www.neuroplasticarts.org. Accessed 18 Apr 2013.

18. Noë, A. (2009). *Out of our heads: Why you are not your brain, and other lessons from the biology of consciousness*. New York: Hill & Wang.
19. Schiphorst, T. *The Whisper[s] Research Group*. Simon Fraser University, Canada, 2005. http://whisper.iat.sfu.ca. Accessed 18 Apr 2013.
20. Freeman, J. CEEDS: The collective experience of empathic data systems. http://ceeds-project.eu. Accessed 18 Apr 2013.
21. Heidegger, M. (1982). *The questions concerning technology, and other essays*. New York: Harper Perennial.

Part III
Seeing Motion

Kia Ng

Continuous advancements in scientific and technological innovation have resulted in digital technologies that are ubiquitous in a wide range of domains and sectors, exploiting new forms of data, contents and knowledge, and influencing and impacting many aspects of our lives [1–5]. This part focuses on "Seeing Motion". Its four chapters showcase research projects that explore methods of capturing and visualising data from motion, and effectively communicate meaning. They draw together science and the arts by using visualised motion as a new form of artistic expression.

Vision is a dominant sense for human beings. Yet, we do not fully understand how it functions and how we are influenced by this sense [6], over which we have only partial conscious control. Clearly, there remain many exciting areas to explore. This theme has long been grounded in the EVA conferences (see http://www.eva-london.org) as part of its interdisciplinary remit: there are many examples of varied and exciting research outcomes in past EVA London conference proceedings (http://www.eva-london.org/past-eva-londons/).

Fernanda D'Agostino and her colleagues present, in Chap. 9, visualisation techniques using volumetric data capture of the airflow surrounding a bird's flight. The system uses laser reflectance to track oil droplets interacting with the bird's motions. This is an example of artistic visualisation combining scientific data visualisation with art, to create a series of beautiful results for exhibition and installation.

Various motion capture technologies, particularly in the game control and interface industry, have recently led to breakthroughs due to progress in the development of sensor and processor technologies. Of particular note are the Wii™, incorporating a combination of sensors and visual tracking (infra red), and the Kinect, which uses a depth camera with laser projection. These technologies have been adapted and utilised in many different contexts including health [7], robotics [8], music [9, 10] and many more. In Chap. 10 the authors present a low cost motion capture system which integrates both these technologies (Wii and Kinect) in order to track human motion for application in the arts and humanities.

Chapter 11 presents a system to capture the gestures of a music conductor, using an inertial measurement unit (IMU) sensor that is embedded inside the handle of a baton. The chapter describes its overall design and development together with a review of related literature. Several examples of using motion data are discussed, including technology-enhanced learning with a 3D visualisation of the conducting gesture data and in the context of a distributed performance.

A process using static photography to represent the gestures in sign language is described in Chap. 12. The authors suggest that their photographic images can be considered to be a form of written sign language. The subjects were found to modify their signing so that the gestures are recorded more clearly. The processes of capturing sign language gestures are described, and several examples demonstrate the outcomes and communicative values. This chapter shows the usefulness of 2D photographical techniques for communicating expressive gestures.

References

1. Guerrieri, P. (2011). *The economic impact of digital technologies: Measuring inclusion and diffusion in Europe*. Cheltenham: Edward Elgar Publishing.
2. Mohammed, S., & Jinan, F. (2010). Ubiquitous health and medical informatics: The ubiquity 2.0 trend and beyond. *Medical information science reference*, Hershey.
3. Chandy, R., & Kamalini, R. (2013). From zero to ubiquity. *Business Strategy Review, 24*(1), 14–25.
4. Turner, F. (2009). Capturing digital lives. *Nature, 461*(7268), 1206–1208.
5. Ng, K., & Nesi, P. (2008). Interactive multimedia music technologies. *Information science reference*, New York.
6. Frisby, J. P., & Stone, J. V. (2010). *Seeing: The computational approach to biological vision*. Cambridge, MA: The MIT Press.
7. Winkels, D. G. M., Kottink, A., Temmink, R., Nijlant, J., & Buurke, J. (2013). Wii™-habilitation of upper extremity function in children with cerebral palsy. An explorative study. *Developmental Neurorehabilitation, 16*(1), 44–51.
8. Brunner, G. (2013). Researchers use Kinect to create precog robots that know when you want abeer.ExtreamTech,29May2013.http://www.extremetech.com/computing/156910-researchers-use-kinect-to-create-precog-robots-that-know-when-you-want-a-beer. Accessed 30 May 2013.
9. Bradshaw, D., & Ng, K. (2008) Tracking conductors hand movements using multiple Wiimotes. *International conference on automated solutions for cross media content and multi-channel distribution (AXMEDIS'08)*. IEEE, pp. 93–99.
10. Solis, J., & Ng, K. (Eds.). (2011). *Musical robots and interactive multimodal systems. Springer tracts in advanced robotics*, vol. 74. Heidelberg: Springer.

Chapter 9
Motion Studies: The Art and Science of Bird Flight

Fernanda D'Agostino, Harry Dawson, and Bret W. Tobalske

Abstract This chapter presents *Motion Studies*, an artwork that brought together investigations into bird flight, at the intersection of art and science. At the core of the project were *motion studies* undertaken in a flight laboratory and translated into video. *Motion Studies* used a fluid dynamics imaging system known as digital particle velocimetry to compare the nature of birds' flights in different conditions. The footage was later edited into an experimental art video that combines location footage, archival imagery and a digitally altered sound track of wild birds' calls. *Motion Studies* has been exhibited around the world as both a single-channel video and as part of a video installation. Insights gained while working on the art video have led to promising new scientific research directions for the team and to a series of related art works.

This chapter is an updated and extended version of the following paper, published here with kind permission of the Chartered Institute for IT (BCS) and of EVA London Conferences: F. D'Agostino et al. "Motion Studies: an Art and Science Collaboration." In A. Seal, J. P. Bowen, and K. Ng (eds.). EVA *London 2010 Conference Proceedings*. Electronic Workshops in Computing (eWiC), British Computer Society, 2010. http://www.bcs.org/ewic/eva2010 (accessed 26 May 2013).

F. D'Agostino (✉)
Fernanda D'Agostino Studio, 5711 SW Boundary Street, Portland, OR 97221, USA
e-mail: nandada@aol.com; www.fernandadagostino.com

H. Dawson
Dawson Media Group, USA
e-mail: harry@harrydawson.com; www.harrydawson.com

B.W. Tobalske
Division of Biological Sciences, University of Montana,
Missoula, MT 59812, USA
e-mail: bret.tobalske@mso.umt.edu

J.P. Bowen et al. (eds.), *Electronic Visualisation in Arts and Culture*,
Springer Series on Cultural Computing, DOI 10.1007/978-1-4471-5406-8_9,

Introduction

The Artists and scientists share a desire to see beneath the surface of things. Observation and experimentation are at the heart of both fields, and so artists and scientists can be natural allies. Recent developments in specialised digital imaging systems offer a new ability to reveal the processes underlying the beauty and mystery of nature. The authors, Fernanda D'Agostino, a video installation artist, and biomechanics scientist Bret Tobalske have formed an alliance together with cinematographer Harry Dawson to create work which brings new developments in our understanding of the physics of flight to a wider audience.

Motion Studies is an artwork that investigates the intersection of art and science. Ornithological motion is captured in a flight laboratory wind tunnel. The data are translated into video in the laboratory and in the artist's studio and combined with video footage of birds in flight to be displayed in a number of innovative ways (Fig. 9.1).

Motion Studies has been exhibited as a single track video of just over 12 min, and also as a video installation projected onto sculptural screens. In the installation, the footage was projected onto a series of stainless steel and hand painted Mylar "wings" suspended in the air. The wings responded to the slightest air current, creating an

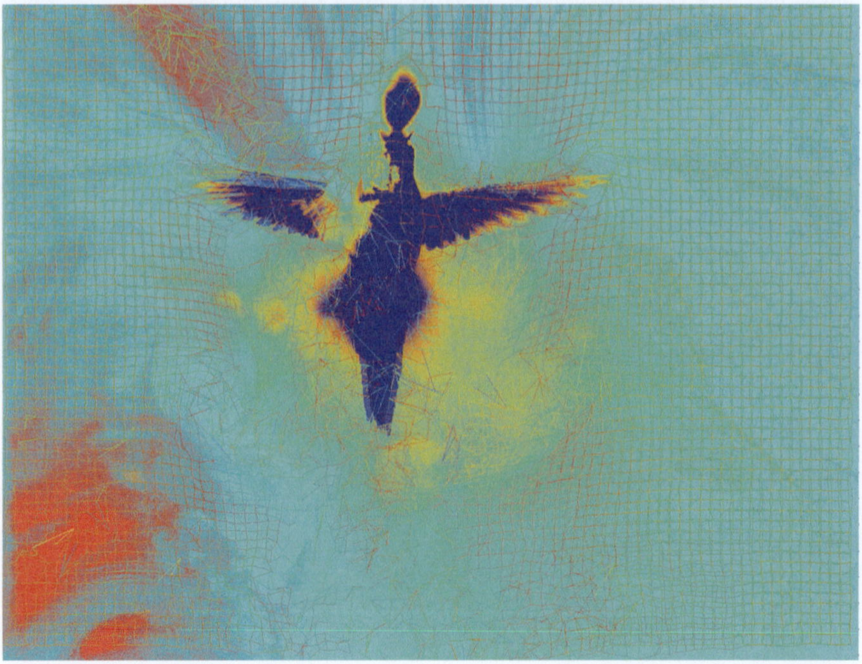

Fig. 9.1 Still from *Motion Studies*

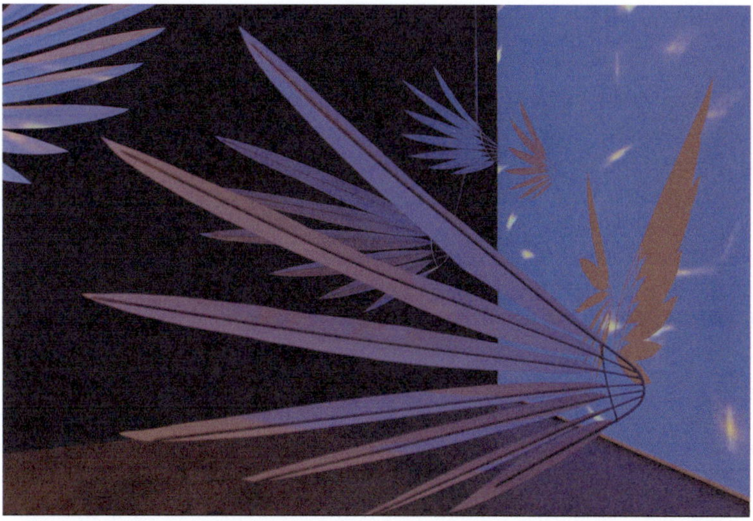

Fig. 9.2 Scale played an important role in viewers' experience of the *Motion Studies* installation [1, 2] (Courtesy of Brian Foulkes Photography)

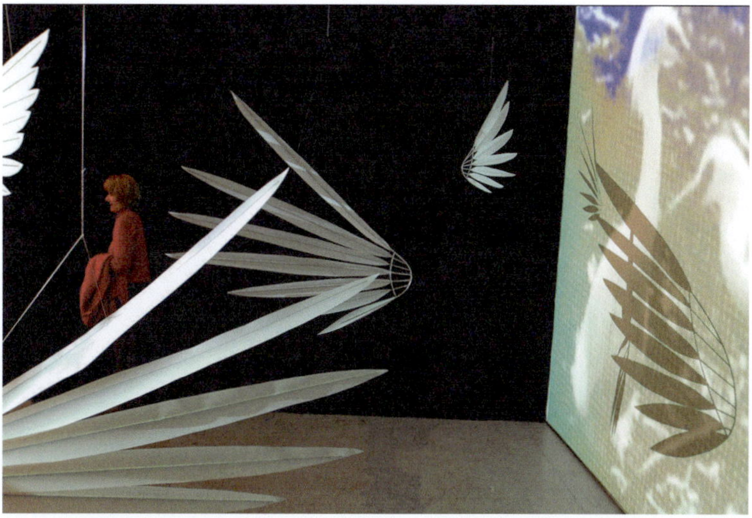

Fig. 9.3 Scale played an important role in viewers' experience of the *Motion Studies* installation [1, 2] (Courtesy of Brian Foulkes photography)

experience analogous to the wind tunnel investigations of the role of air currents in birds' flight. The video projections onto translucent surfaces created a dynamic space in which visitors could move around and through, giving them a physical feeling of being within the flock of birds (Figs. 9.2 and 9.3).

Creating the *Motion Studies* Artworks

The structure of the air currents in the wake of a bird flying in a laboratory wind tunnel is recorded and analysed using a fluid dynamics imaging system (digital particle image velocimetry). The system records the fluid motions of the air currents around the bird by tracking submicron droplets in a mist of olive oil suspended in the air. The software digitally applies colours and grids to the resulting video imaging data to visually show the flows of air generated by the bird's flight. This air movement is the result of the bird generating lift, applying energy to the air. At times this footage is like a moving abstract painting; at other times the bird's flight itself is more evident (Fig. 9.4).

The *Motion Studies* artworks combine these laboratory images with footage of bird mating dances and flights shot during the migration of cranes along the Columbia River, and of Vaux's Swifts *Chaetura vauxi*) returning to their roosts during their annual migration. This footage was shot on location from a distance with a high speed, high definition camera that renders playback in slow motion. Fuller technical details are provided in the Annexe at the end of this chapter.

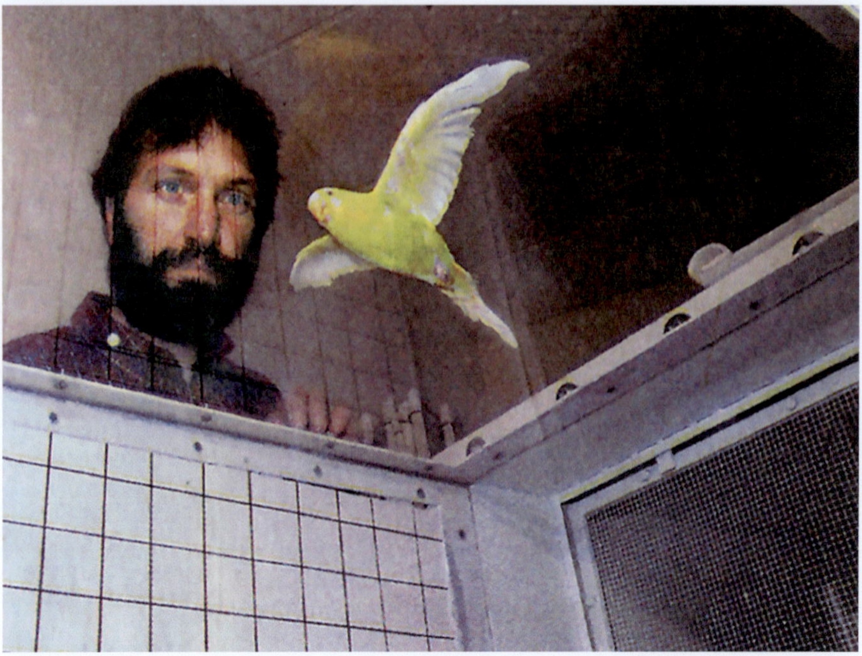

Fig. 9.4 Tobalske with one of his subjects, a budgerigar (*Melopsittacus undulatus*) flying at 10 m s^{-1} in the flight chamber of the wind tunnel [3] (Courtesy of Michael Llyod, The Oregonian)

Art and Science Collaboration

Our collaboration began in 2001, in joint work using flight video in an earlier Installation (*Theatre of Memory*). Although we come from radically different disciplines, we have in common a deep commitment to intense observation, and to using digital imaging to reveal phenomena. One facet is the wish to understand the biological mechanics of bird flight, using scientific observation, recording and analysis. A second facet is the artist's observations of birds, and their presence as a motif in her work for over 20 years, based more on intuition and a sense of wonder that their migrations, flights and rituals can be so beautiful, and yet so utterly foreign to our own experience.

When Tobalske began using digital particle velocimetry in his research, he noted the aesthetically striking layers of colour and grids that were generated to visualise previously invisible phenomena. In 2005, D'Agostino began observing experiments in the wind tunnel and learning to use the LaVision software (DaVis 7.1) that provided the digital imagery and computational analysis. An initial 5 min clip was produced using only imagery from the flight laboratory. The footage from the flight laboratory recordings was somewhat repetitious, because of the scientific requirement for repeatable results. To create a more varied piece and to suggest a sense of mystery, D'Agostino began layering archival footage of wild birds with the more controlled flights from the laboratory. Cinematographer Harry Dawson joined the team, capturing some of the migratory bird flights along the Columbia River (Fig. 9.6).

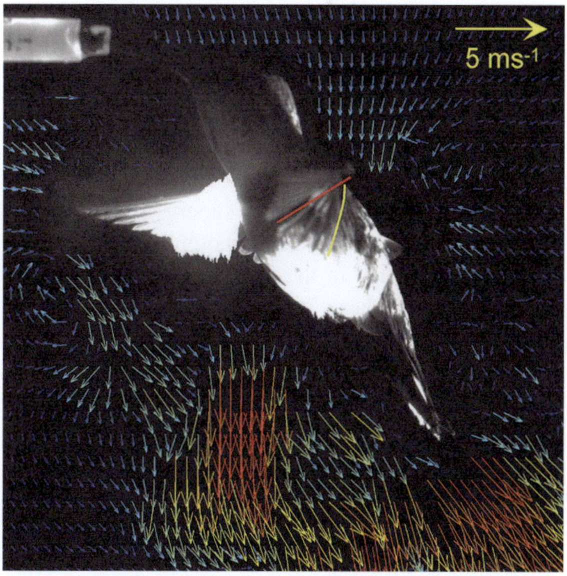

Fig. 9.5 Image of the near wake of a hovering rufous hummingbird (*Selasphorus rufus*) as it is typically seen in the scientific literature [4]. Note the application of colours and grids indicating movement and velocity (Courtesy of Dr. Bret Tobalske)

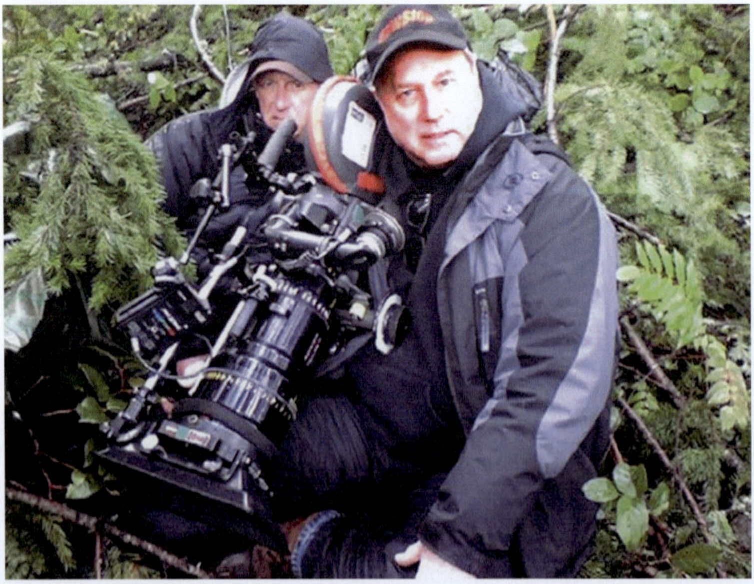

Fig. 9.6 Cinematographer Harry Dawson [5]

As a motion picture cameraman, Dawson has the knowledge, skills and photographic equipment to be able to capture movement and behaviours in wild birds that are difficult to catch with the naked eye. Shooting from a quarter mile distance, he was able to capture mating dances, flocking behaviour and individual flights of Sand Hill Cranes during their annual migration along the Columbia River (Fig. 9.6). This footage became the wild heart of the *Motion Studies* installation, providing the longest segment of the video. From this, freeze frame images of wing movement were abstracted into the stainless steel and Mylar wing/screens that animated the installation space for viewers to move through.

Each member of our team – scientist, cinematographer and artist – brings different skill sets and motivations. A synergy has emerged that has brought new developments in both art and science. Insights gleaned by the artist into the pervasive role fluid dynamics play in the organisation of the natural world have led to new artworks for public places and even to engineering innovations in the development of artist designed structures.

Fluid Dynamics and Public Art

Several large scale artworks based on fluid dynamics have been created as a result of the collaboration. *Celestial Navigations*, a permanent outdoor video installation at Seattle's SeaTac airport, has recently been installed, and includes footage from *Motion Studies* (Fig. 9.7).

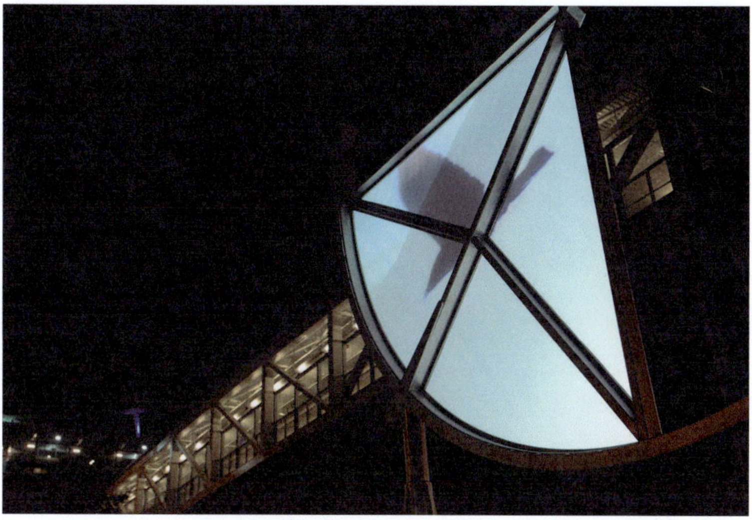

Fig. 9.7 Celestial Navigations; Seattle's SeaTac Airport Plaza [6]

The footage shown within the context of an international airport offers a peripheral awareness, at least, of the science of flight to thousands of viewers a day.

In Phoenix, Arizona, a mile-long migratory pollinator habitat *Linear Oasis* was constructed which incorporated the principals of fluid dynamics into design for an interpretive landscape. Using research on the biomechanics of hummingbird flight by Tobalske, and on the role of migratory pollinators at the Sonoran Desert Museum in Tucson, Arizona, a sceptical Park Department was persuaded to plant a mile-long pollinator habitat corridor in place of previously specified decorative plantings.

At a habitat restoration project at Smith and Bybee Lakes, in Portland Oregon, wing images from flight studies were incorporated into carved cedar *Habitat Trees* for migratory birds, and the forms of the engineered wetlands were based on the fluid dynamics of flight.

Fluid Dynamics, a wildlife viewing area on San Francisco Bay, is of particular interest. Sited on a critical node of the Pacific Migratory Bird Flyway, the entire site design is based on the principals of fluid dynamics, drawing on both the characteristic shapes of the flyway itself and on the form of the Pacific Current as it sweeps up the California Coast not far from the project site. The 26 ft long stainless steel viewing shelter takes its overall form from the Pacific Current (Figs. 9.8 and 9.9). Structural engineering for the shelter is also based on fluid dynamics and uses the characteristic currents and cross currents of fluid motion as its primary structural design principal.

Working with scientists and structural engineers, the team (Fernanda D'Agostino and Valerie Otani) was able to achieve a structural design that reflects the natural dynamic of the bay side site. The shelter contains not a single right angle. The surrounding terraced landscape, also based on fluid dynamics, was reclaimed from an urban spoil dump and has been replanted with native species used as food sources by migrating birds.

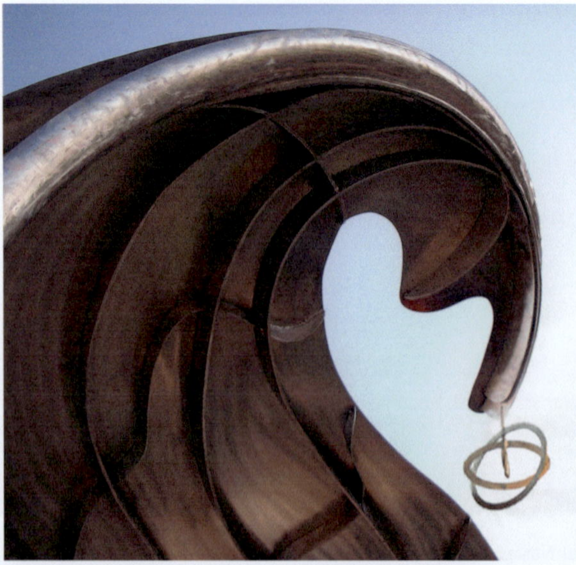

Fig. 9.8 *Fluid Dynamics* – Viewing shelter on San Francisco Bay. Both design and structural engineering are based on fluid dynamics (w Otani) [7, 8]

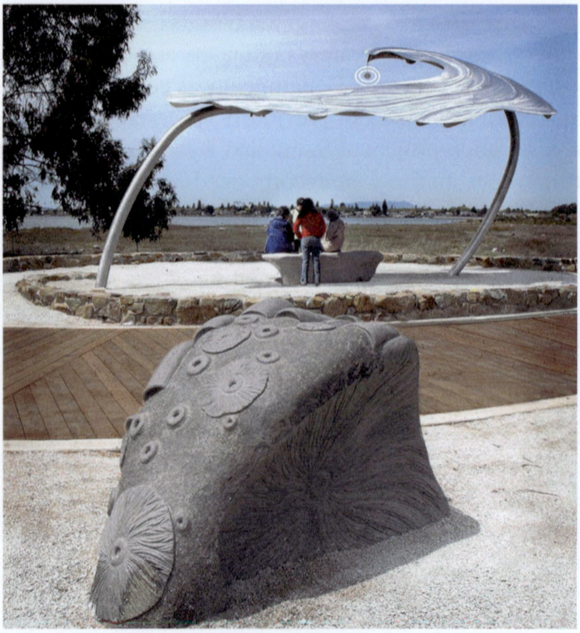

Fig. 9.9 *Fluid Dynamics* – Viewing shelter on San Francisco Bay. Both design and structural engineering are based on fluid dynamics (w Otani) [7, 8]

Next Steps: Art Processes and Practice

The LaVision software is used not only for ornithological flight studies but for the analysis of airflow and fluid dynamics in a host of other sciences, as well as many engineering fields. For example the Boeing Corporation in Seattle uses the identical software with a much larger wind tunnel to engineer its aircraft.

In the art world the software's ability to visualise the velocity and direction of motion in vivid colours, and to plot the flow of air, makes it an intriguing tool for the abstraction of any moving image, once its use is learnt. It has an infinitely expandable and variable palette, ranging from the vivid colours and grids of *Motion Studies* to effects which take on the look of charcoal drawings or monoprints. The range of subjects is planned to extend to include a contemporary dance collaboration. Like bird flight, this would also be recorded in a wind tunnel.

In another public art commission, for Portland State University, fluid dynamics theory becomes an organising metaphor for the project as a whole: it is an important factor in the meta patterns that underlie ecological processes. *Intellectual Ecosystem* (Fig. 9.10) involved working with university scientists, many of whom use scientific video imaging software. *Intellectual Ecosystem* was selected for *Americans for the Arts 2011: Public Art Network Year in Review*, for its innovative use of scientific imaging and the extensive collaboration involved in its creation.

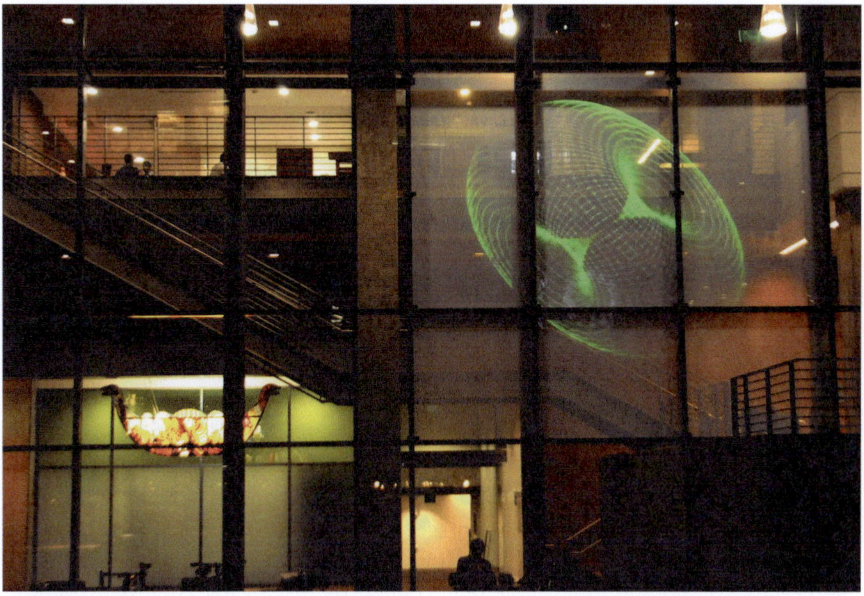

Fig. 9.10 *Intellectual Ecosystem* – Scientific video projected onto a holographic screen [9] (Courtesy of Brian Foulkes photography)

To expand the interactivity of this and other video installation projects, the integration of programming with Max MSP Jitter into a new series of art works is being investigated.

Next Steps: Scientific Research

Generally, studies of wing and body motion in birds require manual digitisation of video or film images [5, 7, 9]. This work is tedious, and it is limited in the extent to which multiple animals may be tracked simultaneously. For our next efforts, we propose to adapt the use of our digital particle image velocimetry equipment to auto-track birds as they fly in the field. We have previously successfully used this method to obtain preliminary (non-calibrated) data of swifts coming in to roost at the Portland, Oregon field site [1].

The LaVision DPIV system that we use will track any objects that may be distinguished via contrast, from sub-micron oil particles imaged using a laser in an interrogation area that is 20 × 20 cm in size [2, 4, 10, 11], to birds illuminated by sunlight within a flock in an interrogation area of 100 × 100 m [1]. To date, DPIV software has not been used to track bird velocity in the field. Our proposed research will provide several advances in our understanding of bird flight. Additionally, this research will advance the use of technology by demonstrating that software and video equipment presently used for detailed studies of particle movement in the wake of flying animals [2, 4, 8, 10] may be adapted to auto-track small animals flying together in a flock. Ultimately, the ability to auto track animals in a flock will further our understanding of the ecological and evolutionary significance of flocking behaviour [12–14].

These new possibilities for research arose from the artistic impulse to expand the range of subjects. Inevitably, there are constraints associated with working with wild animals in a laboratory. Much of the recent research on flying birds involves the use of wind tunnels in which the animal flies within a chamber through which air is drawn using a powerful fan [5, 7–9]. There may be effects of the wind tunnel upon flight performance due to the confined area in which the birds are flying, the peculiar aerodynamics due to being surrounded by walls [6], as well as the stress upon the animal due to being in a noisy environment and being surrounded by humans. Almost no studies have explored the effects of the wind tunnel upon flight performance.

The wild bird footage was shot by Dawson from a distance where the birds' behaviour was not disturbed by our presence. At 1,000 ft per second, the footage was captured with nearly as much control and precision as that from the laboratory wind tunnel. Viewing the location footage, Tobalske saw that it could be used to research the biomechanics of birds' flight in their natural habitat, something he had previously thought impossible due to the difficulty of tracking their flight in an uncontrolled situation. The flocks of Vaux's Swifts spiralling around a huge chimney/roost in Portland seemed to be moving as a vortex, obeying some of the

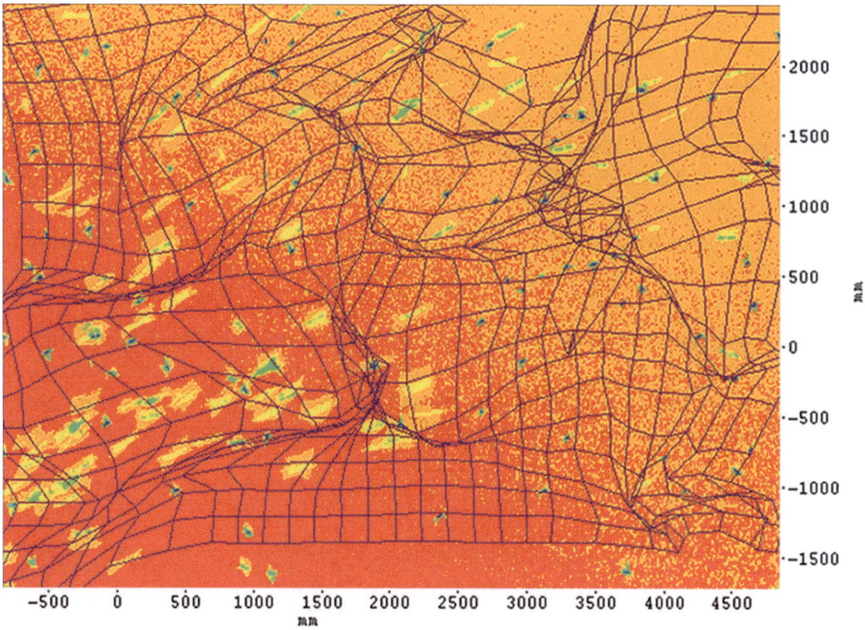

Fig. 9.11 Preliminary experiment analysing location footage to understand the physics of flocking behaviour (Courtesy of Dr. Bret Tobalske)

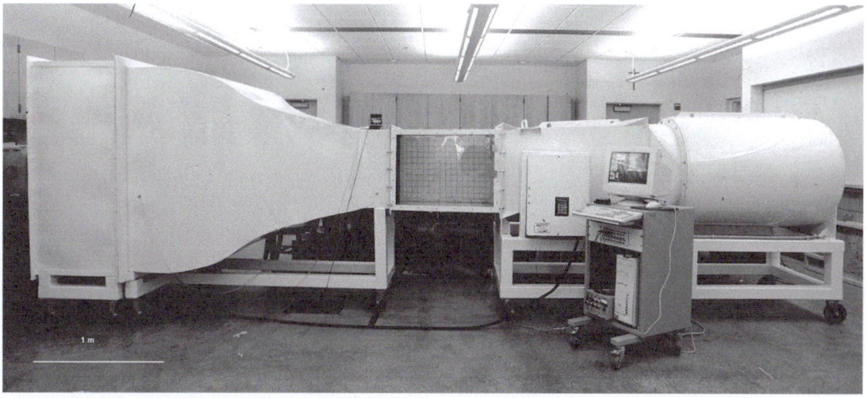

Fig. 9.12 The wind tunnel at the flight laboratory [10] (Courtesy of Dr. Bret Tobalske)

same rules of fluid dynamics that he had found to be associated with the wings of individual birds in flight. Figure 9.11 illustrates a preliminary attempt to analyse the body motion of birds engaged in flocking behaviour.

In the laboratory wind tunnel (Fig. 9.12), the bird flies through a mist of submicron-sized particles of olive oil. The LaVision software tracks individual droplets as they move through the air in response to the wind and the wing beats of the bird (see Fig. 9.5). From this tracking, the software generates moving wireframe grids. Tobalske treated the individual birds in the footage of bird flocks as particles, using the software to map the dynamics of the flock's motion around the roost. Hence, there are new research possibilities for using a large-scale fluid-motion model to study the biomechanics of bird flight in natural habitats, and the physics of flocking behaviour.

Footage shot under controlled conditions in natural settings will allow us to compare flight behaviour in the wild with data from the controlled environment of the laboratory.

In 2008 Tobalske moved to the University of Montana, Missoula. Near campus, a mixed flock of aerial insectivores including Vaux's swifts, the species we did our preliminary flocking experiment on, as well white-throated swifts (*Aeronautes saxatalis*) and a diverse array of swallows roost and forage at the top of a sheer cliff.

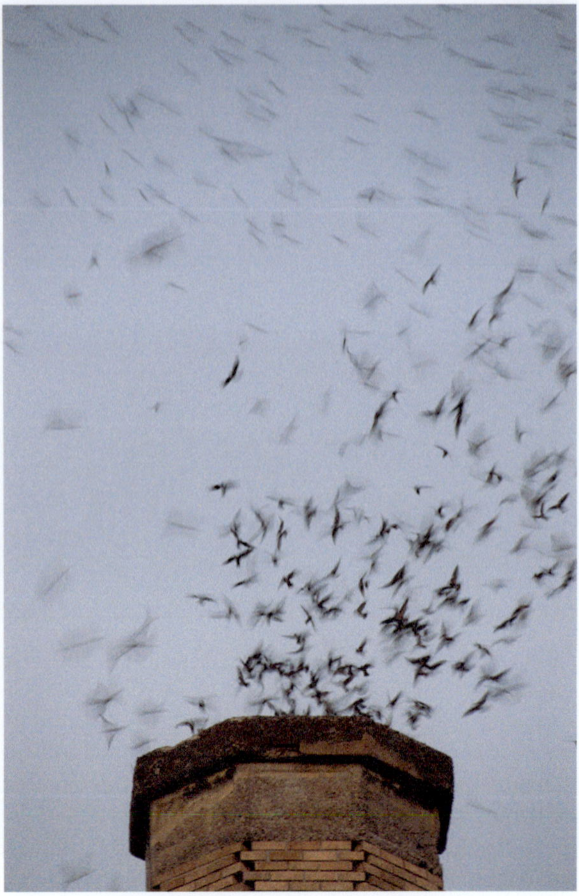

Fig. 9.13 Vaux Swifts flocking at Chapman School, Portland, Oregon, USA (Photo courtesy of Kat & Sam photography) [14]

They take advantage of upwash to dynamically soar at the cliff face. In consultation with a colleague who previously studied flight in these species [15]. It has been determined that it would be possible to lay out, using rock climbing pitons and rope, an accurate grid on the cliff face. This was the missing piece of our first flock tracking experiment. A preliminary proposal has been submitted to the National Science Foundation to begin experimenting using the DaVis system of Digital Particle Velocimetry to track flocking behaviour (Fig. 9.13).

Conclusion

At the start of the collaboration, Tobalske expressed the hope that better understanding of their flight might ultimately help preserve the habitat of the birds he studies. In a small way, the subsequent art projects in galleries and as public art have been able to further this goal, by giving viewers an experience of moving through space along pathways and through landscapes more in tune with natural principals.

Our collaborative work on the experimental video and installation *Motion Studies* speaks strongly to the fertile cross pollination that is made possible by the digital revolution. In the course of our shared work intriguing new directions for investigation opened up for both the artists and the scientists involved in the project. The ability to convey scientific insights to the general public in a compelling way is one outcome of the collaboration. New ways to see and attempt to express both the naturally invisible and the poetically ineffable are perhaps the most exciting outgrowth of our shared work. We see *Motion Studies* as a beginning. We hope to create many more works of art and science collaboration.

Technical Annexe

Flow Visualisation and Particle Image Velocimetry

The birds were flown in a variable-speed wind tunnel that features a 6:1 contraction. The birds fly within a clear working section that is 60 × 60 cm in cross section.

To visualise and measure the flow of air around a flying bird, the air is seeded with a fog of sub-micron sized particles of olive oil. Then a dual-cavity pulsed laser is used to illuminate the flow field. The oil particles reflect the 532 nm (green) laser light. These particles are nearly neutrally buoyant, so they move freely along with the air.

A computer-based system (LaVision, GmbH, DaVis 7.1 software) is used to synchronise the laser flashes with pairs of digital video images (1,376 × 1,040 pixel). The technique of synchronising is called "frame straddling" because one laser flash occurs at the end of the exposure time for the first image in a pair, and the second laser flash occurs at the start of the exposure time for the second image. The time between laser flashes varies from 200 to 400 microseconds. To calculate particle velocity, the paired images are cross-correlated. We employ an adaptive multipass with an initial interrogation area of 64×64 pixels and final area of 16×16 pixels with 50 % overlap. Vector fields are post-processed using a median filter (strong removal if difference relative to average more than 2 * r.m.s. of neighbours and iterative reinsertion if less than 3 * r.m.s. of neighbours), removal of groups with less than 5 vectors, fill of all empty spaces by interpolation, and one pass of 3×3 smoothing. The error estimated for the velocity (m s^{-1}) measurements is 5 % ± 0.5 % including contributions due to a correlation peak of 0.1 pixels, optical distortion and particle-fluid infidelity.

The first scene in the *Motion Studies* video combines scientific imagery captured and edited in the Ornithology laboratory at the Biomechanics Field Research Station. A LaVision, GmbH digital particle image velocimetry system (DaVis 7.1 software) was employed.

The archival footage of egrets in the Everglades was captured at the turn of the twentieth century. The contemporary location footage in the second half of the video was of Sandhill Crane migration shot on location at Sauvie Island Wildlife Refuge, outside Portland, Oregon, and Vaux Swift Migration in Portland, using a Panasonic HDX900 camera at 1,000 frames per second at full DVCPROHD1080. Using the Panasonic HDX900 camera, a telephoto lens and shooting from a quarter mile distance.

The location footage was formatted in Adobe After EffectsCS3 (Adobe Systems, Inc.) to match the pixel aspect ratio, aspect ratio and frame size native to the LaVision system.. The location footage was then analyzed using DaVis.

Creating the Motion Studies Artworks

When used in scientific applications, LaVision software applies colours and grids to footage of flying birds photographed in rigorously controlled conditions. This enables researchers to analyze both the bird's movement and the direction and velocity of the surrounding air. Much of the first part of *Motion Studies* employs the LaVision software system in precisely this way.

In working with the location footage, D'Agostino used the colour palettes of the LaVision software in a more intuitive, aesthetically driven way. The artist's work, however, opened up the potential new areas of scientific research described above. Finally location footage, archival footage and flight laboratory footage were all brought together in Adobe Premiere Pro CS3 (Adobe Systems, Inc.) editing software to create the 12 min 24 s long experimental art video. The LaVision DPIV system only renders 12 s segments of imagery; continuity was achieved through frame matching in both the LaVision software and in Premiere during editing and post production. A digitally altered sound track of bird calls accompanies the video and underscores the mysterious mood the artist sought to create.

Exhibition Installations

For the installation exhibition of the project, at the Elizabeth Leach Gallery in Portland in April 2008, nine wing forms based on stills from the video were fabricated using stainless steel rods and hand painted velum. The vellum acted as a dual sided projection surface and yielded a viewing angle of 180°. The wings were ceiling mounted in a room 16 ft high × 16 ft wide by 22 ft long, using monofilament and swivel mounts at each attachment point, so that each wing rotated independently with the slightest air current. The largest wing spanned 7 ft with a 4 ft depth. As viewers moved about the room the perceived architecture of the space was always in flux as the movement of the wings constantly reshaped the space. Two of the walls of the gallery were draped with light absorbing fabric while the third wall acted as another projection screen. The fourth wall was used for a complementary installation on scientific glass blowing based on the principals of fluid dynamics. As the wings moved in the air, they caught the video projections and created a mesmerising space for the viewer to enter, investing the science of flight with a sense of mystery.

Acknowledgements Our shared exhibitions, artists' talks and participation in conferences and film festivals around the world have been made possible by the National Science Foundation grant requirement to make academic work accessible to a general public. Our further research proposal was awarded a Lindbergh Foundation Honour Award in 2009. A grant from The Regional Arts and Culture Council of Portland supported both the *Motion Studies* exhibition at the Elizabeth Leach Gallery and D'Agostino's attendance at the EVA conference.

References

1. D'Agostino, F., Tobalske, B. W., & Dawson, H. (2008). *Motion studies: Elizabeth Leach Gallery*, Portland, 3–26 April 2008.
2. Henningsson, P., Spedding, G. R., & Hedenstrom, A. (2008). Vortex wake and flight kinematics of a swift in cruising flight in a wind tunnel. *The Journal of Experimental Biology, 211*, 717–730.
3. Hedrick, T. L., Tobalske, B. W., Ros, I. G., Warrick, D. R., & Biewener, A. A. (2011). Morphological and kinematic basis of the hummingbird flight stroke: Scaling of flight muscle transmission ratio. *Proceedings of the Royal Society B: Biological Sciences*. doi:10.1098/rspb.2011.2238.
4. Warrick, D. R., Tobalske, B. W., & Powers, D. P. (2005). Aerodynamics of the hovering hummingbird. *Nature, 435*, 1094–1097.
5. Park, K. J., Rosén, M., & Hedenström, A. (2001). Flight kinematics of the barn swallow *Hirundo rustica* over a wide range of speeds in a wind tunnel. *The Journal of Experimental Biology, 204*, 2741–2750.
6. Rayner, J. M. V. (1994). Aerodynamic corrections for the flight of birds and bats in wind tunnels. *Journal of Zoology, 234*, 537–563.
7. Rosén, M. W., Spedding, G. R., & Hedenström, A. (2004). The relationship between wingbeat kinematics and vortex wake of a thrush nightingale. *The Journal of Experimental Biology, 207*, 4255–4268.

8. Spedding, G. R., Rosén, M., & Hedenström, A. (2003). A family of vortex wakes generated by a thrush nightingale in free flight in a wind tunnel over its entire natural range of flight speeds. *The Journal of Experimental Biology, 206*, 2313–2344.
9. Tobalske, B. W., Olson, N. E., & Dial, K. P. (1997). Flight style of the black-billed magpie: Variation in wing kinematics, neuromuscular control, and muscle composition. *Journal of Experimental Zoology, 279*, 313–329.
10. McCullough, E. M., & Tobalske, B. W. (2013). Elaborate horns in a giant rhinoceros beetle incur negligible aerodynamic costs. *Proceedings of the Royal Society B: Biological Sciences, 280*.
11. Raffel, M., Willert, C., & Kompenhans, J. (2000). *Particle image velocimetry: A practical guide*. Berlin: Springer.
12. Caraco, T., Martindale, S., & Pulliam, H. R. (1982). Avian flocking in the presence of a predator. *Nature, 285*, 400–401.
13. Lee, S. H., Pak, H. K., & Chon, T. S. (2006). Dynamics of prey-flock escaping behavior in response to predator's attack. *Journal of Theoretic Biology, 240*, 250–259.
14. Usherwood, J. R., Stavrou, M., Lowe, J. C., Roskilly, K., & Wilson, A. M. (2001). Flying in a flock comes at a cost in pigeons. *Nature, 474*, 494–497.
15. Warrick, D. R. (1998). The turning- and linear-maneuvering performance of birds: The cost of efficiency for coursing insectivores. *Canadian Journal of Zoology, 76*, 1063–1079.
16. Warrick, D. R., Tobalske, B. W., & Powers, D. P. (2009). Lift production in the hovering hummingbird. *Proceedings of the Royal Society B: Biological Sciences, 276*, 3747–3752.

Chapter 10
Game Catcher: Visualising and Preserving Ephemeral Movement for Research and Analysis

Grethe Mitchell and Andy Clarke

Abstract This chapter discusses the design and development of the Game Catcher, a low-cost markerless motion tracking research tool and computer game, built using open source software (Processing) and hacked games hardware (Kinect and Wiimotes), that allows the recording, playback, visualisation and analysis of movement in 3D. This fully-functional proof of concept, using children's clapping games as an example, provides researchers in the Arts and Humanities with a new and innovative way of preserving, visualising, and analysing gestures and movement, and opens up possibilities for other applications in movement, music and the performing arts.

Introduction

The Game Catcher is a low-cost markerless motion tracking application for capturing, visualising and analysing movement, developed with widely available computer game hardware and open source software. It was developed as part of the "Playground Games and Songs in the Age of New Media" project [1] (funded by the UK Arts & Humanities Research Council (AHRC) as part of the Beyond Text Programme). The "Playground Games and Songs" project as a whole involved four institutions: the Universities of East London, London, and Sheffield, and the British Library.

This chapter is an updated and extended version of the following paper, published here with kind permission of the Chartered Institute for IT (BCS) and of EVA London Conferences: G. Mitchell and A. Clarke, "Capturing and visualizing playground games and performance: A Wii and Kinect based motion capture system." In S. Dunn, J. P. Bowen, and K. Ng (eds.). *EVA London 2011 Conference Proceedings*. Electronic Workshops in Computing (eWiC), British Computer Society, 2011. http://www.bcs.org/ewic/eva2011 (accessed 26 May 2013).

G. Mitchell (✉) • A. Clarke
Lincoln School of Media, University of Lincoln, Brayford Pool, Lincoln LN6 7TS, UK
e-mail: gmitchell@lincoln.ac.uk; staff.lincoln.ac.uk/gmitchell

J.P. Bowen et al. (eds.), *Electronic Visualisation in Arts and Culture*, Springer Series on Cultural Computing, DOI 10.1007/978-1-4471-5406-8_10,

The development of the Game Catcher was supervised by Grethe Mitchell (then at the University of East London, now at the University of Lincoln), and the final version of the application was developed by Andy Clarke.

Children's playground games and songs are complex activities and can therefore be difficult to study. They are ephemeral performances involving both physical gesture and speech/song as integral components, and can lack a clear beginning or end as the play can be initiated, abandoned, or shift from one activity to another without a clear signal. They may involve patterns or structure, but also allow for variation on, or improvisation around, these structures, and although some variation is conscious and deliberate, other occurs through a process of sedimentation over a longer timescale that the participants may not be aware of.

In producing the Game Catcher, we had two main aims. The first was to provide a way for the physical movements of clapping games (as a subset of playground games in general) to be recorded and analysed by researchers, thereby addressing some of the issues in the previous paragraph and providing a proof of concept for the use of movement capture technology more widely in the Arts and Humanities. The second was to "port" a real-life playground game to a computer game so as to better understand the differences between the physical game and the virtual game, as well as their points of similarity. We describe each these aims in more detail in the next section.

Although using playground games as a case study, the Game Catcher has applications (as a research and visualisation system) in a wide range of disciplines within the Arts and Humanities, not just in ones where movement or gesture is the topic of study (or closely related to it), but also potentially in areas such as performance and music where it can facilitate new forms of creativity or interpretation.

Game Catcher Aims and Context

Preservation and Analysis

There are many fields within the Arts and Humanities which involve the recording and/or analysis of movement. These include the visual arts, dance and choreography, drama and music teaching, learning and performance, childhood development and play/games, material and lived cultures, ritual, poetry literature (for a discussion of movement capture in the Arts and Humanities, see Mitchell [2].)

In some cases, the intention may be short-term analysis or immediate comparison. An example – taken from folklore studies or musicology looking at children's games and rhymes – would be where researchers wish to record a single game so that it can be analysed within a project to identify, classify and quantify individual moves used in it and to compare these to other versions of the same game or other games (see, for instance, Bishop [3] in folklore and Marsh [4] in musicology). In other cases, however, the focus may be on the long-term preservation, so that future researchers can see how a particular clapping game was played in a particular location, at a particular moment in time. This is useful when there are distinctive regional forms of games, or rhymes in transition or at risk of dying out; movement is ephemeral and, unless recorded, rarely leaves traces from which the activity can be reconstructed. Peter and Iona Opie's research across four decades of children's play in England from the 1940s to the 1980s [5–7], and the video documentary and ethnographic study from the "Playground Games" project from 2009 to 2011 [1], demonstrate the sometimes rapid changes and variations of playground games, both in terms of gesture and text.

Although video is now widely used for recording movement for both analysis and preservation because of its ease of use, convenience (both for researcher and subject), and relatively low cost, a variety of other techniques are also still practiced. These include written descriptions (whether done from life, or based on the transcription of video recordings) and formal notation systems (such as Labanotation). Photos and drawings can be used, either on their own or to supplement other techniques, such as written descriptions or sound recordings, like those made by Iona Opie in her field research [8]. In the Playground Games project, both video and note taking was used in the ethnographic study, along with the video recording for the ethnographic documentary. Children in the two participating schools also used Flip cameras to video record their games [1]. High end motion capture is possible, though has disadvantages in terms of its initial cost and the complexity of its setup and use.

Even when other techniques are used for documenting movement, video recording is often used as an intermediary step or a supplementary process. A written description will often be made from a video recording, rather than from life (particularly if a detailed description is needed, as this may require more detail than can be identified and transcribed in real-time), and even if a written description is produced at the time of the event, it may still be evaluated against a video recording to check for errors or omissions.

Nonetheless, the techniques for recording and documenting movement are patchily distributed, with bodies of knowledge siloed within certain fields and little known (or little used) outside of that particular field. For instance, formal movement notation systems such as Labanotation are used within dance, but not outside of it, even though they could have application elsewhere. Commercial motion capture systems are likewise used in the entertainment industry and in high-end medical or sports research and development, but are not generally used in the Arts and Humanities. This disciplinary isolation of techniques for recording movement was one of the subjects of discussion at the AHRC-funded 2-day symposium: The Theory, Practice and Art of Movement Capture and Preservation (IOE, London Knowledge Lab, January 2012) [2, 9].

While different areas of the Arts and Humanities may settle on a particular form of motion capture and/or analysis because it suits their tracking/analysis requirements, is appropriate for the type of movement in question, or matches other criteria (often financial or technical constraints), it is nonetheless possible to make some higher level observations.

When thinking about the design of a system for recording movement, we were guided by a number of criteria which we considered to be important. Firstly, there is the issue of ease of use – which applies to both the researcher and the subject – and in particular to researchers and participants who may be unfamiliar or uncomfortable with complex technology. For the researcher, there are issues of whether the system requires an excessive level of knowledge, training, setup or effort on their part. For the subject, there is the issue of whether the system encumbers or restricts their movements or otherwise inconveniences them (for instance, by requiring them to pause or repeat their movements while they are being recorded).

Secondly, there are issues such as accuracy (how precisely movements are recorded), fidelity (how closely the recording portrays events), resolution (the level of detail recorded) and completeness (whether significant moves are omitted). Resolution can also be split into spatial resolution (how precisely details can be observed) and temporal resolution (how frequently measurements are taken).

Although these properties are related, it is important to note that a good performance in one does not necessarily mean a likewise good performance in another. A series of still photos, for example, will have high accuracy, but a low temporal resolution and a low level of completeness (as there are gaps in time between the photos). Conversely, an animation may have high resolution and completeness (as is shows all of the movement at a high frame-rate), but low accuracy (unless it was produced by rotoscoping) as what is shown on screen may not faithfully portray what actually occurred.

The properties also are not fixed, but also depend, in part, on how the system is used. With regard to its recording of movement, a video will have a high spatial resolution if it is taken from close up (excluding extreme close-up), and a low spatial resolution if it is taken from far away (even though the accuracy and fidelity remain constant) – in other words, it is dependent on viewpoint. This resolution is not necessarily constant as the camera may, for example, move closer to the action during the course of the sequence. Similarly, a series of photographs may vary its temporal resolution if instead of taking photos at regular intervals, there are more photos taken at a time of faster or more significant movement.

Flexibility is also an issue, both with regard to the type of movement that can be recorded and to the uses to which data can be put afterwards. Confidentiality and anonymity can also be a concern, particularly when dealing with children, and even if one takes care to leave the child's face obscured, it is easy to inadvertently leave in other details which might identify the school or location.

We felt that a low-cost markerless motion tracking system could potentially have the ease of use of video whilst overcoming its shortcomings with regard to spatial resolution and flexibility. Video provides a level of spatial resolution which is chosen at the time of shooting (through the choice of viewpoint) and which cannot subsequently be changed. This viewpoint may, therefore, either be too close and leave essential details off-screen or too far away and leave them indistinct. Motion capture, on the other hand, allows the movement to be viewed from any angle or distance, not just the one that it was recorded from. By recording raw movement data in a computer-readable format, there is the potential for it to be subsequently transformed into any other notation system (e.g. Labanotation); it can also be used to generate animations which faithfully portray the subject's movements, but leave them unidentifiable. Furthermore, if the motion capture system was markerless, it would not encumber the user, nor require any lengthy setup on the part of the researcher.

The Game Catcher was therefore developed with these ideas and principles in mind and intended to act as a fully functional proof of concept of such a system. Another design principle that we had in mind was that the system should be low cost and robust, and this lead to our decision to use modified game hardware to create the Game Catcher. This is discussed in greater depth later in the chapter.

Game Prototype

The second main aim of the Game Catcher project was to "port" a real-life playground game to a computer game, since this process would force us to think more formally about what these games consist of and about the relationship between physical and virtual games (see [10, 11]).

In the case of the clapping game, this raises questions – for instance, what is its vocabulary of moves? More generally, one can think about what components can be removed, reduced, enhanced, and added, as well as whether any can be substituted or combined. In the context of the project, it was also conceived as a form of "cultural intervention" positioned to investigate the differences between physical and virtual forms of play, and to investigate the possibilities of producing a modifiable and open-ended game application.

But it was not just an intellectual exercise; we also wanted to make a game which was enjoyable, as this would generate additional synergies. We therefore felt it important to combine these two functions – game and preservation tool – in one application as this allowed us to explore these synergies and exploit them to the full. We envisioned that it would be possible to create a virtuous circle with the Game Catcher, as shown in Fig. 10.1.

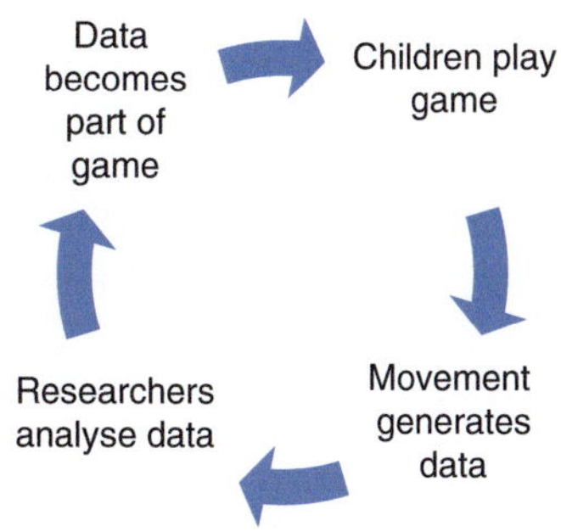

Fig. 10.1 Synergies between play and research in the Game Catcher application

As the children played the game, it would record their movements and this would form raw data which could then be analysed by the researchers. This same data would also form part of the game itself, adding to the library of clapping routines available within it. The Game Catcher was designed so that children could replay any previously recorded clapping game and see the moves of it acted out by an onscreen avatar, who they could play "with".

We envision that there would be a "snowballing" effect over time as the Game Catcher accumulated more and more recordings, and that this would in turn make the Game Catcher more appealing to children, who would then want to add their own games to it. This "snowballing" effect would be particularly strong when, over time, the Game Catcher had been taken to a greater number of locations as this would add to the quantity, depth and variety of the clapping games. Clapping games (as a genre of game) are very widespread but, as found in our project [1], individual variants of them can be geographically and temporally isolated. Pupils at one school may, for example, not be aware of a clapping game played at another school in the same city unless there is a mixing of their pupils outside of school, for example, amongst cousins. Likewise, children may not know the version of a clapping game or song played at their own school a few years previously, as the rate of evolution and mutation of clapping rhymes may be rapid.

Clapping games were chosen for the first version of the Game Catcher as they offer challenges, but also have constraints which make these challenges manageable within the timescale and budget of the research project. With regard to the challenges, clapping games feature fast and unpredictable hand movements, with a high potential for occlusion or misrecognition; they also require a tracking system which doesn't impede the player excessively. On the positive side, clapping games take place within a limited playing area, with a player standing still and just moving their hands. Clapping games also have some conventions about how the hands move, with certain hand positions, orientations and movements being common and others not used.

The Process of Adaptation

As we began the process of adapting real-life clapping games to a computer game, we began to consider the most appropriate terminology for it. One can, for example, think of it as "porting" – in the sense that a piece of software is ported from one operating system to another. This implies that having a similar appearance/behaviour is most important, even though what is happening behind the scenes may be different. "Adaptation", on the other hand, implies something different – it suggests that what is important is the sense or the feeling, rather than the look, and that some degree of flexibility allowed in order to achieve this. "Translation" tends to imply more of a literal process, while "inspired by" is at the other extreme, suggesting that there is a relatively weak connection between elements in the source material and those in the final product.

The difficulty in finding the ideal term stems in part from the fact that although these each come from different areas, they all apply, for the most part, to the process of transferring an object from one field to another, not something as ephemeral as a game. Perhaps the most appropriate concept for the process is that developed by Kress [12] (p. 47) where he describes as transduction the process whereby something which has been configured or shaped in one set of modes (in this case, playground gaming) is then reconfigured and reshaped according to the affordances of a different mode (screen-based computer gaming).

The transduction of the clapping game from playground to screen, is accompanied by a change in modes and interaction. In the playground version, the player uses both visual and tactile modes to make contact with the hands of the other player (some "eyes-closed" clapping games exist and use only touch, but they are rare), whereas in the screen version the tactile mode is omitted and the visual mode becomes more emphasised. This has implications both for the design of the interface and for the "reading" of the action or interaction. Another example is the location of the gaze of the player. In the playground version this is towards the other player, but in the screen version, the player's gaze is towards the screen and in particular directed towards the position of the hands. This brings up interesting questions about the relationship of the player to the on-screen visualisation of play/player and questions as to how one designs a user-experience that is different, but intended to be no less satisfactory, than the playground version of the game. The reconfiguring and reshaping of modes affects the experience, reading and meaning of the "transducted" text – and this also has implications for how the rules of the games are affected by the move from playground to computer screen.

We also had to think about, at a very fundamental level, what the essence of a clapping game is. In terms of hand orientations, there are five main hand orientations when the players clap, as shown in Fig. 10.2. These are:

(i) Palm down, fingers pointing at other player (clapping vertically with other player)
(ii) Palm up, fingers pointing at other player (clapping vertically with other player)
(iii) Palm facing other player, fingers up (clapping horizontally with other player)
(iv) Palm to side, thumb up, fingers pointing at other player (clapping horizontally with self)
(v) Palm to side, fingers up, thumb pointing at self (clapping horizontally with self or diagonally with other player)

The repertoire of moves used in a clapping game is, however, far higher. Firstly, these are just end positions – the orientation of the hand between claps is important as it indicates the next action. Secondly, there is non-clapping contact between players – for instance, in one of the schools studied in the project, there was what we referred to as a "three way clap" where the players place the backs of their left hands together while they perform a sequence of three claps with their right hand. Thirdly, there are gestures in clapping games which don't involve clapping, but are drawn instead from dance routines or from elaborate handshakes.

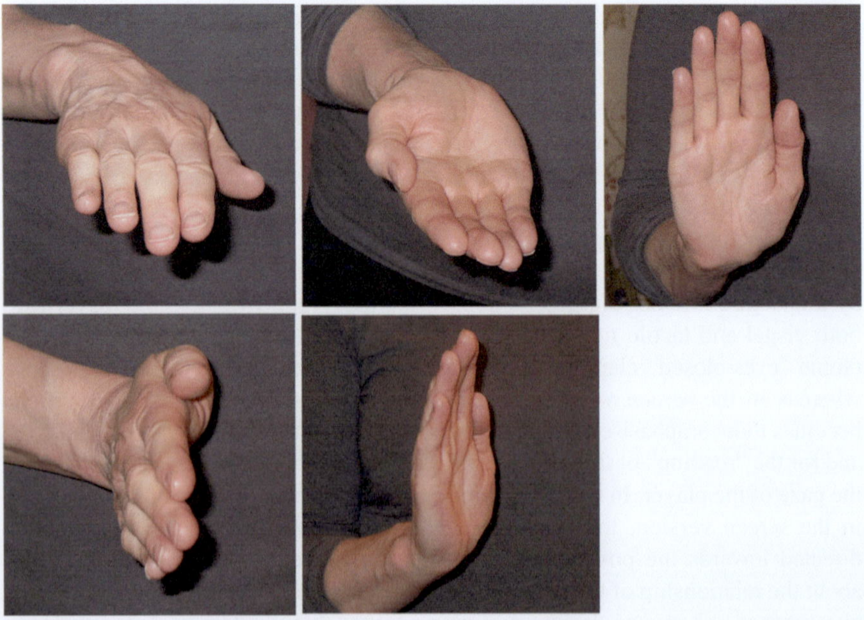

Fig. 10.2 Hand positions in clapping games

The Choice of Technology

Developing the Game Catcher involved finding both the position of the hands in 3D space and their orientation, with enough accuracy and resolution to enable them to be used to produce accurate animations (both at the time of recording and during playback) and to generate meaningful and useful data. The system had to be robust, and not susceptible to background noise which would show itself as a random "juddering" of the hands. In addition, all of this had to be done at a sufficient frame-rate – and with sufficiently low latency – to allow the application to feel responsive to the user.

Videogame hardware offers a number of benefits which were felt to be highly applicable to these aims: it is robust, widely available, and offers an extremely high price to performance ratio (low price, high performance) which can be lower than the cost of buying its individual components separately. During the course of developing the Game Catcher, we used a number of different solutions before adopting a "best of breeds" approach which used the Kinect sensor to track hand position and Wiimote controllers to track hand orientation. But even once we had settled on this combination, we still experimented with a number of different libraries and coding techniques to interface the Kinect with Processing. It is useful, therefore, to discuss briefly the strengths and weaknesses of each of these approaches for the benefit of the wider community.

The Game Catcher was intended to provide a robust motion tracking system which would work in a variety of locations, with minimal setup and calibration, and provide an adequate frame-rate on a relatively low-cost/low-spec computer (ideally, a laptop). Some tests were done with OpenCV, but this was found to be too slow on the target hardware. Simpler video tracking (tracking areas of bright light or colour) was also eliminated as it is too easily affected by outside conditions such as the brightness and colour temperature of the ambient lighting or the colour of the clothing worn by the person being tracked. Because of these issues, we rapidly adopted an approach which used infra red LEDs, rather than visible spectrum light, as this also allowed us to also exploit the strengths of the Wiimote.

The Wiimote is normally used with a sensor bar which sits just under (or just over) the television screen. This sensor bar is, in fact, not a sensor and actually contains just a set of infra red lights. The lights are used by the Wiimote, which has a relatively low resolution IR camera in its tip (128×96 pixels, interpolated within the device before analysis to give an effective $1{,}024 \times 768$ pixels) to more accurately measure the orientation of the Wiimote when it is being used to point at or select items on the screen.

We attached an infra red LED to the Wiimotes in the player's hands and used a third Wiimote as a camera pointing at the player to track the position of these LEDs (an approach similar to that used for the "Brain Baton" in Marrin [13], and by Lee [14, 15] to create an interactive whiteboard). The advantage of this approach is that it is very fast and accurate as the Wiimote has a dedicated built-in chip which is optimised to do this type of image analysis in hardware.

Being infra red, the tracking is unaffected by lighting conditions (providing it is not pointing at a bright, hot, light source), making it more reliable than tracking a visible colour. One negative aspect of this system is that because it is tracking a point source, it can't use the apparent size of an object to calculate depth (as the Sony Move controller can do), and so can only track movement in the XY plane. Researchers at the University of Cambridge [16] have, however, demonstrated that is possible to track the position of an infra red LED in 3D space using a pair of Wiimotes by triangulating its position. We were therefore confident that we could, if necessary, adopt the same approach.

In the end, the release of the Kinect – and the fact that it was hacked on its first day of release – rendered this approach unnecessary. We were therefore able to abandon this approach centred on IR LEDs and adopt a markerless system based on the Kinect (this projects a pattern of infra red dots on the subject, rather than relying on infrared lights or reflectors attached to them). The OpenKinect project's libfreenect drivers gave very high frame rates, but did not provide any built-in functions for performing the hand tracking as it only gave access to the depth map generated by the Kinect. As a result, it was initially necessary to write bespoke code which would track the hands.

A substantial amount of time was devoted to this, but the difficulty in writing routines which were sufficiently resilient to issues such as occlusion meant that we switched to OpenNI once it became possible to access it in Processing (the Java-based programming language used to develop the Game Catcher). This was achieved

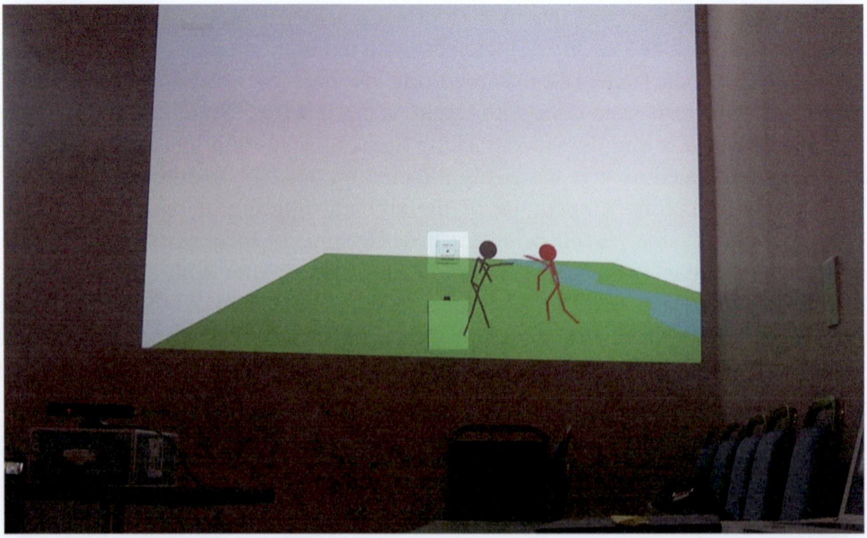

Fig. 10.3 The multi-player version of the Game Catcher in use at the Sheffield Children's Conference March 2011

first by accessing it through the OSC protocol, and then more directly using the Simple-OpenNI library.

OpenNI provided functions to track the whole body and could also track multiple users, providing a persistent ID for each. This lead us to expand our work on the Game Catcher and to develop a second version which was capable of tracking several users in a larger area and was therefore suitable for recording and preserving the movements of other playground games such as skipping, hopscotch, etc.

This multiplayer version (Fig. 10.3) was intensively user tested at the Children's Conference for the project, being used by three groups, each of 15 children, in three 45 min sessions, but following this conference, development effort shifted back to the single user version of the Game Catcher. This was because allowing the user to play against the recorded version of a clapping game presented distinct challenges that the multiplayer version could not.

The key issue here was hand orientation. Although the Kinect libraries allow us to track the skeleton, they did not give the hand orientation which was essential if we were to faithfully and accurately record clapping games. We did investigate whether one could assume the hand orientation from its direction of movement, but although this approach was initially promising, it did not seem to be reliable in every case. For instance, when the hand is moving forward (away from one's body), one can assume that it will be palm out with the fingers up, but if it is moving across the body, it could be in one of several different orientations. This meant that a hybrid technique was necessary, using the Kinect to track the body position and the Wiimotes to track the hand orientation. This proved to be an ideal solution, as it allowed the strengths of each system to be used.

Table 10.1 Theoretical performance of Game Catcher

Dimension	Performance	Notes
XY position	3 mm	Using Kinect
Z position	1 cm	Using Kinect
Z range	1.2–3.5 m	
Orientation	<1°	Using Wiimote accelerometer only (not Wii Motion Plus)

There were a few issues with the Wiimote which it is appropriate to point out from a technical point of view. Although the Wiimote can detect relative motion in all three axes, it does not, on its own, track absolute yaw position (rotation about the Y axis). It relies on accessories to do this – either the Wii Motion Plus add-on (which contains a gyroscope) or the so-called Sensor Bar (which, as already mentioned, is actually a set of LED lights, rather than a sensor, and helps the Wiimote determine its real-world orientation and positioning). Neither of these were suitable in this case. Using the Sensor Bar would have required the user to keep their hands pointing at the bar, and was therefore clearly unsuitable for a clapping game which required free movement in all axes. Using the Wiimote with the Wii Motion Plus would add additional bulk and weight which we felt was not appropriate (though we did briefly investigate whether it would be possible to use the Wii Motion Plus without the Wiimote).

A consequence of this was that we could not tell the differerence between two key hand the palm out, fingers up, position when one is clapping with the other player (position iii in Fig. 10.2), and the similar position with the palm facing sideways used when one is either clapping obliquely with the other player or clapping with oneself (position v in Fig. 10.2). In addition, the Wiimote suffers from a gimbal lock problem when pointed vertically upwards, meaning that in this position, the Z and Y rotation axes are aligned; this makes the data returned by the Wiimote erratic and meant that as the player's hand approached this position, the rotation of the on-screen hand could flip uncontrollably by 180°.

These issues were solved by paying attention both to the limits of human movement and to the conventions of the clapping game and using these to provide an additional level of interpretation. For instance, when the hands are vertical (fingers pointing up) in a clapping game, it is unlikely that the player's palms are facing their body. Likewise, when the hands are clapping obliquely with the other player (palm sideways as in position v in Fig. 10.2), they will have gone through different intermediate positions than when they are doing the normal palm out clap (position iii in Fig. 10.2). These rules are used to make the hand "snap" to certain hand orientations (though it should be noted that this only affects the on-screen display of the hand as the text file always records the raw orientation data).

The theoretical performance of the Game Catcher – based on the published performance data of the Wiimote and Kinect (and/or their components) – is shown below in Table 10.1. These figures are for the accuracy at a typical operating distance as the resolution at which movement in the Z dimension is measured varies with range, and a more detailed study of the resolution of the Kinect can be found, for example, in Mankoff [17].

The presence of unavoidable system noise in the depth map reduced these figures slightly in practice, but XYZ accuracy still remained well within acceptable levels (detecting smaller movements than might be detectable through watching the video recording of a clapping game, for example). The figure given in Table 10.1 for orientation is the raw measurement and in some hand orientations the hand will snap to 90°. As mentioned above, this orientation measurement is obtained using the built-in accelerometer, not the Wii Motion Plus accessory.

Visualisation and Analysis

As the player records a clapping game using the Game Catcher, two files are generated: a plain text file containing the movement data and an audio file containing the associated sound recording. These files are used to provide the movement and sound when the clapping game is played back. A third file can be created manually and is used, if present, to display textual information when the game is played. In the Game Catcher, this was used to show the words of the clapping song/rhyme on screen with a "bouncing ball" effect, but the same technique could be used to show annotations, cross-references, etc. synchronised with the movements on screen at that moment.

In addition to allowing the user to play any previously recorded clapping game, the Game Catcher also provides tools with which to analyse and visualise the game. These use the same movement data files as the game and therefore close the loop portrayed in Fig. 10.1. During the "Playground Games" research project, an initial form of visualisation was implemented as a proof of concept, which indicated the usefulness of the system and generated further ideas.

This initial visualisation (Fig. 10.4) shows a stick figure performing the moves of the clapping game with lines showing the path taken by the hands throughout the entire game (the right hand – and its path – are shown in red and the left hand/path in green). The display can be toggled to show the figure, the paths, or both together (the latter being the default). The movement itself can be played at normal speed, rewound, paused at will, or advanced/reversed frame by frame. In addition, the scene can be rotated in all axes and viewed from any angle while doing this.

Showing the path of the hands throughout the game provides a useful visual summary and enables the most predominant moves from it to be recognised at a glance. By comparing two images side by side, it should be possible to recognise related clapping routines with similar moves, even though they may have different clapping rhymes (or at least eliminate ones which are clearly dissimilar) and this would be a significant breakthrough. Currently, this type of comparison would involve watching two videos side by side and to be able to identify similarities, the videos would have to be shot from similar angles/distances and feature clapping

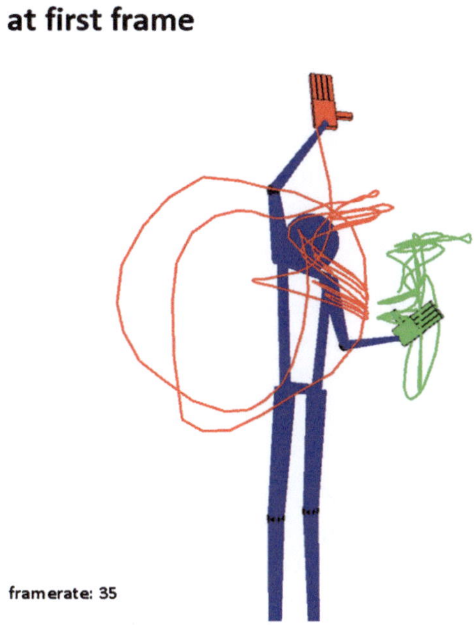

Fig. 10.4 The Game Catcher's "analysis mode" showing the paths taken by the hands

rhymes of similar length performed at a similar tempo (otherwise they would slip out of sync with one another). These difficulties explain why the tracing of variation in clapping games has tended to focus on the words with accompanying descriptions of gestures, rather than primarily on the movements (see Bishop [3]).

Another way in which these similarities could be identified would be through superimposing figures from two different recordings. We believe that this type of visualisation would be most useful in detecting subtle difference and variation, such as that which might occur in a particular clapping game in a particular location over time. Other uses would be in identifying changes in the movement of a single person over time (e.g. to study the learning or unlearning of a gesture or the adaptation of a movement over time in response to local conditions) or a pair of people (e.g. a teacher and pupil, to study the transfer and learning of skills). Further visualisations have been implemented, including one – inspired by the work of Muybridge [18] and Marey [19] – which displays a series of figures separated by a constant interval (say, one every half second).

Each of these two visualisation formats has its own strengths. The initial "trace" visualisation is most useful in situations – such as the clapping games which formed the initial inspiration for the Game Catcher – where the subject is relatively static and it is their gestures which are of most interest. The "Muybridge/Marey" type visualisation is more useful when the subject is moving through space. The distinction between these two visualisation forms is not clear-cut, however. It is, for example, still useful to provide a trace on the latter form of visualisation as it makes the order of frames in the animation clearer.

In addition to the visual analysis, other forms of analysis are also possible. As the movement has been translated into numerical data, it is feasible for it to be analysed automatically by computer using statistical/mathematical analysis or artificial intelligence (e.g. hidden Markov models) to identify similar gestures, patterns or rhythms (even if this is just to narrow down and highlight areas of potential interest, for researchers to watch and analyse manually).

Simpler forms of computer-based analysis could also, on their own, provide useful information. It would, for example, be relatively straightforward to identify clapping rhythms using simple arithmetic and trigonometry, as the claps can be detected by sudden changes in velocity and direction of movement (during the game itself they are identified by an increasing proximity of the hands as this allows us to, in effect, recognise a clap before it occurs).

Conclusions

The development of the Game Catcher prototypes (the single player and multiplayer versions) has proven that a low cost motion capture system built around videogame hardware is both (a) technically viable and (b) useful in practice as a tool for recording, preserving and analysing movement. This setup provides tracking which is sufficiently precise and robust under a variety of conditions.

A viable data format has been developed which allows players in the multiplayer version of the Game Catcher to appear and disappear (as they are picked up by the tracking, or lost as they disappear out of frame) and this data format is also suitable for the single player version. We have provided a sample of the ways in which this data can be visualised – this is useful in itself and also suggests further enhancements and alternative uses. With regard to the Game Catcher hardware, we have identified the size and shape of the Wiimote as a slight issue and are investigating ways to miniaturise this functionality. We envision that a Seeeduino Film offers the most viable solution (probably communicating with the PC via Xbee rather than Bluetooth, as is used by the Wiimote). This should provide a solution with minimal weight which will fit onto a child's hand, as well as providing a compact and robust solution which will be suitable for other uses and scenarios.

In parallel with updating the hardware of the Game Catcher, we also intend to consolidate and merge the codebases of the single player and multiplayer versions so that it is can provide a greater degree of flexibility to the researcher and allow them to change from one mode of use to another without switching applications. The aim of this process is to provide a robust, low-cost, motion capture system for the Arts and Humanities (what we have termed a "solution-in-a-suitcase") that can be easily used in the field, both indoors and outdoors, in a variety of scenarios.

References

1. Burn, A., Marsh, J., Mitchell, G., Robinson, J., Willett, R. *Children's playground games and songs in the New Media Age 2009–2011 project report*. Beyond text, UK, 2011. http://projects.beyondtext.ac.uk/playgroundgames/uploads/end_of_project_report.pdf. Accessed 17 Apr 2013.
2. Mitchell, G. (Ed.) (2014). *The theory, practice and art of movement capture and preservation* (provisional). Newcastle-upon-Tyne: Cambridge Scholars.
3. Bishop, J. C. 'Eeny Meeny Dessameeny': Continuity and change in the 'backstory' of a children's playground rhyme. In *Children's playground games and songs in the New Media Age: Interim Conference*, London Knowledge Lab, Institute of Education, London, 25 February 2010. http://projects.beyondtext.ac.uk/playgroundgames/uploads/bishop_playground_interim.pdf. Accessed 17 Apr 2013.
4. Marsh, K. (2008). *The musical playground: Global tradition and change in children's songs and games*. New York: Oxford University Press.
5. Bakanas, P., Armitage, J., Balmer, J., Halpin, P., Hudspeth, K., & Ng, K. (2012). mConduct: Gesture transmission and reconstruction for distributed performance. In P. Nesi & R. Santucci (Eds.), *International conference on information technologies for performing arts, media access and entertainment (ECLAP2012)* (pp. 107–112). Florence: Firenze University Press.
6. Anglin, G. J., Vaez, H., & Cunningham, K. L. (2004). Visual representations and learning: The role of static and animated graphics. In D. H. Jonassen (Ed.), *Handbook of research on educational communications and technology* (2nd ed., pp. 865–916). Mahwah, NJ: Lawrence Erlbaum.
7. Opie, I. (1993). *The people in the playground*. Oxford: Oxford University Press.
8. British Library (2010). Opie collection of children's games & songs. In *Oral history*, British Library, UK. http://sounds.bl.uk/Oral-history/Opie-collection-of-children-s-games-and-songs. Accessed 17 Apr 2013.
9. Mitchell, G., & Denmead, T. *MovCap: Movement capture in the arts and humanities*. http://www.movcap.org. Accessed 17 Apr 2013.
10. Mitchell, G. (2010). Porting playground games into a computer game environment: Game Catcher concepts, aims and issues. In *Children's playground games in the age of New Media Interim Conference*, London Knowledge Lab, The Institute of Education, London, UK, 25 February 2010. http://projects.beyondtext.ac.uk/playgroundgames/uploads/mitchell_playground_interim_copy.pdf. Accessed 17 Apr 2013.
11. Mitchell, G. (2013). The Game Catcher: A computer game and research tool for embodied movement. In A. Burn (Ed.), *Children's games in the New Media Age: Childlore, media and the playground*. Farnham: Ashgate Books.
12. Kress, G. (2009). *Literacy in the New Media Age*. London: Routledge.
13. Marrin, T. (1996). *Toward an understanding of musical gesture: Mapping expressive intention with the digital baton*. M.Sc. thesis, MIT Media Lab, MIT, Cambridge.
14. Lee, J. C. Johnny Chung Lee>Projects>Wii. http://johnnylee.net/projects/wii/. Accessed 17 Apr 2013.
15. Lee, J. C. (2007). Low-cost multi-touch whiteboard using the Wiimote. *YouTube*, 7 December 2007. http://www.youtube.com/watch?v=5s5EvhHy7eQ. Accessed 17 Apr 2013.
16. Hay, S., Newman, J., Harle, R. (2008). Optical tracking using commodity hardware. In *IEEE international symposium on mixed and augmented reality 2008*, Cambridge. 15–18 Sept 2008.
17. Mankoff, K. D., Russo, T. A. (2012). The Kinect: A low-cost, high-resolution, short-range 3D camera. *Earth Surface Processes and Landforms*. Wiley, 14 November 2012. doi:10.1002/esp.3332
18. Adam, H. C. (Ed.). (2010). *Eadweard Muybridge: The human and animal locomotion photographs*. London: Taschen.
19. Braun, M. (1994). *Picturing time: The work of Etienne-Jules Marey (1830–1904)*. Chicago: University of Chicago Press.

Chapter 11
mConduct: A Multi-sensor Interface for the Capture and Analysis of Conducting Gesture

Joanne Armitage and Kia Ng

Abstract The art of conducting has a long and well-established history, as both a technical and expressive art form, using physical gesture to convey musical intent and expression. Conducting relies on visual communication to direct the individual instrumentalists of an ensemble as a single, coherent unit. The aim of this project is to capture and analyse the hand gestures of conducting in order to provide real-time, interactive multimodal feedback. The system encompasses a number of application contexts including gesture visualisation for conducting analysis, pedagogy and preservation. This chapter presents the design and development of the interface involving hardware sensors and software analysis modules, and discusses the application of visualisation for conducting. Visualisation software has been designed to produce a sculpture of the conductor's gesture, to reflect the individual conductor's style and technique. The chapter concludes with latest findings, future directions and the impact the research may have outside the realm of gesture communication application.

This chapter is an updated and extended version of the following paper, published here with kind permission of the Chartered Institute for IT (BCS) and of EVA London Conferences: Armitage et al., "mConduct: A multi-sensor interface for the capture and analysis of conducting gesture." In S. Dunn, J. P. Bowen, and K. Ng (eds.). *EVA London 2012 Conference Proceedings*. Electronic Workshops in Computing (eWiC), British Computer Society, 2012. http://www.bcs.org/ewic/eva2012 (accessed 26 May 2013).

J. Armitage • K. Ng (✉)
ICSRiM – University of Leeds, School of Computing, School of Electronic and Electrical Engineering & School of Music, Leeds LS2 9JT, UK
e-mail: mconduct@icsrim.org.uk; www.icsrim.org.uk

J.P. Bowen et al. (eds.), *Electronic Visualisation in Arts and Culture*, Springer Series on Cultural Computing, DOI 10.1007/978-1-4471-5406-8_11,

Introduction

The gestural precision, practice and techniques of modern conducting style have developed over approximately 300 years [1]. Whilst conductors employ many different techniques, there is a large amount of literature that describes its basic principles, including Green [2] and Boult [3]. This literature has established a common agreement: distinct gestures have specific interpretations and meanings for the performer. These foundations provide a basis for researchers to further explore and analyse the implications of conducting gesture. Attempts to interpret and quantify conducting gesture have significance outside the art, in the understanding of gesture communication.

Conductors direct musical performances through visual gesture. While the performers look to the conductor for tempo, dynamics, and unified entrances and exits, audiences can look to the conductor for a summative representation of their auditory experience. The mConduct project is developing a real-time interactive multimedia system that captures and analyses a conductor's gesture to offer multimodal feedback including visualisation, sonification and haptics. The system is designed for several different application scenarios including distributed performance, conducting pedagogy and enhanced performance environment interactions.

This chapter provides an overview of the system design and development, with a focus on the impact of the gesture visualisation system module. Section "Background" of the chapter presents a background literature survey, including an overview of conducting history and technique, conductor tracking systems and visualisation techniques. Section "Design and Development" presents the design and development of the mConduct system. Section "Validation" discusses evaluations and validations of the system, and the final section concludes by describing the projects latest findings, contextualising application scenarios and discussing future directions.

Background

This section presents a brief historical progression of conducting practice in relation to the development of musical form in order to contextualise the system. Identifying this relationship presents methods of integrating the system into modern performance environments. After this, previous conductor tracking systems that have informed the design are discussed. The background section concludes with an overview of related visual feedback technology applications.

Conducting

Modern conducting technique has developed over the past 300 years, and a number of earlier practices have influenced the role, technique and equipment of the conductor. The conductor's gestural language has adapted to facilitate the communication of complex musical direction required for an accurate and balanced performance. A brief history of conducting is provided, followed by the evolution of the baton and a description of modern conducting technique.

History of Conducting

The role of the conductor evolved slowly through a variety of practices, influenced by political, economic and technological change [4]. The use of hand gestures to coordinate musical ensembles can be traced back to cheironomy in ancient Egypt [5]. Before melody was notated in a written score, cheironomy hand signs indicated the melodic shape of phrases. Cheironomy was widespread in the ancient world, enduring into medieval times to direct singers of Gregorian chant [6].

During the middle ages, the complexity of music increased. Cheironomy could not facilitate this development, leaving this practice redundant. The complexity of polyphonic music compelled the development of staffed musical notation [6]. In the fifteenth century, it became common practice for the role of the conductor to be focused on timekeeping.

Through the first half of the nineteenth century, there was much experimentation within conducting practice. Formerly, the orchestral leader was rotated within ensembles, as a pianoforte or violin player. By the mid nineteenth century, it became common practice to have a dedicated conductor, an individual who did not play in the ensemble. Other more technical considerations included whether beats should be silent or audible, and with what implement to conduct. Another important refinement was the position of the conductor, or leader, within increasingly large ensembles [4].

In the nineteenth century Wagner developed a theory that shaped the role of conductors today [7]. He believed that conductors should not only keep time but also impose their own interpretation of the piece. Modern conducting is built upon the techniques founded by Wagner and other early conductors. However, conducting is still an evolving art form. Not only does modern music necessitate the use of new conducting techniques, technology is opening doors for new musical forms and interpretations of conducting.

The Baton

The baton, as the conductor's technical instrument, has developed through experimentation with a number of different forms. One of the earliest reported examples of a handheld device being used for conducting is a golden staff, in 709 BC [4]. Pherekydes of Patrae, "Giver of Rhythm", gestured the staff up and down to keep an ensemble of eight hundred performers in time. However, it was in medieval choirs that role of the staff as a conductor's tool gained prominence. Staffs or sticks were used to signal beat and tempo. Longer sticks were often used, allowing the gestures greater audibility and visibility. During the seventeenth century, implementation of these tools grew in prominence, and their use spread to other ensembles. Famously,

Jean-Baptiste Lully (1632–1687), the Maitre de Musique for Louis XIV, kept time by banging a very large stick on the floor. Lully was also, unfortunately, the first to realise the disadvantage of such implements, contracting gangrene after accidentally hitting his own foot [8].

In the eighteenth century the form of the conducting device evolved from the staff to a rolled up piece of paper and then to the baton in the nineteenth century. The first usage of the baton in its current form is unclear, but accounts identify the early nineteenth century. The baton's first use has been attributed to a number of conductors including Haydn, Spohr, Mendelssohn and Spontini. It was repeatedly 'introduced' into the orchestra due to some, including Schumann, disapproving of it [4]. In present times, the use of the baton is left to the discretion of the conductor; it is generally used in instrumental conducting but absent in choral performance. Green identifies the primary advantage of the baton as being its ability to convey a concise and defined message to performers [2]. Individual conductors generally have a preference for overall shape, length and weight of the baton.

Conducting Technique

Conducting is a highly technical and expressive art form that takes years of practice and training to master. For this reason, a succinct analysis of conducting technique is presented, related to the project's requirement. The techniques defined in this section are based upon those outlined by Green [2].

In 1701 lexicographer, Thomas Janowka, described *tactus* for an ordinary measure as a right-hand movement of down, left, right and up. This pattern became standard and is the basis of modern conducting methods. The precise details of these gestures have developed, described in the aforementioned literature.

The beat is indicated through movements in the right hand. Each time signature is defined by a different pattern of movements. The arm moves through the pattern, and wrist motions allow the hand to precisely 'tap' each beat as it occurs. Beat-points are marked by a sudden change in direction or 'rebound'. The instant at which the beat occurs is the known as the '*ictus*', and the reiteration of these beat-points is the '*takt*'. A downward, vertical motion defines the first beat of a measure, and an upward motion the last. Some conductors may use both hands, with the left mirroring the right. The left hand is normally used for cueing the entrances of individual players or sections and aiding indications of dynamics, phrasing and expression.

Conductor Tracking Systems

A number of different conductor tracking systems have been developed. The design of these systems is dependent on their aim, application, and available technologies. Important design considerations include the technical requirements and method of motion capture. Most commonly, their objectives are to identify and analyse gesture for conductor training programs, or control interfaces for live electronic performance and virtual orchestras.

The first documented mechanisation of the conducting baton was during the 1830s in Brussels. The system relayed the conductor's tempo to an offstage chorus through an electromechanical device, similar to a piano key, which would turn on a light when pressed. Berlioz documented the use of this device in his essay, 'On Conducting', published in 1843.

There have been many other attempts to automate and analyse the process of conducting for conductor training programs and virtual orchestras. Bianchi and Smith first introduced the term 'virtual orchestra' into the musical lexicon in the early 1990s [9]. They developed an interactive computer music system that was used in the Kentucky Opera's 1995 production of Hansel and Gretel. This marked one of the first uses of technology by a major performing arts organisation.

Another example of an early virtual orchestra is the system created by Morita et al. [10]. Their electronic orchestra responded to a conductor's gestures. Movements were tracked through a Charge-Coupled Device (CCD) camera and sensor glove. Morita et al. categorise the tracked conducting information into two main functions:

1. Basic, that includes notes, pitch, frequency, duration.
2. Musical performance expression, such as *ritardando*, *sostenuto*, *dolce*.

The basic information is quantifiable and necessary when performing a piece. The expressive information is subjective and creates the artistic essence of the performance. Ascertaining beat points to indicate tempo is a minimum requirement for this system. Expanding upon this to measure gestural expression is fundamental in creating an authentic reconstruction.

In 1996, the 'Digital Baton' [7] was designed as a multipurpose device to control electronic music using traditional conducting parameters. Gestures are tracked using accelerometers, infrared LED and piezo-resistive strips. A similar array of sensors has been used in this project. However, due to advancements in technology, the dimensions and weight of the device will be significantly reduced, allowing the conductor more traditional movement.

Other systems have focussed on conductor analysis; in 1998, Nakra designed the 'Conductor's Jacket', a physiological monitoring system built into clothing. It was designed to study the conductors' technique in their working environment, mapping the conductor's expressive features to a musical score [11].

Other systems aim at conducting pedagogy. Examples include Peng and Gerhard [12] and Bradshaw and Ng's [13] conducting analysis systems. These two projects used a Wii-based tracking system to capture the conducting gesture.

Mapping and Visualisations

In this system, mapping is implemented to translate gestural conducting data using several feedback technologies including visualisation. Through effective mappings, visualisation can enhance aspects of the data that are not apparent in its raw form. The techniques have been applied in a wide range of application contexts including multimedia performance and technology-enhanced learning.

In technology-enhanced learning, both Oliver and Aczel [14] and Ng [15] reported accelerated learning using visualisation. Ng [15] discusses the i-Maestro 3D Augmented Mirror system, which increases awareness of bowing gesture and body posture using real-time visualisation and sonification. MacRitchie et al. [16] visualise musical structure through motion capture of a pianist's performance gestures. This visualisation confirmed a relationship between upper body movements of a pianist and compositional structure.

Gestural controls are commonly integrated into mobile devices; this has influenced much research into the visual implications of gesture. Witt et al. [17] suggested that user satisfaction could be increased by heightening awareness of movements in space. Several previous projects have specifically focussed on conductor gesture visualisation research, notably, Bradshaw [13] and Garnett et al. [18]. Both projects focus on conducting pedagogically. As well as graphing the trajectory of the conducting motion, they designed multiple representations of a single aspect of the gesture. This allows the user to focus on a specific part of their gesture when practicing. Conducting gesture is an effective way of deriving visualisations that relate to sound due to it encompassing all aspects relating to the performance.

Design and Development

This section outlines the design and development of the mConduct baton with a particular focus on its implementation in the visualisation of conducting gesture. Requirements of the system are discussed, alongside hardware and software development and integration with the visualisation module.

Requirement

The design of the system can be divided into four distinct modules:

- Input module – first captures data from the conductor, including intricate data such as movement and acceleration
- Data analysis module – analyses this data to detect features such as beat points, before the –
- Mapping module – maps the analysed data for reconstruction in accordance to the selected mapping strategy
- Feedback module – reconstructs data appropriately for the chosen application.

To realise the aim of the project, the system needed to capture the delicate motions of the conductor with sufficient accuracy and precision required for the visualisation analysis. The sensors measuring the conductor's motion must be sensitive enough to capture sufficient detail in the gesture. It is equally important that the

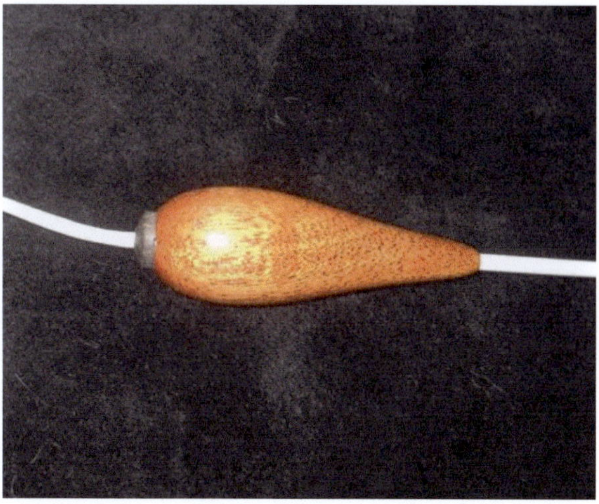

Fig. 11.1 mConduct baton containing IMU sensor

device is non-intrusive and lightweight so the data collected is not compromised by the conductor adjusting their technique to compensate for the hardware.

Once the data has been captured, the system requires algorithms that are capable of analysing the identifying features of conducting movements, particularly at the turning point of the gesture where a beat is indicated. A method of communication is required between the different modules, allowing the integration of hardware and software components.

For the final feedback modules, a variety of software packages are required that are suited for each application. The system requires a set of different mapping strategies in order to translate the detected gesture features to suitable feedback control parameters. Specifically, visual mapping strategies are required in order to translate the gestural data into visual parameters. This project is particularly interested in visualisation strategies that emphasise and highlight differences in conducting gesture. Allowing the system to reflect different expressive and interpretative features of an individual's conducting style.

Baton Development

The characteristics of the conductor's gesture are determined using multi-sensor data fusion. An inertial measurement unit (IMU), consisting of an integrated accelerometer, gyroscope, and magnetometer, is implemented to capture the conductor's gesture in real-time. The IMU is enclosed within the base of a conductor's baton (see Fig. 11.1); a separate design has been implemented for users who conduct without a baton. The device was designed to be as lightweight and nonintrusive as possible, allowing the conductor greater freedom of, and more traditional, movement.

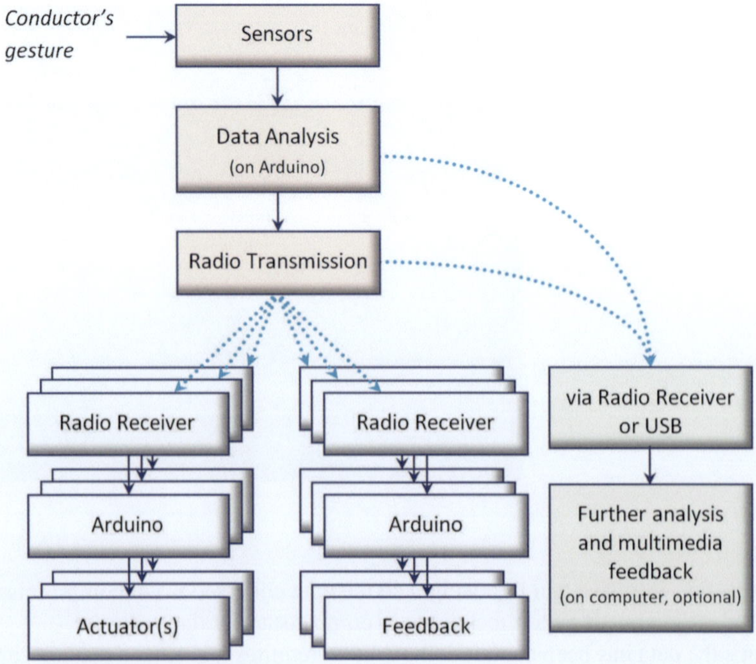

Fig. 11.2 Overall system architecture

Previous projects at ICSRiM have used Vicon motion capture systems, Wiimotes and Kinects; however, the IMU implementation allows greater portability [13, 15, 19].

The Arduino reads the accelerometer and gyroscope values from the IMU and processes them before they are sent to the various applications. Real world accelerometer coordinates are also calculated on the Arduino microcontroller (http://www.arduino.cc/). The IMU unit measures 3D vectors depending on its orientation. In order to find the global movement, quaternions [20, 21] are calculated using the accelerometer and gyroscope data. The effect of gravity on the accelerometer is calculated using the quaternions. This is performed on board the Arduino microcontroller. The accelerometer data is then used to determine the strength and intensity of a conductor's gestures, whilst gyroscope data is used to determine the directionality of these motions. These two data streams together provide a sufficient representation to analyse and understand the baton movement.

After the sensor data has been processed and analysed, the information is broadcast wirelessly, using the ZigBee wireless protocol. The system adopts the 'Music via Motion' (MvM) framework design that facilitates the trans-domain mapping of movement to other multimedia domains [22]. The modular architecture of the systems using MvM has influenced the design of this system, particularly in respect of its potential for multiple applications and multimodal reconstructions. The data that is received by the computer is then utilised in the visualisation and sonification software. Simultaneously, an actuator unit physically translates the data into haptic feedback. The overall system architecture is shown in Fig. 11.2.

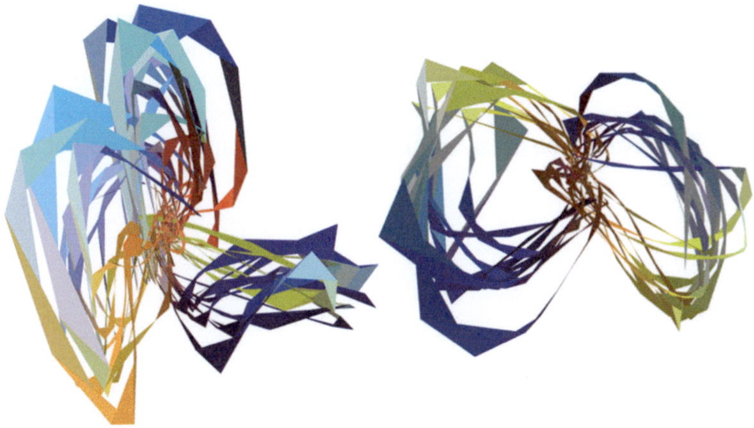

Fig. 11.3 *Left* shows example visualisations for a sequence of gesture in 3/4 time and *right* in 2/4 time

Visualisation Module

Conducting gesture is an effective way of deriving visualisations that relate to a performance as a whole. The overall representation of the gesture in 3D space is influenced by previous projects such as Bradshaw [13] and Garnett et al. [18]. These projects are more pedagogically focussed, including visual representations of single aspects of a gesture. However, this project is particularly interested in visualisation strategies that reflect the expressivity and interpretations of individual conductors. For this reason, a mapping strategy has been developed to form a 3D sculpture that represents the overall shape and structure of a piece.

The system design enables the stream of gestural information to be broadcast and received by multiple actuator units and computers in order to provide distributed processing and multimodal feedback. The visualisation software receives a real-time data stream through the serial port. A minimum baud rate of 57,600 bps is required to allow a reliable connection up to 104 frames per second (fps) for the visualisations, assuming each frame includes up to nine 32-bit floating-point values (3D accelerometer data etc.).

Data is then analysed and mapped to visual parameters including three-dimensional shape, size and colour. The gyroscope data informs shape boundaries and size. 3D acceleration data is mapped to red, green and blue pixel intensity values. This mapping strategy visualises repetition patterns of the acceleration in the gesture through clusters of colour. The overall intention of the visualisation is to create a three-dimensional sculpture of the user's overall gesture. This encompasses musical parameters such as structure, expression, tempo and time signature.

The visualisation software contains user-definable controls that allow fine-tuning and custom display modes for greater freedom in performance. Camera view settings in software allow the user adjustable zoom and other 3D controls. Snapshots of the shape can be taken throughout the performance for comparative analysis of specific sections of a performance, see Fig. 11.3 for an example output.

The shape of the 3D graphical sculpture creates a clear visual distinction between the different time signatures. The number of distinct 'loops' visualised is congruent with the number of beats per measure. The colour mapping strategy of the acceleration data identifies clusters of colour at the same position on different measures. The distribution of colour intensity suggests the user's gestural accuracy and consistency.

Validation

To ascertain the system's performance and establish its capabilities, tests and validation procedures were applied. Trial runs of evaluations were performed and refined for a user group to ensure they were accurate and meaningful. The subjects were given a questionnaire, which outlined questions relating to system's functionality and user experience. Initial evaluations have verified the system as sufficient for the purposes specified above.

An evaluation was designed to assess whether musical features could be identified from a visualisation. A random selection of ten students with musical backgrounds varying from 'expert' to 'proficient' participated in the experiment. The subject was asked to identify a visualisation created from a gesture. The subject was presented with an audio recording and score of a piece of music, and asked to identify the corresponding visualisation. Mapping strategies were explained to the subject, and they were asked to identify the reasoning behind their selection.

Analysis of the results identified that 62.5 % of visualisations were assigned to the correct piece of music. Kallio et al. [23] suggest that people perceive a 3D gesture with greater accuracy when it is translated into 2D space, which could explain misinterpretation in some of the gestures. Overall, subjects were able to identify tempo (83 %) with a greater degree of accuracy than time signature (75 %). The subjects perceived a clear correlation between colour intensity and tempo; 92 % of answers correctly identified the pieces' tempos in the visualisations as 'fast' and 75 % 'slow'. The time signature '4/4' was identified with the least degree of accuracy (67 %). This is most likely caused by the reduced definition in the loops of this time signature. A number of subjects identified that a real-time video rendering would improve their understanding; this would be the case in live performance.

Preliminary tests have found that the visualisation can provide insightful understanding of the gesture by comparing the sculpture-like graphical output. It is a timeless representation of time-based musical performance that is able to communicate certain aspects of the gesture style, consistencies and patterns depending on the mapping strategy applied. This is currently being trial as an aid within a technology-enhanced learning system in Leeds. We are also working with a composer who is writing a piece that combines the visualisation element of the system into a performance.

Conclusion

This chapter proposed the mConduct system to capture and analyse the hand gestures of conducting in order to provide real-time, interactive multimodal feedback with particular focus on visualisation.

The chapter reviewed the evolution of conducting and the baton; discussed the design and development of the tool involving multiple hardware sensors and software analysis modules; examined the parameters for the visualisation software; and discussed evaluations and validations and next steps in the development.

With initial evaluations, we believe the mConduct system can increase conductor communication, aid pedagogical purposes and provide a means for gesture comparative analysis.

It has been proposed that people remember information when it is represented and learnt both visually and audibly [24, 25]. The use of visuals helps build mental models by directing attention to important information and organising data in a meaningful way. Visuals and corresponding auditory information are integrated into one comprehensive mental model. The mental model can be a powerful tool in pedagogical context for the interpretation and understanding of a performance. Conducting gesture visualisations were found to have a similar impact when combined with live audio. Together they provide an enhanced mental model of the performance elements including expression, tempo, time signature and mood. Visualisation of conducting gesture expands live performance by engaging the audience in an additional sensory domain.

The visuals created by mConduct can be used to summarise a conductor's performance. Both conducting patterns and deviations from the normal conducting movements are represented. Students can use the mConduct system to visualise their own conducting patterns and evaluate their consistency and variation of gesture as well as compare their motions to others.

The visualisation of gestures can also be used for comparative analysis. The images formed from the visualisation can be stored and then compared. This can be used for technology-enhanced learning: First, a user can evaluate their consistency by comparing visuals from a series of performances of the same piece. Secondly, a user can track their development by looking at visuals of their conducting over time. Third, users can compare the visual of their performance to others' in order to study differences in techniques and interpretations.

The value of mConduct goes beyond gesture communication applications. The system will benefit cultural heritage through performance preservation. The collected data, analysis and visualisations can be stored for future generations. Future musicians can retrieve the visualisation data and discover how previous conductors shaped a piece.

References

1. Nakara, T. M. (2000). *Inside the conductor's jacket: Analysis, interpretation and musical synthesis of expressive gesture*. Ph.D. thesis. Department of Media Arts and Sciences, MIT, Cambridge.
2. Green, E. (1981). *The modern conductor*. Englewood Cliffs: Prentice Hall.

3. Boult, A. C. (1976). *A handbook on the technique of conducting*. Lakeland: Patterson.
4. Bowen, J. A. (2003). The rise of conducting. In *The Cambridge Companion to Conducting*. Cambridge: Cambridge University Press.
5. Randhofer, R. (2004). By the rivers of Babylon: Echoes of the Babylonian past in the musical heritage of the Iraqi Jewish diaspora. *Ethnomusicology Forum, 13*, 21–45.
6. Haïk-Vantoura, S. *Chironomy in the ancient world*, 17 December 2012. http://www.rakkav.com/biblemusic/pages/chironomy.htm. Accessed 22 Mar 2013.
7. Marrin, T. (1996). *Toward an understanding of musical gesture: Mapping expressive intention with the digital baton*. M.Sc. thesis, MIT Media Lab, MIT, Cambridge.
8. Jacobson, B. (1979). *Conductors on conducting*. Frenchtown: Columbia Publishing.
9. Bianchi, F., & Smith, D. B. *Virtual orchestra*. http://www.virtualorchestra.com. Accessed 22 Mar 2013.
10. Morita, H., Hashimoto, S., & Ohteru, S. (1991). A computer music system that follows a human conductor. *Computer, 24*(7), 44–53.
11. Nakra, T. M. (2000). *Inside the conductor's jacket: Analysis, interpretation and musical synthesis of expressive gesture*. Doctor of Philosophy, Massachusetts Institute of Technology, Boston.
12. Peng, L., & Gerhard, D. A wii-based gestural interface for computer-based conducting systems. In *Proceedings of the 9th international conference on new interfaces for musical expression (NIME)*, Pittsburg, 4–6 June 2009.
13. Bradshaw, D., & Ng, K. (2008). Analyzing a conductors gestures with the Wiimote. In S. Dunn, S. Keene, G. Mallen, & J. P. Bowen (Eds.), *Proceedings of electronic visualisation and the arts (EVA London),* BCS, Electronic Workshops in Computing (eWiC).
14. Oliver, M., & Aczel, J. (2002). Theoretical models of the role of visualisation in learning in formal reasoning. *Journal of Interactive Media in Education (JIME),* 2. The Open University, UK.
15. Ng, K. (2011). Interactive multimedia for technology-enhanced learning with multimodal feedback. In J. Solis & K. Ng (Eds.), *Musical robots and interactive multimodal systems (STAR 74)* (Springer tracts in advanced robotics, Vol. 74, pp. 105–126). Berlin: Springer. Chapter 7.
16. MacRitchie, J., Buck, B., & Bailey, N. J. Visualising musical structure through performance gesture. In *Proceedings of the 10th international society for music information retrieval conference (ISMIR),* Kobe, 26–30 October 2009.
17. Witt, H., Lawo, M., & Drugge, M. (2008). Visual feedback and different frames of reference: The impact of gesture interaction techniques for wearable computing. In G. H. ter Hofte, I. Mulder, & B. E. R. de Ruyter (Eds.), *Proceedings of the 10th conference on human-computer interaction with mobile devices and services (Mobile HCI)*, Amsterdam, 2–5 September 2008, pp. 293–300, ACM International Conference Proceeding Series, ACM.
18. Garnett, G. E., Malvar-Ruiz, F., & Stoltzfus, F. (1999). Virtual conducting practice environment. In *Proceedings of the international computer music conference (ICMC)*, (pp. 371–374).
19. Bakanas, P., Armitage, J., Balmer, J., Halpin, P., Hudspeth, K., & Ng, K. (2012). mConduct: Gesture transmission and reconstruction for distributed performance. In P. Nesi & R. Santucci (Eds.), *International conference on information technologies for performing arts, media access and entertainment (ECLAP2012)* (pp. 107–112). Florence: Firenze University Press.
20. Diebel, J. (2006). *Representing attitude: Euler angles, unit quaternions, and rotation vectors*. Technical Report, Stanford University, USA.
21. Madgwick, S. (2010). *An efficient orientation filter for inertial and inertial/magnetic sensor arrays*. Technical Report, Department of Mechanical Engineering, University of Bristol, UK.
22. Ng, K. (2004). Music via motion: Transdomain mapping of motion and sound for interactive performances. *Proceedings of the IEEE, 92*(4), 645–655.

23. Kallio, S., Kela, J., Mäntyjärvi, J., & Plomp, J. (2006). Visualization of hand gestures for pervasive computing environments. In *Proceedings of ACM working conference on advanced visual interfaces (AVI)*, (pp. 480–483). ACM.
24. Anglin, G. J., Vaez, H., & Cunningham, K. L. (2004). Visual representations and learning: The role of static and animated graphics. In D. H. Jonassen, (Ed.), *Handbook of research on educational communications and technology* (2nd ed., pp. 865–916). Mahwah, NJ: Lawrence Erlbaum.
25. Arcavi, A. (2003). The role of visual representations in the learning of mathematics. *Educational Studies in Mathematics, 52*(3), 215–241.

Chapter 12
Photocaligraphy: Writing Sign Language

Roman Miletitch, Claire Danet, Morgane Rébulard, Raphël de Courville, Patrick Doan, and Dominique Boutet

Abstract The *de facto* language of deaf people is sign language, a gesture based communication process. Being quite different from oral languages (grammar, modality, syntax), it needs a writing system of its own. Despite a few attempts, no clear writing system for sign language has emerged. The work we present in this chapter constitutes a contribution to its formation through a graphic design approach. Our hypothesis is as follows: in its execution, the gestural signs contain readable graphic traces. In order to visualise them, we use a photographic system based on long exposure, creating graphic objects we name photocalligraphies. We experimented with deaf people and created two corpora made up of isolated signs. With the first one we study the legibility of such a representation of a sign: how well it is recognised, how well its meaning is conveyed. With the second we deepen the study of something we observed during the realisation of the first corpus: during the photographic capture of the signs, the sign language speaker makes alterations to the prototypic sign, signing it differently in order to make its graphic rendering more readable. We then discuss potential structures for those alterations that we call graphic inscribing strategies.

This chapter is an updated and extended version of the following paper, published here with kind permission of the Chartered Institute for IT (BCS) and of EVA London Conferences: R. Miletitch et al., "Eliciting writing-like behaviour in sign language through photographic representation of movement." In S. Dunn, J. P. Bowen, and K. Ng (eds.). *EVA London 2012 Conference Proceedings*. Electronic Workshops in Computing (eWiC), British Computer Society, 2012. http://www.bcs.org/ewic/eva2012 (accessed 26 May 2013).

R. Miletitch (✉) • C. Danet • M. Rébulard • R. de Courville • P. Doan
GestuelScript, ESAD Amiens, Amiens, France
e-mail: roman.miletitch@gmail.com

D. Boutet
UMR 7023 SFL, CNRS, Université Paris 8, France

Introduction

French sign language is the first means of communication of the French deaf community, representing around 120,000 people in France. A law passed in 2005 recognised it as a full language [1], which was the starting point for broader recognition from the public and its use in the public school system and in administration. Signed languages are analog, visual-gestural and multilinear (meaning that they allow the simultaneous transmission of several pieces of information) languages. Thus, they are distinct from vocal languages which are arbitrary, acoustic-vocal and monolinear. Up to now, due to this complexity, no satisfactory writing system has been created for sign language, and yet written sign language would offer deaf people the conditions for an unprecedented cultural enrichment.

Signed languages cannot be written with existing writing symbols, as they do not have the same roots and modality as their vocal counterparts. Studies have shown how a harmonious development of conceptualisation relies on a sign language-based education [2]. A writing system needs to be engineered to fit specific characteristics, including grammar, vocabulary and multilinearity among others. However, most endeavors in this direction have resulted in graphic codes for linguists [3, 4] rather than a practical writing system that could be used every day by the deaf community.

We aim at contributing to the creation of a handwriting system for sign language through a graphic approach. We base our work on a visualisation of movements through extensive techniques of investigation and experimentation. Our working hypothesis is that gestural signs produce readable graphic structures comparable to the characters used in writing [5]. We believe that in this particular case, the language and its writing could have much more in common than do vocal languages and their scripts. We have chosen to focus on gesture as a whole and not on one of the various parameters of sign language, so that our study departs from the traditional dissection of sign language [6, 7].

In this chapter we present photocalligraphy, a method aimed at exploring the graphic structures of movement in sign language, which relies on photography using long exposure times. Through the creation of the two corpora and their evaluation by the deaf community we noted that the sign language speakers modified their gestures to make their photographic representation clearer, thus adopting a writing-like behavior. After studying those modifications, their repetitions and patterns, we structured the consistent ones that we call graphic inscribing strategies.

We will begin by clarifying the context of our research: sign language and its current representation and capture, and then writing and movement visualisation. In the second section we will present our main contribution: our photocalligraphic tool and the resulting representations of sign language. We will then present both our corpora, the first one representing legibility (as defined in [8]) while the second deals with the sign modifications made by the speaker in order to increase this legibility. Before concluding we will focus on a particular concept that emerged through both corpora: graphic inscribing strategies.

Contextualisation and State of the Art

Sign language. It is important to keep in mind two major factors before investigating a writing system for French sign language. One is the means of communication. The visuo-gestural mode used in sign language differs from the voco-acoustic one in spoken language. Sign language uses gestures to produce signs, and vision to perceive them. The entire upper body acts as a medium. Taking only manual gestures, we have hand shapes, movements, orientation (of the palm) and location. The capacity to use several parts of the hand at the same time brings us to the second factor: multi-linearity. Sign languages can express a lot of information simultaneously, as opposed to spoken languages which are monolinear, making visualisation of sign language a challenge. Up until now none of the existing transcription systems has the qualities necessary to translate efficiently into written sign language.

Representing Sign Language. In order to keep a written record of French sign language, annotation systems such as HamNoSys [3] or SignWriting [4] have been created, the latter more visual than the first. Neither of these highly schematic systems can properly represent the richness of sign languages. They use more or less arbitrary representations to depict the sign, with a strong tendency towards geometrisation, making them closer to a notation than to a writing system. Most of the existing graphic transcription systems have been devised as scientific tools. The purpose is often to serve as an annotation system [9]. Those systems are successful mostly when used in a narrow, specialised context, and confirm the view that traditional linear writing is not suited for sign language [10].

For that reason, we needed to research a transcription system able to cover various levels of complexity that are communicated simultaneously. We focused on a graphic approach (as opposed to verbal description and subdivision) that takes into account multi-linear communication. By claiming that french sign language, in its gestural dimension, represents graphic structures comparable to writing, our research attempts to go beyond the traditional parametric organisation of sign language described by Stokoe [7, 11] and in France with Cuxac [12].

Captation and corpora. The existing corpora mostly rely on video recording of sign language and on motion capture. Their focus on sign language ranges from its vocabulary or its emergence (Creagest Project: [13]) to its grammatical structure [14], or even a comparison between signs or structures from different countries [15] (MARQSPAT Project [16]). The specific form of the corpus determines the corpus itself and the type of analysis it will allow [17].

Our method of capture differs from those used in existing corpora [13, 18] by moving away from annotating purpose to concentrate on the visualisation of movements. Inspired by cognitive science's enaction paradigm [19], we also wonder about the feedback such a representation can make to the user. We focus especially on the trace the hands leave, and draw an analogy with the stroke of a pen which is regarded as the foundation for formalised writing according to G. Noordzij [20].

Writing. Latin languages are broken into phonemes and their writing systems are separated into small discrete sets of glyphs, like atoms, evolving from the pictograms of proto-sinaitic writing to more complex shapes [21] and to eventually represent sounds or, as we might say, shapes of sounds, pure conventional forms. Unfortunately, such simplicity and economy cannot apply to sign language, as sign language is closer to a continuous mode of communication, defined by its four manual parameters.

The Chinese writing system, on the other hand, appears to be closer to sign language with its phono-semantic compound nature. It developed, while maintaining consistency, by using simple rules of construction and graphic semantics. In Chinese calligraphy, the supple brush is meant to sense every modulation of the body and transfer the movement freely, allowing an infinity of variations in the stroke. This connection between the body, the tool and the sign gives the gesture authority over the sign and not the contrary [22].

Both models help us to reflect on the principle of the stroke of the pen (or brush) and the role of the body in the writing process or performance. It is the formal semantic and structural features of the Chinese writing system that came to be the main source of inspiration in our research, as it associates different graphic modes with the movements of the hand. Far from the conventional alphabetic forms of the glyphs in the transcription of vocal languages, there is the potential to write sign language as we speak it, with the same tools: the hands and the eyes.

Visualisation of Movement. By picturing various factors in movement simultaneously in legible photography, the work of the physiologist E. J. Marey is a milestone in many ways [23]. Next to Eadweard J. Muybridge's sensational chrono-photography, Marey gave birth to the modern, scientific observation of the body in movement.

At a formal level, the work of Anton Giulio Bragaglia [24] crystallised our reflections. By using long exposure and welcoming the blur that results from fast movement, his technique, photodynamism, rejected Marey's analytical methods and focused on capturing the sensation of movement rather than breaking it apart. More than a sequence, this visualisation depicted movement as an indivisible reality and form.

Unlike Picasso and Mili in 1949 [25], the process of photocalligraphy is not painting with light. The movement itself is clearly the origin of the traces in our process, extending the concept of the stroke by capturing the various dimensions of the hands.

Aside from this photocalligraphic representation, we acknowledge the various digital methods of rendering movement, and their advantage (easier manipulation, modification and prototyping). While in this work we focus on analog capture, with the blur of movement characterising our renderings, we are also exploring the digital dimension of movement: its various representations and the manipulation of such a graphic digital object.

Photocalligraphic Capture

We devised a photographic process allowing us to visualise hand movement in space specifically in the context of sign language. We call this technique of visualisation *photocalligraphy*, referring to the formalism of our images. The photocalligraphy method focuses on isolated signs and gestures and turns them into a graphic imprint. This way of representing the gestural dimension of sign language envisions the hand as a graphic tool, similar to a living brush.

In order to isolate the hands and the face, the sign language speaker wears a black garment with long sleeves and stands in front of a uniform black background. A camera frames the upper body plus the space necessary to perform large signs, thus capturing the meaningful signing space and defining our frame of reference. We use a digital camera (Nikon Dsign languageR D90) to shoot long exposure images (duration around 2 s., depending on the sign), in order to capture the entire duration of the sign. This records the continuous trace of the hands in movement without the need for post-editing. Avoiding post-editing enables the sign language speaker to see instantly the graphic potential of their movements. It proved in our experience and in feedback from the sign language speakers that the system was very close to a process of writing. An exposure of 2 s was found to be the optimal value. Because the speaker cannot hear the noise made by the camera shot, we indicated it by opening and closing a hand (start and end of the exposure). This is important, to synchronise the duration of the shot and to convey the time available to perform the sign. Sessions are recorded on video so as to save discussion and keep track of the evolution of the sign language speakers' behaviour.

In our set-up, a screen faces the sign language speaker and displays the image just taken. This visual feedback enables the sign language speaker to see what they have produced, bringing the experience even closer to writing. This process also instigates the exploratory aspect of our work, as the sign language speaker often reacts to his creation and tries to give the next gesture a particular scriptural direction. Without being an actual writing tool, photocalligraphy using this particular set-up demonstrates the concept that French sign language gestuality includes a scriptural dimension.

Visualising Sign Language Gestuality

We focused our research on movement, the most graphically dense parameter of sign language. Yet, we have realised that the object of our study is not this parameter alone. Indeed, changes in configurations and orientation both have an impact on the rendering (see Fig. 12.1), and the positions of the hands over the body are implied in the location of the movement. Facial expression can also be represented if recorded.

In the end, what we capture focuses more on gesture as a whole than on movement as defined in the context of sign language. The resulting object is a picture, a projection of the 4D (space, time and depth) space of sign language on the 2D space of photography. Being 2D, we had to compensate for the loss of two other dimensions (time and depth). Long exposure was intended to compensate for time while the freedom given to sign language speakers to choose how to face the camera partially compensated for depth. Yet, in our case, dynamics and depth are still the main

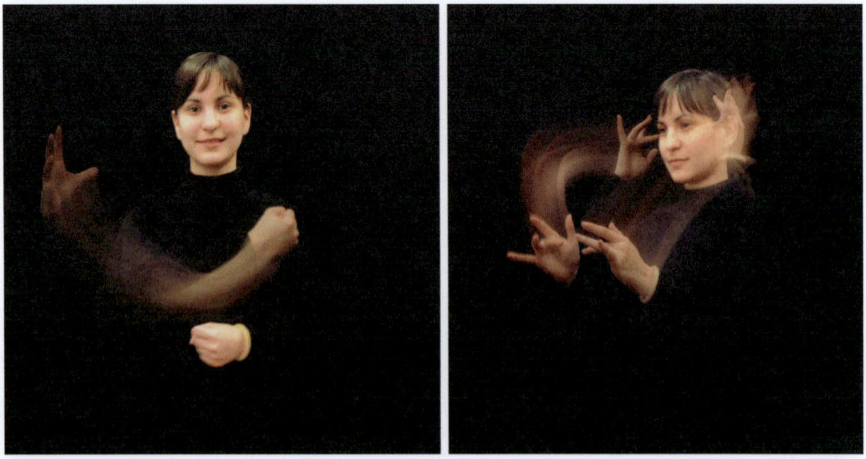

Fig. 12.1 Photocalligraphies of the signs [TO SUCCEED] and [CLEVER]

issue in sign language representation. In the next sections we will see how the sign language speakers used our system to overcome these limitations.

We don't deny the major part exploration plays in our work and in the sign language speakers' experience of our set-up. While spoken language and writing traditionally use completely different modes (voco-accoustic and gestuo-visual), in sign language there is the theoretical potential to use a common channel for writing and speech. Eventually, such an experimental approach pushes the boundary of how we define writing and puts the writer in the situation of recalling his gestural language as the act of writing: an analogical graphic transcription of an oral sign. We aim to show the impact of associating this graphic inscription with a sign from the sign language vocabulary in a future publication.

Signer/Writer Dilemma. The graphic dimension that we perceive in oral speech justifies the dual nature of our two corpora: collecting images that record the execution of a gesture or oral communication, and a scriptural performance. Such a procedure confronts the sign language speaker, who is an expert in their language, with a situation where they have to develop a critical sense of their scripting capability. We name this double ability: signer/writer. The dilemma for the signer/writer is to inscribe a mark that will respect the natural shape of the sign, and yet also result in the greatest legibility in the final picture (Fig. 12.2).

Corpora and Evaluations

For our corpora we chose a representative sample set of 100 signs in French sign language, aiming to represent the different forms in the vocabulary of French sign language [26]. Signs were selected based on their graphic parameters (dimensions,

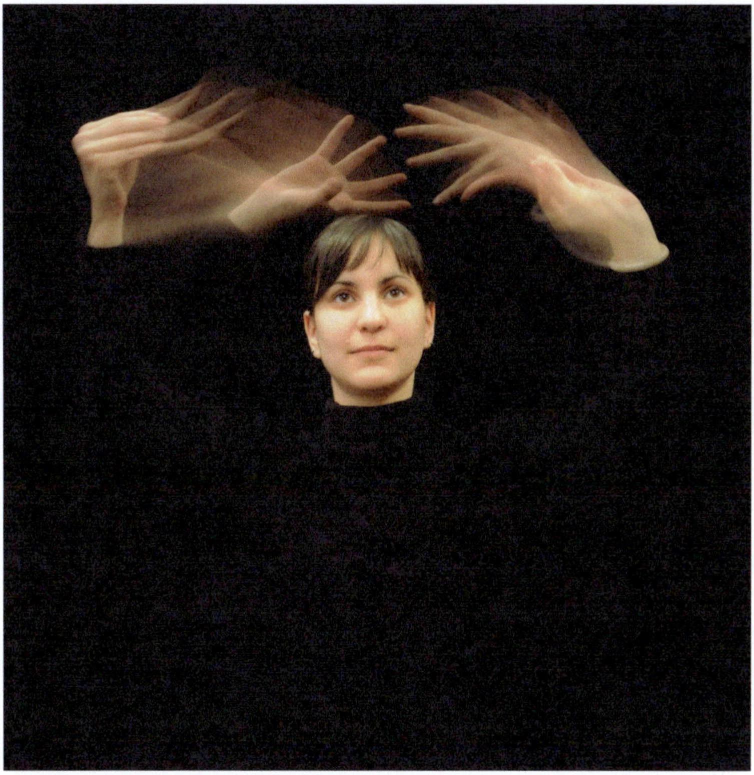

Fig. 12.2 Photocalligraphy of the sign [Abstract]

dynamic, symmetries, rotation and shapes) as well as gesture parameters (one or two hands, mouth movements, repetitions, change in hand configuration, contact with the body, position, spreading of the movement). Once we chose our set of signs, we made a list using illustrations from a dictionary that is considered as a reference in French sign language: the IVT (International Visual Theater) dictionary [27]. During sessions with sign language speakers, we presented them with the pictures from the IVT dictionary as reference to avoid influencing them with our concepts of the signs.

We produced two photographic corpora. Using the first one we were able to study a broad range of photocalligraphies and then test their legibility with sign language speakers. The second corpus focused on the variation and alterations in photocalligraphies among sign language speakers. In both cases we worked with native speakers of sign language. In this way we were able to test both whether our research direction was meaningful and whether it was acceptable to the sign language community. Both corpora will be available in the near future.

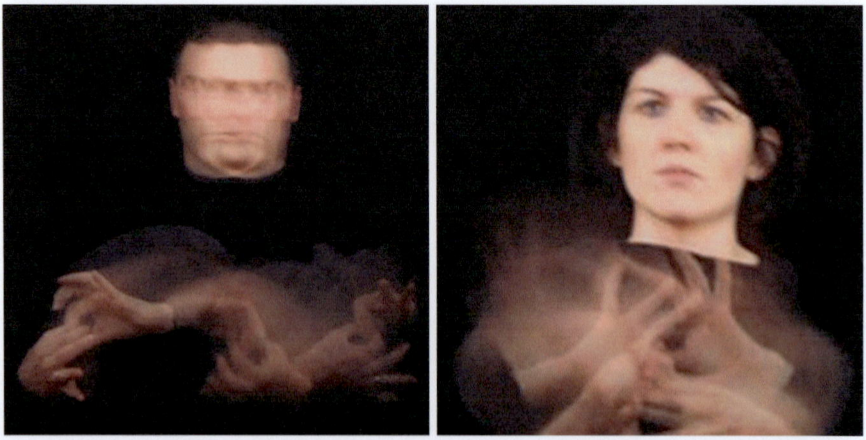

Fig. 12.3 Two different realisations of the sign [CHAIN]

First Corpus: Angle and Legibility

For this corpus, we set up 12 viewpoints spread over a 150° arc in order to photograph the sign language speakers (a man and a woman for this corpus) from different angles. This was to capture the dimension of depth and to explore there was an optimal angle, defined by each sign's various parameters. As it was our first large scale experiment, the main objective for the first corpus was to test the legibility of the graphic records. Despite some limitations in this first set-up, we already found that the sign language speakers were intensely involved, ascribing great importance to their realisations and making good use of the visual feedback to improve them.

Legibility. The next step was to test the ability of those graphic records to convey the original meaning of the sign. For that, we conducted an online evaluation that we describe in [5]. Eighty sign language speakers of various levels of skill participated, resulting in an average 63 % comprehension. By *comprehension* we mean that the subjects were able to recognise the sign depicted in a photocalligraphic. These results confirmed our research direction but above all exposed the progress yet to be made.

Angle. In the end, the angle proved to be a non-variable. Rotation did help legibility by giving the photocalligraphies a feel of 3D when viewed successively as a short animation. No definite rule appeared for an optimal angle other than simply that which the sign language speaker would have chosen by instinct.

Variations. We saw a huge difference in legibility between the two sign language speakers in some signs, as can be seen for instance with the sign [CHAIN] in the Fig. 12.3, with 100 % recognition for the realisation on the left and 60 % for the one on the right. As our system does not instantly create an instant visual representation of sign language for every sign, the sign language speakers themselves took to distorting some signs, making them different from the prototype but improving their graphic representation.

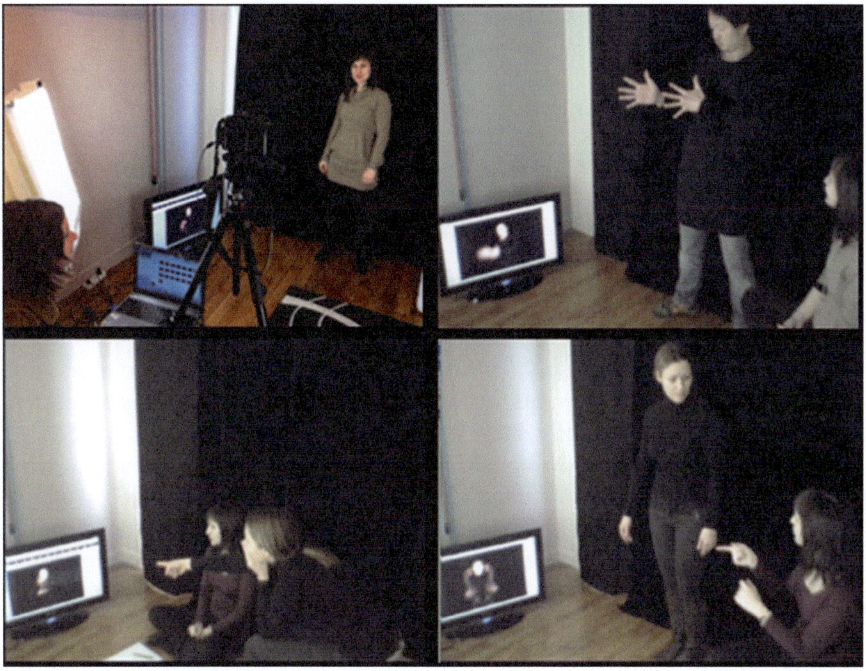

Fig. 12.4 The setup for the second corpus

Those variations implied the existence of rules for improving the legibility of our photocalligraphies; our understanding was that these same rules might apply in a possible gesture based sign language writing system. This new direction prompted us to devise a second corpus aimed specifically at the study of these alterations.

Second Corpus: Alterations

In order to study variations in the performance of signs, we worked this time with eight native sign language speakers, men and women: some, from deaf families, had learnt french sign language since they were born while others had learnt it in high school or even when they reached adulthood. For this corpus the setup (Fig. 12.4) was simpler. We only captured the image from one angle, trusting the sign language speaker to choose the best angle. As in the first set-up, visual feedback was given and the sign language speaker could create a different version of a sign if they wished, by modifying the angle, speed or dynamic. Our aim here was not so much to achieve the best graphic imprint but to study the processes themselves and their evolution.

Each speaker performed 25 signs out of the whole sample set. The resulting corpus comprises a series of 200 images covering the 100 signs, and over 25 h of annotated video.

A session took place as follows:

- Explanation of the project, presentation of the different working steps;
- First capture of the 25 signs in video as a reference;
- Experimentation with the photocalligraphic set-up;
- Second capture of the same 25 signs with the photocalligraphic set-up;
- Selection of the best pictures for each sign taken during the session;
- Discussion of the working session.

The protocol was organised to allow the sign language speaker to master the set-up with minimum intervention from us. We did not express any subjective judgment on the quality of the images produced, even when asked to by the sign language speaker. When they were uncertain, we advised them to think of what they would want to see in the image. Then, we could assist with technical advice on how to realise their vision. When we felt that the speaker had developed a particular process of modification for the photocalligraphy, we asked them to describe it.

At the end of the session, the pictures were displayed again and we discussed with them the question of legibility and the potential offered by the set-up. We also watched another series of pictures produced by a different sign language speaker and ask the subject to identify the meaning, to pick out the most legible ones sign by sign, and to explain their choice.

We noticed that similar strategies (observed earlier) were used spontaneously by most participants without any direction from us. This would imply that these techniques are a generic response to the writing/performance process rather than arising from the individual alone.

Alterations used for a specific visual purpose were identified and an underlying structure emerged. Because of that structure and the recurrence of these purposeful modifications of the signs, we decided to call those alterations strategies of graphic inscription. By this, we mean all the techniques of production of the sign used in order to make its graphical representation more legible and closer to the mental visualisation the person has of the sign.

Graphic Inscribing Strategies

Sign language speakers can see the result of their trials and variations in the visual feedback. If a variation is considered effective it is integrated, and can reveal a specific process. When this process proves itself to be common to a variety of signs and speakers, it becomes a graphic inscribing strategy as seen in Fig. 12.5. Those strategies are connected to the set of parameters that those various signs share, implying the existence of possible generic rules.

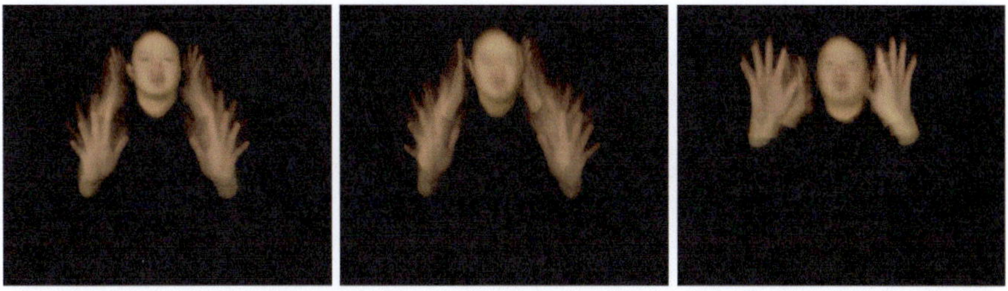

Fig. 12.5 Evolution in the realisation of the sign [FOREST]

As sign language speakers build up an understanding of the set-up and skill in using it, they are able to improve their production by recalling acquired strategies, showing that a learning process has occurred. The first underlying structure we found in the inscribing strategies related to the two missing dimensions of the projection: time and depth.

Time Related Strategies

With an exposure longer than 1/4 of a second, a moving object produces a motion blur. The stiller an object remains, the sharper and brighter it will appear. In contrast, movement will make it blurry and under exposed. This gives the speaker freedom to shape the dynamic of the photocalligraphy by accentuating different parts of the sign.

One of such strategy is to break down some of the sign into key positions. Those key positions are either a strong variation in direction or a modification of the hand's configuration. The emphasis of key parts eases the analysis of the sign as a whole as it sharpens the most revealing components.

Some strategies were used to define the flow of the sign: where it begins, where it ends. This is in fact a piece of information our photocalligraphies do not record, and feedback from our first corpus indicated that its absence reduces legibility and makes it harder to recognise the sign. Most sign language speakers dealt with this issue by making the end configuration of a sign brighter in order to hint at a direction of the movement. Finally, when there was any kind of repetitive motion in a sign, sign language speakers usually chose to remove it in order to avoid graphical overlays of hands or movement trail.

Space Related Strategies

By default, the sign language speaker puts themself in front of the camera during the shot. This promotes a face-to-face position similar to the natural communication stance in sign language. In the case of movements on the axis of the camera, the loss of information related to depth impairs the legibility of the sign. A line becomes a dot and the entire movement is flattened into a blurry form. Here, the sign language speaker can choose to turn slightly sideways in order to present the movement from a better angle.

Moreover, some movements are too slight, and this creates overlays. In this case the movement can be exaggerated to reduce overlays.

The speaker can rotate not only the body at the beginning of the sign (thus impacting the whole sign) but also the hands during the sign. This way, they can choose the best angle for their current specific hand configuration, to maximise legibility and recognition while not altering the trail too much.

Conclusion

In this chapter we presented our photocalligraphic set-up as well as the graphic inscription strategies that emerged from both our corpora. We hope to offer a valid approach to creating a script that takes graphic design into account. We feel that this is a multidisciplinary field of study where the importance of exploratory graphic design is under-represented.

The list of strategies we have are only those that arose from our sessions. The next step will be to broaden the field and search for more of those strategies, which will help us to better understand the structure of this first set. We will also carefully associate these strategies with the parameters of the sign with which they were used in our sample set. Then we will test for generalisation by searching signs with similar parameters in our sample set, check whether the strategies are applicable to those, and observe their effects.

Perspectives. The next logical step will be to measure the impact of those strategies on legibility. Once we have assembled enough of them, we will again evaluate them and compare signs with and without the graphic inscribing strategies. This will also be the occasion to make this evaluation using higher resolution images. Because of the set-up, the quality of pictures from the first evaluation was low. We hope that this improvement in quality, together with the use of graphic inscribing strategies, will have a positive impact on legibility.

The photocalligraphic inscription system shares certain characteristics with writing tools, hopefully implying that the rules developed for one medium will also apply to the other. We are interested in learning from the strategies developed through our visualisation technique and applying this knowledge to a writing system. The strategies would be translated into rules of composition, harmony, balance, etc.

We will have to overcome some problems if we want to propose relevant answers to the challenge of graphic visualisation of french sign language. For example, how do we choose which are the meaningful parameters in a spacially performed gestural sign in order to translate it into a graphic sign that is static and flat? We can also question the status of those images. Are they a representation of the gesture, or a representation of the language? How do they affect the cognitive model of language? It also begs the question of articulation between signs. This would imply taking into account the segmentation and grammar of the language itself.

References

1. Legifrance.gouv.fr. *LOI n° 2005–102 du 11 Février 2005 pour L'égalité des Droits et des Chances, la Participation et la Citoyenneté des Personnes Handicapées*. France, February 2005. http://www.legifrance.gouv.fr/affichTexte.do?cidTexte=JORFTEXT000000809647. Accessed 13 May 2013.
2. Courtin, C. (2002). Le développement de la conceptualisation chez l'enfant sourd. La Nouvelle Revue de L'adaptation et de la Scolarisation.
3. Prillwitz, S., Leven, R., Zienert, H., Hanke, T., & Henning, J. (1989). *HamNoSys version 2.0. Hamburg notation system for sign language: An introductory guide*. Seedorf: Signum.
4. Sutton, V. (1995). *Lessons in SignWriting – Textbook and workbook*, 2nd edition. Deaf Action Committee for SignWriting, La Jolla.
5. Danet, C., de Courville, R., Miletitch, R., Rébulard, M., Boutet, D., & Doan, P. (2010). Un Système Analogique Visuo-gestuel pour la Graphie de la LS, Traitement Automatique des Langues des Signes. Montréal, Canada.
6. Hoiting, N., & Slobin, D. I. (2002). Transcription as a tool for understanding: The Berkeley Transcription System for sign language research (BTS). In G. Morgan & B. Woll (Eds.), *Directions in sign language acquisition* (pp. 55–75). Amsterdam: John Benjamins.
7. Stokoe, W. C., Jr. (2005). Sign language structure: An outline of the visual communication systems of the American deaf. *Journal of Deaf Studies and Deaf Education, 10*(1), 3–37. doi:10.1093/deafed/eni001.
8. Connolly, G. K. (1998). Legibility and readability of small print: Effects of font, observer age and spatial vision. University of Calgary, Canada.
9. Projet LS-COLIN. Quel outil de notation pour quelle analyse de la LS? In *Recherches sur la Langue des Signes (RLSF'01)*, Toulouse, 23–24 November 2001.
10. Garcia, B., Brugeille, J.-L., Kellerhals, M. P., Braffort, A., Boutet, D., Dalle, P., & Mercier, H. (2007). *Rapport du Projet LS Script, 2005–2007*. Agence Nationale de la Recherche.
11. Stokoe, W. C., Jr. (1976). *A dictionary of American Sign Language on linguistic principles*. Silver Spring: Linstok Press.
12. Cuxac, C. *La Langue des Signes Française (LSF): Les voies de l'iconicité*. Paris-Gap, Ophrys, Bibliothèque de Faits de Langues, no. 15–16, 2000.
13. Balvet, A., Courtin, C., Boutet, D., Cuxac, C., Fusellier-Souza, I., Garcia, B., & L'Huillier, M.-T. (2010). Sallandre, M.-A. The Creagest project: A digitized and annotated corpus for French sign language (LSF) and natural gestural languages. In *Proceedings of LREC*.
14. Liddell, S. K. (2003). *Grammar, gesture, and meaning in American Sign Language*. Cambridge: Cambridge University Press.
15. Zeshan, U. (2006). *Interrogative and negative constructions in sign languages* (Sign language typology series). Nijmegen: Ishara Press.
16. Blondel, M., Boutora, L., & Parisot, A.-M. (2009). Inventaire et mesures du marquage spatial dans la grammaire des langues des signes. *Communication Orale*. CILS, NAMUR, Belgium.
17. Johnston, T. (2008). Corpus linguistics and signed languages: no lemmata, no corpus. In O. Crasborn, E. Efthimiou, T. Hanke, E. D. Thoutenhoofd, & I. Zwitserlood (Eds.), *3rd workshop on the representation and processing of sign languages* (pp. 82–88). ELDA, Paris.
18. Hanke, T. (2002). iLex-A tool for sign language lexicography and corpus analysis. In *Proceedings of the third international conference on language resources and evaluation* (pp. 923–926). Las Palma de Gran Canaria.

19. Varela, F., Thompson, E., & Rosch, E. (1996). *L'inscription Corporelle de L'esprit: Sciences cognitives et expérience humaine*. Paris: Seuil.
20. Noordzij, G. (2005). *The stroke: Theory of writing*. London: Hyphen Press.
21. Calvet, L.-J. (1998). *Histoire de L'écriture*. Paris: Hachette.
22. Bara, F., & Gentaz, E. (August 2011). Haptics in teaching handwriting: The role of perceptual and visuo-motor skills. *Human Movement Science, 30*(4), 745–759.
23. Marey, É.-J., & Demeny, G. (1883). *Etudes Photographiques sur la Locomotion de l' Homme et des Animaux*. Paris: Gauthier-Villars.
24. Bragaglia, Anton Giulio. "'Futurist Photodynamism' (1911)." *MODERNISM-MODERNITY* 15.2 (2008): 363–379.
25. Life Magazine. Behind the picture: Picasso 'draws' with light. Time, USA. http://life.time.com/culture/picasso-draws-with-light-1949/#1. Accessed 13 May 2013.
26. Lefebvre-Albaret, F. (2010). Segmentation de la Langue des Signes Française par une Approche basée sur la Phonologie. Doctoral thesis, Université Paul Sabatier, Toulouse.
27. Moody, B., Vourc'h, A., Girod, M., & Dufour, M.-C. (1998). La Langue des Signes, vols. 2 & 3. International Visual Theatre.

Part IV
Interaction and Interfaces

Jonathan P. Bowen

Interactivity in particular and interaction in general are an increasingly important aspect of electronic visualisation. In this Part of the book, we consider human–computer interaction and the associated interfaces when using Information Technology for visualisation. Interaction with visualisation facilities is an increasingly important technique in allowing people to manipulate data in a way that aids in understanding information that may be hidden in the data otherwise [1, 2]. The design of interactive systems is interdisciplinary in nature due to the combination of humans and technology. It involves, for example, disciplines such as cognitive psychology, graphic design, user interface design, etc. [3, 4]. Knowledge visualisation can also be used in different fields, including arts and cultural applications, sometimes in an interactive manner [5].

IT-based interactive devices have developed and changed significantly over the years. Initially there involved expensive workstations, only available to researchers and industry, beyond the reach in terms of cost and ease of use for most in arts fields. The development of the personal computer, soon with enough power to support windows-based interaction through a mouse, allowed more access for those with limited means, although software and computational power was still a limiting factor.

More recently, the development of extremely portable tablets and smartphones, typically including a digital camera of increasing resolution, has enabled artists to use these devices with suitable interactive apps as an creative medium, transforming what is possible, in much the same way that paint technology development enabled the Impressionists to paint outdoors easily in the nineteenth century (see the introduction to Part II on *New Art Practice*). For example, the British artist David Hockney has been an enthusiastic user of such technology to produce electronic "paintings" that can easily be sent directly to friends on other similar mobile devices. Examples were exhibited at the Royal Academy in London at a solo show by Hockney in 2012 entitled *A Bigger Picture*. Many were enlarged and printed for the exhibition as a series of outside scenes, much like the series by Monet of haystacks, etc., in different lighting conditions and at different times of the year.

Interaction using mobile devices is becoming progressively more important in cultural applications in general. For example, museums are finding this technology an increasingly worthwhile way to augment the visitors' experience [6]. In Chap. 13, Matt Benatan and Kia Ng present the use of mobile devices for musical applications. In particular, the combination of standard technology with customised hardware to allow the interface to break away from the standard screen-based approach (e.g. using gestures) is suggested as a worthwhile approach, enabling multimodal interaction through a variety of input mechanisms. Thus the interface can become more physical than virtual.

In Chap. 14, Jeremy Pilcher presents an interesting and novel approach to visualising legal networks in an interactive manner. He views law as a social system. As a case study, he analyses the artwork *They Rule*, which visualises data involving legal relationships. He argues that the interface is as important as the data itself in this artistic context.

Steve DiPaola is a long-time attendee at EVA conferences. In Chap. 15, he describes his approach to manipulating faces, synthesising and visualising them in an artistic manner using computer-based tools. The faces can be realistic or more abstract, depending on the desired effect. Interactivity allows the viewer to change the character of the face, unlike in a traditional portrait that is fixed in nature. Issues include the fact that any computation must be done in real-time to achieve true interactivity.

In Chap. 16, Sophy Smith presents the experimental use of Facebook for artistic interacting collaboration. A social network like Facebook allows artistic contributions to be made by geographically separated participants. The chapter covers different models of collaboration. The results of a specific project, the Feedback Project, is also reported. The processes employed by users in their collaboration and how well these integrate with the available technology are critical to success.

In summary, the chapters in this part of the book illustrate the great diversity of ways that interactivity and interaction can be used to artistic ends using the variety of Information Technology that is now available.

References

1. Zudilova-Seinstra, E., Adriaansen, T., & van Liere, R. (Eds.). (2008). *Trends in interactive visualization: state-of-the-art survey*. Berlin/Heidelberg: Springer.
2. Ferster, B. (2012). *Interactive visualization: Insight through inquiry*. Cambridge, MA: The MIT Press.
3. Pannafino, J. (2012). *Interdisciplinary interaction design: A visual guide to basic theories, models and ideas for thinking and designing for interactive web design and digital device experiences*. Lancaster: Assiduous Publishing.
4. Pratt, A. (2012). *Interactive design: An introduction to the theory and application of user-centered design*. Beverly: Rockport Publishers.
5. Marchese, F. T., & Banissi, E. (Eds.). (2013). *Knowledge visualization currents: From text to art to culture*. Berlin/Heidelberg: Springer.
6. Tallon, L., & Walker, K. (Eds.). (2008). *Digital technologies and the museum experience: Handheld guides and other media*. Lanham: AltaMira Press.

Chapter 13
Mobile Motion: Multimodal Device Augmentation for Musical Applications

Matt Benatan and Kia Ng

Abstract Mobile devices have become an integral part of the twenty-first century lifestyle. From social networking and business to day-to-day scheduling and multimedia applications, smart-phones and other portable handsets are now the go-to devices for interaction in the digital world. Currently, mobile devices typically utilise direct user interfaces, such as touch screens or keyboards, where interactions are performed directly by controlling graphical elements or controls on the interface. This project looks to bring device interaction out of the virtual world and into the physical world. Through augmenting existing mobile technologies with custom electronic hardware, it is possible to create a system that can incorporate free gestures within a portable context. With this approach, portable applications can break away from the virtual world and enable the mobile platform to be harnessed as a physical augmented interface. This concept can be exploited for applications within a wide range of contexts including musical performance, games, learning and teaching, and beyond.

This chapter is an updated and extended version of the following paper, published here with kind permission of the Chartered Institute for IT (BCS) and of EVA London Conferences: M. Benatan, I. Symonds and K.Ng, "Mobile motion: multimodal device augmentation for musical applications." In S. Dunn, J. P. Bowen, and K. Ng (eds.). *EVA London 2011 Conference Proceedings*. Electronic Workshops in Computing (eWiC), British Computer Society, 2011. http://www.bcs.org/ewic/eva2011 (accessed 26 May 2013).

K. Ng (✉)
ICSRiM – University of Leeds, School of Computing, School of Electronic and Electrical Engineering & School of Music, Leeds LS2 9JT, UK
e-mail: www.icsrim.org.uk

M. Benatan
ICSRiM – University of Leeds, School of Computing & School of Music,
Leeds LS2 9JT, UK
e-mail: mobilemotion@icsrim.org.uk

J.P. Bowen et al. (eds.), *Electronic Visualisation in Arts and Culture*,
Springer Series on Cultural Computing, DOI 10.1007/978-1-4471-5406-8_13,

Introduction

Over recent years mobile devices have increased dramatically in popularity, becoming central to the way many users experience the web, multimedia and more. These devices rely largely on touch-based interfaces, often with several other sensors, such as accelerometers, being used for different forms of user input. Through augmenting existing technologies with local position-aware sensor capabilities, this project looks to further explore mobile device interaction and enable users to engage with virtual technologies through physical gestures. This has already proven to be hugely successful in the realm of gaming, with products such as Microsoft's Kinect and the Nintendo Wii. However, this approach has yet to be explored on mobile devices. The current limitation is largely due to the fact that these technologies rely on static hardware units to provide a point of reference – something that poses a challenge for the mobile platform, as these devices cannot rely on stationary components. Through this project we are developing a prototype to offer a solution to the challenge.

To ensure that the project results in a system that positively enhances the user interaction experience, key requirements include:

- Precision: the system should be able to consistently provide data on the location of the device relative to the user.
- Portability: the physical gesture mechanism should be capable of working anywhere the device goes, without being bound to stationary hardware.

Related Background

Although there is a vastly expanding range of smart phones and mobile devices, none of these has implemented a comprehensive local positional tracking mechanism. However, they are all equipped with a global tracking mechanism, GPS. In order to survey current trends in local tracking systems, a number of motion control technologies are discussed in this section.

One commercially available product that is closest to the project idea is the Nintendo Wii [1]. It combines physical input with accelerometer and infrared sensors to provide a gesture-based control system. The principle behind the motion detection component is simple: a sensor bar is placed in a fixed position, which emits infrared beams. The beams are tracked by the Wii remotes (wiimote), and triangulated to work out their position relative to the sensor bar.

Following in Nintendo's footsteps, two other major console developers, Sony and Microsoft, have also released motion control interfaces. In Sony's case, their PlayStation Move system [2] relies on tracking an LED orb. To enable it to work successfully in a range of environments, the colour of the orb changes dynamically to allow it to be easily distinguishable by the camera. The controller also houses an accelerometer, an angular rate sensor and a magnetometer, which provide further gestural information. To enable the controller to function in three dimensions, Sony's PlayStation Eye (the camera) determines the distance of the controller from the camera via the size of the image corresponding to the orb.

Microsoft has further developed light-based approaches through their Kinect system [3, 26]. Unlike the Wii and PlayStation Move, this system uses a range-camera system. By combining the depth sensor technology and model based computer vision techniques, this system is able to follow user movement with a body model. Thus, the system is capable of recognising and tracking different parts of the users, such as hands and heads.

Although there are currently no portable local motion tracking systems for the mobile environment, there have been a number of developments in the area of multimodal mobile device interaction. For example, the Multimodal Home Entertainment Interface [4] uses mobile device interaction within a home entertainment environment. This system utilises speech input from the user as well as touch-based interaction to navigate a television programme guide.

With the current advancements in sensor technology there has been increased interest in sensor-based gesture interfaces in a wide range of research applications, such as Young's work on the augmented violin bow [5]. Through the use of accelerometers and strain sensors, Young developed a system capable of measuring the gestures of violinists. This enabled gesture pattern data to be used for a range of purposes, including pedagogical applications.

These examples demonstrate the interests and trends in creative new developments in the field of user interaction via mobile devices. Gesture-based motion control is a natural and engaging approach [6], with great potential to be adapted to a vast variety of applications; for a diverse range of industries, education and entertainment.

Gesture-Based Interaction

Defining Gesture

The simplest way of defining a gesture is as the movement of a part of the body, such as the hand or foot. However, problems arise from using such a definition due to the over-simplification of the process. Defining a gesture as a movement fails to take into account the intention of the gesture (the meaning behind the movement). In order to fully appreciate and understand the use of gestures, both the primary (movement) and secondary (intention) focuses need to be considered. Doing so gives context from which more information can be extrapolated. Gestures can be classified within one of three core categories: communication, control and metaphor.

Communication gestures include movements used within social interactions. These consist of gesticulations which aid speech, such as hand motions, or entirely self-sufficient non-verbal communication, such as commonly understood signals (such as waving) or sign language.

Control gestures consist of actions used to physically influence a system. This includes the movement associated with controlling electronic devices, such as computers, musical instruments and a broad range of other interactions. Control gestures are generally entirely functional, with no ancillary motive.

Metaphorical gestures are the psychological responses to a form of stimuli, such as the mental reaction a listener perceives in response to a piece of music. While these are not physically quantifiable, they hold significance from a psychological point of view, and can be used to better understand the motives behind, as well the perception of, other associated gestures.

With the continued advancement in gesture-based technologies, the line between communication and control gestures, within the context of Human-Computer Interaction (HCI), has begun to blur as computer systems become more adept at interpreting a broader range of physical interactions – allowing users' communication gestures to be used as a means of control. However, in many applications, such as within the development of virtual musical instruments, it is equally important for technology to be able to recognise the control gestures used with existing instruments, in order to ensure that the interaction is as natural and intuitive as possible.

Gesture in Music

Understanding types of gesture is useful when studying musicians, as this enables the intention behind various movements to be determined, and the gestures to be classified. Jensenius et al. [7] proposed the following categories to define musical gesture:

- Sound-producing: gestures responsible for sounding the note;
- Communicative: gestures intended for communication with others;
- Sound-facilitating: gestures which facilitate the performance but do not directly produce sound;
- Sound-accompanying: gestures made in response to the sound.

Being aware of the different functions of gesture allows for more accurate analysis of gestures. For example, it would be obvious when observing a guitarist that the movements of hands and arms are directly influencing the sound, and thus fall within the category of sound-producing; whereas the movement of his head would be an ancillary gesture, fulfilling a communicative function though not contributing to the production of the sound itself. Thus the critical, functional gestures can be differentiated from those which do not directly influence the musical output. This is important when designing a gesture-based system, as these gesture classifications need to be taken into account when considering which movements the system should be configured to detect, and which it should ignore.

Gesture in Human-Computer Interaction

In the past, human-computer interaction has typically involved basic interface devices such as a keyboard and mouse. Due to the limitations of these technologies, the gesture of the user can neither be observed nor processed by the system, making

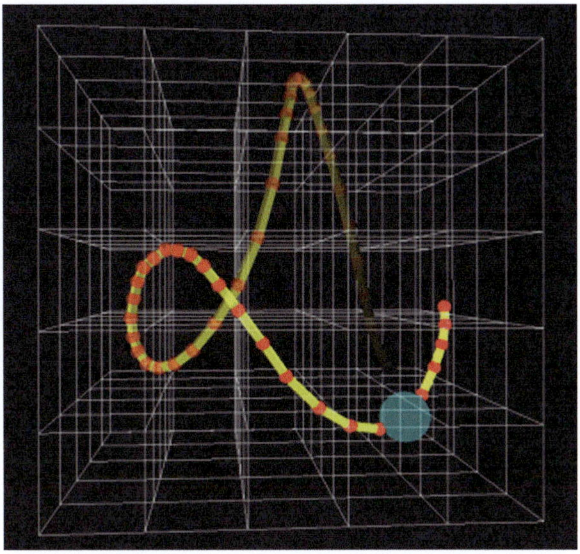

Fig. 13.1 Visualisation of conducting gesture using Open NI and Microsoft Kinect. *Yellow* trace: gesture curve. *Blue circle*: detected beat point

the mechanical process of clicking the mouse or pressing a key the only significant component of the user's motion. As such, in the context of HCI, the interactions are entirely governed by the limitations of the machine. Over recent years a number of new sensor technologies have been introduced and exploited to enhance the capabilities of computers with regard to observing and responding to user gestures. These technologies, such as those discussed earlier, have made it possible to convert users' movements into data that can be analysed and interpreted by computer systems [8–10]. Other developments within gesture recognition algorithms have enabled this data to be effectively processed, allowing computer systems to not only track movement, but to identify patterns and respond to the intentions of the users [11–13]. These algorithms monitor the data corresponding to the user's movement in order to identify turning points (see Fig. 13.1) – thus allowing the system to recognise and track conducting gestures [14, 15]. In this case, the beats have been used to control tempo within a virtual conducting program [16].

Design and Development

Mobile Device Technologies

Several mobile device platform technologies were investigated to determine which would be most suitable for the development of the motion control system. These technologies fell within two categories, defined by two of the most popular mobile device operating systems available at the time: Google's Android OS [17, 25] and

Apple's iOS [18]. Due to the extensive features available on each of the devices, several key features were decided upon for consideration:

- CPU: the faster the CPU, the more efficiently the device would be able to run custom programs and process data.
- Connectivity: the connectivity options would be central for communicating with other components of the system.
- Sensors: the sensor technologies available on the device would indicate the device's current motion control capabilities, and thus dictate what additional sensor technologies may be required.
- Programming environment: the way in which the device is programmed would be central to the development process, so it was essential to evaluate both the programming language and development environments associated with the devices.

iOS Devices

Over the years Apple has released a number of iOS devices. With each iteration, they have continued to add features and enhance functionality. The available iOS devices fall into two categories. These are the iPod Touch and the iPhone, the latter of which adds phone functionality to the iPod Touch's capabilities. As the iPhone functionality was not necessary for this project, the iPod Touch alone was considered.

At the time of writing, Apple's most recent iteration of the iPod Touch was the 4th generation iPod Touch [19]. This incorporates a 1 GHz ARM Cortex-A8 processor running at 800 MHz. The device's connectivity options are fairly broad, supporting Wi-Fi, USB 2.0 and Bluetooth 2.1. The iPod Touch also has a variety of on-board sensor systems, including a multi-touch touch screen, three axis gyroscope, accelerometer, and ambient light sensor. This version of the device also includes front and back facing cameras and a microphone.

Applications for iOS are developed in Objective-C using Apple's Xcode [18] development suite. Objective-C is an object-oriented programming language which, unlike other OOP's such as Java, functions as a strict superset of C, making it possible to freely include C code within an Objective-C class.

One of the disadvantages noted for the iPod Touch was the cost associated with developing for the platform [20].

Android Devices

Following the popularity of the iPhone and iPod Touch, Google soon entered the scene with a variety of mobile devices designed to compete directly with Apple's products. Over the years the devices have converged in functionality, demonstrating fairly similar capabilities across the board, with Google's Android devices now providing mobile solutions for playing media, gaming and accessing the internet.

At the time of writing, the most recent Android devices were the HTC Desire [21] and Samsung Galaxy S [22]. These devices both boasted almost identical features, with the core considerations being the processor speed, connectivity and sensor capabilities. Both devices had 1 GHz processors, supported USB, Blue-tooth and Wi-Fi and had all desired sensor capabilities, namely: a multi-touch touch screen, ambient light sensor, microphone, three-axis accelerometer, three-axis gyroscope and camera. Due to the similarity of the features across both devices, neither exhibited any particular advantage, and both were level with the iPod Touch for the purpose of this project.

Android applications are programmed using the Android SDK, which is based on Apache Harmony, an open source Java implementation. Typically applications are developed within the Eclipse IDE, as recommended by the Android Developer site. Due to Java being open source, it is free to develop and release applications for the Android operating system. This was viewed as a clear advantage over using Apple's iOS.

Selecting a Device

Due to the similarities in functionality between the iOS and Android devices available, there was no clear advantage from this perspective on either side. As such, the decision as to which to use fell to some of the less critical factors. These factors were the ease of developing for the platform and the ease of which the device could be attained. As there was an Android device readily available, it would not have to be bought, and thus Android was the more cost effective option. Another advantage, as mentioned earlier, was the fact that there was no cost associated with developing for Android. Hence, the HTC Desire was the device chosen for the project.

Sensor Survey

In order to choose a suitable method of sensor augmentation, this section surveyed a number of sensor technologies.

Infrared

A popular example of infrared motion-detection technology is the Nintendo Wii [23]. The primary weakness here is its susceptibility to visual light interference. Infrared systems require specific lighting environments to perform consistently, and would thus work inefficiently outdoors, making it a poor choice for a mobile device system.

Near Magnetic Field Coupling

Another approach considered was to use near magnetic field coupling, as demonstrated by M. Bezdicek's hand tracker [24]. This system provides coordinates of finger positions and transmits them via Bluetooth, thus making it an appropriate approach for hand-specific gestures within computer interaction. However, with the effective range of near magnetic field coupling being approximately 15 cm, in the case of this project this approach would not satisfy the distance requirements.

Ultrasonic Sensors

A popular technique for acquiring positional information within robotics is through the use of ultrasonic transceivers. This approach is used for a broad variety of range-finding applications, and has a number of qualities that make it ideal for use in this project. The range of ultrasonic devices varies according to the frequency used. There are a range of ultrasonic sensors available, the most common being 40 kHz and 125 kHz transducers. Due to the short wavelength emitted by the 125 kHz models, the signal dissipates rapidly, resulting in a range of approximately 10 cm. Therefore the 40 kHz model was used, as it provides an effective range of up to 150 cm, thus fulfilling the range requirements for this project. Ultrasonic sensors are also far less susceptible to noise than infrared, as the ultrasonic receiver is tuned to receive within a narrow frequency band, resulting in a particularly high level of noise rejection. These factors make ultrasound an attractive option when compared to other available technologies, providing both the necessary range and accuracy required. Additionally, the ultrasonic components are small, lightweight and can be easily powered by batteries, making them highly portable.

In order to provide user-relative positional tracking, the system required one ultrasonic transmitter, two ultrasonic receivers and a radio system. The receivers are worn on the body of the user, and the transmitter attached to the device (Fig. 13.2). This enabled the ultrasonic signal's time of flight to be calculated relative to the two receiver points.

Ultrasonic Distance Measurement

The system works by sending 50 Hz bursts of 40 kHz ultrasonic signals from a single transmitter (Fig. 13.3). 50 Hz was chosen as the optimal burst frequency as it was the highest frequency tested to maintain a low error rate; frequencies of 60 Hz and 70 Hz resulted in significant loss of accuracy. The same 50 Hz timer also triggers the transmission of a radio signal. The bursts are then intercepted by the two receiver units, and their time of arrival is compared with the radio signal on the Arduino board.

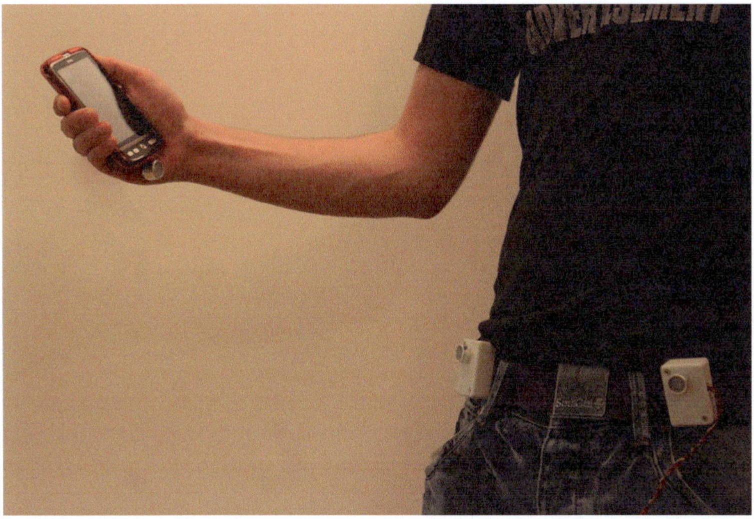

Fig. 13.2 Mobile motion prototype

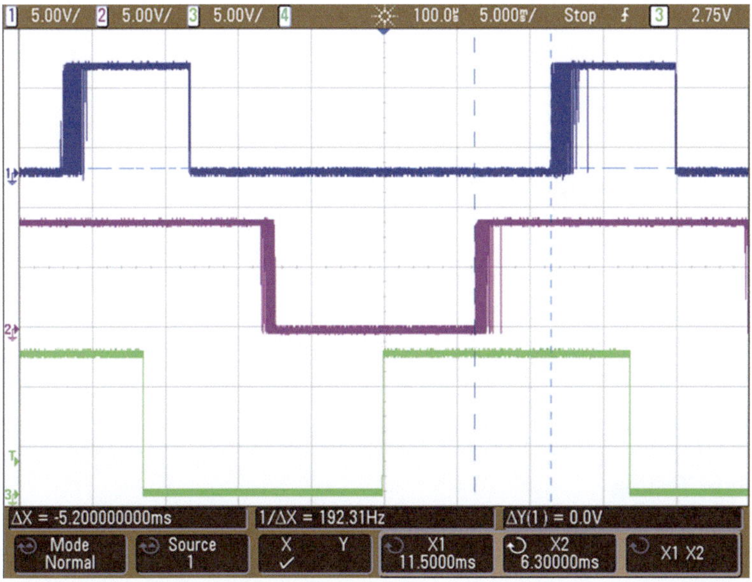

Fig. 13.3 Signal trace using an oscilloscope

Figure 13.4 illustrates the different positions of the units, that result in the ultrasonic pulse reaching the receivers at different times. The position of the transmitter is then calculated by comparing the times of interception with the radio signal. From this, the propagation time for each ultrasonic signal can be determined, and the position of the transmitter calculated.

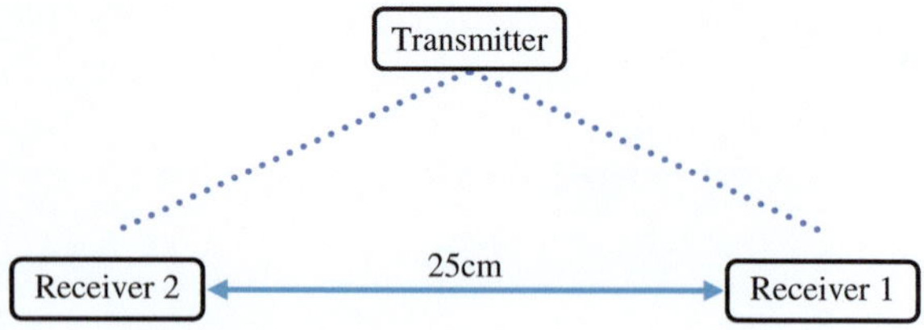

Fig. 13.4 Ultrasonic sensor setup

Accessing Mobile Device Sensors

The mobile device's on-board accelerometer was key to providing information on the forces acting on the device, and thus essential for providing another representation of gesture information. In order to access this information, a custom Android application was developed.

The application 'Sensor Control' streams the device's sensor measurements wirelessly via UDP. These are then intercepted and processed by a computer for real-time processing to collate and interpret the data within the prototype system.

Gesture Recognition

Once the sensor information could be streamed from the mobile device, it was possible to analyse the data for the development of gesture following algorithms. These algorithms could then be used to identify specific gesture patterns and trends and use them to trigger actions within the software for multimedia mapping. Gestural following techniques are also central to reducing latency: through detecting the gesture onset, the system is able to dynamically predict the motion, rather than waiting for the entire gesture to be enacted (Fig. 13.5).

Prototype Testing

To provide a platform for qualitative testing, a virtual xylophone program was conceived to enable the user to play a xylophone using the mobile device as a virtual beater (Fig. 13.6). The software uses ultrasonic data to compute the position of the device in relation to the user, increasing the note pitch to the right, and decreasing it to the left, just as with a real xylophone. The trigger (hit) and velocity (force) data are determined using the device's accelerometer, allowing the user to virtually tap gently for softer/quieter strokes, and harder for louder strokes. The audio samples are then triggered accordingly, providing realistic sonic feedback to the user's virtual interaction.

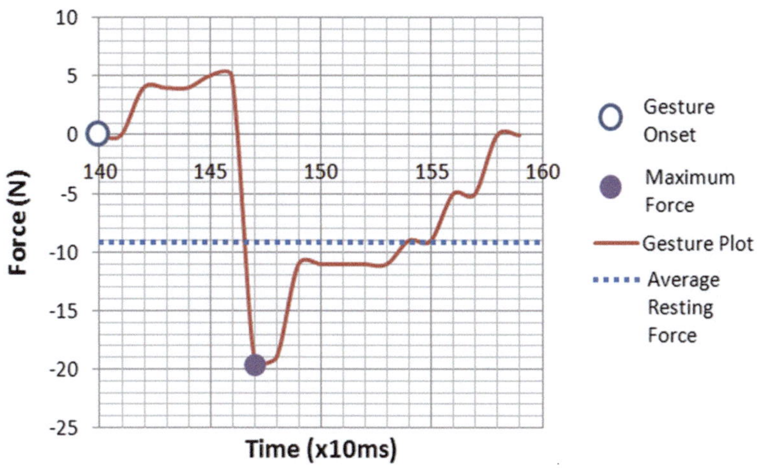

Fig. 13.5 Graph depicting forces acting on the accelerometer sensor's X-axis

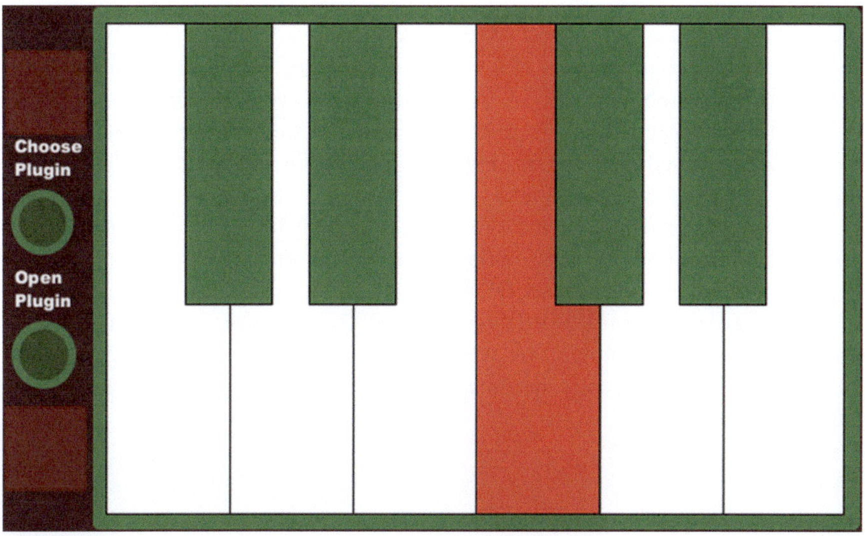

Fig. 13.6 Virtual xylophone graphical user interface

Conclusion

This chapter has presented the design and development of a position-aware motion control interface. The multi-modal approach has shown that ultrasonic sensors can be used to augment existing devices to enhance their capabilities and produce a usable interactive system. User testing was carried out to evaluate user response to

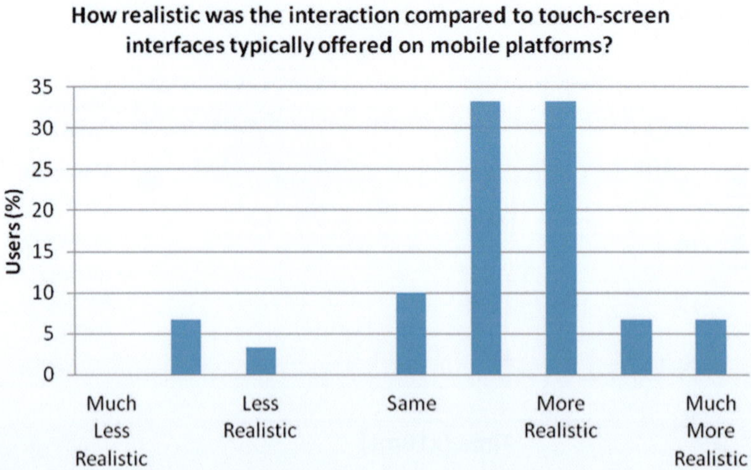

Fig. 13.7 User evaluation results: realistic interaction comparison

the system. This was carried out over a group of 30 individuals, all of whom had some musical background and had used mobile-device based music applications. The system was highly successful, with a majority of users agreeing that the interface provided a more realistic form of physical interaction when compared to other mobile-device based instruments (Fig. 13.7). Users also felt that the system was intuitive, engaging and fun to use.

The technology also lends itself to a range of applications beyond the test case. As a gesture analysis tool, it could prove useful for studying the movement patterns of percussionists, an application that could be used in a similar way to the i-Maestro project for music pedagogy [27]. With further development, it would also be possible to combine this with other sensing and tracking technologies, including global positioning systems, to create a connected world of augmented gesture communication.

References

1. Nintendo of Europe GmbH. *Wii – Nintendo* (2011). http://wii.nintendo.co.uk. Accessed 31 Mar 2011.
2. Micah, M. *PlayStation move explained: An interview with Anton Mikhailov, 2010.* http://www.gamexplain.com/article-72-1272999307-playstation-move-xplained-an-interview-with-anton-mikhailov.html. Accessed 18 May 2013.
3. Shotton, J. et al. (2011). Real-time human pose recognition in parts from single depth Im-ages. In *IEEE computer vision and pattern recognition* 2011, Colorado, 21–25 June 2011. IEEE, 2011.
4. Gruenstein, A. et al. A multimodal home entertainment interface via a mobile device. In *Proceedings of the 9th SIGdial workshop on discourse and dialogue*, Columbus, 19–20 June 2008, (pp.11–29). Stroudsburg: Association for Computational Linguistics.

5. Young, D. (2003). Wireless sensor system for measurement of violin bowing parameters. In *Proceedings of Stockholm Music Acoustics Conference*, Stockholm, 6–9 August 2003. KTH Speech, Music and Hearing.
6. Wilson, F. (2000). *The hand*. New York: Vintage Books.
7. Jensenius, A. R. et al. (2010). Musical gestures: Concepts and methods in research. In R. I. Godøy, & M. Leman (Eds.), *Musical gestures: Sound, movement, and meaning*. London: Routledge. ISBN 978-0-415-99887-1. Chapter 2.
8. Baillie, L., Schatz, R., Simon, R., & Grassner, A. (2005). Designing Mona: User interactions with multimodal mobile applications. In *Human computer interaction*, Las Vegas.
9. Kopp, S., & Wachsmuth, I. (2010). Gesture in embodied communication and human-computer interaction. In S. Kopp, & I. Wachsmuth (Eds.), *8th international gesture workshop, GW 2009*, Bielefeld, Germany, 25–27 February 2009, revised selected papers. Lecture Notes in Computer Science, vol. 5934, Berlin: Springer. doi: 10.1007/978-3-642-12553-9
10. Wachsmuth, I., & Sowa, T. (2002). Gesture and sign languages in human-computer interaction. In *International gesture workshop, GW 2001*, London, 18–20 April 2001, revised papers. Berlin/New York: Springer.
11. Junker, H. (2005). *Human activity recognition and gesture spotting with body-worn sensors*. Konstanz: Hartung-Gorre.
12. Yang, M.-H., & Ahuja, N. (2001). *Face detection and gesture recognition for human-computer interaction*. Boston: Kluwer.
13. Müller, M. (2007). *Information retrieval for music and motion*. Berlin: Springer.
14. Bradshaw, D., & Ng, K. (2008). Tracking conductors hand movements using multiple Wiimotes. In *International conference on automated solutions for cross media content and multi-channel distribution*, Florence.
15. Bradshaw, D., & Ng, K. (2009). Motion capture, analysis and feedback to support learning conducting. In *International Computer Music Conference*, Montreal, Quebec.
16. Leonard, J., & Ng, K. (2011). Music via motion: A distributed framework for interactive multimedia performance. In *Distributed multimedia systems*, Florence.
17. Android. *Android Developers*, 2013. http://developer.android.com. Accessed 11 May 2013.
18. Apple. *Apple Developer*, 2013. http://developer.apple.com. Accessed: 11 May 2013.
19. Apple. *iPod Touch*, 2013. http://www.apple.com/ipodtouch/. Accessed 11 May 2013.
20. Keene, T. The Apple barrier: an open source interface to the iPhone. In *Proceedings of electronic visualisation and the arts (EVA 2011), EVA* London, 2011. http://ewic.bcs.org/content/ConWebDoc/40651. Accessed 18 May 2013
21. HTC. *HTC Desire Product Overview*. http://www.htc.com/www/smartphones/htc-desire-c/. Accessed 18 Mar 2013.
22. Samsung. *Samsung Galaxy S*. http://galaxys.samsungmobile.com. Accessed 7 Mar 2011, now SII http://www.samsung.com/global/microsite/galaxys2/html/index.html. Accessed 18 May 2013.
23. Nintendo. *Wii*, 2007. http://wii.nintendo.com. Accessed 11 May 2013.
24. Bezdicek, M. et al. Portable absolute position tracking system for human hand fingertips. In *Proceedings of Virtual Concept 2006*, Cancún, 27 November–1 December 2006.
25. Meir, R. A beginner's guide to Android. *Google I/O 2010*, San Francisco, USA, 19–20 May 2010. Session Video. http://www.google.com/events/io/2010/sessions.html. Accessed 12 May 2013.
26. Leadbetter, R. *Tech analysis: Kinect*, EUROGAMER.net, 15 June 2010. http://www.eurogamer.net/articles/digitalfoundry-kinect-tech-analysis. Accessed 12 May 2013.
27. Ng, K. (2008). Technology-enhanced learning for i-Maestro framework and tools. In S. Dunn, S. Keene, G. Mallen, & J. P. Bowen (Eds.), *Proceedings of EVA London 2008 Conference: Electronic visualisation and the arts*, London, 22–24 July 2008. London: British Computer Society. http://ewic.bcs.org/content/ConWebDoc/20604. Accessed 18 May 2013.

Chapter 14
Legal Networks: Visualising the Violence of the Law

Jeremy Pilcher

Abstract Data visualisation techniques have been used as a means to critique society and in particular capitalism. The possibilities for interaction with data and its malleability in digital form make the internet an effective site for the technique. Art online that employs data visualisation is commonly approached in terms of the understanding that the data may bring and its aesthetic appeal. However, I propose that the impact of a work may also be engaged with in terms of the interface that it provides, which enables interaction with the data. In this chapter, I explore this possibility through an analysis of the artwork *They Rule*, which visualises data about legal relationships. I propose its interactive interface provides a context for accessing data in a way that directs attention to the contingency of the legal system that permits the generation of the data visualised. In the process, I argue that *They Rule* may be understood to invite a critical engagement with the constructed nature of social systems, such as the law, and how they seek to justify their foundation and maintain their validity.

Introduction

The use of the web as a site for commercial exchange and profit has increasingly undermined perceptions of the internet as a space in which the influence of established institutions and networks of power may be questioned by means of

---

This chapter is an updated and extended version of the following paper, published here with kind permission of the Chartered Institute for IT (BCS) and of EVA London Conferences: J. Pilcher, "Legal networks: visualizing the violence of the law." In A. Seal, J. P. Bowen, and K. Ng (eds.). EVA *London 2010 Conference Proceedings*. Electronic Workshops in Computing (eWiC), British Computer Society, 2010. http://www.bcs.org/ewic/eva2010 (accessed 26 May 2013).

J. Pilcher (✉)
Independent scholar, London, UK
e-mail: jdkpilcher@gmail.com

J.P. Bowen et al. (eds.), *Electronic Visualisation in Arts and Culture*,
Springer Series on Cultural Computing, DOI 10.1007/978-1-4471-5406-8_14,

"immediate access to and transparency of data" [1]. However, the visualisation of data continues to be perceived as a potent means to critique free market conduct and values. The technique, by which the morass of data online is visually transformed into orderly forms, is typically understood to enable patterns to be seen in large quantities of data that may otherwise appear to be random. This reductive approach to the visualisation of data has also been adopted towards art that employs the technique. However, it has also been argued that vast quantities of data may stimulate a different, more intuitive and less rational understanding. I propose that irrespective of which approach is adopted both involve a focus on data.

In this chapter, I argue that it is equally as important to engage with the interface provided to data as it is with the data itself. In order to explore what this may involve I shall discuss in detail the artwork *They Rule*. This work is typically engaged with as a critique of capitalism by allowing people to become aware of links between directors and companies through visually engaging network diagrams. The focus of such interpretations remains the way the data employed by the work can be used to uncover the real nature of the capitalist system. By contrast, I examine the implications of approaching *They Rule* in terms of both the data it employs and the ways in which its interface enables people to interact with the data from which meaning is sought to be extracted. I propose that it is through the work's interface that users may come to engage with the contingency of a specific social institution, which in this case is the legal system of the United States of America. I conclude by suggesting that this may lead people to reflect both on the existence of an established social system and how it might be constructed differently in the future.

Visualisation and Art

The visualisation of data has been employed by art on the internet, where it seeks to subvert the use of the web as a "mere marketing tool that turns us into transparent customers" [1]. The technique, typically understood in terms of disclosing systems that generate overwhelming amounts of data, which may otherwise remain invisible, is not confined to art that employs digital and online technologies [2].

Mark Lombardi's pencil network diagrams of crime and conspiracy networks have been described as combining the "feeling of discovering new beauty with a political undertone – the idea that the world has become less hierarchical but, on the other hand more highly networked" [3]. The earlier social system work, Shapolsky et al. *Manhattan Real Estate Holdings, a Real-Time Social System, as of May 1, 1971* by Hans Haacke employed a series of bland photographs, charts and network diagrams about the real estate holdings of slum tenements in New York. The piece is notorious because the Guggenheim found it so provocative that the museum stated it was concerned legal action for libel would be brought by those referred to in the work and refused to allow it to be exhibited.

The power of art that employs data visualisation techniques is understood in a variety of ways. Lev Manovich suggests that new media data mapping projects which are motivated by efforts to engage rationally with the complexities of the world tend to miss the opportunity to "show us other realities embedded in our own, to show us the ambiguity always present in our perception and experience" [4]. Manovich calls for work that does more than show "how to map some abstract and impersonal data into something meaningful and beautiful – economists, graphic designers, and scientists are already doing this quite well" [4].

There are a number of sites readily available online that seek to make commercial activity more transparent. Some of the currently available websites that are used to investigate corporations include: Opencorporates [5]; Duedil [6]; Companycheck [7]; and Corporationwiki [8]. The site Corporationwiki is particularly relevant to Manovich's point because it provides, for example, an interactive tool called a 'Connection Visualiser', which generates graphs that show the relationships between companies.

Manovich invites an understanding of art that employs data visualisation in terms of the sublime and the beautiful. As Jean-François Lyotard identified: "there is even something of the sublime in the capitalist economy" with its regulation by the Idea of "infinite wealth or power" [9]. While Lisa Jevbratt agrees that the argument made by Manovich against data visualisation enabling an experience of the sublime is logical she is troubled by his approach. Jevbratt comments "Many strategies for aiding people in the task of turning any large set of data into knowledge assumes that they should be presented with less information and fewer options in order to be able to make sense out of the data" [10].

Jevbratt claims support from Kant to argue that "under the right circumstances, drawing on sensations of the sublime, people can, when faced with huge quantities of data, be mobilised to make intuitive understandings of the data" [11]. In short, data visualisation should not seek to reduce, but instead increase, the amount of what is presented to view. Brett Stalbaum similarly considers that although the sublime overwhelms the viewer with data it nevertheless results in the viewer's senses being "mobilized in a special kind of cognition that allows them to carry on with the formation of an understanding" [12]. The underlying similarity of such approaches to data visualisation used in art is a focus on the data that is employed.

They Rule

The online potential of data visualisation may be approached in terms of the paradigmatic shift between the computer database and other more traditional collections of documents. The use of databases allows huge quantities of records to be quickly accessed, sorted, and reorganised. It may also contain different media types, and it allows the multiple indexing of data [13]. Moreover, because the data is in digital form it is susceptible to being manipulated very rapidly by users.

An understanding of data visualisation in such terms invites art that employs the technique to be engaged with as much in terms of the ways it enables data to be navigated as it does with the data itself. The combination of both data and the ways in which users are able to interface with that data may invite critique of an underlying (social) system that gives rise to the data that is visualised. The adoption of such an approach requires detailed attention to both the data and the ways any given piece enables people to interact with the data employed by the artwork. In this chapter, I explore what such a process may involve by means of the analysis of one particular work: *They Rule* [14].

Networks of Directors

They Rule by Josh On has been critically acclaimed for the way in which it provides the viewer with the opportunity to interact with data about major institutions and the boards of directors of some of the largest companies in the United States of America. Users are able to trace links between company directors and so discover, for example, that "the members of the boards for the so-called competitors Coke and Pepsi actually sit together on the board of a third corporation, Bristol Myers Squibb" [15]. Connections can be identified using the work by employing "the features of networked technologies, such as dynamic mapping, hyperlinking, and instant searches" [16] in combination with data.

They Rule has been described as "one of those rare sites where the content material is actually so interesting that it matches the design. If only the economic realities it depicts were as transparent and intuitive as its navigational structure, this would be a more benevolent world" [17]. *They Rule* won the Golden Nica award at the Ars Electronica Festival in 2002 for 'Net Excellence' and has been exhibited at various digital art festivals including among others, DEAF03 organised by the Dutch V2 centre and at the Whitney Biennial [18].

Networks of directors and companies can be visualised by using *They Rule*. The process of creating a simple diagram is illustrated below in Figs. 14.1, 14.2, and 14.3 with images I generated using the work. One way to start using *They Rule* is by selecting the name of a corporation from a list, which is then represented on screen by an icon of a company board table. Visitors to the work reveal the directors who are members of that board by clicking on the board table of the chosen corporation (Fig. 14.1). Once this is done, users see that that the avatars of board directors come in various sizes. A large avatar for a director indicates that person sits on more than one company board. It can be seen from Fig. 14.1 that L. John Doerr is the largest director on the board table of Amazon.com.

Clicking on individual directors reveals any other boards of which that director is a member. *They Rule* discloses that Doerr also sits on the board tables for Google and the Aspen Institute, as can be seen in Fig. 14.2.

As users move through this process the connections between directors who sit on different company boards become apparent and a network diagram may start to form. In Fig. 14.3 the board table for Google has been expanded. All the directors of the Amazon.com board, except Doerr, have been moved closer to its board table in order that it can be more easily seen that Doerr is the connection between that

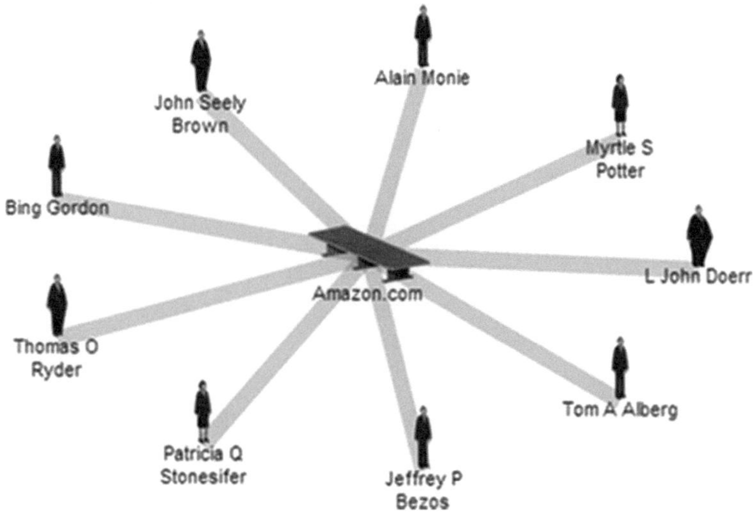

Fig. 14.1 The expanded view of the board table of Amazon.com (generated using *They Rule* [14])

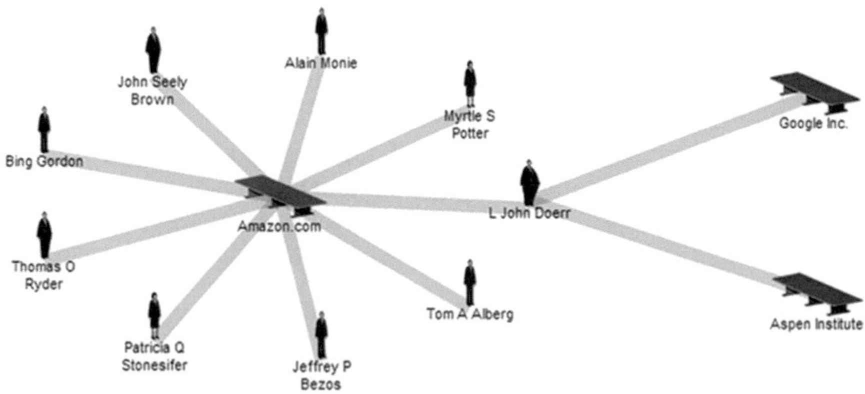

Fig. 14.2 The company boards of which L. John Doerr is a member (generated using *They Rule* [14])

company, Google and Aspen Institute. Once a user has finished exploring and arranging the connections between directors and companies the results can be saved.

They Rule is typically understood to reveal the extent to which there are interconnected networks of directors who control what is supposed to be a free-market economy. The work exploits the same principle as the database used against Slobodan Milosevic at The Hague: when enough information is gathered together it is possible to find connections that might not otherwise be apparent [15]. As such, it is understood to enable a critical engagement with capitalism. However, it is also relevant that the networks of links between companies visually depict relationships

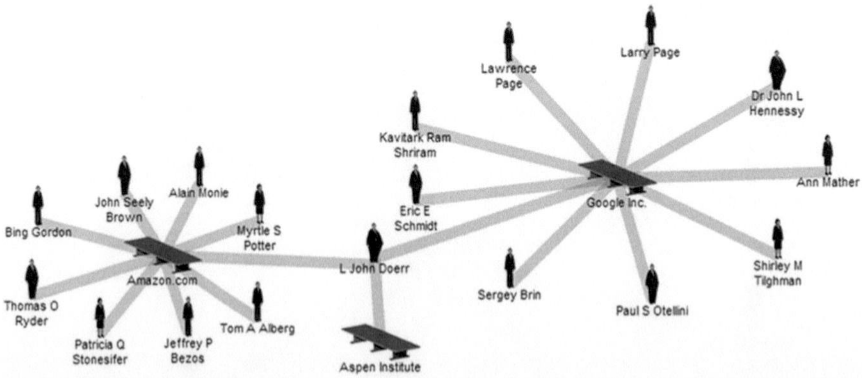

Fig. 14.3 Amazon.com, Aspen Institute and Google are connected by L. John Doerr (generated using *They Rule* [14])

whose existence depends on the legal system of the United States of America. Companies, and the concomitant roles of directors of such organisations of capital accumulation, are brought into being by reason of the operation of the law.

Corporations as Legal Entities

In law, companies are recognised as individual legal entities. As business organisations, corporations have a number of advantages because of the operation of the law. The liability of a shareholder in companies is limited to the sum of money invested by that person. A company can potentially continue to trade indefinitely. Although companies are frequently criticised for neglecting their social responsibilities in favour of making profits they are regulated specifically in order to protect investors and, more widely, the economy.

They Rule is substantially based on data that is legally required to be publicly available by being filed with a government agency, the United States Securities and Exchange Commission ("SEC"). The SEC's mission is to "protect investors, maintain fair, orderly, and efficient markets, and facilitate capital formation" [19]. As its website states, the SEC is responsible for enforcing and regulating the laws and rules that govern the securities industry in the United States and these "derive from a simple and straightforward concept: all investors, whether large institutions or private individuals, should have access to certain basic facts about an investment prior to buying it, and so long as they hold it" [19].

The SEC states that it considers the best way for investors to protect their money is to do research and ask questions. In order to facilitate this, the SEC operates a database called EDGAR, which is comprised of disclosure documents that companies are required to file. It is regularly updated and enhanced.

Although *They Rule* is acknowledged as an activist work it may be regarded as expressing a common concern with the SEC. The artwork states on its website: "*They Rule* is a starting point for research about these powerful individuals and corporations." [14]. Irrespective of whether the work is approached in terms of a representation of reality or as a platform from which to carry out further inquiries, *They Rule* and other data visualisation artworks are faced with difficulties that may significantly undermine their effectiveness.

Barriers to Data Visualisation

Online works that visualise data typically have to resolve difficulties relating to acquiring and processing data (not digitally generated) [20]. It is acknowledged on *They Rule* that the data represented by the network diagrams is in a constant state of flux, given that there are changes in the composition of boards of directors and companies may stop trading. *They Rule* does not employ a live database of board members and companies. There are three versions of the work, with the first two being based on data from 2001 to 2004. Since 2011 *They Rule* has provided the ability to interface with information about the top 1,000 companies in the United States.

The data about corporate boards provided by *They Rule* is based on information filed with the SEC. The information available from EDGAR is regularly updated because companies have statutory obligations to file information within certain specified time frames. However, ensuring that data is both current and accurate is not simply a matter of resolving technical issues associated with inputting data and converting it to a format that may be accessed. The availability of information will always depend on the extent to which there is compliance with the relevant filing requirements placed on companies. Any network which *They Rule* enables a user to locate may already be out of date by the time connections are visualised, even if only because of lag in the time within which information is required to be filed or delay in compliance with those obligations.

While the amount of data that may be accessed through *They Rule* is large, what can be visualised is selective. In terms of the myriad connections that may exist between companies and directors that could be traced and depicted, the work's scope is limited. This may be illustrated by reference to the way in which *They Rule* does not provide for visualisations of networks of shares owned in corporations. These connections are as central, if not more so, to the issue of who 'rules' the global capitalist economy as the links between company boards through directors that corporations have in common. There are extensive networks of companies connected by reason of the common ownership (which is also a legal relationship) of shares by a vast range of different people and corporate entities.

Approached only in terms of the extent to which it makes reality more transparent the continued relevance of *They Rule* may be suggested to lie, to some extent, on the assumption that any given specific network of inter-connected companies continues to exist, which may not be the case. An understanding of the work in terms of the way it enables viewers to engage with a structural reality underlying a very large quantity of data is of more force. It may be said that the work directs attention to the fact that the legal system of the United States of America allows companies that are competitors to have common directors on their boards.

Interfacing with Data

I suggest, however, that the power of *They Rule* is understated if it is understood solely in terms of opening an awareness that the legal system of the United States of America permits directors to sit on the boards of competitor companies. The generic possibility of the existence of such networks is readily conceptualised and identified without the diagrams *They Rule* enables users to construct. Once somebody is interested in knowing what boards a given director sits on it is relatively straight-forward to use information filed the SEC to obtain the relevant information. However, I propose that through the combination of its interface and databases *They Rule* goes further and actively encourages a critical engagement with the legal system of the United States.

My argument in this regard depends on an acknowledgement of the interface provided by the work to its data. The meanings available from interacting with data are not only a product of the nature and the quantity of data that is accessible in a database [21]. Manovich has discussed how the process of rendering large amounts of data into meaningful information is a product of the interface provided to users of the database. It is possible to construct a narrative by using the interface to create a cause-and-effect trajectory of seemingly unordered items.

Manovich points out that different interfaces, which provide access to the same data, may translate a database into very different user experiences [22]. However, a database and the narrative that is generated by an interface that mediates an experience of the data are not discrete and mutually exclusive [23]. Each new media work may be understood as combining both database and narrative to varying degrees somewhere along a spectrum with these two respective aspects at either extreme.

By way of contrast with *They Rule*, EDGAR presents companies as individual organisations to users of the site. The interface of EDGAR provides access to data to companies as isolated legal entities. EDGAR is invested with the authority of the state and, as such, privileges one way of accessing data about companies. The legal system that enables such companies to form networks of power is not brought into question. The process by which a website may assert such an 'unassailable voice' [24] may also be found in the context of other institutions, which I have discussed with Saskia Vermeylen in the context of museums [25, 26].

Before the Law

Those who access EDGAR, Corporationwiki or *They Rule* with a focus solely on the truth value of the data may circle around endlessly looking for combinations of companies and directors that exist. On occasion a specific set of relationships will be found, which may be pointed at as an example of a network of power privileged by the law. Understood in this way *They Rule* may be regarded as providing an example of an experience of the law that has been encapsulated by Douzinas and Gearey: "The law remains temporally and spatially deferred. Law's secret, its essence and principle is always one door further away, there is always one more guard or judge to persuade" [27]. The legal system, which lies behind and authorises the existence of the relationships visualised by *They Rule*, remains inaccessible behind seemingly endless webs of directors, companies, and the property that these entities own.

The quote from Douzinas and Gearey relates to Derrida's reading [28] of the tale told by Franz Kafka, *Before the Law* [29]. The work was published as both a short story of the same name, and as part of the novel, *The Trial*. The story concerns the encounter between a man from the country and the law. The man comes to the law, but when he asks to be admitted by the doorkeeper he is told to wait. The guard does not physically prevent the peasant from entering the doorway, but rather he suggests that the door is only one of many, all of which are guarded by other more powerful doorkeepers.

Although the man is never forcibly prevented from entering the door, he spends his entire life before it awaiting admission to the law. Shortly before his death the man is told by the doorkeeper that the door was meant only for him and that now the door will be closed for good. The law is before the man but is not present; it forever recedes to some other place and time. It seems to me that to repeatedly access *They Rule* or any other website simply in order to obtain locate an (historically) factual state of affairs, created in accordance with a given legal system, is to grow old sitting before one of the many doors of the law.

Data Contexts

The significance of *They Rule* includes the way it invites users to reflect on the process of manipulating data to form meaning through the realisation of network diagrams. It is a work that broadens the focus of attention outwards from the truth of the data to include the ways in which that data is engaged with by users of the work. It is a work that contextualises data in such a way as to invite users to think about the ways that meaning is produced by using the interface of a site [30].

In *They Rule*, as users click on the icons, the screen typically quickly becomes cluttered with data after expanding a few boards of directors. In order to enable

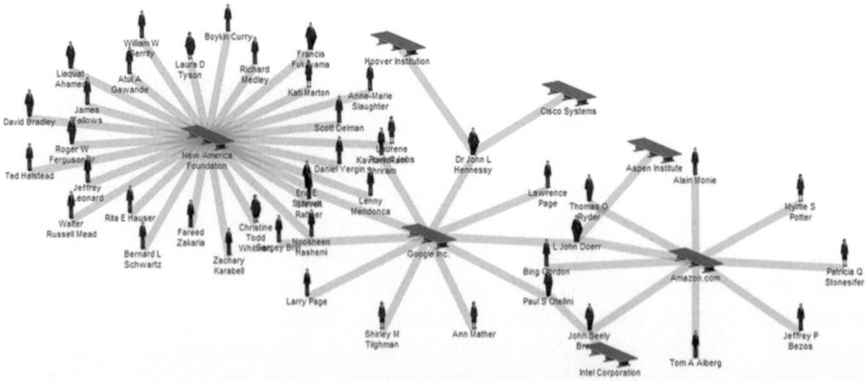

Fig. 14.4 The icons of the boards of Google, New America Foundation; and Amazon.com expanded without selection or arrangement (generated using *They Rule* [14])

networks to be visualised, users are more or less compelled to delete (unconnected) data from the screen. Furthermore, in the event that users then want the avatars and the lines of connection between them to appear in the form of a visually appealing diagram, the directors and board tables that remain have to be moved around until the desired pattern for the network is achieved. Figure 14.4 is a simple example of the sort of clutter I was able to generate using *They Rule* without being selective about data or moving it around the screen.

There are many fascinating diagrams saved on *They Rule*, but investigations using the work will not necessarily establish the existence of striking network connections. The work invites its users to become aware of the need for the selection and organisation of data in order to find and make the type of network diagrams that have been saved as part of *They Rule*. Actively using the work, as distinct from accessing previously saved diagrams, draws attention to the way in which the meaning of data is constructed. *They Rule* does not reveal that companies always have boards of directors that are interlinked. It actively encourages people to realise that both data and its manipulation are required to discover which companies **may** be connected in this way.

The likelihood of constructing a diagram with clear and visually elegant connections is improved by employing knowledge not necessarily available from the work itself. *They Rule* explicitly invites users to search elsewhere on the web. This may take place whilst a diagram is being formed and so assist in its construction, or it may occur after the site has been visited. The SEC also encourages such further investigations but it does so in the context of a very different interface than that provided by *They Rule*. EDGAR provides users with information about a given state of affairs. By contrast, I propose that amongst other things, *They Rule* provides a space to reflect on the extent to which the meanings constructed from data in an archive are a product of pre-existing knowledge or information subsequently obtained from other sources.

They Rule invites reflection about the way in which database interfaces affect data manipulation and the meaning that the process may construct. The user might begin by moving icons around on screen in *They Rule* but they may then continue with investigation to discover, for example, the historical circumstances in which the law came to recognise companies as legal entities. In its various versions *They Rule* combines this with data that relates to specific years (e.g. 2001, which is the date of the first version). As such, the work permits the exploration of data about individual companies and networks of directors, which are examples of connections that it has been possible to create at a given point in time and place by reason of the law.

The significance of the way that data about companies and directors is re-contextualised in *They Rule* at fixed points in time and the critical engagement which this invites may be approached through the work of Jacques Derrida on iterability. Derrida argues in *Limited Inc* that communication, whether by means of real-time technologies or not, is fissured from its inception by iterability [31]. In brief, for anything to be what 'it' is it must be possible for that thing to be repeated, but each repetition results in it being slightly different from the time before. Every network must in some way be the same as every other network in order to be recognised as such. Yet, at the same time, that repetition creates a difference in space and a deferral in time, which means that the meaning of any given network will be (even if only marginally) different.

In the process of moving through iterations of data using *They Rule,* users may give thought as to whether the relevant laws are still in force and whether, at the time and in the place a given network is visualised, it should still be possible for that set of relationships to be created. *They Rule* opens a space in which users may reflect on whether it is acceptable that any given network that is identified should still now exist, or indeed should ever have been allowed by the legal system to have existed.

Once attention is directed toward such issues this may give rise to a range of questions: by whose authority do individuals become directors; according to what laws are they qualified to control companies that are recognised as separate legal entities? Eventually, the user, by following ever receding lines of inquiry, may arrive at the question: by whose authority did the legal system, which enabled these entities to be created, itself come into being and continue to exist?

They Rule invites users to reflect on the persistence of the laws that enable individual networks to be brought into being and the enforcement of rights and obligations arising out of them. This process may ultimately lead to an awareness of the contingency of underlying institutions, such as the law, and how society could be constructed differently.

The Violence of the Law

The founding moment of the law is itself unfounded [32]. There is an abyss underneath the foundation of all laws given that every legal system has a point at which its own (il)legality is undecidable [33]. A successful revolution, for example, is "defined by the fact that an act which is illegal under the pre-existing legal order retrospectively becomes the source of all legality" [34]. Social institutions, such as legal systems, produce their own grounds of legitimation [35] and [36]. In order to do so, a legal system may invoke self-evident truths, God, or appeals to natural law in order to justify its authority, despite the violence inherent in its inception.

Every legal system is entangled in a bind, an aporia, which means that the law is not only founded on, but also conserved by, violence [37]. The aporia involves the need, on the one hand, for laws to be sufficiently general so as to allow them to be enforced equally and in a way that is not arbitrary [38]. At the same time, any given law also has to be responsive to individual circumstances as it must be applied in quite specific situations, which cannot all be anticipated at the time it is created [39].

The difficulty is that all laws have to be applied at a time that is different from that at which they were formulated and brought into being. The more established and general laws are, the more apparent become the difficulties associated with trying to reconcile the general with the particular. Ultimately it is impossible for the universality of laws to be maintained at all times given the need for decisions to be made as to the legal merits of individual cases. Exceptions will always need to be made in an attempt to give effect to justice in specific situations. The law is violent in asserting the authority to make and enforce such decisions.

I suggest that *They Rule* invites people to engage with the aporia of the law by judging whether it might be possible to frame laws that always prevented competing companies from having common directors. This could involve reflecting on whether it would be just to make an exception to a general rule prohibiting, for example, directors to sit on more than one board of directors and if so in what circumstances. In the process, the work opens a space in which to reflect on the violence of the law in claiming the ongoing power to frame and adjudicate on such issues.

By contrast, the univocal power of EDGAR may be understood to be one means by which the law underpins its continuing claims to legitimacy. Hillis Miller points out that Lyotard, in a "prophetic statement" [40], foresaw that the power of self-legitimation would be strengthened by "taking the route of data storage and accessibility, and the operativity of information" [41]. EDGAR, in the way it enables access to an archive of records about companies and directors, does not direct attention to the aporia of the law. In the process, the contingency of the legal system of the United States is disavowed.

In directing attention toward the violence of the law, *They Rule* is a powerful work because to do so provides "a space for reconceptualising and reliving the relationship between homogenous law and the others which it presently excludes" [42]. An acknowledgement of the violence that is inherent in the law from its inception opens up an awareness of the need to be constantly vigilant of the possibilities for the construction of a different legal system and society.

To approach *They Rule* only as allowing beautiful and accurate representations of some underlying reality is to restrict its power to uncovering the existence of specific networks or a given legal system. The effect is to focus on cognition, or determinate judgments, as the work is used to engage reductively with data in order to understand the commercial world. However, as Lyotard has argued, this is incommensurable with an attempt to bring about a transformation of reality. For Lyotard improving existing institutions such as the law requires indeterminate judgments to be made as to what is just in a given set of circumstances [43, 44]. The interface of *They Rule* invites, not simply an engagement with accurate historical data, but also reflections on the way the legal system that enables those relationships to exist could be other than the way it functions.

Conclusion

In this chapter, I have proposed that where art visualises data the focus should not only be on its data but also on the way the interface re-contextualises that data. My argument has been that through the combination of data and its interface *They Rule* allows interactions that give rise to reflections on whether a legal system should enable the creation of networks of connecting companies and if so, what exceptions there should be to the law. The work actively encourages critical questions to be asked about both specific network diagrams and the legal system that enables the generation of the data that is visualised. *They Rule* opens a space in which to consider the constructed nature of the law and the possibilities for change which that implies.

My exploration of *They Rule* suggests to me that art which visualises data about social systems may bring about an awareness of the "contingency of every form of community in the light of our separateness and singularity" [45]. This contingency exists because everything, including institutions and systems, is subject to iterability [46]. An awareness of iterability and its implications invites reflection on the way that any given social institution is susceptible to being differently constructed. By unsettling claims by social systems to historical transcendence, art that visualises data may invite transformations of society [47].

References

1. Paul, C. (2003). *Digital art*. London: Thames & Hudson. 205.
2. I have discussed the art historical precedents for the visualisation of data in so called 'new media art' and Arthur Danto's theoretical engagement with what differentiates art from other forms of representation in. Pilcher, J. (2012). Network art unbound?. *Leonardo, 45*(5), 470–471.
3. Bednarzek, W. (2005). The art and promise of network analysis. *IEEE Multimedia, 12*(3), 19–21. 20.
4. Manovich, L. (2002). *Data visualisation as new abstraction and anti-sublime*. http://www.manovich.net. Accessed 28 Jan 2013.
5. Opencorporates. http://opencorporates.com. Accessed 20 Apr 2013.
6. Duedil. https://www.duedil.com. Accessed 31 Jan 2013.
7. Companycheck. http://companycheck.co.uk. Accessed 31 Jan 2013.
8. Corporationwiki. http://www.corporationwiki.com. Accessed 31 Jan 2013.

9. Lyotard, J. F. (1991). *The inhuman: Reflections on time*. Cambridge: Polity. 105.
10. Jevbratt, L. (2004). The prospect of the sublime in data visualisations. *Ylem Journal, 24*(8), 4–14. 6.
11. Jevbratt, L. (2004). The prospect of the sublime in data visualisations. *Ylem Journal, 24*(8), 4–14. 7.
12. Stalbaum, B. (2006). An interpretative framework for contemporary database practice in the arts. http://www.cityarts.com/paulc/database/database.html. Accessed 28 Jan 2013.
13. Manovich, L. (2001). *The language of new media*. Cambridge: MIT Press. 214.
14. On, J. *They rule*. http://www.theyrule.net/. Accessed 18 Apr 2013.
15. Ippolito, J. (2002). Ten myths of internet art. *Leonardo, 35*(5), 485–498. 496.
16. Whitney Artport, On, J., & Futurefarmers. (2002). http://artport.whitney.org/exhibitions/biennial2002/on.shtml. Accessed 28 Jan 2013.
17. Johnstone, D. (2005). Webwork4: They rule. http://magazine.ciac.ca/archives/no_21/en/oeuvre4.htm. Accessed 28 Jan 2013.
18. Derivart. (2006). Derivatives, new financial art visions. http://www.artificial.dk/articles/joshon.htm and also http://we-make-money-not-art.com/archives/2006/07/art-finance-and.php#.UQbZu7_tQWY. Accessed 28 Jan 2013.
19. United States Securities and Exchange Commission. http://www.sec.gov/. Accessed 28 Jan 2013.
20. The chapter in this volume by Michael Lesk discusses both the opportunities of, and the barriers to, digitisation.
21. The chapter in this volume by Steve DiPaola engages with a number of ways in which an interface may impact on the meaning taken from data.
22. Manovich, L. (2001). *The language of new media*. Cambridge: MIT Press. 181.
23. Paul, C. (2007). The database as system and cultural form: Anatomies of cultural narratives. In V. Vesna (Ed.), *Database aesthetics: Art in the age of information overflow*. Minneapolis/London: University of Minnesota Press. 100.
24. This is a term used by. Walsh, P. (1997). The web and the unassailable voice. *Archives and Museum Informatics, 11*, 77–85, p. 77 to refer to the authoritative meaning given by museums to cultural objects.
25. Pilcher, J., & Vermeylen, S. (2008). From loss of objects to recovery of meanings. *M/C Journal, 11*(6).
26. Vermeylen, S., & Pilcher, J. (2009). Let the objects speak: Online museums and indigenous cultural heritage. *International Journal of Intangible Heritage, 4*, 60–71.
27. Douzinas, C., & Gearey, A. (2005). *Critical jurisprudence: The political philosophy of justice*. Oxford/Portland: Hart Publishing. 357.
28. Derrida, J. (1992). Before the law. In D. Attridge (Ed.), *Acts of literature*. New York/London: Routledge.
29. Kafka, F. (1994). *The trial*. London: Penguin.
30. The chapter in this volume by Jeremy Gardiner and Anthony Head, in its discussion of the artwork *Light Years: Jurassic Coast*, also comments on the way in which an interface may bring into question perceptions of those who are interacting with a work that employs a database.
31. Derrida, J. (1988). *Limited Inc*. Evanston: Northwestern University Press.
32. Sokoloff, W. W. (2005). Between justice and legality. *Political Research Quarterly, 58*(2), 341–352. 343.
33. Beardsworth, R. (1996). *Derrida and the political*. London/New York: Routledge. 25.
34. Davies, M. (2001). Derrida and law: Legitimate fictions. In T. Cohen (Ed.), *Jacques Derrida and the humanities: A critical reader*. Cambridge: Cambridge University Press. 225.
35. Lyotard, J. F. (1984). *The postmodern condition: A report on knowledge*. Manchester: Manchester University Press.
36. Miller, J. H. (2001). Derrida and literature. In T. Cohen (Ed.), *Jacques Derrida and the humanities: A critical reader*. Cambridge: Cambridge University Press.

37. Douzinas, C., & Gearey, A. (2005). *Critical jurisprudence: The political philosophy of justice*. Oxford/Portland: Hart Publishing. 71.
38. Sokoloff, W. W. (2005). Between justice and legality. *Political Research Quarterly, 58*(2), 341–352. 342.
39. Derrida J. (1990). 'Force of law': The mystical foundation of authority. *Cardozo Law Review, 11*: 919–1045. As Derrida points out at p. 961: "Each case is other, each decision is different and requires an absolutely unique interpretation, which no existing, coded rule, can or ought to guarantee absolutely".
40. Miller, J. H. (2007). Performativity as performance/Performativity as speech act: Derrida's special theory of performativity. *South Atlantic Quarterly, 106*(2), 219–235. 223.
41. Lyotard, J. F. (1984). *The postmodern condition: A report on knowledge*. Manchester: Manchester University Press. 47.
42. Davies, M. (2001). Derrida and law: Legitimate fictions. In T. Cohen (Ed.), *Jacques Derrida and the humanities: A critical reader*. Cambridge: Cambridge University Press. 228.
43. Lyotard, J. F. (1985). *Just gaming*. Minneapolis: University of Minnesota Press.
44. Readings, B. (1991). *Introducing lyotard: Art and politics*. London/New York: Routledge.
45. Gere, C., & Corris, M. (2008). *Non-relational aesthetics*. London: Artwords Press. 21.
46. Beardsworth, R. (1996). *Derrida and the political*. London/New York: Routledge. 18.
47. Shortly before publication my attention was drawn to the fascinating work by Blakely, R., & Raphael, S. *The rendition project*. http://www.therenditionproject.org.uk/. Accessed 23 May 2013. This "acts as a hub for accessing publicly available data relating to the global system of rendition and secret detention". It provides a site that may be used to investigate the way the corporate structure has been used by the CIA to obscure its ownership of aircraft linked to renditions.

Chapter 15
Face, Portrait, Mask: Using a Parameterised System to Explore Synthetic Face Space

Steve DiPaola

Abstract New technological tools are allowing the authorship of computer-generated faces that can easily move between very realistic, to cartoon-like, to painterly or even iconified, in both depiction and movement. These systems are beginning to allow artists, scientists and scholars to explore the notion of "face space", whether as a realistic emotive character, an artistic portrait or symbolic facial mask, in new ways that give a deeper understanding of how the concept of faces work as an expressive and communicative medium. We overview our computer facial suite of tools, which using a hierarchical parameterisation approach, gave been used as a comprehensive framework in several interdisciplinary, industrial and cognitive science applications.

Introduction

We overview our interdisciplinary computational face authoring tools that build a parameterised synthetic facial rendering and animation system for learning, artistic, expression and research systems. It allows artists, scientists and scholars to move through a space of faces from artistic to realistic. With new computational systems it is possible to conceptually compose and explore in higher-level conceptual spaces – with our system that space is facial emotion and depiction. We are interested

---

This chapter is an updated and extended version of the following paper, published here with kind permission of the Chartered Institute for IT (BCS) and of EVA London Conferences: S. DiPaola, "Face, portrait, mask – using a parameterized system to explore synthetic face space." In A. Seal, J. P. Bowen, and K. Ng (eds.). EVA *London 2010 Conference Proceedings*. Electronic Workshops in Computing (eWiC), British Computer Society, 2010. http://www.bcs.org/ewic/eva2010 (accessed 26 May 2013)

S. DiPaola (✉)
Simon Fraser University, 250 - 13450 102nd Avenue, Surrey, BC V3T 0A3, Canada
e-mail: sdipaola@sfu.ca

J.P. Bowen et al. (eds.), *Electronic Visualisation in Arts and Culture*,
Springer Series on Cultural Computing, DOI 10.1007/978-1-4471-5406-8_15,

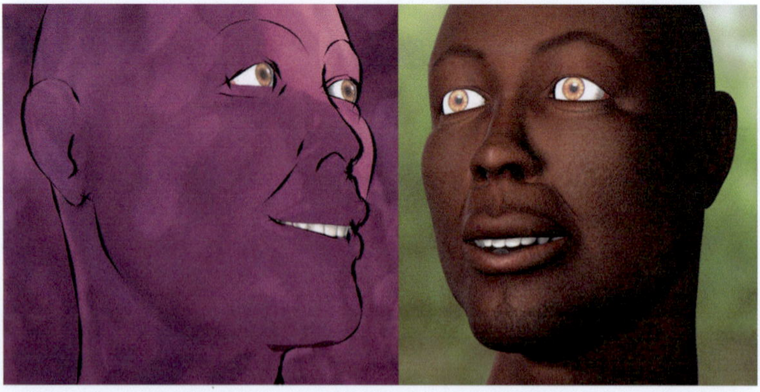

Fig. 15.1 Same face model rendered (1) as a portrait and (2) realistically; stills from the autism research work

in building art and science systems that support exploring these spaces and in particular report on our software-based facial toolkit and resulting experiments using parameter spaces in face based new media.

With new technological artistic tools that allow us to author computer generated and manipulated faces that can be as real or as abstract or as iconified as we choose, what aesthetic and cultural communication language do we elicit? Is it the historically rich language of the fine art portrait – the abstracted artefact of the human face (Fig. 15.1)?

What happens when this portrait animates, conveying lifelike human facial emotion – does it cease to be a portrait and instead move into the realm of embodied face – when it begins to emote and feel and possibly react to the viewer? Is it then more in the language of the animated character, or as we make it photo-realistic, the language of the video actor with deep dramatic back-story, or simply as real as a person on the other side of the screen? A viewer cannot be rude to a portrait but can feel that they are being rude to an interactive character in an art installation. When does it become not an embodied face nor portrait but a mask – the icon that speaks of face but is never embodied? Masks also have a deep cultural, historic and ethnic language far different from that of human faces or art portraits, more eastern than the western portrait. Iconised faces such as the smiley face or the emoticon face takes the mask full through to the western modern world of technology.

With animated and interactive artwork, what is to stop a piece from fluidly moving between all these forms? This chapter explores the synthetic face in art and science in all its forms and more importantly explores the virtuality of the face, for true art has one soul that can be manifest in many realisations and aesthetic communication forms.

The chapter will discuss where these forms differ and intersect both culturally and in relation to new technology (i.e. – is the robot face more a face or more a mask, what about a game avatar). We then overview our computer facial application toolkit, which, using hierarchical parameterisation can provide a comprehensive and open ended synthetic facial depiction, expression and communication system via: (1) the use of higher-level parameters which apply lower level ones in combination and with constraints, and (2) defining time-based parameters that control facial actions. The system allows for experiments and questions that can be explored by traditional and new media artists, art historians, cognitive scientists and other scholars.

Faces and Parametric Face Space

The face is one of the most important surfaces we deal with. It is the showcase of the self, displaying our sex, age, and ethnic background as well as our health and mood. It also is our main vehicle for transmitting our feelings and explicit communications to others. We are all experts in interpreting and communicating through the human face. We can recognise the face of someone we knew in the fifth grade 20 years later. We can read volumes through one glance into our father's stare. Ironically, this universal expertise comes with little common understanding of what the mechanisms are that govern such talent [1]. Most people cannot even describe the features of a loved one's face accurately nor can they dissect how it is that they know when someone is lying to them; they just know.

Visualising and, more recently, animating faces have long been a challenge to visual artists, animators and communication professionals. The advent of computer-based tools opened a new chapter for this challenging task. Computer-generated face-based multimedia presentations play an increasing role in applications such as computer games, movies, communication, online services, as well as artistic endeavours. Delicate features and expressive capabilities make human faces both difficult and attractive to visualise and animate using computer based tools. There are many authoring tools for facial animation, but they are based on general modelling and animation techniques such as key framing, point morphing or boning systems. Very few can be used in an intuitive way specific to facial creation and understanding. A comprehensive and specially designed system for facial authoring can be used by expert and novice alike to explore how we use and perceive human facial communication, as well as to create and control synthetic faces for a myriad of industry, art and research applications. The primary requirement for developing such a system is to build in the knowledge space face modelling, both anatomically and behaviourally. We introduce FaceSpace as a basic face model in the form of a multidimensional parameter space that is a language for and controls facial geometry and behaviour. Our face-based systems, described later in the chapter, are built on top of the FaceSpace model.

After earlier work by Parke [2], many researchers have worked on different approaches to modelling the human face for creation and recognition purposes [3]. One common approach to facial animation is to model the underlying structure and interaction of bones, muscles and skin [4, 5]. This approach is based on the idea that simulating the underlying mechanisms of facial changes will lead to realistic visual results.

However, the complexity and subtlety of the human facial system along with the hypersensitivity of the viewer to the state of the face make this approach computationally prohibitive for interactive applications. Furthermore, a simulation approach is difficult to apply generally to a character with features that are impossible within real-world constraints, such as oblong eyes as well as other non-real or cartoon-like features. Another limitation of the simulation approach is that a particular expression is composed only of physical state (i.e. a set of tensed muscles, etc.) and is not linked to any semantic framework such as the associated emotional state of the character (e.g. sad, happy, quizzical, etc.)

Parameter Spaces

Direct parameterisation models [3] address the computational problems of simulation modelling by applying simple and efficient transformations of a head model through simple parameters such as eye-width, lip-thickness, or jaw-open. These parameters encapsulate high-level knowledge about the combined effect of skin and muscle movement along with knowledge of the underlying mesh topology. They define the state of the head and act as "dimensions" in a "face space".

We believe that direct parameterisation can provide a comprehensive and effective authoring system if extended through: one, the use of higher-level pseudo-parameters which apply lower level parameters in combination and with constraints in order to produce complex expressions, and two, defining time-based parameters that control actions and behaviours as an addition to the spatial geometry (for example parameters that control how expressions are performed or what typical head movements are to be created based on a personality type).

Major contributions of this model are the inclusion of temporal and spatial parameters (e.g., expressions over time), intuitive parameter spaces (e.g. personality space), and hierarchical parameters with different levels of abstraction (e.g. heroicness built on top of simpler behaviour types). Besides the face-centric knowledge approach and weighted towards communication and behaviour of faces, another goal of the FaceSpace model has been to decouple output details from the face-centric core, allowing for intuitive face oriented authoring which can be applied at any level, to any model, with any emotion. For instance, first add this expressive audio sequence to this cartoon face type but add more goofiness with a little heroicness to the personality as it animates through the given sequence outputting it as a 3D rendered movie; now take that same 'knowledge' sequence and try it on a realistic face with a more angry tone outputting it as image based movie. Also, because the multidimensional parameters are aligned in a face centric way it is possible to affect a face from another knowledge or expression data stream, for instance one application of FaceSpace has been to remap emotional channels of music to emotional aspects of the face [6, 7]. Newer extensions to the parameter space approach include depiction controls which allow fine art painterly portrait depiction, which is aligned both with artistic painterly knowledge (the cognitive painterly process) as well as knowledge from vision and perception science (how humans see and perceive). In the following sections, we briefly review some related works, describe the basic concepts of FaceSpace, and introduce some FaceSpace-based systems.

The FaceSpace Environment

The essence of the FaceSpace environment is a set of numerical parameters, each of which controls some aspect of a character's face, expression, emotion, movement and depiction. Parameters are typically unitised vectors, each representing a subroutine, which performs some low level complex transformations on the part of the face it controls. Because parameters are abstracted from their low-level techniques they have mathematically rigorous properties such as the ability to be combined, subtracted, and added together, while still maintaining controllable and repeatable effects to their face model.

Parameters can be varied independently to modify specific features of the face (e.g. cheekbone prominence, forehead height, jaw-width, etc.). This authoring paradigm is highly flexible, allowing a wide range of applications. The entire set of parameters can be exposed individually for full low level authoring control or a sub-set of these parameters with constraints can be presented to a novice user for customisation and personalisation. Higher-level constructs can be imposed on the basic parameter scheme by combining low-level parameters to create application-specific descriptive elements. For example, a user could modify the character's appearance from "sophisticated" to "silly" with a single control that simultaneously modifies eye separation, forehead height, nose scale, etc.

Groups of high-level parameters can act on the face simultaneously, creating lip-sync speech with one channel while specifying an astonished look for the whole face on another independent channel. Because of their associative properties and their abstraction from the actual face topology, results typically always look natural, although naturalness can be arbitrary as you move away from realistic – either towards fine art portrait depiction or cartoon exaggeration. In fact, one of the driving forces behind our system is the ability to explore different dimensions of face spaces, to begin to understand faces as a language just like the language of cinema or painting or modern jazz. FaceSpace allows the concept of faces and face expressions to be explored at intuitive level.

Face System Examples

Once a believable, controllable and communicative face environment is available to artists, developers and researchers, we believe new ranges of social-based applications are possible. Most computer based communication systems such as internet-based websites (using HTML, PHP, ASP), information kiosks or ebooks (using PDF, Director, Flash) for example are informational in nature, not socially-based. People however (like teachers, aquarium or science experts, or museum guides) use more socially-based techniques to convey their message – they use their passion for the subject, narrative techniques, lesson plans, flexible content depending on audience or audience feedback, eye contact, humour, voice modulation. We believe these socially-based techniques using a communicative face system can open up more human centric applications in many areas, such as:

- Video games that can convey the subtle dramatic nuances more common to cinema thereby extending games to a wider audience and into the educational and adult realms [8].
- Chat systems that use voice and facial expression for better and deeper communication,
- Education systems that bring the passion of a teacher or expert scientist into distance education.
- Art and science research facial systems to better understand how humans perceive, receive and create social and emotional communication and expressions with faces.

For our example sections, we will concentrate on applications that support more engaging art, learning and research facial systems and will discuss five ongoing application prototypes.

Storytelling Masks

Art and science museums (including zoos and aquariums) mostly still use static displays of text and graphics to explain the deeper historical or scientific concepts about the nearby artefact (i.e. a portrait, a model of a planet) and often the display is not read. The situation is very different when a human guide gives a presentation about that same artefact, engrossing the viewers in that subject as they use narrative, real-time and socially based deliveries.

Can this experience be mimicked with interactive systems allowing students, who do not have geographically or financial access to a science facility a similar level of engagement and educational experience. Can a facility create a better level of engagement when a human guide is not available? We will describe two active prototypes:

Museums of anthropology, especially in North America, display a variety of artefacts from "first nations" (Native Americans). Among the most attractive of these artefacts are masks and head figures presented on objects such as totem poles. Songs, myths, and stories relate these figures to the history of the people who made them. Computer-generated characters with those figure-forms who also tell their stories and sing their songs are appealing and informative for the viewers and also provide a new means of creativity and expression for the native artists. Combination

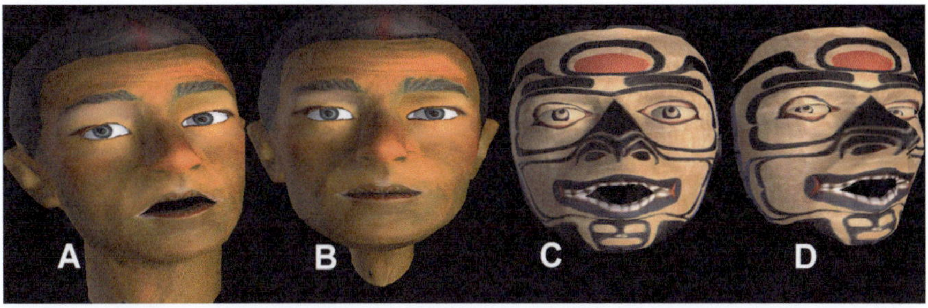

Fig. 15.2 Frames from "storytelling mask" interactive, where a real artist's voice, passion and expression first introduces himself (**A**) transform into his artwork (**B**, **C**) tells it's back story with full voice and expression (**D**) and can return to his persona to interactively give interactive and educational content (**A**)

of FaceSpace design and scripting tools provide such a creative environment. In this specific case we have begun working with the Parks Department of British Columbia, Canada and the indigenous community to create a museum display where a virtual version of an artist appears and tells the story of his work, can virtually turn into the artwork – a native mask – and have a virtual version of the art tell its story (see Fig. 15.2). Because all this is under computer control it is possible to create many of the perceptual and educational techniques that a live human guide/artist could achieve including:

- Introduction: the ability to announce and bring the audience to the work,
- Narrative style: conveying the back-story, passion, timing and expressiveness;
- Multiple contexts: via interactive control, the material can be tailored to different age levels, different perspectives and focus areas, including updating the material;
- Presentation: the exhibit can feel more like a live presentation: for instance the interplay between artist and artefact – i.e. the mask is not displayed until the artist gives sufficient context; afterward the mask returns back to the artist/guide for additional commentary;
- Q&A: at session end, the viewers can pick questions for more tailored commentary.

Evolving Faces

With goals and techniques similar to the *Storytelling Mask* project, *Evolving Faces* attempts to use facial agents to better engage viewers into the content, but in this case the agents are used to describe complicated scientific details, as well as to create agents that are also an integral part of the content. Their appearance evolves to tell the story of humanity's migration out of Africa, based on new DNA techniques. Our FaceSpace systems allow a designer to create head models that correspond to various stages of human evolution, and assign different types of

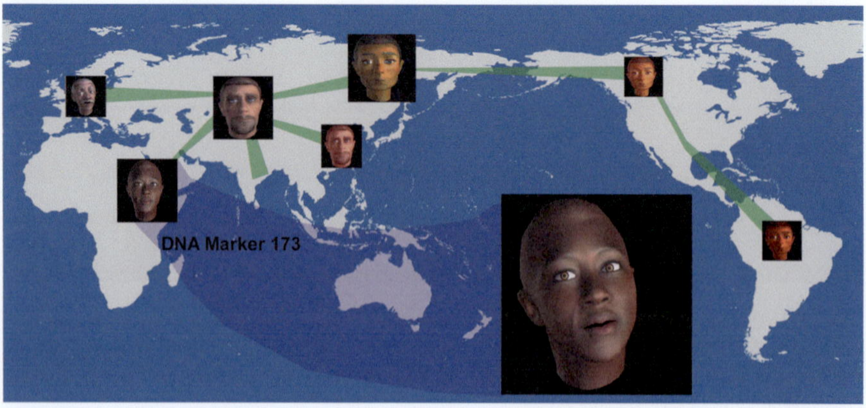

Fig. 15.3 Screenshot of *Evolving Faces* where emotive talking faces describe the DNA science of human migration out of Africa, actively "morphing" facial types

behaviour (e.g. coarse or fine) to them to be expressed during talking or interaction. Such characters are ideal for science booths or online learning. Adding simple or complicated artificial intelligence can improve the behavioural capability of the characters for real-time interaction. The display uses voices, change and expressive faces and maps rather than charts and text.

A screen shot from the *Human Migration* interactive is shown in Fig. 15.3. It demonstrates that complicated subject matter can be engagingly presented (how we migrated from Africa some 50–100,000 years ago, with migration evidence from DNA marker and facial type). Viewers can click on a specific face/area to be told the story of that DNA marker, or click on a migratory path. An evolving face will then explain the science facts of the journey. We have currently begun trials using a similar approach where marine scientist from different parts of the world could discuss their active work through facial systems next to marine displays in a major aquarium. The visitors would receive current (updated monthly) information from the expert, while the scientist would keep their privacy by just supply audio narrative to the education staff of the aquarium, who would put a face persona and behavioural state to the science narrative.

MusicFace Application

Music-driven Emotionally Expressive Face (MusicFace) by DiPaola and Arya, [4, 7] is a multimedia application based on our facial systems, developed to demonstrate the concept of Affective Communication Remapping, i.e. transforming emotional information from one communication medium to another. Emotional information is extracted from a piece of music by analyzing musical features such as rhythm, energy, timbre, articulation and melody which then automatically drives

a

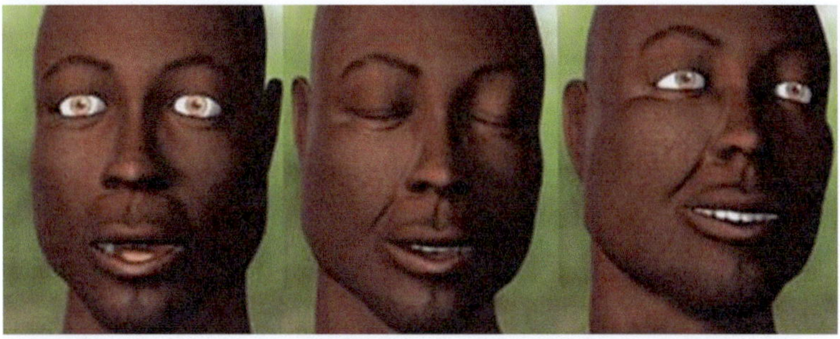

b

Emotion	Feature	Value
Fear	Tempo Sound Level Articulation	Irregular Low Mostly non-legato
Anger	Tempo Sound Level Articulation	Very rapid Load Mostly non-legato
Happiness	Tempo Sound Level Articulation	Fast Moderate or load Airy

Fig. 15.4 (**a**) Sample stills from MusicFace's music controlled animations and (**b**) Example of the parameters of music features and emotions that automatically drive the face animation

emotional face animation (Fig. 15.4). Fine art versions of this work have been shown in galleries in NYC and Los Angles. We have been in discussion with a theatre owner to use the system to drive (computer projected) set design in real-time, as the face reacts to the music much as a dancer might.

Autism Communication Research

Autism is one of the most commonly diagnosed developmental disorders in children. It is characterised by severe impairment in the domains of social, communicative, cognitive, and behavioural functioning. Despite inconsistent profiles across individuals with autism, recent research reflects a developing consensus that the central behavioural symptom of autism is the impairment of social behaviour, such as the social use of gaze, failure of joint attention interaction, lack of interest in peers, difficulty initiating communication, preference for solitary play [9]. Autism affects from 5 % to 17 % of the population.

Research has shown that individuals with autism fail to understand the emotional state expressed by another person [10]. Whether individuals with autism rely on isolated parts of the face, such as eyes or bushy eyebrows to recognise faces rather

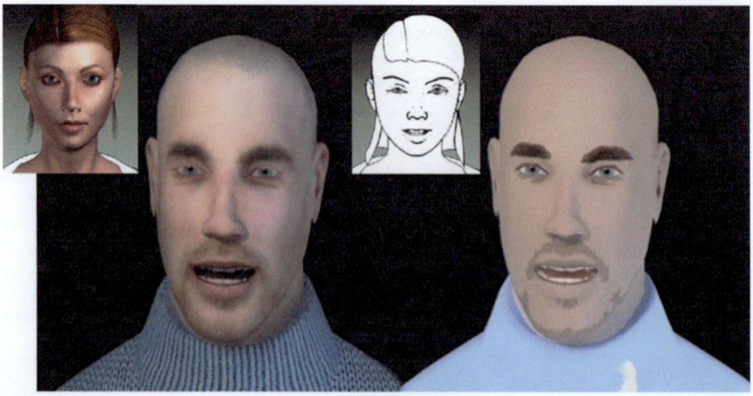

Fig. 15.5 Stills from our facespace based TASIT social sequences using expression units of 3D rendered realistically (*left*) and low texture rendering (*right*) for the male, and realistic and line drawing for the female

than whole faces is not clear. That is because static images do not provide realistic assessment of face processing and emotion recognition.

Our research is in studying social competency and facial expression awareness in autistic children by combining our configurable 3D facial communication input system with a real-time eye gaze measurement system. This set of studies involves varying the visual and social complexity of a dynamic 3D face in discrete steps to measure facial awareness and social competency (emotional recognition). The goal of the work is to both better understand this issue from a scientific and clinical point of view and to build a computer based communication and serious game systems that take advantage of the clinical and technical results of the research.

Our study investigates whether different facial image rendering styles, as well as varying levels of expressions scenarios (such as percent of direct eye gaze and normal to dampened mouth movement) can affect autistic children's visual perception and their social competence. We are using 'The Awareness of Social Inference Test' (TASIT), to measure results. The TASIT test comprises videoed sequences that can measure social and emotion recognition. By presenting each social sequence under controlled face animations with differing rendering styles and levels of expression situations on high developed autistic teenagers, we can firstly monitor eye-gaze patterns and retention time and secondly assess how well they correctly identify the emotion associated with TASIT animated sequence. Since children can be distracted by details, one study in progress seeks to understand face-to-face comprehension by varying the level of realism and detail in a facial sequence, comparing the same communicative short sequence with three different rendering styles: realistic detail or removing details (textures), or line drawing of the face (Fig. 15.5).

Currently most autistic individuals miss important eye/eye brow expression cues by concentrating their gaze on the quick movement in the mouth area

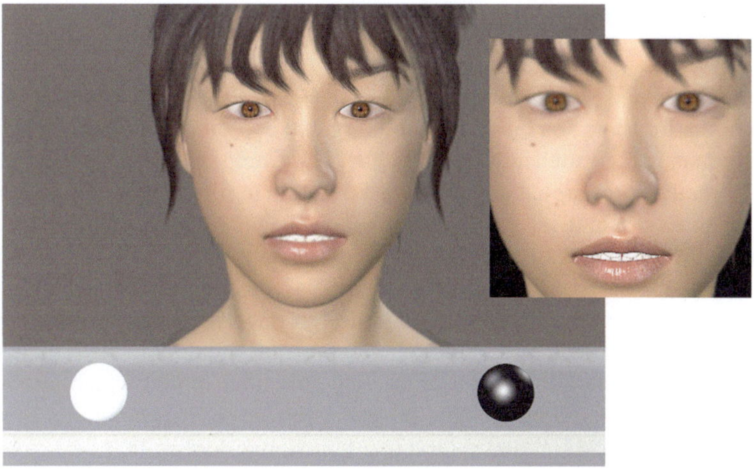

Fig. 15.6 Two stills from our study using 64 movie variations of eye/mouth blurring where a living talking characters can gaze at either white or black ball in a simple 'pick the correct ball' quiz. Early results show that it is possible to significantly influence children with autism gaze away from the moving mouth where they typically over look to the eyes when the mouth is blurred and the eyes are sharpened (*Left*) compared to the no blurring or if we reverse the blurring (*right*)

(during speech). One completed experiment systematically dampened mouth movements in perceptually valid ways, so the lip-syncing looked natural, but was progressively less overwhelming to the subject. At the same time, the eye area was sharpened. We than tracked at what level of mouth movement dampening a balanced eye gaze between eye, mouth and other head areas returned (see Fig. 15.6). Initial results showed that mouth dampening with eye sharpening draws the eye gaze of autistic individuals towards the subject's eyes, giving them a heightened awareness of, say, someone's eye gaze and emotional communication. The techniques are being refined to create, 1 day, a simple smartphone or tablet app. for parents. If instructions seem particularly tricky, for instance for daily dressing, they could pull out their phone and show a video of the instructions on the phone. Our app. would process the video of the parent's face to emphasise the eyes and de-emphasise the moving mouth. The phone would then be handed to the child to watch and better retain.

The goal is to understand how the complicated factors of social complexity versus visual complexity affect face-to-face communication in autistic subjects. Because autism is on a spectrum, individuals vary widely in how they perceive faces. Being able to deconstruct, output and modify expression units at any level of the animated 3D face animations allows us to conduct very detailed and modifiable experiments as well as easily to transfer knowledge from the experiments to consumer learning, to develop serious games toolkits like the smartphone app. described above for autism communication and understanding.

Art and Vision Research: Rembrandt's Genius

Portrait artists and painters in general have developed over the centuries a little understood, intuitive and open methodology that exploits cognitive mechanisms in the human perception and visual system [11]. Compared with the original live sitter or their photograph, the portrait artist is able to filter and manipulate using what cognitive scientists only recently have begun to understand about our visual and perception system including shape and edge detection, centre of vision focusing and eye movement as well as colour temperature relational space. Our research, by first collecting through interviews and reference data a 'soft' qualitative knowledge space of how portrait painters achieve their craft, converts that soft data into a parameterised computer model which sits on the rigor of vision, image processing and facial knowledge. This computer model is the basis for our XML based interactive knowledge toolkit that has a twofold interdisciplinary goal. First, it is able to generate a correlated space of painterly rendered portraits from input photographs in a large style set which has applications in computer based rendering, often called Non Photorealistic Rendering (NPR), for games and multimedia. Second, it can be used by traditional and new media artists, art historians, cognitive scientists and other scholars as a toolkit to explore interdisciplinary questions about the act of portrait painting. For the latter area, it can begin to bridge these areas and show how artistic knowledge can lead to discoveries about cognitive processes and the human mind. It can lead to an understanding of the deeply creative, intuitive and human process of creating visual art.

Our research system uses a parameterised approach to approximate a knowledge domain for the painterly rendering of portraits. The knowledge domain uses fuzzy knowledge rules gained from interviews with oil portrait painters, data from the traditional 'portrait painter process' combined with human vision techniques and semantic models of the face and upper torso. By knowledge domain, we mean that the system attempts to act on the same semantic level as a human painter, such as human vision techniques, facial planes and expression, tonal masses, and colour temperature control. The system also relies on an historical, open methodology that artists have created and passed down from one to another. This qualitative knowledge is parameterised into an n-dimensional space of low-level rules that can be accessed at different semantic levels. Non-professional photographic imagery of people's heads is used as input. Figure 15.7 shows the process, starting at the top left. This can be summarised as collecting a knowledge space of the painterly process (qualitative at this point – lower left) from interviews with artists, reference materials and user studies, then (centre) parameterising the knowledge using known computer science and cognitive science models and methods, into the NPR system (lower left). This can be used for better and wider NPR results as well as to acquire data and clues to human vision and perception theory. This can be mapped back into the system.

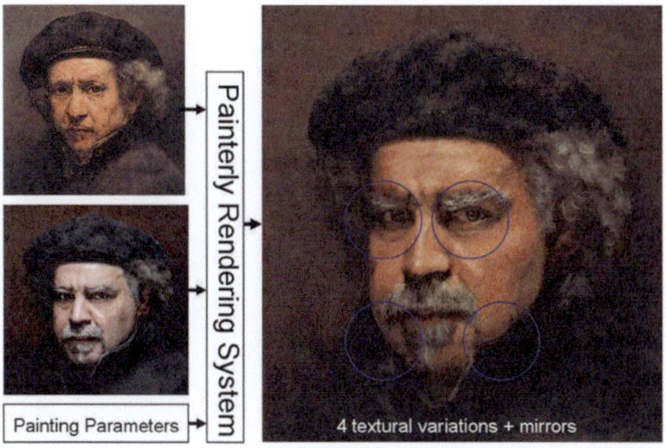

Fig. 15.7 Using the painterly extension of our facespace system for scholarly analysis of a Rembrandt portrait, to test the intuited vision science, through painterly portrait simulation with eye tracking

A painted portrait differs from a photograph in that the artist intentionally selects only specific regions for fine detail (i.e., narrow versus broad brushwork) and the level of contrast of edges. Although artists and art critics have claimed that these choices guide the viewer's eyes, this claim has not been thoroughly tested. In past studies of viewers gazing at original works of art, interpretation is complicated because regions of fine and coarse detail also differ in other ways (e.g., whether they are foreground or background). Here we monitored the gaze of participants viewing photos and paintings of the same portrait view, inspired by Rembrandt's portraits (e.g., *Self Portrait with Beret*, 1659). The paintings were created by a face space based non-photorealistic rendering technique to mimic Rembrandt's style [12, 13]. In each painting, four regions of interest were selected for systematic variation in level of detail: left versus right eye region in finer detail and left versus right collar region in finer detail. Participants viewed each portrait for a 5 s period, in the context of viewing many portraits rendered in a wide range of styles, assigning ratings of artistic merit to each portrait. Analysis of the gaze patterns showed that fewer fixations were made overall when viewing paintings than photographs, and that viewers' eyes were both attracted to and dwelt longer in the eye region of a portrait that was rendered in finer detail. Even regions of paintings that were rarely fixed on directly (i.e., collar regions below each face) nevertheless guided the gaze of viewers, specifically enhancing the salience of eyes rendered in fine detail on the same side of the portrait. This implies that Rembrandt and other master portraitists used an effective implicit theory of gaze direction [13]. Results from this study, which show how artists can significantly influence a viewer's eye path by using edge placement and detailing in specific areas to better convey a mood or narrative, can be used in many fields. Besides the benefit directly to art history criticism and understanding, we are using these techniques for better face to face communication tools for autism systems (above) and in affect mood and narrative in game characters (Fig. 15.8) [14, 15].

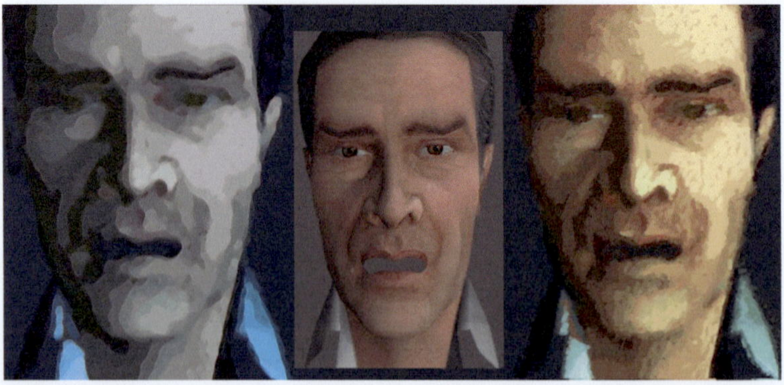

Fig. 15.8 Lessons learned from our Rembrandt work to create mood/narrative emotion through artist techniques, is being used within video game research to show that the same game character (*middle*) can appear to have different moods by changing the palette to cool colors and round brushes (*left*) compared to warm palette with jagged strokes

Conclusion

It is well known that we humans have specific neuro-programming for recognising and interpreting faces. It is hoped that we can use the FaceSpace systems to better understand the conscious and intuitive meaning of faces and the universal language they appear to represent (facial meaning, inter-relationships and expressions) for use in the arts, cultural theory, science research and communication/expression systems. We hope that by creating a development kit that our team or other developers can use and customise, it will be possible to gain a greater understanding of how we communicate and beguile using our faces. We also hope to create an authoring environment that will let us take advantage of this new understanding via intuitive synthetic facial systems. In this chapter, a modular multi-dimensional parameter space for face creation, animation and depiction is described as an underlying structure that will allow for this face-centric, knowledge-based, approach. We try to look at this parameter space not as a pure graphic model but an expressive and behavioural one for a "communicative face". The foundation of our model is a hierarchical geometry. Parameters are encapsulated within objects in a tree structure that allow local control of level-of-details both for animation and depiction.

The main advantages of our model are modular design, efficient and local control of geometric and depiction details, and inclusion of behavioural time-based extensions. Future work will focus on a more systematic parameterisation of facial emotions and personality in order to simplify navigation through the spatio-temporal face space. This modular face centric approach, we hope allows for more open ended research and exploration into the language of facial expression which hopefully can be used to both provide intrinsic knowledge to scholars and allows for creating new and innovative human centric expression systems.

References

1. McNeil, D. (1998). *The face*. Little Brown and Company. New York.
2. Parke, F. I. (1998). Computer generated animation of faces. In *Seminal graphics: Pioneering efforts that shaped the field* (pp. 241–247). New York: ACM.
3. Parke, F. I., & Waters, K. (2008). *Computer facial animation*. A. K. Peters. Natick, MA.
4. Kähler, K. (2007). *3D facial animation – recreating human heads with virtual skin, bones, and muscles*. VDM Verlag Dr Mueller e.K. Saarbrücken.
5. Li, L., Liu, Y., & Zhang, H. (2012). A survey of computer facial animation techniques. In *2012 International Conference on Computer Science and Electronics Engineering (ICCSEE)* Vol. 3, (pp. 434–438). Hangzhou, China.
6. DiPaola, S., & Arya, A. (2004). Affective communication remapping in music face system. In *Electronic imaging and visual arts*. London: EVA Conferences International.
7. DiPaola, S., & Arya, A. (2006). Emotional remapping of music to facial animation. In *ACM SIGRAPH video game symposium proceedings*. Boston, USA: ACM.
8. Arya, A., DiPaola, S., & Parush, A. (2009). Perceptually valid facial expressions for character-based applications. *International Journal of Computer Games Technology 2009*: Article ID 462315. doi:10.1155/2009/462315.
9. Rose, F., Lincoln, A., Lai, Z., Ene, M., Searcy, Y., & Bellugi, U. (2007). Orientation and affective expression effects on face recognition in Williams syndrome and autism. *Journal of Autism and Developmental Disorders, 37*(3), 513–522.
10. Joseph, R., & Tanaka, J. (2003). Holistic and part-based face recognition in children with autism. *Journal of Child Psychology and Psychiatry, 44*(4), 529–542.
11. Cavanagh, P. (2005). The artist as neuroscientist. *Nature, 434*(7031), 301–307.
12. DiPaola, S. (2009). Exploring a parameterized portrait painting space. *International Journal of Art and Technology, 2*(1–2), 82–93.
13. DiPaola, S., Riebe, C., & Enns, J. (2010). Rembrandt's textural agency: A shared perspective in visual art and science. *Leonardo, 43*(2), 145–151.
14. Seifi, H., DiPaola, S., & Arya, A. (2011). Expressive animated character sequences using knowledge-based painterly rendering. *International Journal of Computer Games Technology, 2011*, 7. doi:10.1155/2011/164949.
15. Seifi, H., DiPaola, S., & Enns, J. T. (2012). Exploring the effect of color palette in painterly rendered character sequences. In *Proceeding 8th annual symposium on computational aesthetics in graphics, visualization, and imaging* (pp. 89–97). Annecy, France.

Chapter 16
Facebook as a Tool for Artistic Collaboration

Sophy Smith

Abstract Since its foundation in 2004, Facebook has become a major force in social networking, claiming to give people "*...the power to share and make the world more open and connected.*" How can these tools be used by artists to connect and share with collaborators? Can Facebook be used to aid creativity, as a collaborative artistic tool or environment? Based on a practical performance-based research project 'Feedback', this chapter focuses on the use of Facebook as a tool for creative collaboration and explores a number of possible models of artistic collaboration using the online social network.

Introduction

Since its foundation in 2004, Facebook has become a major force in social networking, stating its mission as *"to give people the power to share and make the world more open and connected"* [1]. The success of Facebook has been unprecedented, allowing millions of members to upload photographs and share links and videos, as well as personal information about themselves and their lifestyle preferences. How can these tools be used by artists to connect and share with collaborators? Can Facebook be used as an aid to creativity, as a collaborative artistic tool or environment?

This chapter is an updated and extended version of the following paper, published here with kind permission of the Chartered Institute for IT (BCS) and of EVA London Conferences: S. Smith, "The creative uses of Facebook as a tool for artistic collaboration." In A. Seal, S. Keene, and J. P. Bowen (eds.). *EVA London 2009 Conference Proceedings*. Electronic Workshops in Computing (eWiC), British Computer Society, 2009. http://www.bcs.org/ewic/eva2009 (accessed 26 May 2013).

S. Smith (✉)
Institute of Creative Technologies, De Montfort University, Leicester LE1 9BH, UK
e-mail: ssmith05@dmu.ac.uk

J.P. Bowen et al. (eds.), *Electronic Visualisation in Arts and Culture*,
Springer Series on Cultural Computing, DOI 10.1007/978-1-4471-5406-8_16,

The social tools of Web 2.0 offer to be "*powerful platforms for cooperation, collaboration and creativity*" [2] (p. 278) and this developing technological infrastructure not only allows people to access digital content relatively cheaply and simply, but also makes it simpler to distribute and share that work. Web 2.0 technologies have led to an explosion in the amount of user generated content, created in and then shared with groups with similar interest areas. The book *The Art of Participation* describes an 'explosion' of user generated content that has unleashed a new media environment, replacing the mass consumption of commercial culture with mass production of cultural objects [3] (pp. 67, 71). New tools of production and distribution are making the distinctions between producer and consumer, professional and amateur, less clear. Sporton reflects how, as these distinctions break down, we are presented with new challenges for creative practice [3] (p. 61). Some present user generated content as a threat to professional practice [4], but this is not necessarily the case. As part of the wider society, professional artists also create content as users and are members of the social networking sites that host such content. Rather than being threatened by the increase in creative content arising from users, how could artists employ the context of user generated content as an opportunity for artistic collaboration, harnessing the new tools to support their practice?

In the same way that the Internet has led to changes in the nature of social relationships [5] (p. 21), it has also caused alterations in the character of working relationships and processes. A number of benefits have been outlined for different players in the user generated content chain including professional content creators, for whom they see the benefit as "*reinventing business models to compete with free web content*" [5] (p. 54). However, these benefits may not be restricted to new models for business environments that support user generated content. For example social networking sites have also led to new models of collaboration across the sectors. This social phenomenon and the new ways of creating, sharing and interacting it enables may have far reaching cultural impacts [5] (p. 64).

This chapter focuses on Facebook as it is, to date, the most commonly used social online tool in the UK. According to the 3-month Alexa Internet traffic rankings, Facebook is currently the second most popular site in the world, with 44 % of global Internet users visiting the site for the 3 months to January 2013 [6]. Although recently it seems that users have been leaving Facebook, it may remain a useful tool for artistic collaboration. The research results from a practical project carried out by the author in 2010, while undertaking a collaborative performance project 'Feedback' with the live art company Assault Events. The Feedback Project investigated the potential of online social media to create and develop collaborative artistic content, exploring new methodologies for collaborative creation supported by online social media, asking how Facebook could support collaboration between artists in different geographic locations and working in different disciplines and how it could be used to create and develop collaborative artistic content. This chapter is intended as a starting point for discussions around the creative use of online social media, establishing a number of possible models of artistic collaboration using Facebook.

Facebook as a Collaborative Tool

When discussing the effects of the web, focus is often on the tools rather than the way in which those tools are being used. The potential uses of web tools are not always implicit in the tools themselves (for example [7], p. 14). This is certainly true in the case of Facebook, which though originally created as a social network has been used by a number of different professional groups across different sectors as a tool to support collaboration.

For example, Facebook has been used for worker collaboration and improved communication with customers [5] (p. 63). Business-related reports and research papers also offer examples, such as harnessing the online content available in Facebook to assist idea creation for collaborative brainstorming [8] (p. 1). Facebook has been used as groupware for relationship building to improve the performance of Global Virtual Teams [9]. It was found that Facebook can provide an 'immense degree' of support through multimodal communication tools, as well as through the ability to add-on third party applications including schedules and tasks, polling, discussion and file sharing [9] (p. 6). They suggested using Facebook tools to increase social capital, using Status updates and the Notification facility to develop trust, photo-sharing and tagging to develop reciprocity, the Profile, Friends and Newsfeed to develop group identification and the Wall to develop a shared language [9] (p. 7).

The potential of Facebook as a collaborative tool is also being explored within the science sector. In one system designed for distributed collaboration, the use of structured updates was inspired by status updates in social networking sites such as Facebook [10] (p. 38). As biomedical research becomes increasingly interdisciplinary, collaboration is ever more crucial to project success. Science professionals are beginning to use social networking technologies including Facebook to extend professional networks, locate experts and find collaborators. Social networking sites the authors claim, have the potential to make the process of finding scientific collaborators quicker and more effectively than traditional methods [11].

Facebook is also being considered as a tool for creative collaboration. Members of The Open University Design Group established a Facebook Group to explore and evaluate its potential for creating a community of distance design learners by using it to mirror the characteristics of a traditional design studio [12] (p. 2). The project found that student interaction was characterised by a number of themes – communication and facilitation, identity and community, awareness, confidence and enjoyment [12] (p. 4). The idea of using Web 2.0 technologies for virtual design studio teaching was also explored by Shao et al. [13], who reflected that the flexible structure of Facebook is readily adopted by those for whom social networking sites are an integral part of daily life, and that the openness provided by Web 2.0 provides an innovative foundation for Virtual Design Studios [13] (p. 919).

Facebook and Artistic Creation

Facebook Groups and Pages have been used by many groups of artists to share and develop work. Some of these have been more informal, created to connect artists, for example the Facebook Page 'Creative Collaboration' and the Facebook Group 'Creative Artists'. These groups have had a number of purposes including self-promotion, networking and the provision of critical feedback. 'Creative Collaboration' [14] described itself as a collaborative page for connecting artists of all abilities and invites members to share their work in the Discussions section. Similarly, the 'Creative Artists' Group [15] was formed to connect artists interested in collaboration and sharing industrial knowledge. Some Facebook Pages existed to support specific collaborative projects, for example two education-led pages, Media Arts and Drama Collaboration group [16] (run by undergraduate students from Plymouth University to share project ideas and create collaborative opportunities) and Arts Collaboration Lab at Columbia [17] (established by the School of the Arts at Columbia University to enhance an intensive collaborative arts programme). Other Facebook pages, for example 'Collaboration Project – Los Angeles' [18], act to support a larger physical group who meet face-to-face but who use Facebook as an online dimension to their physical meetings.

Some groups have used Facebook as a creative environment within which to create artistic work. A collaborative poetry project took place on Facebook involving 19 poets from five cities who contributed to a multimedia poem [19]. The project investigated the potential and limitations of creative collaboration using Facebook, and how Facebook can affect the form and content of the created work, although lacking an analysis. Students at the University of California, Santa Barbara, have also explored the idea of using Facebook to create content, as part of their undergraduate studies. Students were asked to choose a literary work and treat it according to research paradigms prevalent in other disciplines, resulting in a project entitled "*Romeo and Juliet: A Facebook Tragedy*" which explored non-linear storytelling and character development, using Facebook to make the text more interactive for users [20].

To date, the creative uses of Facebook have split mostly down amateur/professional lines. While the worlds of professional business, science and education have explored the use of Facebook as a collaborative tool, this is not so true of the professional arts sector. Professional arts organisations primarily use Facebook to share information about their work online, and it has tended to be amateur groups that use Facebook to share and develop work or to meet other collaborators. As the amateur and education groups have demonstrated, Facebook and other online social tools can offer more than merely providing alternative ways for arts groups and organisation to promote their work with a larger audience, and may have the potential to support creative collaborative production. In 2010, the Feedback Project took place to research this potential use.

The Feedback Project

The Feedback Project investigated the potential of online social media to create and develop collaborative artistic content, rather than as a teaching and learning tool. It explored new methodologies for creative collaboration supported by online social media. Feedback was developed and delivered by the University of Ulster's dance outreach team Satellite, in partnership with artists from dance company Assault Events, with support from the Institute of Creative Technologies, De Montfort University, UK. Two further education colleges in Northern Ireland nominated a group of ten students with music or dance specialisms to take part in the project. Under the guidance of four professional artists/facilitators they became co-creators and performers in a new piece of performance work, supported by using the social networking site Facebook as a virtual studio environment. The professional artists facilitated the participant's engagement with the project and did not collaborate in the creation of the performance work themselves. Data on the project was gathered through analysing the use of the Feedback Group (http://www.facebook.com/groups/374472110584/) and through responses to questionnaires and interviews with participants during and after the project.

All participants worked together on the same project, and through existing online social media sites were able to share and develop ideas and creative 'products'. These were then drawn together under the guidance of Assault Events to create a piece of original performance produced using the material that had been collaboratively created or developed. Many of the project participants were new to collaborative devising processes, and online tasks were devised to support them through the creative process. 95 % of the participants had previously collaborated with other people to make creative work, but always face-to-face. 95 % of project participants used online social media, primarily for social networking and watching videos, as well as for finding out about bands and learning drama techniques.

The project was structured as four stages, including both synchronous and asynchronous collaboration. There were four face-to-face workshops and 13 online creative tasks, the latter undertaken each week that there was no face-to-face workshop. In the first phase, an initial workshop day for briefing and training was held with artists from Assault Events and a social media worker. In Stage 2 both groups continued to engage in creative tasks and activities via a Facebook closed group, facilitated online by artists from Assault Events. A new creative task was set weekly. Thirteen tasks were divided almost equally between music, dance and joint music and dance. Two more face-to-face workshops were held to draw together the ideas and tasks. In the third stage of the project, the participating groups met for a '*Creative Think Tank*' day where they joined together to collaborate, share and develop their experience and create more work to share online. The final stage of the project saw the launch of the final online archive.

Facebook was chosen to be the central hub to the project because it was familiar to most participants, and would therefore support natural working processes and provide a "*common context or framework within which to interact*" [21] (p. 27). For this reason, other online networks tools for collaboration, for example LinkedIn, Teambox, and Basecamp, were not used, since they were unfamiliar to the participants.

Use of the Feedback Facebook Group

Data on the use of the Feedback Facebook Group was collected in a number of different ways. Following the project, the Feedback Facebook Group was analysed for data primarily relating to task type and collaborator response. Collaborators completed questionnaires before, during and after the project. Individual participants and staff from the participating colleges were interviewed.

By creating a Facebook Group for the project, Assault aimed to offer an online studio where collaborators could share and develop ideas without having to physically meet, open 24 h a day. Members could drop in and see work, share ideas with each other, leave video clips and pictures, play music, ask questions and chat. A number of Facebook tools were offered: the Discussion, Wall, Photos, and Video tools.

The Discussion Tool

Through the Discussion tool on the Facebook Group, collaborators were set 13 online tasks to support and develop the collaborative process of creation, sharing and development. They included tasks such as generating concepts and ideas, dance recap, discussion boards for photo and music upload, online research, publicity design and advance preparation. Tasks were completed within the Facebook Group, using either the Discussion or the Photos tool.

The 13 tasks included three different types of activity – creating new ideas through online research, developing ideas shared in workshops, and developing ideas shared online. All tasks were set through the Facebook Group and all responses were to be shared through the Group. The most popular tasks were those that involved the creation of ideas using online research (73 collaborators participated), followed in popularity by the development of ideas shared online (ten participants). The development of ideas shared in workshops was least popular (four participants).

Of the activities that involved the creation of new ideas through online research, the most popular were those that were related to general concept development, followed by joint music and dance activities and then music activities. There were no specific online dance activities set, but the activities involving the development of ideas shared in workshops were solely dance-based. Tasks that involved the development of ideas online were all either music, or music and dance-related.

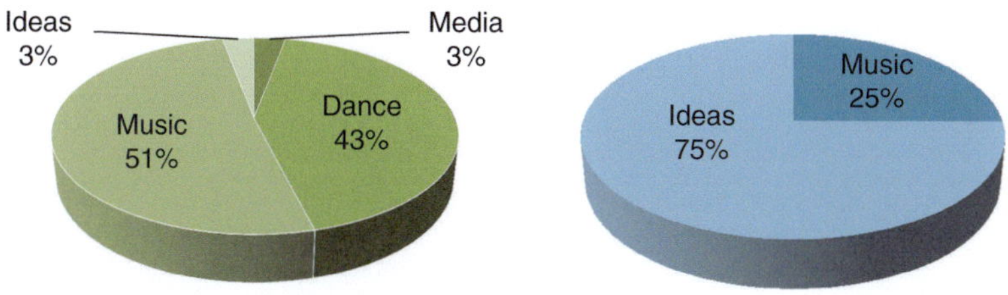

Fig. 16.1 Use of the photos tool, relating to the creative process. *Left*, by facilitators; *right*, by collaborators

The Wall

I categorised the posts to the Wall as relating to course content or course context, following Schadewitz and Zamenopoulos [12]. Content-related posts included topical messages, specific questions, relies to questions, advice on problems and solution suggestions. Context-related included work learners done, learning problems, complaints, enjoyment and mood. I sub-divided these activities into dance, music or the project concept. A 'social-related' category was also included, for posts that were not specifically related to the project.

The Wall was mostly used for socialising between the collaborators, general discussions and chitchat. However, nearly a quarter of wall posts involved discussions and comments around project content, and about half of these were specifically music-related. The Wall was least used for discussing dance content, but a couple of posts did discuss the more contextual aspects of dance elements, for example expressing enjoyment about the dance workshops and the uploaded dance videos. Content related postings included all the music-related Wall activities and 72 % of project concept-related posts. Only 25 % of dance-related activities were concerned with content.

Photos and Video Tool

The Photos page included 57 photographs uploaded by both facilitators and collaborators (Fig. 16.1). The majority of these documented the collaborative process and were images taken during physical workshops, creating an archive to aid reflection. However, some of the photos were part of the creative process itself and were uploaded by collaborators as part of one of the online tasks relating to theme development.

The Videos page included 23 videos, all uploaded by the project facilitators (Fig. 16.2). Three related to process and the film of the final product. Although collaborators uploaded photographs, they chose not to upload any videos. Possibly the choice of media created and uploaded may have been influenced by the ease of use of each of the technologies. Many mobile phones have integrated cameras, making it easier for participants to create and upload photographs, where video technology was more difficult to access.

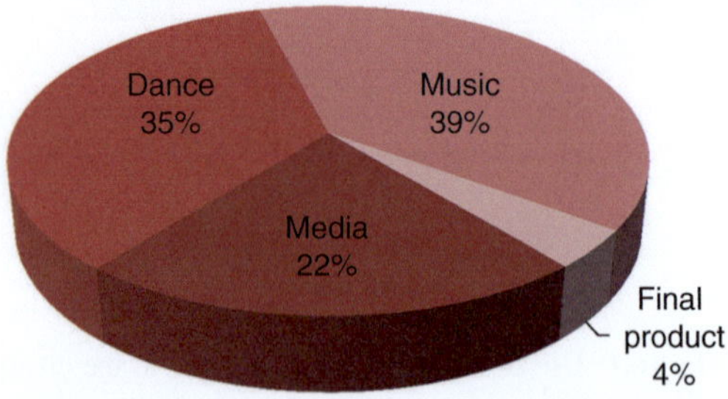

Fig. 16.2 Use of the videos tool, relating to the creative process, by facilitators

How Was Facebook Used as a Tool for Artistic Collaboration?

From analyzing which tasks were the most popular and how the different tools were used in this project, it is possible to draw some conclusions about using Facebook as a tool for artistic collaboration.

Patterns of Task Response

The Feedback Facebook Group was most useful as a vehicle to develop the overall concept of the piece, share ideas about the work and create a bond between collaborators separated geographically. As is evident from the data presented above, the most popular tasks were those that related to the generation of new ideas and the development on the concept of the piece, followed by tasks that related to the sharing of creative content. The online tasks that involved general project concept development or music activities were designed to be completed online, so online discussion naturally followed. In terms of discipline specific activities, dance tasks were the least favourite activity. The majority of online tasks that involved dance activities were related to physical work that either had to be done in physical groups and uploaded or reflected on online, and this proved problematic as collaborators found it difficult to physically meet. When responding to project questionnaires, the majority of collaborators communicated that they preferred to do the online tasks individually, identifying that it was difficult to complete tasks in groups due to scheduling issues. As these were the least favourite tasks, they were also therefore the tasks with the lowest response.

Different Tools Supported Different Parts of the Collaborative Process

During the project, tasks were set and responded to using the Discussion tool, and the Wall was used to strengthen social relationships between collaborators as well as to support discussion relating to project content and context. The process of Wall posting has been identified as developing shared meaning between collaborators [9]

(p. 8). The strength of relationships developed through Wall postings may have been relatively weak, but weak ties may still significantly increase an individuals' ability to solve problems [12, 22]. Half of the wall posts related to social comments and general chit-chat rather than specific information about the project, and this use of the Wall helped to give the collaborators the feeling of being a member of a larger group and to enhance engagement with the project as a whole.

The Photos and Video tools were used to aid reflection and assist review, to document the process by creating an archive, and to share ideas and points of inspiration. Respondents to the project questionnaires identified how the online videos had helped collaborators to recall what had taken place in the physical workshops. One of the group leaders commented, "*It's a great idea, purely because if they [the participants] rehearse/record something, and it's constantly there on Feedback, they can keep going to it… keeping an online archive has been helpful.*" Photographs and videos were shared and commented upon, an activity that Tan et al. [9] suggest may develop a habit of reciprocity. Such dialogical modes of interaction encourage collaborators to engage in more reflective modes of conversation [23] (p. 87), and I would suggest that the process of commenting on each other's work supports the development of the skills of reflection as well as critical analysis. The Photos tool was popular for sharing initial ideas between the collaborators, and unsurprisingly the video tool was the ideal medium to share audio and visual work such as dance and music. Another of the Feedback group leaders reflected on the importance of the video tool: "*it's great for them* [the participants] *to see what the other collaborators are doing… and it raises competition as well – it's great!*" The ability to host and share a variety of media types through different tools was important in supporting collaboration between artists from different disciplines: they could share their work in a range of ways. Collaborators added content in whatever format they felt was most suitable and they were able to discuss it in the same forum. This enhanced and supported communication between collaborators working in different disciplines, as it offered an independent, non discipline-specific environment in which to share a range of work in different ways.

Support for Different Working Methods

By working separately and then later sharing ideas collaborators can avoid many of the communication problems that can arise when people work together from the outset [24] (p. 160). The asynchronous nature of the Feedback Facebook Group clearly benefitted the creative collaborative process. The term 'collaboration' is often misused to mean all collaborators working on the same part of the project at the same time [25] (p. 426). But in collaborative projects, individuals are not all necessarily equal in activity intensity or responsibility. The Feedback Facebook Group supported different intensities of interaction between collaborators and different levels of input over the duration of project and allowed the collaborators to move back and forth between working with others and working alone: one of the "*holy grails of collaboration*" [21] (p. 27).

Convenience of Access

The act of joining the Feedback Facebook Group enabled the collaborators on the Feedback Project to be in direct contact with each other without having to physically meet. They could keep in touch with each other, share and develop ideas both before meeting in person and between rehearsal periods, and establish and build project momentum. Collaborators were able to participate whenever and from wherever it was convenient for them. Where creative collaboration is long-term and distributed, as in the Feedback Project, breakdowns in creativity can be alleviated, as individual collaborators have a context for their work [10] (pp. 31, 38). 'Activity awareness' enables collaborators to monitor and understand the development and selection of ideas and task allocation within the group [10] (p. 36). 'Ambient awareness' of peer activity helps to build trust, a key element in collaboration [12, 26]. The asynchronous nature of the Feedback Facebook Group and its ability to archive practical work and discussions supported such ambient awareness.

Conclusion

Successful collaboration is not dependent on the features and functions of the chosen technology, but on how well the technology integrates with and supports the processes of the users, enabling sharing and coordination [21] (pp. 22–23). It is evident that different artistic groups that use Facebook for artistic collaboration have different models of online collaboration, depending on their specific needs. However, it is possible to determine a number of characteristics and potential uses.

The different Facebook tools, including the Wall, Discussion, Photos and Video, can be used to support different elements of the collaborative and creative process. Facebook's independence of space and time enables it to support collaboration across different geographical locations and in different timeframes. Facebook Groups enable collaborators to meet to share and develop ideas without having to physically interact, whenever their time permits. Collaborators can work alone or together and are able to share work and ideas. This can provide many of the benefits of a physical studio but without the costs and complications of getting collaborators together in one place at a certain time. Facebook tools to host and share a range of media, coupled with the use of discussion groups to facilitate communication and understanding, can support collaboration, enhance project ownership, and help to create and develop a concept for creative work from a range of different disciplines.

The Feedback Facebook Group logged and retained ideas and discussion, and archived work. This repository feature enables collaborators to access inputted and uploaded material in order to reflect or recap, so that collaborators remain engaged with the progress of the project even when they are not active in it.

Clearly, using Facebook as a tool to support creative collaboration also poses challenges. Difficulties in meeting face-to-face restricted participants' abilities to collaborate in the virtual space, and their freedom to respond to tasks was affected by the tools used. However, although it is not without challenges, Facebook can be used as a tool to support collaboration in creative projects.

The Feedback Project was the first research project to explore the potential of online social media to create and develop collaborative artistic content, using Facebook as the central project hub. This restricted focus could be widened, for example to explore and develop the interplay between collaboration in the physical space and that in the virtual space. I plan to develop this through a research project that these research findings to explore how UGC could be used for artistic collaboration in the creation of a wholly professional piece of work.

It has been observed that many of the characteristics we consider new to the Internet are not new at all [27] (p. 11). Distributed collaboration on an artistic product is not new, but the Feedback Facebook Group provided a new environment to support collaborative creation by enabling collaborators from different arts disciplines to work both synchronously and asynchronously in a flexible and cost-effective creative space. Online collaboration may not be uncommon in other sectors, but within arts practice it offers a new way to work collaboratively. It is the everyday nature of these online relationships that makes it surprising that social media tools are not generally used for this purpose. We shall wait and see how artists develop their use of Facebook and other online social tools, perhaps not only to do what they are already doing in a different way, but also to do new things in new ways.

References

1. Facebook. Facebook. Product/Service, Facebook, USA. http://www.facebook.com/facebook. Accessed 26 Jan 2013.
2. Fraser, M., & Dutta, S. (2008). *Throwing sheep in the boardroom*. Chichester: Wiley.
3. Manovich, L. (2008). Art after Web 2.0. In R. Frieling et al. (Ed.), *The art of participation: 1950 to now*. London: San Francisco Museum of Modern Art/Thames & Hudson.
4. Keen, A. (2008). *The cult of the amateur*. London: Nicholas Brealey.
5. Vickery, G., & Wunsch-Vincent, S. (2007). *Participative web and user-created content*. Paris: OECD Publishing.
6. Alexa. Site info: Facebook.com. http://www.alexa.com/siteinfo/facebook.com. Accessed 21 Jan 2013.
7. Shirky, C. (2010). *Cognitive surplus*. London: Penguin.
8. Gartrell, M., Beach, A., Ramanarayanankrishnaniyer, J., Xing, X., Han, R., Lv, Q., Mishra, S., & Seada, K. (2010). Integrating wikipedia and facebook context into collaborative e-brainstorming. Department of Computer Science, University of Colorado at Boulder/Nokia Research Palo Alto. USA. http://www.parc.com/content/events/attachments/Gartrell_revised_Group10.pdf. Accessed 21 Jan 2013.
9. Tan, W. K., Nguyen, T. T. D., Tha, K. K. O., & Yu, X. (2009). Designing groupware that fosters social capital creation: Can facebook support global virtual team? In *Proceeding Americas conference on information systems (AMCIS 2009)*, paper 525. http://aisel.aisnet.org/amcis2009/525/. Accessed 21 Jan 2013.
10. Farooq, U., Carroll, J. M., & Ganoe, C. G. (2007). Supporting creativity with awareness in distributed collaboration. In *Proceeding 2007 international ACM conference on supporting Group Work (GROUP'07)* (pp. 31–40). New York: ACM.

11. Schleyer, T., Spallek, H., Butler, B. S., Subramanian, S., Weiss, D., Rattanathikun, P., & Mueller, G. (2008). Facebook for scientists: Requirements and services for optimizing how scientific collaborations are established. *Journal of Medical Internet Research, 10*(3), e24. doi:10.2196/jmir.1047.
12. Schadewitz, N., & Zamenopoulos, T. (2009). Towards an online design studio: A study of social networking in design distance learning. In *International associated of societies of design research conference (IASDR)*. Seoul, 18–22 October 2009.
13. Shao, Y., Daley, L., & Vaughan, L. (2007). Exploring Web 2.0 for virtual design studio teaching. In *Proceeding Australian society for computers in learning in tertiary education conference*. Singapore.
14. Creative Collaboration. Creative collaboration. Facebook, USA. http://www.facebook.com/creativecollabz. Accessed 24 May 2011.
15. Kiu, R., et al. Creative artists group. Open group, Facebook, USA. http://www.facebook.com/groups/53578934168. Accessed 27 Jan 2013.
16. Plymouth University. Media arts and drama collaboration. Open group, Facebook, USA. https://www.facebook.com/groups/185413704790/. Accessed 15 July 2011.
17. Arts Collaboration Lab. Arts collaboration lab at Columbia. Facebook, USA. http://www.facebook.com. Accessed 15 July 2011.
18. The Collaboration Project. Collaboration project – Los Angeles. Facebook, USA. http://www.facebook.com/collabproject. Accessed 14 Jan 2013.
19. Hamidi, F., & Baljko, M. (2010). Collaborative poetry on the Facebook social network. In *Proceeding 16th ACM international conference on Supporting Group Work (GROUP'10)* (pp. 305–306). New York: ACM.
20. Skura, H., Nierle, K., & Gin, G. (2008). Romeo and Juliet: A Facebook tragedy. In A. Liu (Ed.), *Literature+: Cross-disciplinary models of literary interpretation*. PBWorks. http://english149-w2008.pbworks.com/Romeo-and-Juliet:-A-Facebook-Tragedy. Accessed 24 Jan 2013.
21. Coleman, D., & Levine, S. (2008). Collaboration 2.0. In *Happy about, silicon valley* (p. 27). Cupertino: HappyAbout.info.
22. Thompson, C. (2007, September 5). Brave new world of digital intimacy. *The New York Times*. http://www.nytimes.com/2008/09/07/magazine/07awareness-t.html. Accessed 21 Jan 2013.
23. Bennett, R., & Dziekan, V. (2005). The omnium project: Forming online communities of students, educators and professionals to explore collaborative modes of creative interaction and practice. In *Proceeding 8th international electronic theses and dissertations symposium (ETD2005)*. Sydney.
24. Dennis, A., & Williams, M. (2003). Electronic brainstorming: Theory, research and future directions. In P. B. Paulus & B. A. Nijstad (Eds.), *Group creativity* (p. 160). New York: Oxford University Press.
25. Bennett, R., & Polaine, A. (2006). Online collaboration and creative processes. In *Enhancing curricula: 3rd international conference*. Lisbon: Centre for Learning and Teaching in Art and Design.
26. Kvan, T. (2001). The pedagogy of virtual design studios. *Automation in Construction, 10*(3), 345–353.
27. Silverstone, R. (1999). What's new about new media? *New Media and Society, 1*(1), 10–82.

Part V
Visualising Heritage

Suzanne Keene

This Part presents recent work on graphical representations of the past. Artists' impressions have long been a major way to present archaeological sites to the public – but the arrival of the technologies of 3D virtual reality has been irresistibly enticing [1]. With deep roots in cinema, including the horror genre [2], the technologies of visualisation have been used to present reconstructions of famous sites the world over, from Stonehenge to Pompeii to the Dunhuan caves in China. The Computer Applications in Archaeology (CAA) conferences have charted their developing use [3]. Now, convincing reconstructions are becoming easier to create, using game engine software, and virtual archaeology is moving to become a respectable academic research tool [4], worthy of public funding; the UK Heritage Lottery Fund offers an invaluable guide to good practice in using digital technology [5].

Looking further into the past, many philosophers and authors have found different ways of visually representing time itself. Historically, notions on depicting the passage of time developed from Euclid onwards, and particularly by Descartes in the seventeenth and Newton in the eighteenth centuries. The passage of time and events have been represented cyclically, as in analogue clock dials; in a linear fashion – timelines, often used for historic representations; as a stream; as arrangements of words; and in many other ways. In Chap. 17 the authors explore the history of the representation of time in visual space. As a working example of how digital media could be used for this, they constructed a time based interface to a database of a collection of wallpaper, fabric and designs from the nineteenth and twentieth centuries. The interface enables curators and other users to interrogate the database in various time related ways, such as to investigate when floral patterns were most popular.

While virtual 3D reconstructions of buildings are commonplace, the recreation of landscapes is much less familiar. Since the mid-1990s, researchers have virtually reconstructed places such as gardens, archaeological landscapes and the Everglades, using ever more sophisticated and usable game engine software. The authors of Chap. 18 recount how they employed the game engine, CryEngine, to reconstruct a whole landscape constructed for William Beckford in the nineteenth century on his estate near Bath. This historic designed landscape has now vanished almost without trace beneath later building and development. Using documentary sources and historical evidence that described the features of the landscape, such as a kitchen garden, a picturesque cottage, a pond and a grotto, an interactive installation was made for the Beckford Tower Museum.

The installation is popular with users, who are extremely interested to discover the relationship of the tower to the wider designed landscape. Visitors stay longer in the museum, and pass on recommendations to their friends.

Experimental archaeology is well established as a means of testing hypotheses on how people in the past went about practical activities, such as fabricating implements out of flint and stone or constructing Iron Age round houses. Virtual reality has also been widely used, but mostly to illustrate what sites may have looked like in the past when the buildings were complete and in use.

Part III, above, explores the application of motion capture; here, Chap. 19 explores the use of these technologies to investigate the interaction of people with their physical environment, specifically recreating domestic activities likely to have taken place in these buildings, such as floor sweeping, fetching water, querning and making bread. The movements of subjects carrying out these activities were recorded in a studio virtual reconstruction and in a reconstructed Iron Age round house in Butser Ancient Farm Facility in Hampshire, using motion capture apparatus and software. This enabled movements such as floor sweeping techniques in the studio virtual environment to be compared with that in the 'real' Iron Age house. From this the authors were able to infer how these movements were affected by the different kinds of reconstructed environment. For example, people are aware of the physical structures and environment around them, a point also illustrated by Soltani in comparing embodiment in airborne imagery of places with the sterile depiction of street layout in some modern maps (above, Chap. 4).

References

1. Renfrew, C. (1997). Foreword. In Virtual archaeology: Great discoveries brought to life through virtual reality. London: Thames & Hudson.
2. Keene, S. (2005). *Fragments of the world: Uses of museum collections, Chapter 7*. Oxford: Butterworth.
3. CAA. Theme: Visualisation. *Computer applications & quantitative methods in archaeology*. http://caaconference.org/proceedings/theme/visualisation/. Accessed 31 May 2013.
4. Bonacchi, C. (2012). *Archaeology and digital communication: towards strategies of public engagement*. London: Archetype.
5. Heritage Lottery Fund. *Using digital technology in heritage projects: Good practice guide*, London: HLF, 2012. http://www.hlf.org.uk/HowToApply/goodpractice/Documents/Using_Digital_Technology_Good_Practice.pdf. Accessed 29 May 2013.

Chapter 17
Just in Time: Defining Historical Chronographics

Stephen Boyd Davis, Emma Bevan, and Aleksei Kudikov

Abstract This chapter is historical in two respects. Its first purpose is to enquire how visual representations of historical time can be used to bring out patterns in cultural collections. Such a visual analytics approach raises questions about the proper representation of time and of objects and events within it. It is argued that such chronographics can support both an externalised, objectivising point of view from 'outside' time and one which is immersive and gives a sense of the historic moment. These modes are set in their own historical context through original historical research, highlighting the shift to an Enlightenment view of time as a uniform container for events. This in turn prompts new ways of thinking about chronological visualisation, in particular the separation of the 'ideal' image of time from contingent, temporary rendered views.

This chapter is an updated and extended version of the following paper, published here with kind permission of the Chartered Institute for IT (BCS) and of EVA London Conferences: Stephen Boyd Davis, et al., "Just in time: defining historical chronographics." In A. Seal, J. P. Bowen, and K. Ng (eds.). EVA *London 2010 Conference Proceedings*. Electronic Workshops in Computing (eWiC), British Computer Society, 2010. http://www.bcs.org/ewic/eva2010 (accessed 26 May 2013).

S. Boyd Davis (✉)
Royal College of Art, London, UK
e-mail: stephen.boyd-davis@rca.ac.uk

E. Bevan
Nonsense Ltd., London, UK
e-mail: emmalucybevan@gmail.com

A. Kudikov
SRL Global, London, UK
e-mail: akudikov@hotmail.co.uk

J.P. Bowen et al. (eds.), *Electronic Visualisation in Arts and Culture*, Springer Series on Cultural Computing, DOI 10.1007/978-1-4471-5406-8_17,

Introduction

Our chapter focuses on the 'shape' of time in digital visualisations of history, and considers the positioning of objects and events in documents such as timelines. We exemplify these using a prototype for a museum. Working on it caused us to reflect on the mapping of time to visual space, which we pursued by researching the early days of modern visualisation, which in turn clarified our thinking about the future design of such chronographic forms in digital media. We consider time, not as a more-or-less familiar quantity, but as a 'special dimension'[1] worthy of interrogation.

A Timeline of Museum Objects

Historical Interactive Timeline (HiT) is a prototype chronographic interface to a database at the Museum of Domestic Design and Architecture (MoDA) at Middlesex University in north London, UK. The Museum collection covers the visual culture of everyday domestic interiors from the late nineteenth to mid twentieth century. Its core comprises Silver Studio wallpaper, fabric and designs from 1880 onwards. The Studio designed for clients including Liberty and London Underground until 1963.

MoDA uses a single database for collections management and as its source of public information such as its website. Curators access the data via a basic interface and can only view multiple records as series of lists and 'lightbox' views of small images. The web interface offers similar lists plus simple tabular graphic views. One cannot organise items in relation to one another, place the collection in the context of time, or see at a glance when pieces were produced. Having a chronographic or timeline-based presentation would give curators, historians and other users a sense of the physical size of the collection, an idea of its breadth over time, and enable them to view images within these contexts and to discover periods when production was sparse or intense. They could, for instance, investigate when floral patterns were produced in greatest number, or find the most popular production technique during the Art Deco period. The dataset has approximately 10,500 records of 160 fields: for our prototype we worked with one fifth of these. Figure 17.1 shows a detail of our display in which the lower band offers a miniature view of the entire dataset: patterning and altered densities over time are clearly visible.

Chronographics

Considering the mapping of events and objects to time led us to question some of our basic assumptions. In particular, we became fascinated by the very notion of positioning objects in a fixed, constant timeframe. Clearly there are many ways to visualise time. Some, such as the dials of clocks, emphasise its cyclical qualities;

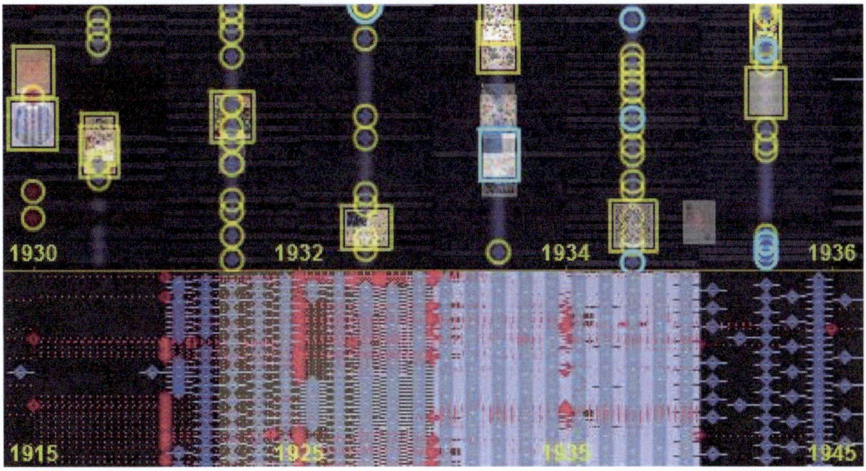

Fig. 17.1 Bevan and Kudikov, 2010: HiT interface for MoDA (detail of screenshot). At *top*, part of the main view spanning 1930–1936; the *lower* part of the display offers a wider view, here encompassing 1915–1945. The changing densities of items through time are made evident

others, such as diaries and calendars, are more linear. In visualising history, strongly linear presentations tend to predominate. Nevertheless there is considerable scope for variation. For example, events may be packed closely, they may be positioned arithmetically along a uniform scale or on a non-linear scale or, as often with paper timelines, may use a scale that is altered pragmatically to accommodate unevenness in the data. These representations of history have a history of their own, which can cast light on some important issues: this chapter is therefore also an argument for the value of historical perspectives on modern visualisation.

Two Historic Examples

In the mid eighteenth century two revolutionary charts appeared. In 1753 in Paris, Jacques Barbeu-Dubourg (1709–1779) created a chart 16.5 m long plotting all history from the Creation to his own date on a uniform timescale (Fig. 17.2) [2]. Also using a uniform scale, in 1765 Joseph Priestley (1733–1804) for the first time represented the duration of individuals' lives using printed lines (Fig. 17.3) [3]. Though these objects are fascinating in themselves, it is their conceptual basis that interests us here.

From Chronology to Chronography

In the eighteenth century, 'history' had connotations of narrative and story, to which chronology contributed rigour: it brought (various authors argued) meaning, vividness, memorability, an evidential basis, and a unifying framework. Locke considered

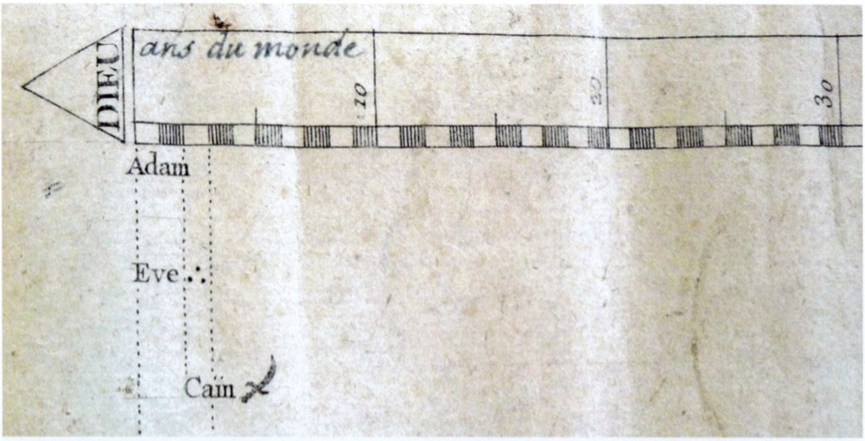

Fig. 17.2 Barbeu-Dubourg: chronographic chart 1753 (detail). The beginning of time, at the left-hand end of a continuous chart 16.5 m long. Rare Book Division, Department of Rare Books and Special Collections, Princeton University Library (Used with permission. Photograph: Stephen Boyd Davis)

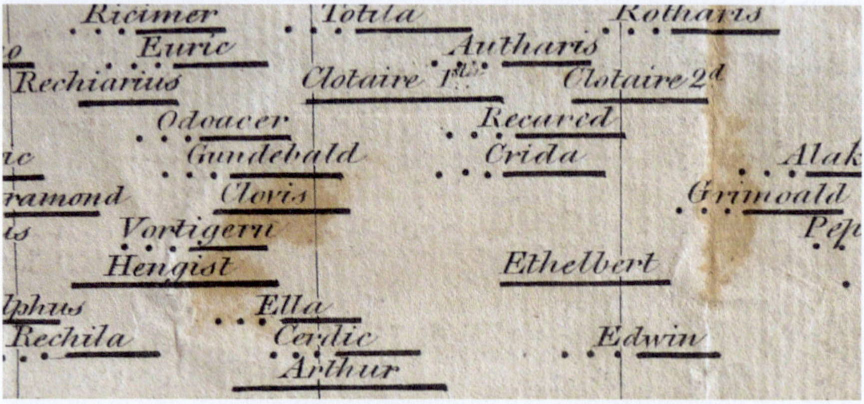

Fig. 17.3 Priestley: chronographic chart 1765 (detail). Priestley invented the use of individual lines to represent multiple lifespans. He also used dots to represent uncertainty (Photograph: Stephen Boyd Davis. With the permission of Chetham's Library, Manchester)

chronology necessary to give form to history, making it more memorable and more productive of moral lessons [4]. A recurrent motif, dating back at least to the mid-sixteenth century, is that chronology and geography are the 'two eyes of history', probably originating in Chytraeus' 1563 phrase 'duos velut oculos historiae' ('two as-it-were eyes of history') [5]. In the Enlightenment, appropriately, the metaphor of illumination is common; historical events are 'cover'd with a Cloud of Darkness […] till the Lamp of Historical Chronology has enlighten'd them' (1754) [6]; without it we will 'wander in the dark, and be always at a loss' (1770) [7].

Mid-century, these metaphors of the visual are actualised: Twyman describes how relationships between sets of information are made visually explicit, including by Lambert's line graphs (1760–70s) and Playfair's 'lineal arithmetic' (1780s) [8].

Chronology becomes chronography when duration is mapped to spatial dimension. Pre-eighteenth century chronologies had almost always packed each entry close upon the previous one. In the early seventeenth century Helvicus [9] had created tables using equal space for equal time, 100 years to a page. Instead of having to read and compute intervals, the user could *see* them. But it would take another 140 years before historic time was mapped arithmetically to space on a continuous substrate, rather than table-wise in pages.

A key innovator was Barbeu-Dubourg. For him, geography is not merely parallel with chronology as in the 'two eyes' metaphor, but the inspiration for change: 'The study of Geography is pleasing, easy, attractive [...] This is not how it is with Chronology, which is a dry form of study, laborious, unforgiving, offering nothing to the mind but repellent dates, a prodigious accumulation of numbers which burden the memory, are difficult to lodge in the mind and escape thence all too easily' [10] (p. 5). His solution is to make time like territory: 'May not duration be imitated and represented as effectively to the senses, as distinctly as space, and may not intervals of time be as easily counted in degrees?' He insists that 'charts of time can and should be constructed all at the same scale, with a constant representation of the years' – because that way we can directly compare intervals. But before time could be conceived as mappable to a uniform space in this way, it had itself to be perceived as a uniform measure. To do so might seem simply natural, but several prior concepts were necessary.

The Origins of Uniform Time

A necessary antecedent to chronography proper is Newton's 'absolute, true, and mathematical' time as the measure of all events [11]. It is hard for us now to capture the excitement of d'Alembert, quoting Newton at the beginning of the article *Chronologie* in Diderot's 1753 Encyclopaedia, 'All things are placed in time as to order of succession; and in space as to order of situation,' but such a view of time as analogous to spatial measurement was an innovation [12]. Yet as Rosenberg points out [13], Newton's chronologies were textual and numeric: no graphical chronologies have been revealed by a recent comprehensive study of this material [14]. For a graphical, visual approach we have to turn to Descartes.

Descartes' writings, particularly the *Compendium Musicae* of 1619, reveal a fixation with the ideas of clear representation, of grasping magnitudes at a glance, and specifically of line-lengths corresponding to number [15]. Euclid had used line lengths to show proportional magnitudes, but Descartes' line is one on which numerical operations are enacted and visualised, echoed by Priestley's explanation [16] (p. 5) that time 'admits of a natural and easy representation in our minds by the idea of a measurable space, and particularly that of a *line*.' By the late eighteenth century William Playfair (1759–1823), the inventor of the line chart, would recall his mathematician brother John teaching him that 'whatever can be expressed in

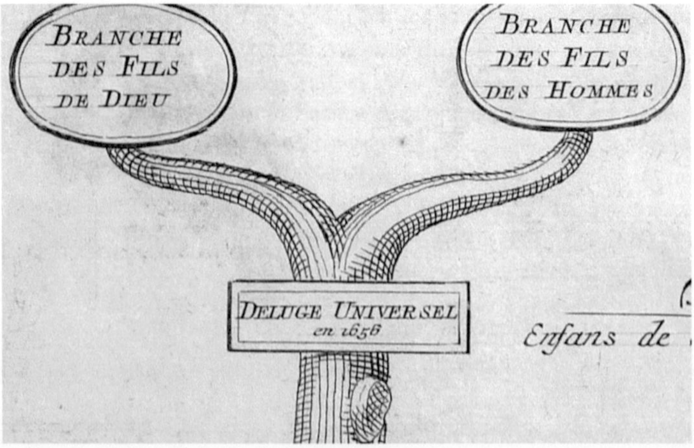

Fig. 17.4 Châtelain, 1721: Chain of Sacred History (detail) from the Atlas Historique. Time as branching plant (Collection: Stephen Boyd Davis. Photo: Stephen Boyd Davis)

numbers may be represented in lines,' [17] (p. 324). Before Descartes' time, this idea could not have been thought. The mechanical uniformity of these arithmetic spaces may also be connected with an enthusiasm among forward-thinking intellectuals for mechanical approaches to knowledge and cognition [18].

Branches, Chains, Streams, Rivers, Arrows

Simplistic distinctions have been made between cultures such as the ancient Greeks, said to have a circular conception of time, and the linear teleological time of Judaism and Christianity, but Feeney [19] (p. 3) points out that we ourselves habitually switch between models depending on context. The eighteenth century balanced metaphors of time's cycle and time's arrow [20], while most modern timelines, including our own HiT, are linear.

One of the simplest time-wise representations is the sequence or procession. Haskell is useful on the Renaissance use of sequenced medals and statues as physical 'lists' [21], while we might also think of Shakespeare's 'show of eight kings' in Macbeth. Such sequences are collated and discussed at length by Eco [22].

Figure 17.4 illustrates a different graphical metaphor for historical events, the branching plant – though the work's title uses the notion of a chain [23]. As in genealogy, the aim is not primarily to show positions in time – the topography of events – as the relations between them – their topology (Rosenberg provides an extended discussion of such metaphors [13]. Priestley favours the *river*: for him universities are pools of stagnant water compared with the Dissenting academies which are 'like rivers which taking their natural course fertilise a whole country' (quoted by Sheps [24], p. 141). Though Priestley avoided any figurative elements in his charts, the metaphor of the river is never far away. In his explanatory 1764 *Description* he explicitly invokes rivers, citing their lack of beginning and end, and likening the lives of men to 'so many small straws swimming on the surface' [23] (p. 24). His chart of biography bears the motto *fluminis ritu feruntur*, evoking Horace's advice to Maecenas to maintain his own position while the world flows around him like a river [25]. In either case, a river is more or less formless: unlike a genealogy or Châtelain's 1721 *Chaine*, it has no internal structures. Though both Barbeu-Dubourg and Priestley impose some order on their streams using banded categories on the non-time axis, there is a lack of explicit structural or relational information. Nevertheless, the river metaphor affords two alternative interpretations, one based on observation, one on immersion.

Observation and Immersion

Priestley's river-of-time metaphor takes two forms. In the *Description*, we seem to stand on the riverbank watching time's flow from without, while with the Horace quotation Priestley puts man within the river as the waters swirl around him. In relation to the first usage, an obvious aspect of the chronographics we have been discussing is that they do indeed provide an overview, seeming to chime with everyday metaphors of standing back in order to get situations in perspective. A less obvious potentiality is to create a sense of immersion in the historic moment. Priestley describes this as follows:

> It is a peculiar kind of pleasure we receive, from such a view as this chart exhibits, of a great man, such as Sir Isaac Newton, seated, as it were, in the circle of his friends and illustrious cotemporaries. We see at once with whom he was capable of holding conversation, and in a manner (from the distinct view of their respective ages) upon what terms they might converse.

Priestley's time charts are static, the flow of his river of time arrested. However, immersion is a strong feature of an extraordinary creation by Barbeu-Dubourg, described in detail by him for Diderot in the 1753 *Encyclopédie* [26]. He inserted his 16.5-m paper roll of time in a *machine chronographique,* with handles to wind history back and forth: about 150 years are visible at any moment (Fig. 17.5). He calls his invention:

> a moving, living tableau, through which pass in review all the ages of the world, where each famous figure steps forth in his rank with the attributes belonging to him, where each Prince is surrounded by his contemporaries and occupies the scene for more or less time according to the duration of his role, where the rise and fall of Empires are acted out in visible form…

Here the sense of history as immersive experience is uppermost.

The visualisations we construct may favour the observational or immersive mode. One factor that differentiates these modes is perceived distance. Seeing the full scope of a comprehensive data-set, patterns emerge for the observer who stands outside time; but when the user moves closer and studies individuals in their context, instead a sense of immersion is promoted. This is an underemphasised aspect of the relationship between focus and context discussed at length, for example, in Card et al. [27].

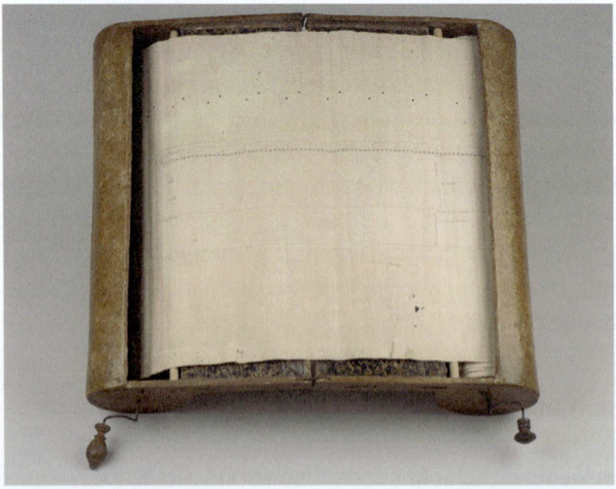

Fig. 17.5 Barbeu-Dubourg: chronographic chart 1753. The 16.5 m long scrolled timeline in its machine. The user may turn the handles to move through time. Rare Book Division, Department of Rare Books and Special Collections, Princeton University Library (Used with permission)

Issues in Visualising Time

Priestley makes a superb case for visualisation [23] (p. 10). He uses the example of trying to figure out the relationship between the lives of five historical figures: he allows his reader to experience the difficulty of answering questions about their relative dates before directing them to look at his chart:

> as soon as you have found the names, you see at one glance, without the help of Arithmetic, or even of words, and in the most clear and perfect manner possible, the relation of these lives to one another.

His short explanatory book offers over 50 thoughts relevant to visualisation on themes including perception, visual metaphors, salience, recall, data integrity, categorisation and problems of objectivity. He was the first and for many years the only chronographer to care about representing uncertainty, something we carried through in HiT, always indicating the (im)precision of our dates by a span rather than a point. MacEachren et al. offer a thorough discussion of modern graphical representations of uncertainty and a useful evaluation [28].

Priestley's understanding of the benefits of a spatial layout is striking: 'the thin and void places in the chart are, in fact, not less instructive than the most crowded' (*op cit* p. 24–5). Absence, he realises, is a form of information, and is most easily brought out by a constant scale. Such patterns are visible in Fig. 17.6, as we also noted above in relation to HiT (Fig. 17.1). He criticises a recent French predecessor to his own chart (not Barbeu-Dubourg's), for its non-linear design. The most impressive point is his reason: 'the notice which is given of this change [in scale] is not sufficient to correct the error of the imagination' (*op cit* p. 8) – he realises that first impressions

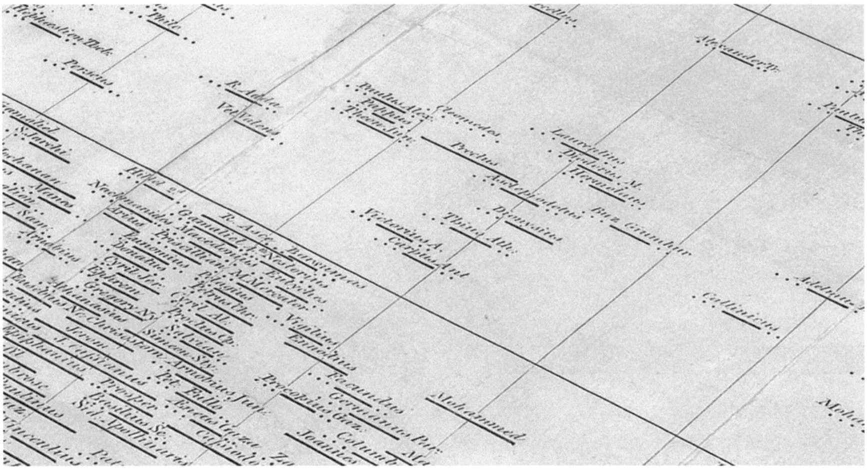

Fig. 17.6 Priestley, 1765: Chart of Biography (detail). Clusters and absences become clear at a distance (Photograph: Stephen Boyd Davis. With the permission of Chetham's Library, Manchester)

resist subsequent attempts to intellectually reinterpret what has been seen. These and his other observations are remarkable at the dawn of modern visualisation.

Despite the cogency of many of Priestley's observations, he and Barbeu-Dubourg present one-sided arguments for uniform timescales. It is worth considering the counter-arguments they chose to ignore.

The Problem of Data Density

In 1838 a second, posthumous edition of Barbeu-Dubourg's *Carte* was produced [29]. Like the first edition, although printed on sheets of uniform height, the timeline proper occupies a narrow band at the Creation which deepens as it approaches the author's own time. Even so, the uniform timescale means that the early period is noticeably lacking in data. This tendency inherent in all historiography reaches an alarming state in Barbeu-Dubourg's second edition, since it includes the recent event avalanche of the French Revolution. At the Creation the timeline is 140 mm high; by the birth of Christ it is 320 mm; in 1000 AD, 385 mm; by 1600 AD, the full 428 mm height of the page – thus far there is no problem. But the attempt to use a uniform scale effectively collapses for the most recent period – virtual extensions to the height, presented sequentially, mean that the height for 1770–1800 is really 1,320 mm, and for 1,800 it is 1,760 mm! An additional difficulty in attempts to map *all* time, is that in just this period time grew dramatically longer. The theories of Hutton and others pushed Creation back by thousands, later millions, of years. Nevertheless timelines fixing the Creation at 4004BC continue to be produced into the nineteenth century, and even recently.

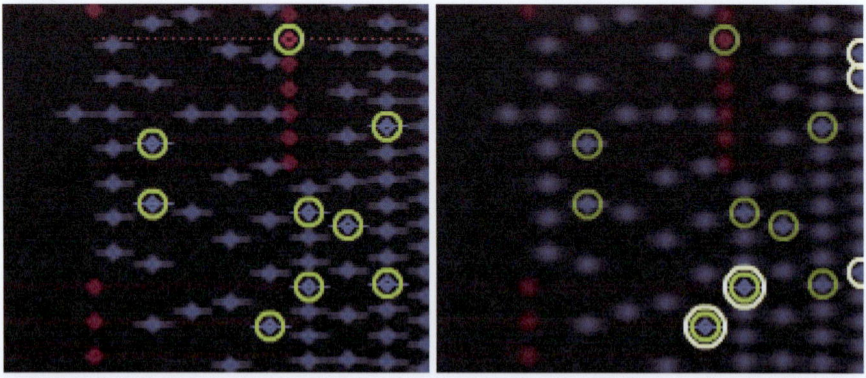

Fig. 17.7 Bevan and Kudikov 2010: HiT for MoDA (detail). Salience for search results. *Left*, designs containing trees are highlighted; *right*, designs containing both trees and fruit now have two highlights, while the remnants of the previous search are reduced in brightness

In digital media an obvious solution to the need for both an overview of all time and a close view of any chosen period is, as in our own HiT, to use two uniform scales together: a miniature chronographic of the whole dataset with an indicator of the portion currently visible in the larger view (Fig. 17.1). This emerging practice is shared by SIMILE (2009) [30] and Continuum (2007) [31]. This step towards a conceptual disconnection between the space to be visualised and the space of the visualisation itself forms part of our proposal for future work below.

The Problem of Navigation

When Helvicus divided history into equal pages for equal periods of time, he knew that the user could flip a handful of pages to jump to any period. Sadly, Barbeu-Dubourg's *machine chronologique* anticipates a problem of many digital interactive timelines: it is almost useless as a reference work, being optimised for the experiential, immersive form of engagement we noted earlier. It is intolerable to wind the crank-handles repeatedly just to look up a different period of history. Digital media of course have a solution: the user can be enabled to jump near-instantaneously from one time to another. However there is a risk associated with this: that the relationship between the time-period in view before the jump and that afterwards is obscured. The context-giving sense of time which is one of the main points of a chronographic approach is lost. Such loss of context is also likely to arise in visualising search results. In HiT we avoided this problem by visualising found items in the ever-present context of the timeline (Fig. 17.7). Rather than making unwanted items disappear, we insert a small frame or halo around items matching the most recent search. Items not selected are repressed: with each new search, the unwanted items have their transparency and blur increased until they reach the maximum level of obscurity at the sixth iteration. The highlight of an item which is part of a previous search is also reduced in alpha, but has no blur applied. The 2.5D visual effect produced by this use of visual salience produces a valuable 'ghosting' or trail of previous searches. Thus the context of time (search history) as well as of space (the surrounding data) is maintained. Search results never appear outside time.

An interesting alternative to navigation between two periods is to graphically omit the intervening period, rather as a spreadsheet does when the user hides columns or rows, an approach taken by *Continuum* [31]. As the authors demonstrate, this means that, for instance, the works of Bach in one century can be juxtaposed with recordings of those works in another: the intervening time is temporarily suppressed. One could say that there is an underlying linear model, but temporarily another view is created. We return to this issue below.

The Issue of Perspective

In his explanatory *Description*, Priestley reveals an interesting aspect of his approach to organising the two thousand names in the biographical chart within six bands of types of individual. He describes how, since the lower part of a large chart will generally be nearer the user's eye, he has in various instances moved the more important data to the lower and therefore nearer part [16]: 'As the Romans come in, they are made to enter by the front line, while the Greeks remove farther backwards' (p. 20). These are literal cases of foregrounding, and reveal an idea akin to spatial perspective. A quasi-perspective is also employed by the French chart of which Priestley disapproved. Organising time vertically, it employs four timescales ranging from 22mm = 500 years to 24mm = 100 years. The effect is a rough gradient from the most recent to the furthest: the changing scale compensates for the fall-off in data in distant times. As we have seen, Priestley objected to the lack of *indication* that the scale is non-uniform. This is a problem with many modern timelines: the reasonable objective in using a non-linear scale is let down by poor visual design. Often the desire to make a tidy, graphically uniform image militates against proper communication that the scale is changing. In HiT, with its fairly short time span, a constant timescale allowed us to avoid confronting this problem.

Such perspective invites consideration of the use of three dimensions. An early innovative 3D digital timeline of photography by Kullberg created a timescape of events, lifelines and associated objects that the user navigates freely [32]. Such use of 3D space for time has been evaluated by Foreman et al. [33] and Korallo et al. [34, 35] particularly in relation to memorability, though with fairly inconclusive results. Such representations offer an important insight: in working with 3D it is clear that there is a conceptual separation between the space of the 'world' to be depicted and the flat space of the display – in computer graphics often conceived as a pipeline, from model to view to rendered image [36] (pp. 334–5, 806–9). We have discussed its implications for depiction generally elsewhere [37]. We revisit this in our third principle below.

Review and Further Work

We present here a brief distillation of our two lines of inquiry, practical development of a working timeline and investigation of earlier chronographics.

Principle 1: the value of linear timescales The 250-year-old arguments of Barbeu-Dubourg and Priestley for linear historic timescales still have some validity. No other rendering can give such a feel for relative intervals and durations; nor can it so accurately disclose the clusters, outliers and lacunae of history.

Principle 2: the value of nonlinear timescales So often is historiography obliged to deal with dramatically uneven densities of data, especially over extended historical periods, that it is impossible to deny the value of various non-linear scales. These include not only logarithmic scales but pragmatic adjustments of scale based on the density of data at that point. Other approaches are more easily conceptualised as changes to the view, for example various kinds of virtual lens, fisheye view etc., which temporarily 'distort' the view in order to optimise the scale for the period currently of interest. We suggest this is the best way to conceive such visual manipulations. Nowviskie [38] (p. 246) and Drucker [39], in making arguments for the digital humanities, have used the word 'inflection' for temporary and contingent alterations to the space or other aspect of a digital surface – a useful term without the pejorative undertones of 'distortion'.

Principle 3: separate model and view Working with physical media, Barbeu-Dubourg and Priestley inevitably conflated three things: their Newtonian mental concept of time, their ideal visual model, and the view they rendered for their users. All were linear. If instead we conceptualise discretely the data, the model, and the view, we can more easily reconcile principles 1 and 2. We can offer users a range of controls to inflect – to bend, stretch or otherwise manipulate – their current view of the model (or part of it), based on their immediate needs, switching instantly or smoothly between views. Digital media facilitate this separation of conceptual shape and rendered shape, because they allow the rendered shape to be contingent on the data, the user's needs or any other factors the designer wishes to take into account. Yet the design of most digital timelines ignores this potential.

Principle 4: indicate scaling As Priestley warned, when non-linear scales are inadequately indicated, many of the advantages of chronographic visualisation are thrown away. If we are to enable users to inflect images of time, the use and zone of influence of these tools must be patent to the user. Any inflections of the linear model should be easily and fluently perceived as such.

When we tackled issues in interactive digital visualisation in the HiT prototype, we were inspired by historical examples and the textual rationales that their designers had set down. This is part of a larger programme of work concerned with chronographics including historical investigation, practical development and the establishment of a research agenda, discussed elsewhere [40]. In HiT we followed the example of the chronographic pioneers in exploring the use of linear timescales and of graphical representations of uncertainty. Rather than break up our constant timescale through navigation we introduced a miniature of the entire dataset; also, rather than break it up when presenting search results, we adopted in-situ salience and recession. Practical development and further historical research led us to seek to combine the advantages of linear and other scales. Rather than thinking of the user simply switching between two or more views, we have adopted a conceptual separation between three things: the data, the ideal model (in our case this is rooted in the Newtonian uniform timeframe whose history we have traced in this chapter) and any number of contingent views upon it. In future work we shall exploit this conceptual architecture more fully, while also tackling some of the other rich issues in visualisation presented by chronographic forms.

Acknowledgments We are very grateful to Prof. Michael Twyman of Reading University for allowing access to his personal collection of chronographic materials, to Prof. Anthony Grafton at Princeton University for valuable advice, to the staff at Chetham's Library Manchester and at Princeton University Library especially Stephen Ferguson, Curator of Rare Books, and to Christine North for advice on translation. We gratefully acknowledge the support of System Simulation, London, software developers, and of the Museum of Domestic Design and Architecture at Middlesex University, especially Zoe Hendon, the curator.

References

1. Aigner, W., Miksch, S., Muller, W., Schumann, H., & Tominski, C. (2008). Visual methods for analyzing time-oriented data. *IEEE Transactions on Visualization and Computer Graphics, 14*(1), 4–60.
2. Ferguson, S. (1991). The 1753 Carte chronographique of Jacques Barbeu-Dubourg. *Princeton University Library Chronicle*, Princeton University. http://www.princeton.edu/~ferguson/PULC_1991_duBourg.pdf. Accessed 22 May 2013.
3. Twyman, M. (1986). Articulating graphic language: A historical perspective. In M. E. Wrolstad & D. F. Fisher (Eds.), *Towards a new understanding of literacy* (pp. 188–251). New York: Praeger.
4. Locke, J. (1693). *Some thoughts concerning education*. Section 172. Churchill, London. British Library General Reference Collection, 1030.f.1.(3).
5. Chytraeus, D. (1563). *De Lectione Historiarum Recte Instituenda*. British Library General Reference Collection, 1030.d.4.(2).
6. Blair, J. (1754). *The chronology and history of the world, from the creation to the year of Christ,* 1753. British Library General Reference Collection, 1852.c.9.
7. Emerson, W. (1770). *Chronology: Or, the art of reckoning time*. London: British Library General Reference Collection, 49.a.4.(2).
8. Twyman, M. (1990, December). Textbook design: Chronological tables and the use of typographic cueing. *Paradigm*, 4. http://faculty.education.illinois.edu/westbury/paradigm/twyman.html. Accessed 20 Apr 2013.
9. Helvicus [Helwig], C. (1609). *Theatrum Historicum* (Historical and Chronological Theatre). Giessæ Hessorum. British Library General Reference Collection, 747.c.22.(1).
10. Barbeu-Dubourg, J. (1753). *Chronographie ou Description des Tems* [sic] (Chronography or Depiction of Time). Paris. Explanatory booklet for Chart. All translations in the text by Stephen Boyd Davis. http://gallica.bnf.fr. Accessed 20 Apr 2013.
11. Newton, I. (1803). *Mathematical principles of natural philosophy*. Book 1. Scholium. Symonds, London. British Library General Reference Collection, 958.c.25. 1687, 1803.

12. d'Alembert, J. L-R. (1753). Chronologie. In *Encyclopédie ou Dictionnaire raisonné des sciences, des arts et des metiers*. Paris, Vol. 3, (pp. 390–400). http://artflsrv02.uchicago.edu/cgi-bin/philologic/getobject.pl?c.2:853.encyclopedie0513. Accessed 5 Aug 2013.
13. Rosenberg, D. (2007). Joseph Priestley and the graphic invention of modern time. *Studies in Eighteenth Century Culture, 36*(1), 55–103.
14. Buchwald, J. Z., & Feingold, M. (2012). *Newton and the origin of civilization*. Princeton: Princeton University Press.
15. Gaukroger, S. (1995). *Descartes: An intellectual biography*. Oxford: Clarendon.
16. Priestley, J. (1764). *A description of a chart of biography*. Warrington. British Library General Reference Collection, 10604.aa.11.
17. Costigan-Eaves, P., & Macdonald-Ross, M. (1990). William Playfair (1759–1823). *Statistical Science, 5*(3), 318–326.
18. Boyd Davis, S. (2010). Time machines. Technology and the 'Death of Art History'. In *Proceedings of the 26th conference of Computers and the History of Art* (CHArt), British Computer Society, London, 10–11 November 2010. http://www.chart.ac.uk/chart2010//papers/toc.html. Accessed 20 Apr 2013.
19. Feeney, D. (2007). *Caesar's calendar: Ancient time and the beginnings of history*. Berkeley: University of California Press.
20. Gould, S. J. (1987). *Time's arrow, time's cycle: Myth and metaphor in the discovery of geological time*. Cambridge: Harvard University Press.
21. Haskell, F. (1993). *History and its images: Art and the interpretation of the past*. New Haven: Yale University Press.
22. Eco, U. (2009). *The infinity of lists*. London: MacLehose Press.
23. Châtelain, H. A. (1721). *Atlas Historique*, Vol. 1. L'Honore & Châtelain, Amsterdam. British Library Cartographic Items, 209.i.4–6.
24. Sheps, A. (1999). Joseph Priestley's time charts. Lumen – *Proceedings Representations of Time in the XVIIIth Century* (pp. 135–144). Canadian Society for Eighteenth-Century Studies.
25. Horace (Quintus Horatius Flaccus). *Odes*, Book 3, 29, 23BCE.
26. Diderot, D. (1753). Chronologique (machine). *Encyclopédie ou Dictionnaire Raisonné des Sciences, des Arts et des Metiers, 3*, (pp. 400–401). Paris. Translated by S. Boyd Davis. The Encyclopedia of Diderot & d'Alembert Collaborative Translation Project. University of Michigan, Ann Arbor, 2009. http://hdl.handle.net/2027/spo.did2222.0001.081. Accessed 20 Apr 2013.
27. Card, S. K., Mackinlay, J. D., & Shneiderman, B. (Eds.). (1999). *Readings in information visualization: Using vision to think*. San Francisco: Morgan Kaufmann.
28. MacEachren, A. M., Roth, R. E., O'Brien, J., Li, B., Swingley, D., & Gahegan, M. (2012). Visual semiotics & uncertainty visualization: An empirical study. *IEEE Transactions on Visualization and Computer Graphics, 18*(12), 2496–2505.
29. Barbeu-Dubourg, J. (1838). *Chronographie, ou Description des Temps*. (Chronography or Depiction of Time). Paris. British Library, 798.l.19.
30. SIMILE Timeline. (2009). http://www.simile-widgets.org/timeline/. Accessed 3 Jan 2013.
31. André, P., Wilson, M. L., Russell, A., Smith, D. A., Owens, A., & Schraefel, M. Continuum: Designing timelines for hierarchies, relationships and scale. In *Proceedings of ACM symposium on User interface software and technology* (UIST) (pp. 101–110). Newport, 7–10 October 2007.
32. Kullberg, R. L. (1995). *Dynamic timelines: Visualizing historical information in three dimensions*. M.Sc. thesis. Massachusetts Institute of Technology, Cambridge.
33. Foreman, N., Boyd Davis, S., Moar, M., Korallo, L., & Chappell, E. (2008). Can virtual environments enhance the learning of historical chronology? *Instructional Science, 36*(2), 155–173.
34. Korallo, L., Foreman, N., Boyd Davis, S., Moar, M., & Coulson, M. (2012). Can multiple 'spatial' virtual timelines convey the relatedness of chronological knowledge across parallel domains? *Computers and Education, 58*(2), 856–862.
35. Korallo, L., Foreman, N., Boyd Davis, S., Moar, M., & Coulson, M. (2012). Do challenge, task experience or computer familiarity influence the learning of historical chronology from virtual environments in 8–9 year old children? *Computers and Education, 58*(4), 1106–1116.

36. Foley, J. D., van Dam, A., Feiner, S. K., & Hughes, J. F. (1995). *Computer graphics: Principles and practice*. Reading: Addison Wesley.
37. Boyd Davis, S. (2007). A schema for depiction. In K. Van der Waarde, & P. Westendorp (Eds.), *Visible language* 41(3), 280–300.
38. Nowviskie, B. P. (2004). *Speculative computing: Instruments for interpretive scholarship.* Ph. D. thesis. Department of English, University of Virginia, USA.
39. Drucker, J. (2011). Humanities approaches to graphical display. In *Digital Humanities Quarterly* 5(1). http://www.digitalhumanities.org/dhq/vol/5/1/. Accessed 21 Apr 2013.
40. Boyd Davis, S. (2012). History on the line: Time as dimension. *Design Issues, 28*(4), 4–17.

Chapter 18
Beckford's Ride: The Reconstruction of Historic Landscape

Paul Richens and Marion Harney

Abstract William Beckford (1760–1844) built a lookout tower and landscape garden in Bath, now almost completely vanished beneath subsequent buildings. Referring to archival documents and a few traces on the ground, we used an advanced video-game engine to reconstruct the landscape, architecture and planting as it was around 1840, for an interactive installation in the Beckford Tower Museum. Bespoke software was developed to handle the wide views and rich planting. The resulting virtual environment succeeds in relating the lost landscape to the intentions and taste of its creator, and to surviving fragments in the real world. It has enhanced the museum visitor's experience in several ways.

Introduction

Compared to the extensive use of real-time virtual environments in architecture and archaeology over the last decade [1], there has been relatively little work on constructing virtual landscapes and gardens. The first example, by Klein [2] applied high-end graphics to the eighteenth-century garden at Wörlitz. Soon after, DeLeon and Berry [3] used the Unreal game engine to project a virtual Everglades in an exhibition setting, and Honjo and Lim [4] used VRML to model a Japanese garden. These early

---

This chapter is an updated and extended version of the following paper, published here with kind permission of the Chartered Institute for IT (BCS) and of EVA London Conferences: P. Richens and M. Harney, "Reconstruction of historic landscapes." In S. Dunn, J. P. Bowen, and K. Ng (eds.). *EVA London 2011 Conference Proceedings*. Electronic Workshops in Computing (eWiC), British Computer Society, 2011. http://www.bcs.org/ewic/eva2011 (accessed 26 May 2013).

P. Richens (✉) • M. Harney
Centre for Advanced Studies in Architecture, Department of Architecture and Civil Engineering, University of Bath, Bath BA2 7AY, UK
e-mail: pnr20@bath.ac.uk

J.P. Bowen et al. (eds.), *Electronic Visualisation in Arts and Culture*, Springer Series on Cultural Computing, DOI 10.1007/978-1-4471-5406-8_18,

attempts used a flat landscape and simplified two-dimensional representations of vegetation. Since then, botanically realistic results have been produced with specialised software, particularly Lenné3D applied for example by Döllner et al. [5] to Sans Souci and proposed by Paar and Blaik [6] for Wrest Park. Modern game engines offer a broader range of capabilities at low cost, and are proving adaptable for landscape and garden reconstruction. Pokladek [7] is revisting Wörlitz using Unity, while CryEngine [8, 9] has been used by Ch'ng [10] to recreate a drowned Mesolithic landscape, and by ourselves [11], in a precursor to the current project, to model a delicate eighteenth-century garden, Prior Park near Bath, including landscape, water features, architecture and planting, for an exhibition at the Sorbonne.

In 2010 we worked on a much larger site on the opposite side of the city. The occasion was the 250th anniversary of the birth of the reclusive connoisseur William Beckford (1760–1844) who had once built a linear garden there, known locally as "Beckford's Ride".

The aim was to produce an interactive installation for the museum, which is situated in the lookout tower that Beckford built at the high point of his ride, with the objectives of attracting visitors, improving their experience, and explaining how the now detached Tower was once related to the wider landscape running down to the City of Bath. Achieving this required substantial research on the one hand into the history, topography and planting of the garden, and on the other, into the design, technology and workflow needed to produce a highly visual and realistic interactive environment.

Historical background: Beckford was born into an immensely rich family [12]. His father, a Lord Mayor of London and owner of some of the largest sugar plantations in Jamaica, died when William was nine. The son was educated privately and well, learning first Latin, Greek and music, then travelling widely, and continuing to study Spanish, Portuguese, Arabic and Sanskrit. In later life he claimed to have been taught architecture by William Chambers and music by Mozart. Already flagrantly bisexual, he celebrated his majority, when he became "the richest commoner in England", with a 3-day mixed party of young friends unchaperoned in the shuttered but mysteriously illuminated rooms of his father's Palladian mansion Fonthill Splendens (in Wiltshire). The peculiar atmosphere of this event was something he tried to recapture throughout his life, and provides some of the impetus for his widely admired oriental-gothic novel Vathek [13].

Scandal necessitated a period of exile, during which he made his first garden, Montserrate, in Sintra near Lisbon. European war in 1797 forced his return to Fonthill, where he engaged on his second and largest, the park surrounding his colossal folly, Fonthill Abbey (Fig. 18.1(left)). Intended to house his huge collections of books, paintings and objets d'art, it was to have had a spire overtopping that of Salisbury Cathedral. Built rapidly and badly by his inattentive architect James Wyatt, it suffered two partial collapses, and consumed the bulk of his fortune, as well as all the stone from his father's house, pulled down for the purpose. Eventually, running out of cash, tiring of exoticism, and chilled by its vast emptiness, he sold the building and most of the contents for a good price, and retired to Bath, buying a property in Lansdown Crescent.

Once settled in Bath (which he did not much like) his enthusiasm for landscape and towers soon revived. He started to acquire all the ground between his house and

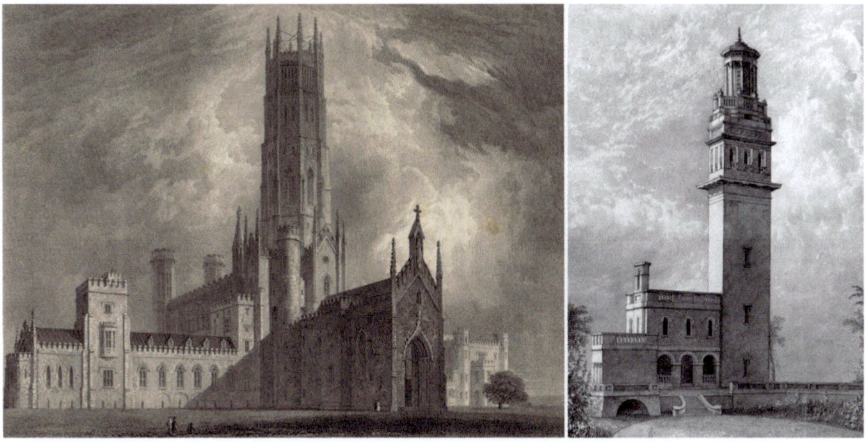

Fig. 18.1 (*Left*). Fonthill Abbey, designed by James Wyatt, from John Rutter's Delineations of Fonthill and its Abbey 1823. (*Right*). Beckford's Tower, watercolour by the architect, Henry Goodridge (Copyright free, images in the public domain)

the top of Lansdown, a distance of about 2 km, and rising 100 m. He engaged a young architect, Henry Goodridge, to build a lookout tower on the summit (Fig. 18.1(right)), with views extending beyond the Bristol Channel to Wales. Only 24 at the time of his commission, Goodridge proved to be attentive and competent, and Beckford's Tower is still standing today. With the help of Goodridge and Vincent, his trusted and very capable gardener from Fonthill, Beckford rapidly developed a landscape garden stretching between his house and the tower. Always a slim and vigorous man, it was his habit to ride each morning up to the tower, there to ascend to the belvedere with one of his treasured books, and afterwards to walk back through the garden to Lansdown Crescent.

Today the house is in private ownership and the tower belongs to a Trust which keeps a small museum there. The garden immediately around the tower became a cemetery, now disused; there is a plantation extant, but all the rest has been built over; a few trees and architectural fragments in suburban gardens are all that survive.

The present work to reconstruct, in a virtual environment, the landscape and the interior of the tower, was commissioned by the Trust, and is now a permanent installation in the museum. The objective was to show it as it was in 1840, a few years before Beckford's death.

Evidence

Most of the garden has been built over, and there is no surviving plan of the whole. So our reconstruction has had to be based on piecing together evidence from documentary sources, and relating these to the ground. Where evidence is scarce, we have looked for comparable designs elsewhere.

Documents: The most instructive source is an account by Henry Venn Lansdown [14] written in the form of letters to his daughter, and published by her 50 years later. Lansdown was himself a topographical painter, and secured an introduction to Beckford through Goodridge, hoping to view the extraordinarily rich collection of old-master paintings in the house. His conversation so impressed Beckford that he was invited back to walk to the tower and view its contents as well, which he did in the company of the architect. Lansdown had a painter's eye for landscape, and a remarkable memory; his description is full and seemingly exact. He describes the sequence walking north from the mews behind Lansdown Crescent as follows:

- A Kitchen Garden of 7–8 acres; magnificent terrace to the north backed by shrubbery, from which arises an Archway of massive proportions.
- A hill with a winding path through short grass, extending half a mile.
- A broad walk between two flourishing plantations.
- A rustic sort of bungalow allowing extensive views to the E, S and W.
- A sort of tableland, containing the picturesque remains of an immense quarry, vividly recalling Roman ruins, such as the Baths of Caracalla.
- A low doorway leading to a lovely shrubbery, a walk composed of small fossils winding under a green arcade of trees flanked by odoriferous flowers.
- A beautiful kitchen garden, a broad and noble straight walk 10 ft in width and 400 long between beds of flowers, with fruit trees and vegetables beyond. The garden is 80 ft wide, and 12 below the down, being in an old quarry, with high walls.
- Garden terminating with a picturesque cottage pierced by a lofty archway, through which the walk passes (Fig. 18.2).
- A pond of gold and silver fish, then a grotto winding 60–70 ft under a public road, emerging up rustic steps to the level of the down.
- A path a quarter mile long parallel to the wall of the public road. Venerable bushes of lavender, rosemary and large roses.
- A wilder garden near the Tower, paths more serpentine, planted with exotic trees.
- Ground broken and diversified, steps leading to an eminence. An apparently old ruin overgrown with shrubs. Easy steps leading to an archway from which the view of the Tower bursts out (Fig. 18.3).
- A long straight walk leading to the entrance.

There are two other printed accounts [15, 16], one with some valuable illustrations which can be related to Lansdown's account. From these we learn that the garden in the quarry is called the Dyke Garden, and the tower garden contained two tombs, one of a favourite dog, the other intended for Beckford himself.

Maps and plans are sadly lacking. There are some useful tithe maps of the right era, which identify roads, property boundaries, building footprints and tenure. They establish the boundary of Beckford's holdings, but do not reveal any internal details of the garden. The earliest Ordnance Survey of 1895 is wonderfully detailed but already much has been built-over. It does give some indication of the quarry, and tree-planting.

There are quite a lot of surviving drawings of the architecture, particularly those by Goodridge for the Tower, and also a plan of the Kitchen Garden, made when it

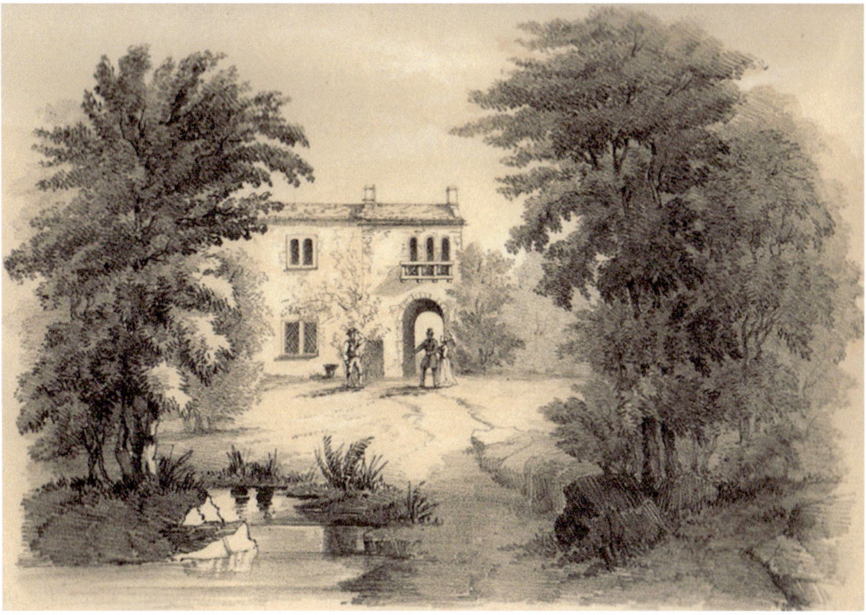

Fig. 18.2 Cottage in the Dyke Garden, lithograph by William Maddox, 1844. Arch and Italianate windows added by Goodridge during the garden development. View taken from the grotto entrance, with fishpond in the foreground (Copyright free, image in the public domain)

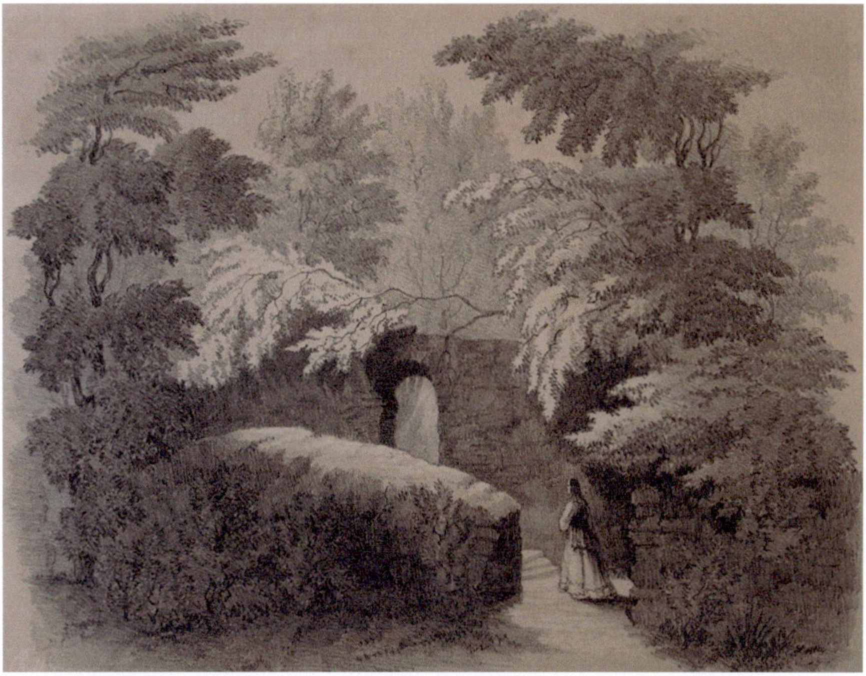

Fig. 18.3 Ruin with arch, lithograph by William Maddox 1844. Probably in the wilderness garden close to the tower (Copyright free, image in the public domain)

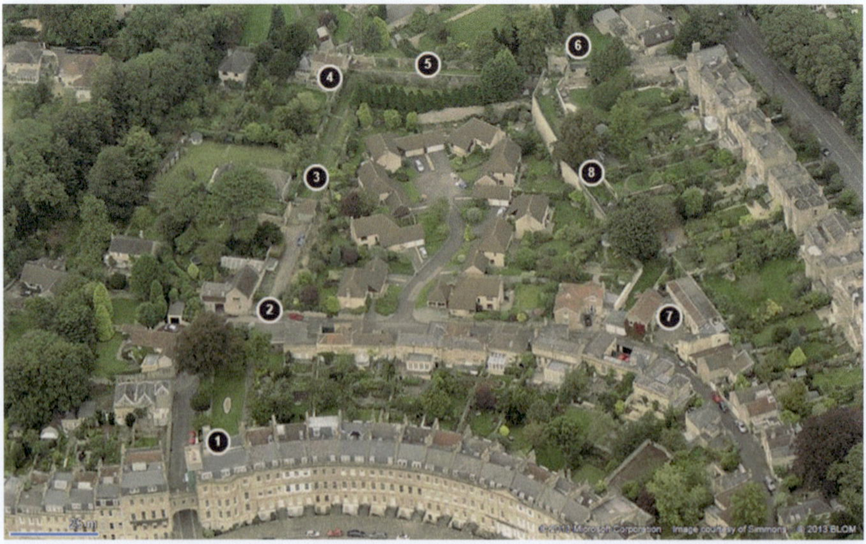

Fig. 18.4 Kitchen garden and ramps today, showing surviving features buried in suburban gardens. (1) house, (2) entrance, (3&8) ramps, (4) gardeners cottage, (5) terrace, (6) archway, (7) stables (Microsoft Bing screenshot reprinted with permission from Microsoft Corporation)

was broken up into allotments after Beckford's death. It survived as a nursery garden until the 1960s, when it is was filled with an estate of bungalows (Fig. 18.4). The lower slopes were built over with suburban villas and the Kingswood School. The quarry garden was initially occupied by a substantial mansion, later replaced by more housing. The immediate surroundings of the tower became a cemetery, and the tower a mortuary chapel, then a private house, and is now a museum, with a holiday apartment leased out through the Landmark Trust.

Physical remains: Our first move was to walk the site, to try and trace the route, and identify architectural remains, viewpoints and traces of planting.

Evidence we found on the ground includes the magnificent terraces and Archway of the Kitchen Garden, now buried in various back gardens, also a pair of ramps, one leading from Beckford's Stable in the mews behind the Crescent to the Archway, and so presumably part of his route uphill (Figs. 18.4 and 18.5). Two out of three cottages mentioned in written accounts survive, and there is a lithograph of the third, with its arch (Fig. 18.2). Various trees survive, including a long line of limes planted when Beckford diverted a footpath to the edge of the turnpike road, and some old ash and cedars. There is still a wood below the brow of the hill, probably much more extensive than the original plantations.

The most difficult feature to locate is the "Rustic Bungalow", and the fossil walk that follows it. There is no surviving point with clear views to E, S and N, so it is most likely buried in the overgrowth of Beckford's plantation. We presume the building was by Goodridge, but there are no surviving rustic structures or designs by him. There are many by contemporaries, which we have used as reference for the reconstruction, adapting the usual gothic style to one a touch more Italianate.

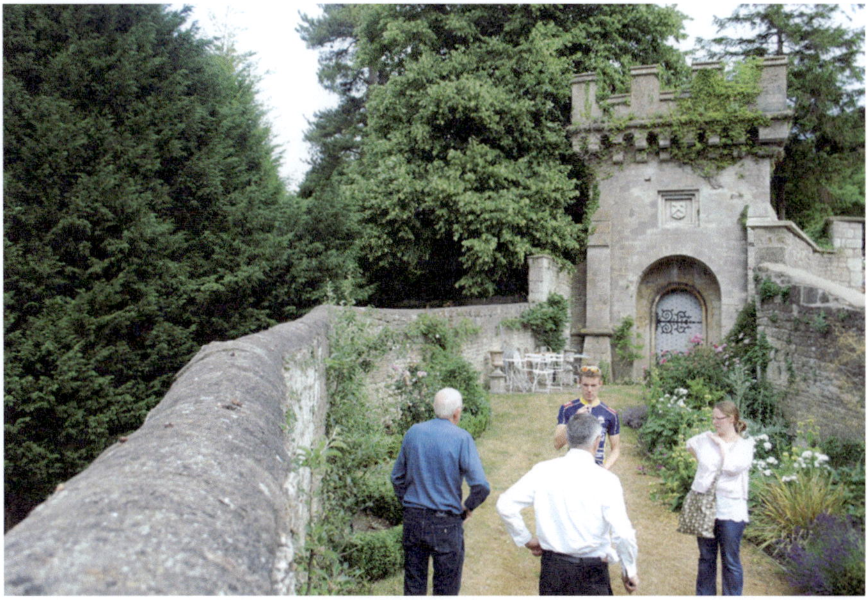

Fig. 18.5 The "archway of massive proportions" today, at the top of the ramp leading up from the stables. The wall on the left was originally lower, allowing a view into the kitchen garden below

The form of the quarry garden is also completely lost; we are using one at Belsay Hall (Morpeth, Northumberland) as a reference. It is exactly contemporary, and its creator, Sir Charles Monck, was inspired by the same Greek marble quarries in Sicily as was Beckford.

Most of the Dyke garden is now filled-in, though one end remains as a visible depression. Nearby, under nettles and brambles and almost impenetrable, we found the exit from what remains of the grotto.

The Tower itself is well preserved, though somewhat altered. It has been the subject of extensive study, and the changes are well documented. Our intention is to model it as it was in 1840.

The views from the tower are very extensive, particularly to the West where they reach over the Bristol Channel to Wales. The landform has barely changed, though there is a great deal of modern development, and to the East a very visible modern road.

Virtual Reconstruction

Technology Following the successful use of CryEngine 2 [9] for the Prior Park project, we opted (rather bravely, as it turned out) to use the nascent Version 3 for this project. The original engine was developed for a game, called Crysis [17], set on a Pacific Island. It is in the category of "first-person shooters", which basically provide the player with an extensive landscape in which to move about and engage in simulated combat. Such games compete in providing very fluid movement through elaborate battlefield and urban environments rendered with a high degree of realism. We are not interested in the war game itself, but in the landscape setting, which we can rebuild to represent the sites we are studying.

From our point of view, Crysis demonstrated a most impressive ability to handle extensive and detailed landscape, water and vegetation. Its lighting of outdoor scenes is spectacular. Trees move gently in the wind, while the sun rises and streams through the leaves to cast constantly moving shadows. It employs High Dynamic Range Imaging (HDRI) to cope effectively with the extreme contrast in light levels such as between a cave and the sunlight outside.

The second very attractive feature of the engine is that it is provided with a completely integrated editor – called *Sandbox* – with which to compose the scenery. The appearance of the scene in the editor is exactly as it appears in the game, which makes an experimental, interactive way of assembling planting and buildings attractive and efficient.

A game engine such as CryEngine has a surprising range of subsystems [18]. The most important for us are concerned with: terrain and its textures, water, vegetation, sky (including sun, moon, stars, clouds and mist), static objects like buildings, particles (for smoke, fire, fountains, fireworks), movable objects, triggers that make things happen, physics (collisions, falling objects, vehicles) and sounds (collisions again, footfalls, ambience, music). We also make use of scripted sequences of events, called *cinematics*. Systems of huge importance in the original game to do with characters, dialogue and artificial intelligence are of less concern, though we do use some flocking birds and other animals.

Building the landscape: The first element to construct is the terrain, as it provides a surface on which all the other elements will be placed. The terrain is textured at two levels of detail – one showing what it looks like from a distance ("blue remembered hills"), and one for close up (turf on the down, leaf litter in the wood). However in the first instance it proved more useful to use an annotated Ordnance Survey map as the overall texture, to guide the placement of other objects. Next comes the establishment of the playing boundary – there has to be some limit on the player's movement to stop them falling off the edge of the world, and this boundary separates the area that must be modelled in full detail from that needing only a partial visual treatment. Roads and paths come next as they establish a framework, and more precise levels for adjacent buildings.

Buildings are assembled; those outside the playing boundary will be like film studio back-lot sets, with only one façade, while those inside are built in the round, and possibly with interiors as well. Buildings are created with architectural modelling software, but their location in the landscape, and interior lighting, is handled in the Sandbox.

Vegetation comes next, along with other kinds of scattered objects like rocks and stones, sticks and leaves, and detail textures known as *decals*.

Ambient sounds such as birdsong, cattle, insects, wind and running water, are edited and formatted with specialist software (SoundForge [19] and FMOD Designer [20]), and then located in the Sandbox.

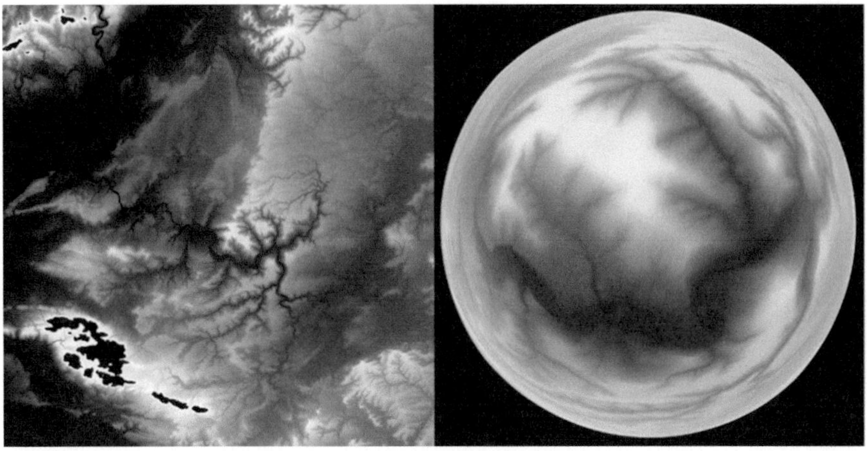

Fig. 18.6 (*Left*). Wide-area Digital Terrain Model showing the Avon river basin draining into the Severn Estuary. (*Right*). The result of hyperbolic compression centred on Bath

Finally, interactive events are constructed, usually by placing an invisible trigger that causes something to happen as the player approaches, which could be a door opening, a sound, an information display, or in the extreme an elaborate cinematic sequence.

Terrain: The Sandbox accepts terrain as a greyscale image, where the brightness of each pixel represents the height – called a Digital Terrain Model (DTM). We had to work with a 32-bit version of the Sandbox, which limited our terrain to an 8 km square, with each pixel representing 2 m of ground. This is sufficient for the playable area, but not for the extensive distant views from the high down, which extend more than 50 km. This was a new problem for us, as the Prior Park site was in a valley, with nearby hills cutting off the horizon in all directions. Scenes in the Crysis game, we noticed, were all in deep valleys, or sea-girt islands, so avoiding the problem.

Two approaches were considered. One would be to take a panoramic photograph from the top of the tower, and use that as a background *skybox*. The second was to find a way to model the distant landscape in some sort of false perspective. Using a conventional skybox would suppress the Crytek HDRI sky (which includes sun, moon and atmospheric effects), which seemed rather a loss. False perspective would require some bespoke programming, but seemed quite feasible in principle.

We acquired a wide area digital terrain map (DTM) from the Ordnance Survey, on a 50 m grid, centred on the Tower, and covering the entire landscape visible from the top (Fig. 18.6). This was input to a bespoke image-warping program that left a central circle of 2 km radius unchanged, but applied a radial scaling to pixels outside that limit so that a pixel originally at r km from the centre moves to $4(1-1/r)$. This maps distances between 2 and infinity to the range 2–4, thereby compressing the entire outside world into the available 4 km. In order to preserve the appearance of the landscape, the height values relative to the central point are also diminished linearly, in proportion to the scale factor applied. So a peak of 3,000 m 40 km away reduces to one roughly 300 m high 4 km away. A similar distortion was applied to aerial photography of the whole region, to be used as a terrain texture map. Then we superimposed higher resolution data, up to our target 2 m per pixel, (both DTM and photography), warped in the same way, to provide better detail in the central regions.

The result was a kind of hyperbolic distortion that compressed 80 km of landscape into a bowl 8 km across (Fig. 18.6(right)). From a selected point the perspective is perfect; and the errors from elsewhere in the playable region (about 1 km radius) are perfectly acceptable. A few oddities were anticipated – the sea is no longer at sea level, or even level – and clouds might appear to swell as they moved towards the horizon. But neither effect has proved troublesome.

Architecture: The preferred "digital content creation" software for CryEngine is AutoDesk 3D Studio Max [21], and all our modelling had to pass through this in order to be exported in a form recognised by the engine – a mesh of connected triangles with textures mapped onto it. We started making the architectural models in SketchUp [22], but found that though they could be imported into 3D Studio easily, they often failed to export into the game. The reason proved to be the poor quality of the mesh exported by SketchUp. The answer was to pass the models through Rhino [23], which can reassemble the SketchUp mesh into planar polygons, then remesh to a high standard. After this discovery we simplified the workflow by originating the architectural models in Rhino itself. So the final workflow was:

- Originate architectural model using Rhino surface modelling.
- Convert to a triangulated mesh and export to 3D Studio.
- Apply texture coordinates and assign materials in 3D Studio.
- Export to the Crytek Sandbox game editor, and finalise the materials.
- If complicated, generate simplified meshes to be used at greater distances (Level of Detail), and for collision detection (Physics Proxy).

Significant judgement is needed in deciding how much to model, and how much detail can be provided by textures. For example, windows in buildings seen only from a distance (like those outside the playable area), can be safely treated as 2D decals applied to the face of the building, thereby saving a lot of modelling effort, and reducing the number of triangles to be rendered. Low-relief architectural ornament is better treated as a texture rather than modelled in full.

Textures: These are needed for all the visible surfaces, and fall into three main categories – building materials like brick and stone, ground surfaces like gravel and earth, and vegetation surfaces such as grass, bark and foliage.

The texture itself is an image (typically 512 pixels square), designed or edited so as to repeat like a wall-paper pattern without obvious seams. These patterns are used to cover surfaces in the model. Fitting the wall-paper to a flat architectural surface is quite easy, but curvy organic shapes (such as the crutch of a tree) can be quite challenging. Unlike real wall paper, computer textures can be stretched to fit, but it can take a lot of work to get a good result.

In addition to the visible pattern, most textures have additional layers containing for example information on the bumpiness of the surface (normal map) or its opacity (alpha mask) – invaluable for partly transparent surface like grilles and foliage. Special photographic techniques were used to generate these. Tree foliage texture was generated by detaching large branches (2–3 m long) and photographing against a blue background. This can be detected in Photoshop to generate an alpha mask. Normal maps were generated by taking stereo pairs of photographs, and processing them with specialist software like PhotoSculpt [24], PhotoSculpt constructs a mesh model of the surface using stereo disparity measurements, and from that derives displacements and surface orientation.

Vegetation: The Crytek development kit contains a number of trees and shrubs derived from the original Crysis game. As this is set on a Pacific Island, the look is distinctly tropical. For Prior Park we had used the more anonymous supplied examples, but for Beckford's Ride we needed some identifiable temperate zone species.

The content creation task for a tree is quite demanding. First of all the trunk and major limbs have to be modelled as a mesh, and then textured. Stretching the texture pattern to fit limbs and forks is tricky. Then smaller branches and foliage are modelled as triangles or small meshes with their textures alpha-masked for partial transparency. The meshes themselves are coloured to indicate how they react to the wind. Then everything has to be repeated at several levels of detail, and supplemented by an approximate collision proxy.

As we needed about six examples of each species, in various stages of growth, and the modelling process was difficult and tedious (and did not appeal to the architecture students we employed for content creation), we decided to treat it as a parametric design exercise, adapting some research software designed for architectural structures, and based on subdivision surfaces.

The parametric tree generator goes through five stages. First the centre-line skeleton of a tree is built as a set of linked bones, like those used in character animation (Fig. 18.7(left)). The parameters are adjusted interactively until it has the desired height, spread and branching posture. Then the bones are thickened up to give limbs with a square cross-section and properly formed joints, represented as a mesh of (mostly) quadrangles. Texture coordinates (in a specially developed cylindrical form) and wind-control parameters are added to this basic mesh, which is destined to be the lowest level of detail. Higher levels are generated by applying one or two rounds of Catmull-Clark subdivision [25] to the mesh (Fig. 18.7(right)). In addition to refining and smoothing the geometrical mesh, this process also subdivides and smooths the texture and wind coordinates. Textured branches and foliage meshes are added, and the whole structure exported as a Collada file [26], to be imported into 3D Studio, matched up with an appropriate material, and re-exported to CryEngine.

Once a single tree has been generated, additional instances of the same species are generated by adding some carefully controlled Gaussian variance to the parameters. Using this process, suites of trees can be generated in hours rather than days, and to a highly consistent standard.

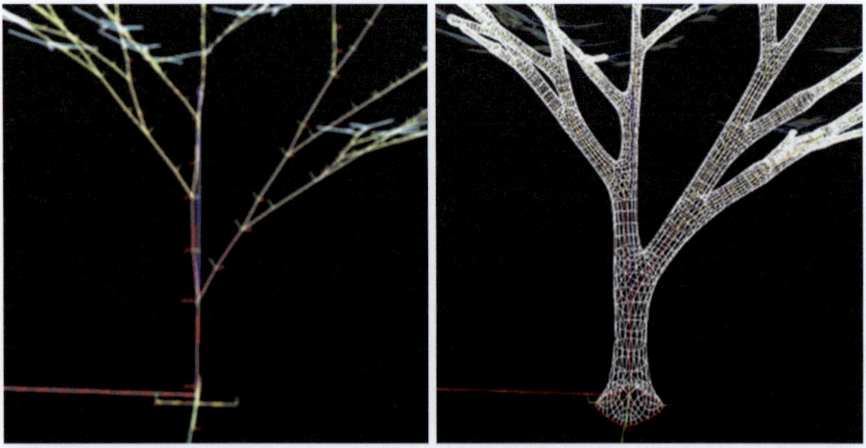

Fig. 18.7 (*Left*). Tree skeleton. (*Right*). Tree developed as a subdivision surface mesh

Interactivity: In both Prior Park and Beckford's Ride, we provide information points which can be approached to give some background on what is seen, for example some text from Henry Lansdown's letters, an illustration from the archives, or a photograph of what the scene looks like today.

In the case of Prior Park we wished to show a more panoramic view of the landscape and so built a cinematic balloon ride, which takes the player up into the air and towards the city of Bath. In the case of Beckford's Ride, we had the problem of a wide expanse of open down between the Embattled Gateway and the wood, where nothing much happens. This has been solved by providing a cinematic horse gallop (Fig. 18.10) across the space, to the tune of *Non più andrai*, which Beckford claimed he had improvised as a boy during his music lesson with Mozart.

The Rustic Bungalow is a circular building which acts as a kind of time machine. Looking out through different windows causes the time of day to change, with the sun moving across the sky, night falling, and the moon rising. The light in turn affects the ambient sound: at dawn the birdsong in the plantation reaches a peak, at midday insects hum on the downs, while at dusk the rooks can be heard settling in the lime trees.

Presentation: The completed virtual environment can be presented in several different formats. The simplest is to play it on a desktop computer, with keyboard and mouse. A darkened room and a pair of earphones improve the experience. In the Beckford Tower Museum it is presented as a "kiosk" with a 60 cm wall-hung display, earphones and a game-pad.

We have shown it quite often in a lecture-room setting, using a large-screen projection. This can be quite impressive, but viewers do not have the chance to interact and explore on their own. Most of them will not be seated in the ideal viewing position, and the presenter has to drive with caution, otherwise the audience may suffer mild giddiness.

Our preferred presentation is to project from overhead onto a large screen, reaching from floor level to 3 m above, in a dark space. A lectern is placed at the exact centre of perspective, with a tethered game-controller and some basic instructions. Audio is channelled through a 5 + 1 surround system. Placing the player at the exact centre of the visual and audio simulation gives a substantial boost to the feeling of immersion. This arrangement was used at an exhibition in Paris in 2010, and proved easy to transport and set up, and capable of working unattended for days at a time.

Conclusion

Leading-edge computer game engines are already finding a number of uses outside their primary entertainment role, such as military training and simulated fire-fighting. Uses in architecture are beginning to emerge, and our experiments have demonstrated a real capability in the area of landscape design and reconstruction.

Our primary aim was to generate interpretive exhibition material for public consumption, to convey in a fully rounded and immersive form what a lost landscape would have been like to enter and walk around, and to relate this visual impression to the intentions and taste of the creator, and also to the surviving scene of everyday experience. It has proved engaging and curatorially successful in the context of the Beckford Tower Museum. The volunteer guides (mostly retired people) have taken to it with surprising enthusiasm, using it to explain the richness of the lost garden. Visitors, both local people and tourists, have been fascinated to discover how the now isolated Tower once related to the wider landscape (Figs. 18.8, 18.9, 18.10, 18.11, 18.12, 18.13, 18.14, 18.15, and 18.16). Young

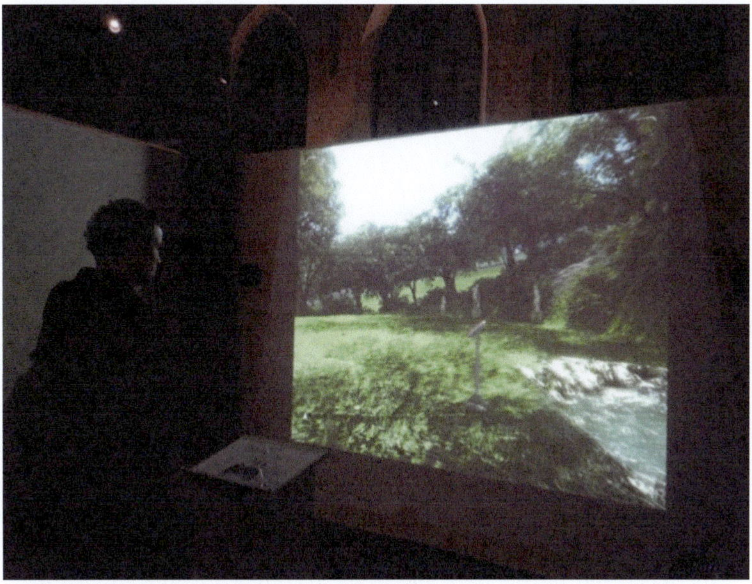

Fig. 18.8 Virtual landscape as an interactive installation

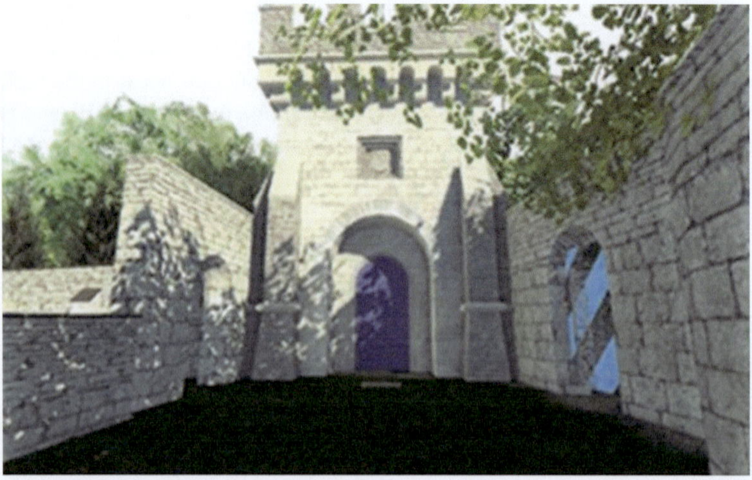

Fig. 18.9 Embattled gateway

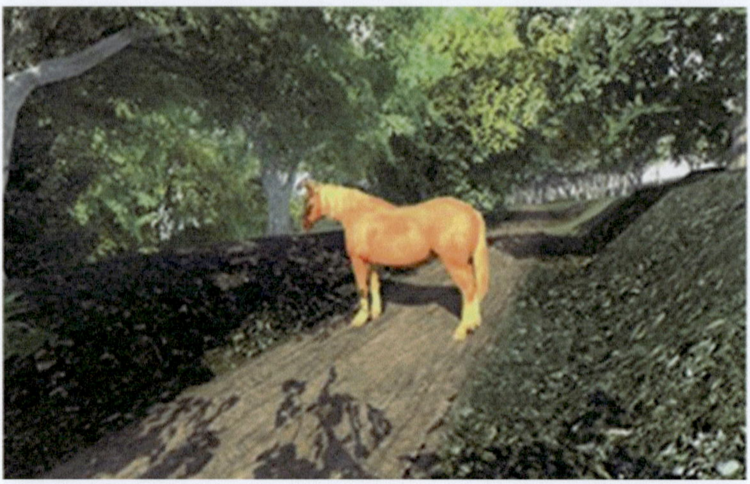

Fig. 18.10 Horse waiting for the cinematic gallop

people, not unexpectedly, spend more time exploring it, but then go outside to the old cemetery to see what is still to be seen on the ground. Visit lengths have increased noticeably for family groups, as parents get a chance to spend time in the museum while their children are playing with the model. This has proved very beneficial to visitor experience and satisfaction, and to the recommendations to visit the Tower that they pass on to friends.

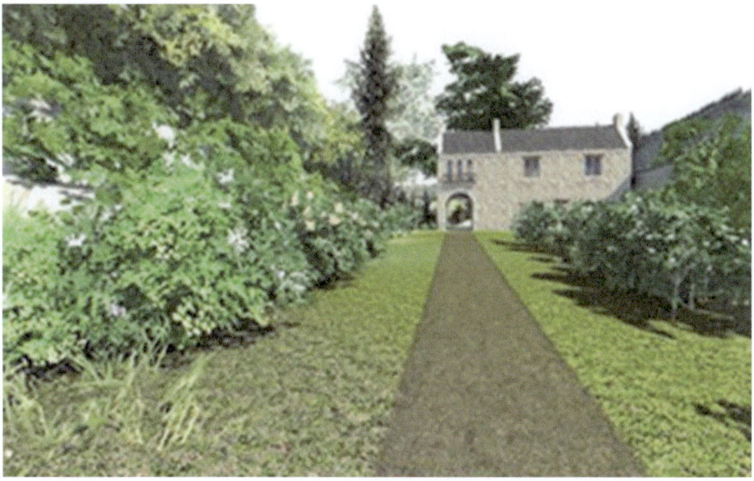

Fig. 18.11 Dyke garden

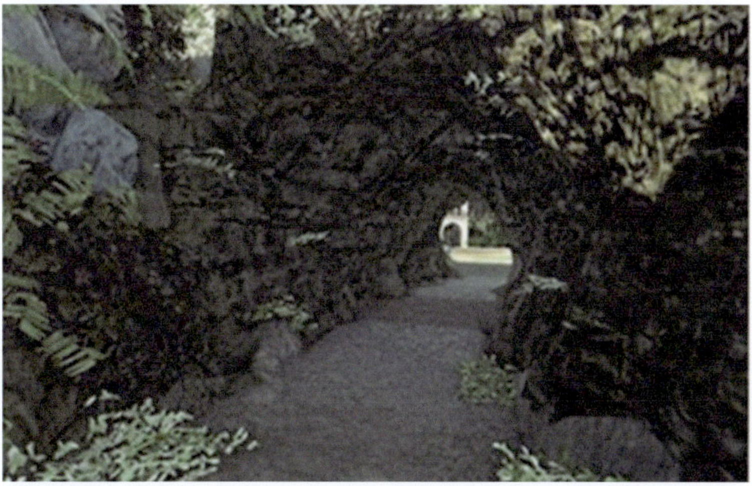

Fig. 18.12 Grotto

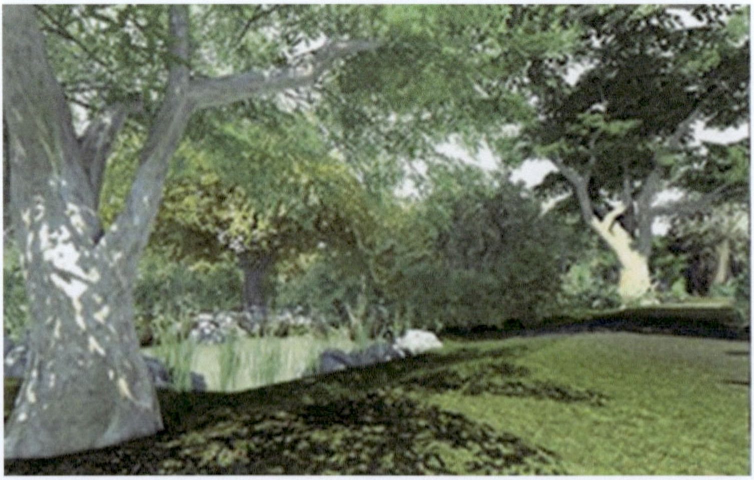

Fig. 18.13 Wilderness

Fig. 18.14 Tower seen through mock ruin

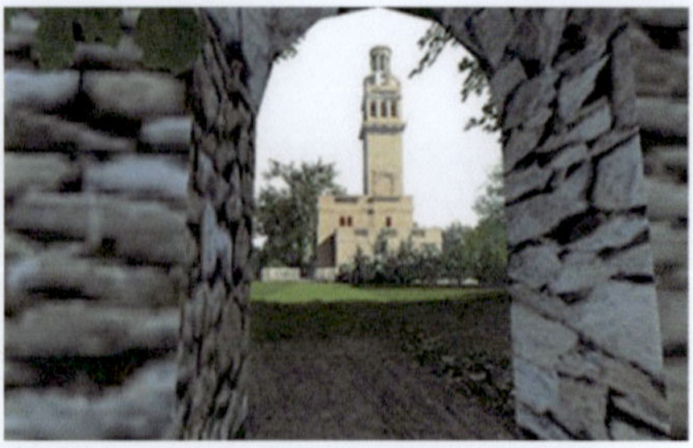

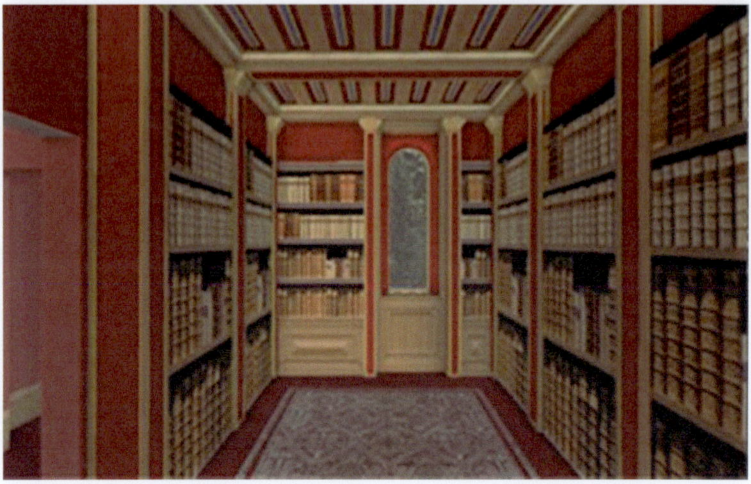

Fig. 18.15 Bookroom in the tower

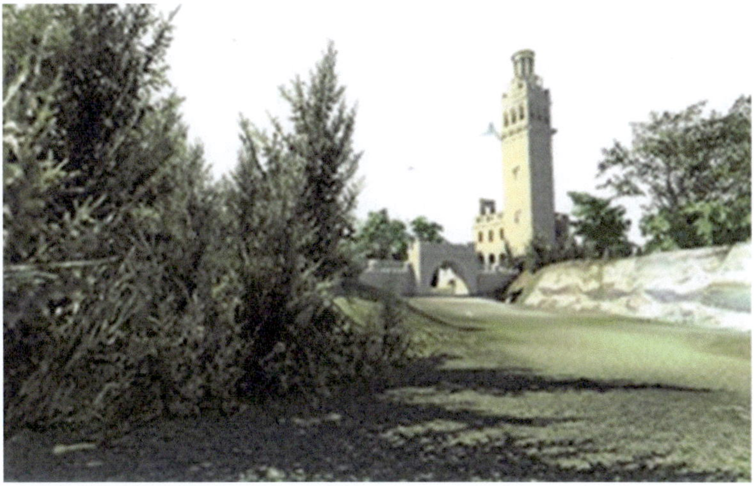

Fig. 18.16 Tower from road entrance

Acknowledgments The project was funded by the Beckford Tower Trust with the help of a grant from the Heritage Lottery Fund. Unpublished reports and bibliographies commissioned by the Trust were invaluable: Pat Hughes on the documentary history of the Tower, Jerry Sampson's Archaeological survey of the Tower, and A S N Lewis and J L Phibbs of Debois Landscape Survey Group on the Landscape surrounding the Tower. Modelling was carried out by three architecture students: James Bailey, Joe Mummery, and Stephan Wasserman-Fry. Paul Shepherd and Simon Hartley helped with programming and animation. John Treddinick pioneered the use of CryEngine for the Prior Park project. DTMs were supplied by Digimap, WIST and NEXTMap, Aerial Photography by Google Earth. Ambient sounds came from the Freesound Project. Additional programming used the Processing environment. Photosculpt provided by Hippolyte Mounier. CryEngine 3 was provided under an academic license from Crytek GmbH Frankfurt.

References

1. Richens, P. (2000). Playing games. *Digital Creativity, 11*(3), 156–160.
2. Klein, M. (1996). Weltbild Wörlitz: Entwurf einer Kulturlandschaft.Institut für Neue Medien. Frankfürt am Main: *INM*. http://www.inm.de/projects/woerlitz/woerlitz_d.html. Accessed 24 Jan 2013.
3. DeLeon, V. J., & Berry, H. R. (1998). Virtual Florida everglades. In *VSMM98 Future Vision: Application realities for the virtual age.*
4. Honjo, T., & Lim, E. (2001). Visualization of landscape by VRML system. *Landscape and Urban Planning, 55*(3), 175–183.
5. Döllner, J., Baumann, K., Buchholz, H., & Paar, P. (2005). Real-time virtual landscapes in landscape and urban planning. In *Proceeding of GIS PLANET*, Estoril.
6. Paar, P., & Blaik, R. (2008). Time-slicing wrest park – Interactive 3D visualization of a historic garden. In E. Buhmann (Ed.), *Digital design in landscape architecture*. Heidelberg: Wichmann.
7. Pokladek, M., Thürkow, D., Dette, C., & Glässer, C. (2012). Geovisualization of the garden kingdom of Dessau-Wörlitz. In E. Buhmann, S. Ervin, & M. Pietsch (Eds.), *Proceeding of Digital Landscape Architecture*. Anhalt University.

8. Mittring, M. (2007). Finding next gen: CryEngine 2. In *Proceeding of SIGGRAPH'07 Courses*, chapter 8. New York: ACM.
9. Crytek GmbH. "CryEngine 3." http://www.crytek.com/cryengine. Accessed 18 Apr 2013.
10. Ch'ng, E. (2007). Using game engines for archaeological visualization: Recreating lost worlds. In *Proceeding of 11th international conference on computer games*.
11. Harney, M., & Tredinnick, J. (2009) An interactive tool for the exploration of contextual architecture: Case study: 18th century Prior Park, Bath. In *27th eCAADe conference*, Istanbul.
12. Fothergill, B. (1979). *Beckford of fonthill*. London: Faber and Faber.
13. Beckford, W. (1823). Vathek. Translated from the original French, (4th ed.). London: Clarke
14. Lansdown, H. V. (1893). *Recollections of the late William Beckford*. Bath: Kingsmead.
15. Maddox, W. (1844). *Views of Lansdown tower, Bath: The favourite edifice of the late William Beckford*. Bath: Edmund English.
16. Redding, C. (1859). *Memoirs of William Beckford of Fonthill, author of "Vathek"*. London: Skeet.
17. Wikipedia. Crysis. http://en.wikipedia.org/wiki/Crysis. Accessed 18 Apr 2013.
18. Sousa, T. Crysis 2 & CryENGINE 3, key rendering features. *Crytek*, Germany. http://crytek.com/assets/Crysis-2-Key-Rendering-Features.pdf. Accessed 2 Apr 2011.
19. Sony. Sound Forge Pro 10. http://www.sonycreativesoftware.com/soundforge. Accessed 18 Apr 2013.
20. Firelight Technologies Pty. FMOD designer 2010. http://www.fmod.org/products/fmoddesign.html. Accessed 18 Apr 2013.
21. Autodesk Inc. 3DS Max. http://www.autodesk.com/products/autodesk-3ds-max/overview. Accessed 18 Apr 2013.
22. Trimble. SketchUp. http://www.sketchup.com. Accessed 18 Apr 2013.
23. McNeel, R., & Associates. *Rhinoceros* 2012. http://www.rhino3d.com. Accessed 18 Apr 2013.
24. Mounier, H. *PhotoSculpt*, 2010. http://www.photosculpt.net. Accessed 25 Jan 2013.
25. Catmull, E., & Clarke, J. (1978). Recursively generated bspline surfaces on arbitrary topological meshes. *Computer Aided Design, 10*, 350–355.
26. Khronos Group. *COLLADA – Digital asset and FX exchange schema*. https://collada.org. Accessed 18 Apr 2013.

Chapter 19
Reconfiguring Experimental Archaeology Using 3D Movement Reconstruction

Stuart Dunn and Kirk Woolford

Abstract The Motion in Place Platform was an infrastructure experiment which sought to provide a 'deep' mapping of reconstructed human movement. It was a collaboration between Animazoo, a Brighton-based motion hardware company, digital humanities and informatics researchers from the University of Sussex, King's College London, and the University of Bedfordshire. Both 3D reconstruction and Virtual Reality (VR) in archaeology have been used to a great extent in the presentation and interpretation of archaeological sites in the past 20 years. However, there remains a predominant focus on their use as a means of illustration which, while enhancing the visual perception of the site, facilitates only passive consumption by the audience. This chapter reports on two linked experiments which sought to use motion capture technology to test the validity of digital reconstruction in exploring interpretations of the use of space, using domestic experimental round house buildings of the British Iron Age. Contemporary human movement was captured in a studio-based representation of a round house, and compared with comparable movements captured in an experimental reconstruction of the same environment. The results indicate significant quantitative variation in physical human responses to the two environments.

This chapter is an updated and extended version of the following paper, published here with kind permission of the Chartered Institute for IT (BCS) and of EVA London Conferences: S. Dunn and K. Woolford, "Reconfiguring experimental archaeology using 3D reconstruction." In S. Dunn, J. P. Bowen, and K. Ng (eds.). *EVA London 2012 Conference Proceedings*. Electronic Workshops in Computing (eWiC), British Computer Society, 2012. http://www.bcs.org/ewic/eva2012 (accessed 26 May 2013).

S. Dunn (✉)
Department of Digital Humanities, King's College London, 26-29 Drury Lane, London, WC2B 5RL, UK

K. Woolford
School of Media, Film and Music, University of Sussex, Falmer, BN1 9RG, UK
www.motioninplace.org

J.P. Bowen et al. (eds.), *Electronic Visualisation in Arts and Culture*, Springer Series on Cultural Computing, DOI 10.1007/978-1-4471-5406-8_19,

Introduction

Experimental archaeology has long yielded valuable insights into the tools and techniques that featured in past peoples' relationship with the material world around them. We can determine, for example, how many trees would need to be felled to construct a large round-house of the southern British Iron Age (over 100); infer the exact angle needed to strike a flint core in order to knap an arrowhead in the manner of a Neolithic hunter-gatherer; or recreate the precise environmental conditions needed to store grain in underground silos over the winter months, with only the technologies and materials available to Romano-Briton villagers [1, 2]. However, experimental archaeology has hitherto confined itself to empirical and quantitative questions such as those posed in these examples. Although this is in line with good scientific practice, which stipulates that any 'experiment' must be based on replicable data, and have a reproducible methodology, it explicitly excludes visualisation of the human element in the interpretation of past environments.

It is likely for this reason that digital reconstruction technologies, including games, have yet to play a significant role in experimental archaeology. Whilst many excellent examples of digital 3D reconstruction of heritage sites exist (for example the Digital Roman Forum project: http://dlib.etc.ucla.edu/projects/Forum) most, if not all, of these are characterised by a drive to establish a photorealistic re-creation of physical features. The Motion in Place Platform project (MiPP: http://www.motioninplace.org) was a capital grant under the AHRC's DEDEFI scheme to develop motion capture and analysis tools for exploring how people move through spaces outside studio environments where, hitherto, most motion capture work had been done. In the course of MiPP, a series of experiments were conducted using motion capture hardware and software at the Silchester Roman town archaeological excavation in Hampshire, and in two 'versions' of the kind of round house widely in use in Britain in the centuries leading up to the Roman invasion in AD 43. One version was reconstructed in a studio in a manner in keeping with 'conventional' motion capture experimentation; whereas the other was a physically reconstructed round house in an outdoor setting, at the Butser Ancient Farm facility, where Romano-British and Iron Age dwellings have been constructed according to the best experimental practice. The aim was to reconstruct the kind of activities that – according to the material evidence – are likely to have been carried out by the occupants, and in the process explore human reactions to 'immersion' in the physical and virtual versions of the round house. Bespoke motion capture suits developed for the project were employed, and the traces captured and rendered with a combination of Autodesk and Unity3D software. Comparing the two sets of traces allowed us to examine how both reconstructed spaces guided human movement. In particular the exercises allowed the evaluation and visualisation of changes in behaviour which occur as a result of familiarity with an environment, and the acquisition of expertise over time.

Understanding Movement in the Past and Present

Understanding movement is a recurrent and topical theme in archaeology. At all scales, how and why humans moved from A to B through a landscape, and what they did in between times, lies at the core of building narratives about the past. However, the evidence on which we can build such narratives is as varied and as patchy as archaeological evidence itself. In more recent periods, the material record can be supplemented with textual narratives, or even oral memory and tradition. Human motion is contingent upon both time and space, and individual movements can be remembered and documented in various ways. For example recent research in performance studies has focused on the ontological and transitory nature of performance pieces, and various ways in which they can be captured through notation and documentation [3]. In the same way, human movement in distant history needs to be understood at some level: a key question for this work is to establish if comparably valuable observations can be made about human movement in periods for which we have no written or social historical records; and if so, how.

3D visualisation has been used to address this elsewhere [4]. However most 3D reconstructions of archaeological features, where they include humans at all, simply include them as decorative accoutrements, as adjuncts to the physical or architectural features being (re)constructed, or at best as measures of scale. Rarely is there any meaningful attempt made to understand or represent how those humans might have interacted with that physical environment, and what might have driven those interactions. Many such reconstructions simply omit humans and human movement all together. As M. Gillings has stated:

> [I]t is worth noting that one of the most striking things about archaeological Virtual-models is the lack of people in them. As a result, wandering around re-creations … can be a ghostly and unsettling experience. [5]

The 'undocumentable' movement of humans in or through their contemporary environments is the product of a combination of those environments' materiality and those humans' experience, personal histories, purposes, intents and other immediate circumstances. There is an important distinction between such unprescribed movement and highly specialised, location-specific instances of ritual and cult activity, which are initiated by imperatives over and above the personal and the material. Such motions provide the focus of most existing research in this area [4, 6]. It is true that the documented presence of such rituals in the historic period allow us to test theoretical and practical aspects of reconstruction. As Johanson and Favro have noted in relation to reconstructing Roman funerary processions: '[t]he consideration of events in situ illustrates how the Romans choreographed their processions to exploit scale, orientation, sequencing and symbolic associations of structures and places' [6]. However, unscripted narratives of the mundane, the day to day, and the domestic, especially from periods of the distant past, remain largely confined to conjecturing what might fill the gaps in our material evidence.

The Motion in Place Project

Methodologies involving experience and interaction in space have been employed in the study and conservation of heritage sites and in museums and galleries for some time. There is recognition that the paths visitors use (or create themselves) to navigate around sites can be used to plan conservation practices, and to design pathways for tours and visitors to follow. The problems of documenting these are not dissimilar to those encountered by performance researchers seeking to document and capture individual performances, as noted above [3]. However, despite numerous innovative and effective ways of gathering such data, the visualised output of such work is almost always static, in the form of maps, plotted pathways and diagrams. Ironically enough, this is the kind of static, positivist form of illustration that has been criticised by researchers who have considered the role of movement in the past and cognitive approaches to it. Witness, for example, Copeland (2009)'s critique of Ivan Margary's 1955 Roman Roads of Britain:

> Clearly the road is being treated as an abstract entity, a form of 'land art' … which could be numbered, listed, quantified, mapped, safe and satisfying. The route of the road is extracted from the landscape, is a measured space, excluded from its surroundings both materially and cognitively'. [7]

Round-House Trial

The round house experiments, conducted in the spring and summer of 2011 compared movement captured in studios with virtual backdrops projected on walls and screens (see Fig. 19.1) with movement captured in 'real world' equivalents of the studio environment at the Butser Ancient Farm facility in Hampshire, where Romano-British and Iron Age dwellings – mainly round houses – have been constructed according to the best experimental practice [1, 2] (see Fig. 19.2). Butser is an example of *experimental archaeology*, the practice of constructing features or artefacts by a process of using trial and error to approximate 'construct' artefacts as accurately as possible, in the process inferring the techniques (including the movements) used in the creation process. We sought to create motion capture data from the studio-based round house and the physically reconstructed version which were comparable in the sense that they represented the same tasks, but we wished to investigate how (or if) they differed according to how the human undertaking them responded the respective virtual and physical natures of the environments themselves.

In contrast, the studio based trial, on the other hand, provided a 'clean' environment in which movement could be captured with few physical or haptic stimuli. A 'footprint' was taped out corresponding to the wall of the roundhouse, and props used to stand in for obstructions such as the hearth (although this seemed to have little impact on the trajectories of the subjects – see below).

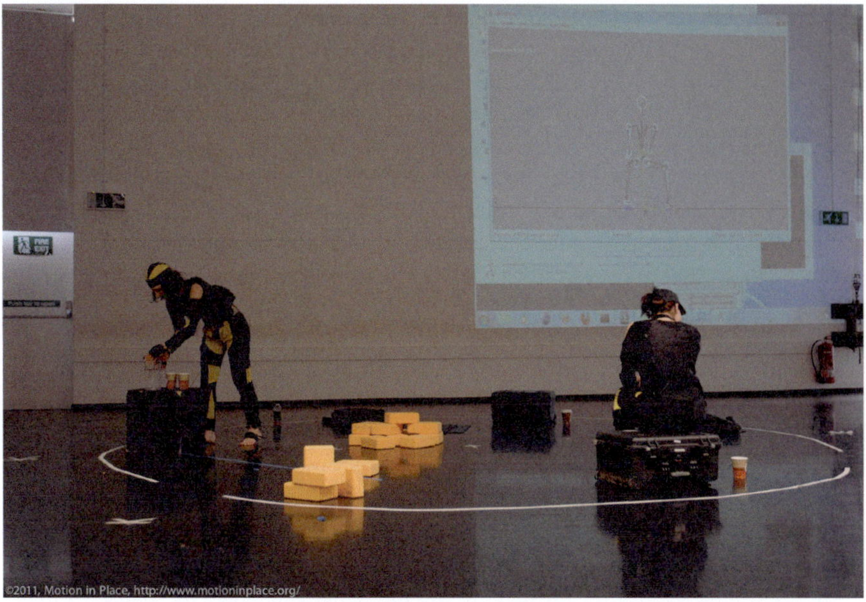

Fig. 19.1 Studio-based reconstruction of scripted movements

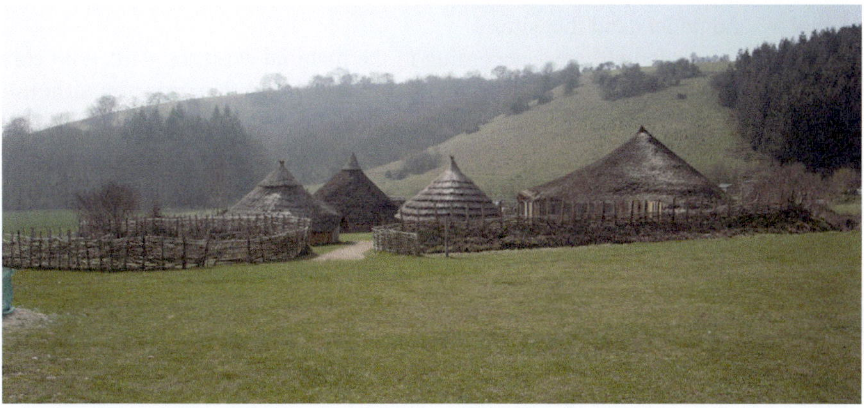

Fig. 19.2 Round houses at Butser farm

In the domestic culture of the British Iron Age, there is no direct archaeological evidence or historic or material evidence of how round houses were built, how they were used, or how artefacts such as arrowheads or ceramics were made. Nor is there any evidence for any rituals which can be reconstructed to the extent of Roman funerary practices alluded to by Favro and Johanson [6]. Reconstructing the use of domestic spaces is therefore fraught, with much attention inevitably being concentrated on the better documented (both materially and textually) Roman periods that followed [8]. The reconstruction process in experimental archaeology has a long tradition of researching and utilising past methods of construction and craft to construct (the term 'reconstruct' is explicitly avoided in the literature – see [2]) non-extant buildings using those methods. However the experimental approach, now well established and widely referred to, requires the 'human factor', in that it requires human intervention in, and interaction with, the physical world. We cannot travel back in time to capture the exact motions involved in archaeologically relevant activities, however we can capture current activities and physical processes in order to gain more insight into probable past activities. Such an approach is particularly useful for testing the validity of different kinds of archaeological evidence, and also the efficacy of means of reconstructing, rendering and visualising past environments in 3D.

The experiment sought to explore how human movement could be visualised and observed directly in the context of these spatial and temporal scales. The remainder of this chapter will focus on the second experiment, at Butser farm, which deployed the methods and hardware developed in the Silchester trial, and used additional techniques for placing the movement in space or "place". In particular, this allowed us to observe the impact on movement of experience and familiarity with an environment gained over time. This is linked to notions of expertise and location-specific knowledge, such as an archaeologist with expertise and experience of a particular site in a particular place employing their knowledge to explore and understand that site.

The activities captured are – according to the material evidence – likely to correspond to those carried out by the occupants who used domestic round house spaces historically (the nature of this correspondence is of course critical). These tasks included querning (grinding flour), sweeping, fetching water (according to available evidence, round houses had no water sources inside, so all water used for cooking, washing and drinking would have been fetched from an external source) and bread making – see Fig. 19.3. The intangible nature of these tasks is intrinsically conditioned by the physical environment in which they are embodied, and the information they receive about it via the media of sight, smell, sound, touch and, to a lesser extent perhaps, by taste. We infer that re-recreating a round house's physical properties also involves creating the conditions parallel to those which provoked cognitive responses to this information in the past.

Two performers were given a broom, constructed using materials and methods sufficiently generic as to approximate to those likely to have been used in historic periods including the Iron Age, to sweep the virtual studio-based round house as well as the physical round house (see Fig. 19.4). In the virtual round house, their movements had no effect on the virtual environment. The lack of haptic feedback clearly meant that influence of the environment was minimal: The smooth, flat floor of the studio offered little resistance to the brooms and the even surface and lack of material barriers such as the inner post ring gave rise to a lack of physical consequences related to sweeping through objects or walking into walls. This appeared to

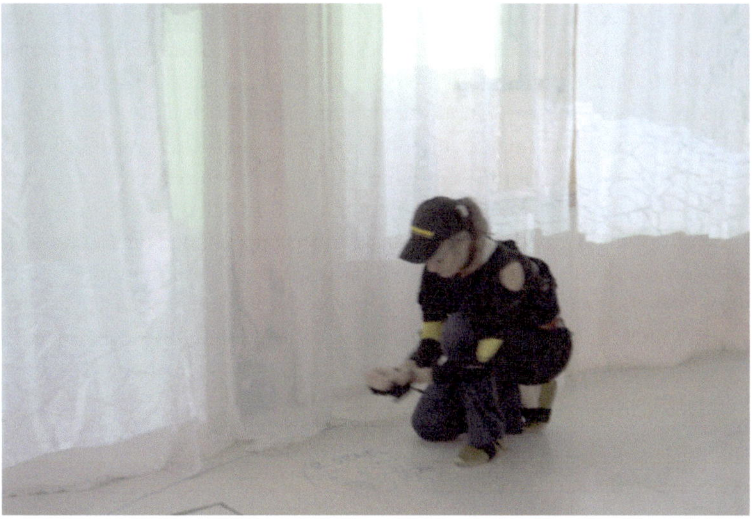

Fig. 19.3 Making bread inside a virtual round house

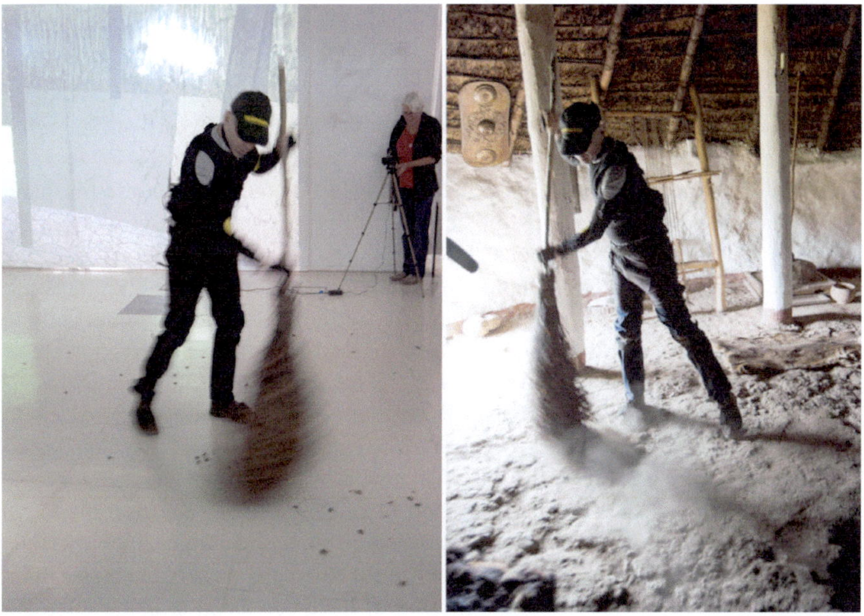

Fig. 19.4 Sweeping with the same broom in both physical and virtual (re)constructions of the same round house

invite the performers to move aggressively and openly. In the physical round house at Butser, the floor was uneven and the performers had to move the broom around inner posts while not stepping into the hearth (this is not accounting for the conjectured possibility that the ring supported by the inner posts may have had objects hanging from it, such as meat being smoked or animal skins, which would have further impeded human motion around the posts). Furthermore, there was great deal of variation in the resistance to the movement of the broom on the floor. At the same time, the performers learned that large, fast movements created dense clouds of dust and damaged the floor of the house; and that an inward sweeping motion, towards the central hearth and away from the walls, was the most efficient way of avoiding large dust clouds. Clearly the 3D rendering of the roundhouse constructed in the studio was unable in any way to capture or represent these haptic response.

Analysis of the Capture Data

The authors developed a bespoke application to track the position of the dancer's hands while sweeping and to determine the distance the hands travelled and the amount of time required for an average "sweeping" motion or cycle. A single sweep motion or cycle was defined as the time between when a broom was placed down on the floor until the next time it was placed on the floor. Figure 19.5 shows a plot of sweeping in both the virtual roundhouse and the physical roundhouse. Both graphs show the position of the dancer's right hand over approximately 45 s of sweeping. This is the most convenient approximation to ascertain the trajectory of the broom itself, and the same point was captured consistently across all traces.

The plots in the bottom right show the composite 3D motion trajectories the hand (i.e., its position in 3D space). The other two graphs plot the distance away from the centre of the body. The top graphs show these positions on a traditional timeline while the graph in the bottom left plots y-offset, (the height above the body's centre) on the y-axis against xy-offset (the length of a vector from the centre of the body to the body part being tracked). This plot also highlights the current sweep cycle or stroke and the current position in this cycle.

The layout of round houses makes them interesting environments in which to experiment. As Webley has noted [9], most round houses are usually configured with the door facing to the south east. This means that most advantageous use is made of daylight, and this is generally reflected in the layout of finds from structures of this type. Finds reflecting domestic occupation, such as ceramics, loom weights and cooking paraphernalia typically cluster in the eastern section of the house, with the western section, which is often inferred to have contained sleeping quarters, relatively free of finds [9]. It has been argued that this so-called 'sunwise' model of configuration reflected not only a practical solution to the problem of round houses not containing windows, but also that it may have reflected the cycle of life and death, given that some contain burials of humans and dogs in the northeast

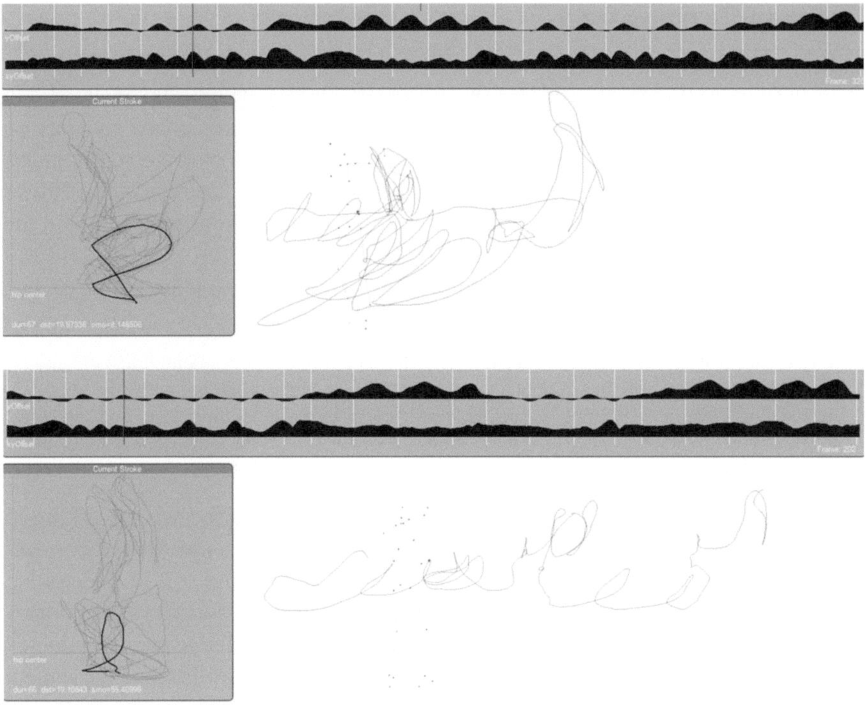

Fig. 19.5 Sweeping in both the virtual roundhouse and the physical roundhouse

quadrants. It was not our intention to test such hypotheses in the Butser experiment, but rather to test the execution of domestic, and seemingly mundane, tasks referred to above, and how familiarity with the environment might impact on that execution. We were, in essence, interested in what Eugene Ch'ng has termed 'experiential archaeology', which is explicitly differentiated from experimental archaeology by its focus on the immaterial rather than the material [10]; although we would hesitate to go as far as Ch'ng and argue that advances in visual technology will make possible 'virtual time travel'.

What does this mean? This data demonstrates that the performer did, indeed, make larger sweeping strokes in the virtual roundhouse (as expected). However, the performer also made sweeping strokes of shorter duration in the physically reconstructed roundhouse. This may be a result of the dust stirred up by sweeping in the physically constructed space, or it may be a result of the amount of resistance of the rough, uneven floor. Because the sample size is so small, it is not possible to make any definitive statements, but the data does appear to demonstrate that engagement with the environment has altered the performer's movement: in other words their internal spatial configuration has changed.

Geographic Knowledge

In our experiment, we captured three types of person: performers who are trained to respond with physical expressiveness to their physical environs; two students on internship placements, with very limited previous familiarity of the round house environment; and finally an experimental archaeologist who has worked at Butser for many years, and who is intimately familiar with the environment, and with the tasks involved in maintaining it (see Fig. 19.6a, b).

This coincides with much writing on movement and environments as summed up by the architecture theorist, Juhani Pallasmaa:

> Our bodies and movements are in constant interaction with the environment; the world and the self-inform and redefine each other constantly. The percept of the body and the image of the world turn into one single continuous existential experience; there is no body separate from its domicile in space, and there is no space unrelated to the unconscious image of the perceiving self.' [11]

If the in situ aspect of which kind of environment the performer is working in affects their internal spatial referencing with consequent impact on their documentable movements, then another fact which is like to change the spatial referencing again is time, and how time and familiarity with an environment alters human interaction with it. The motion experiments detailed in sections above were conducted with trained performers, who were used not because of their virtuosic movement abilities or vocabularies, but because of their ability to take physical direction, and remember and re-create the movements. However, the experience of working with a number of the experimental archaeologists familiar with the site allowed us a broader perspective. In addition, the performers were captured upon first arriving on site, then captured again after having been given training by the archaeologists who worked on the site on a daily basis, performing the same tasks. The dancers' movements were then compared against the archaeologist's movement and their earlier, uninformed motion as depicted in Fig. 19.6a.

The experience with the broom showed that the connection to material objects such as tools and buildings are of crucial importance in elucidating our understanding of possible behaviours, usages of space, and movements in periods for which there is no empirical evidence. In other words, whilst we cannot reconstruct actual day to day events in prehistory, we can infer a broad spectrum of *procedural geographic knowledge*: this is the combination of cues, learned or taught responses, conscious decisions and personal imperatives which people used to navigate their ways around their immediate environments [12]. This adds to an individual's store of *declarative geographic knowledge*, the set of geographic facts, which may be associated with location at any level (*ibid.*). The students and the experienced archaeologist in this experiment had procedural geographic knowledge, but differed vastly in their levels of declarative knowledge. This accounts for the variations visible in the visualisations of their motion traces in (Fig. 19.6a, b).

This is, in effect, an extension of traditional experimental archaeology, which allows us to infer how people are likely to have interacted with their physical

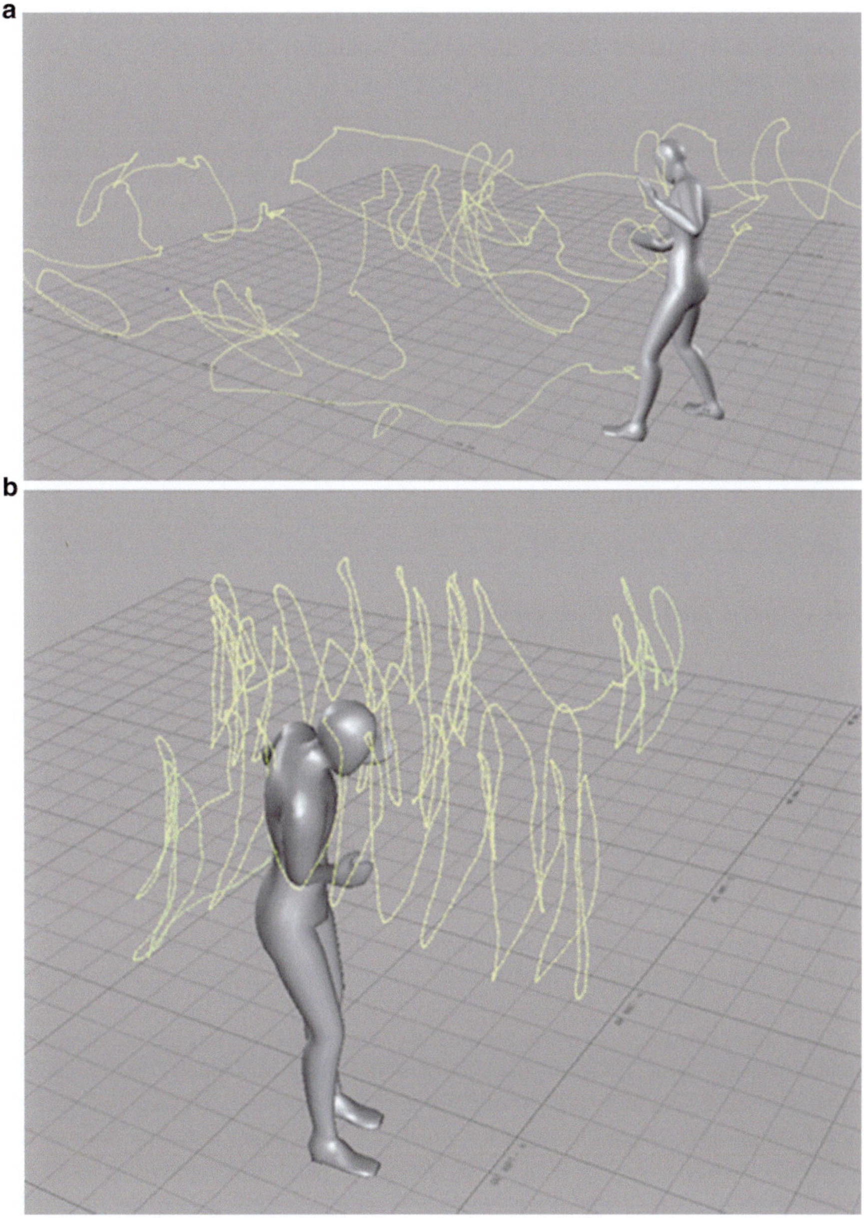

Fig. 19.6 (a) Performer sweeping in physical roundhouse without instruction. (b) Experienced archaeologist performing the same task

environments and how those environments (or tools) were constructed. It also resonates with Marcel Mauss' theory of techniques of the body, transmitted through tradition:

> I call technique an action which is effective and traditional … There is no technique and no transmission in the absence of tradition. This above all is what distinguishes man from the animals: the transmission of his techniques … we are dealing with techniques of the body. The body is man's first and most natural instrument. Or more accurately, not to speak of instruments, man's first and most natural technical object, and at the same time technical means, is his body. [13].

Integrating visualised movement in this way, and applying some basic theory of spatial cognition, sheds new light on how the reconstructed spaces – and, by inference, their ancient counterparts – were likely to have been used. In particular the exercises allowed the evaluation and visualisation of changes in behaviour which occur as a result of familiarity with an environment and the acquisition of expertise over time; and to assess how interaction between different actors affects how everyday tasks are carried out.

Movement and Phenomenology

That knowledge and experience of a landscape alters a human being's relationship with it has long been at the heart of so-called phenomenological archaeology [14], and the limitations of any attempt to investigate experience empirically are well-rehearsed. One could easily argue, however, that even the most conventional analysis of high-status artefacts requires us to make value judgements about the 'quality' of the craftsmanship, and therefore the experience of the craftsman with those materials, or possibly the experience of the wearer in wearing the jewellery. Topology as well as topography also plays a major role in landscape studies. For the 'experience' related to manual tasks in the round house, we have no material object to examine from the past: the use of motion data allows us to create (im)material digital objects from direct observation.

This allows us to make some preliminary observations about the nature of evidence that underpins 3D reconstruction in archaeology, and indeed the humanities more generally. We have argued elsewhere that, in general, 3D visualisations in archaeology have tended towards the positivist, with scant attention paid to the human of such spaces [15]. We propose here that, rather than supporting the establishment of an 'experiential archaeology', the application of motion capture hardware outside the studio expands the capacity of experimental archaeology to allow documentation of the human responses to physical spaces – spaces which are, themselves, artefacts of human creation. This, we would argue, is archaeologically inferential evidence. Conceptually beneath the archaeologically inferential is the archaeologically empirical. An example of this would be the spatial footprint of the round house, which can be determined from empirical observation. We are also able to tell that the house contained 12 posts supporting its inner ring, and that it had a hearth in the centre. Empiricism and objectivity are, of course, notoriously difficult concepts to deal with in archaeology, but these are examples of statements that can be made *for certain*, even if one disagrees with the interpretation placed on these. A third layer is the archaeologically conjectural. Conjecture is widely used in archaeological theory and practice, and in the context of our reconstructions, we had no surfaces from which to make direct observations from which to derive textures. There is no way that we can know that the walls were the same colour, or that their surfaces had the consistency that we attributed to them. We consider that this is acceptable, so long as the lack of certainty is made explicit, and that it is divided out from our motion traces, which are inferred, and the footprint of the structure, which is empirical. This is a useful framework in which to consider 3D reconstruction in archaeology, especially where a more 'constructivist' approach is attempted, where the purpose of the reconstruction is to provoke the audience (whether that audience is public or specialist) into building its own interpretations; rather than simply presenting a positivist interpretation of the structure as a *fait accompli.*

Conclusion

As we have seen, experimental archaeology has a strong emphasis on the *material*. It shares this characteristic with other branches of archaeology, which is, after all, the study of *material* remains. Materiality is an underpinning concept throughout all archaeological interpretation, and it thus influences – often unconsciously or subconsciously – those interpretations. We talk of *material* culture, a term which itself not unproblematic. One attribute inextricably linked with materiality is spatiality: every material thing exists in space and must be located somewhere. Our thesis in this chapter is that we cannot understand places without understanding movement, and the framework of empirical, inferential and conjectural represents an approach which frees us from the 'forced' spatial certainty on (potentially) uncertain data which is implicit in many GIS approaches, and with which 3D visualisation often falls foul.

Some concrete conclusions can be drawn about the how a physical environment affects movement: the example of the sweeping shows that there are attributes to the action involved which are altered when transferred from a virtual/studio environment to a physical one; the shorter brush strokes being a primary example. This shows that the 3D reconstruction of a non-extant round house can be said to adequately represent only the visual aspect of the experience of being in it. The motion data captured from Butser augments this understanding by documenting human interaction with it, a point underscored by the changes observable in the motion as the experience of the person captured is varied. Further investigations might investigate further distinctions: a light environment versus a darker one or warm versus cold. Capturing such traces using the motion hardware we trialled allows us to augment the otherwise static 3D reconstruction of the round house, and communicate more effectively the implications of its physicality.

The obvious limitation of this approach is that it does not provide the kind of direct reconstruction of past construction and manufacturing techniques that experimental archaeology provides for building and artefacts. Our motion traces are one-off embodiments, whereas the physical reconstruction of the Moel-y-Gerddi round house provides a hypothesis which can be tested, examined and reproduced. It will require the development of a large reference collection of traces for any one site before supportable general inferences can be made about that site. These experiments have shown that such information can be gathered from motion capture, they have not shown the effects of growing them incrementally over time.

The purpose of MiPP was emphatically not to attempt to re-enact possible scenarios of history or prehistory, but to capture and visualise human interaction with place and material culture as documented by archaeological evidence, and thus to provide a critique of how well VR represents the experiential past. No, it is not possible to definitively know how Iron Age Britons used their round houses. We can infer past movements from an understanding and analysis of current movement in much the same way we infer the structure of past buildings and material objects through the fragments that have survived to our current time. However, just as archaeologists make clear distinctions between what material objects have actually been uncovered and what contextual information they have based their conjectures upon, we need to be clear about exactly what motion data we are capturing and the contexts in which it has been captured. If we want to understand how motion influences place and place influences motion, we need to capture and study them together.

References

1. Coles, J. M. (1979). *Experimental archaeology*. London: Academic.
2. Reynolds P. (1993). Experimental reconstruction. The report of a specific construction based upon the excavation of a great round house at Pimperne Down in Dorset, including an account of the life of the structure and its final dismantlement. In *An iron age settlement in Dorset: Excavation and reconstruction*. Edinburgh University Monograph No. 1, UK.
3. Blades, H. (2012). Creative computing and the re-configuration of dance ontology. In S. Dunn, J. P. Bowen, & K. Ng (Eds.), *EVA London 2012 conference proceedings* (pp. 221–228). Electronic Workshops in Computing (eWiC), British Computer Society, 2012. http://ewic.bcs.org/content/ConWebDoc/46137. Accessed 22 May 2013.
4. Johanson, C. (2009). Visualizing history: Modeling in the eternal city. *Visual Resources: An International Visualizing History, 25*(4), 403–418.
5. Gillings, M. (1999). Engaging place: A framework for the integration and realisation of virtual reality approaches in archaeology. In L. Dingwall, S. Exon, V. Gaffney, S. Laflin, & M. van Leusen (Eds.), *Archaeology in the age of the internet* (pp. 247–254), BAR International Series 750. ArchaeoPress.
6. Joahnson, C., & Favro, D. (2010). Death in motion. Funeral processions in the Roman forum. *Journal of the Society of Architectural Historians, 69*(1), 12–37.
7. Copeland, T. (2009). *Akeman street: Moving through the Iron Age and Roman Landscapes*. Stroud: The History Press.
8. Percival, J. (1976). *The Roman villa*. London: Book Club Associates.

9. Webley, L. (2009). Using and abandoning roundhouses. A reinterpretation of the evidence from late Bronze Age-Early Iron Age southern England. *Oxford Journal of Archaeology, 26*(2), 127–144.
10. Ch'ng, E. (2009). Experiential archaeology: Is virtual time travel possible? *Journal of Cultural Heritage, 10*(4), 458–470.
11. Pallasmaa, J. (2009). *The eyes of the skin*. Chichester: Wiley.
12. Hill, L. L. (2006). *Georeferencing: The geographic associations of information*. Cambridge: Massachusetts Institute of Technology.
13. Mauss, M. (1973). Techniques of the body. *Economy and Society, 2*(1), 70–88.
14. Brück, J. (2005). Experiencing the past? The development of a phenomenological archaeology in British prehistory. *Archaeological Dialogues, 12*(1), 45–72.

MIX
Papier aus verantwortungsvollen Quellen
Paper from responsible sources
FSC® C105338

FSC
www.fsc.org

If you have any concerns about our products,
you can contact us on
ProductSafety@springernature.com

In case Publisher is established outside the EU,
the EU authorized representative is:
Springer Nature Customer Service Center GmbH
Europaplatz 3, 69115 Heidelberg, Germany

Printed by Libri Plureos GmbH
in Hamburg, Germany